NATASHA.

AN ❧
ACCIDENTAL
AUTOBIOGRAPHY

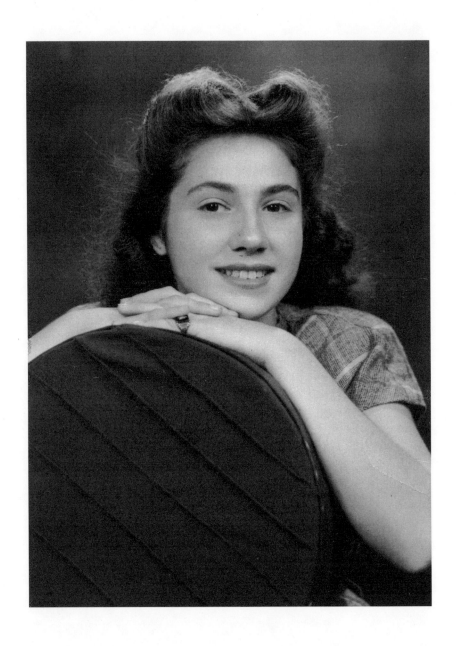

AN ❧

ACCIDENTAL

AUTOBIOGRAPHY

Barbara Grizzuti Harrison

HOUGHTON MIFFLIN COMPANY

BOSTON   NEW YORK

1996

For information about permission to reproduce selections from this
book, write to Permissions, Houghton Mifflin Company,
215 Park Avenue South, New York, New York 10003.

For information about this and other Houghton Mifflin trade and
reference books and multimedia products, visit The Bookstore
at Houghton Mifflin on the World Wide Web at
http://www.hmco.com/trade/.

Library of Congress Cataloging-in-Publication Data

Harrison, Barbara Grizzuti.
An accidental autobiography / Barbara Grizzuti Harrison.
p. cm.
ISBN 0-395-78000-4
1. Harrison, Barbara Grizzuti — Biography. 2. Women authors,
American — 20th century — Biography. I. Title.
PS3558.A664Z4614 1996
818'.5409 — dc20   95-40018   CIP   [B]

Book design by Anne Chalmers

Printed in the United States of America

MP 10 9 8 7 6 5 4 3 2 1

Portions of this book appeared, in different form, in
Condé Nast Traveler, European Travel and Life, Gourmet,
Mirabella, North American Review, and *Diamonds Are*
a Girl's Best Friend: Women Writers on Baseball
(edited by Elinor Nauen).

Credits appear on page 397.

AUTHOR'S NOTE

In recounting my story, I have tried to honor
discretion as much as truth. I have, therefore,
changed the names and identifying details
of certain individuals appearing in this book.

CONTENTS

INTRODUCTION

Memories gather around puzzles, passions, and possessions; they shelter daydreams, which in turn give birth to memories that are new to the conscious mind. Round and round we go. Memory is no more linear than it is hierarchical. Synchronicity and caprice, improvisation and intransigence are the engine by which memory drives and is driven; and so is repetition, and so is contradiction, neither of which I have disavowed. There are in this book different photographs of the same emotional memories; they are all true — by which I mean that I have been conscious only of one imperative, not to corrupt the way my thoughts came to me by seeking to impose upon them a pattern.

I am so much more interested in the improbable juxtapositions of circumstances that make up the warp and woof of natural history than I am in strictly systematizing them. I search for enchantment — for the witch and the wart, the cupboard and the shining treasure, the toad and the prince, the secret door, the golden orb, the magical forest, the silken rain, the riff in the silence, the silence in the riff, the improbable sudden light.

Sometimes, when I wrote, what was meant to be a point of departure became, to my pleased surprise, an end in itself: in such cases the starting point of my reflections (Frederico Secundo, for example) devoured my self (a sensation I quite like); but I am always still there, in the words or in between the words. How could it be otherwise?

I have used, as both safety net and trampoline, a web of quotations drawn from found objects: books that moved me once and books I came upon serendipitously in secondhand bookstores. (Wandering in bookstores without formal purpose is like strolling through the ordered labyrinth of the unconscious, which offers us that which is fixed, defining, inevitable, and associative.)

A linear autobiography would falsify, because it would cast things in a mold and present me with the temptation to find formal patterns where none exist; having imposed the grid of pattern on my work, my self, and my life, I might then, being stubborn, not be able to divorce myself from the pattern. I have no wish to be imprisoned in a frame of my own creation.

The path of memory is circular and coherent:

There is a town in Italy that is made of five concentric circles. It is perfectly logical.

In that town there is a garden not unlike most Italian country gardens: gladioli and basil, roses and squash flowers riot organically together — they make sense of themselves. I know a field in Morocco where onions, poppies, and wheat grow together entangled but each possessed of its peculiar integrity. Memory is like that — surprising, organic, and unhierarchical.

I arranged the material of my life in chapter headings that are alphabetical in order. This gave me room to play and freedom to improvise.

Some time ago I bought several batches of silk swatches; some were from the eighteenth century and some from the twenties, the thirties, the forties, and the fifties; and I did not know what I was going to do with them, or why I had bought them, except for their beauty. The swatches, of a variety so great as to appear almost infinite in design, are floral and geometric, reminiscent of Klimt, reminiscent of Morris, reminiscent of Braque, reminiscent of a child's or a lover's doodling and canoodling — marbled, watered, paisley; silk postcards of idealized court ladies and of Chinese gentlemen and of pheasants and peacocks and fans and lions and pagodas and lilies; they are variously lush and restrained, witty and sentimental. I decided, after some deliberation on my lack of manual dexterity (I was left back in school for being unable to weave a raffia plate), to make a collage of them.

I looked at them and played with them over and over and over again until they organized themselves into the configuration of a design. I hope the design has integrity and that the pieces complement one another. I do like things, however apparently random, to cohere. (And I take a child's pleasure in settling an old score with the teacher who declared me incapable of carrying a thing through to its end.)

> *This perhaps you do not know: I could not use different words.*
> — Italo Calvino

The inferno of the living is not something that will be; if there is one, it is what is already here, the inferno where we live every day, that we form by being together. There are two ways to escape suffering it. The first is easy for many: accept the inferno and become such a part of it that you no longer see it. The second is risky and demands constant vigilance and apprehension: seek and learn to recognize who and what, in the midst of inferno, are not inferno, then make them endure, give them space.

— Italo Calvino

AN ❧
ACCIDENTAL
AUTOBIOGRAPHY

1

BREATHING
LESSONS

*Every organized being always lives immersed in a strong solution of
its own elements. . . . We are perishing and being born again at every
instant. We do literally enter over and over again into the womb of
that great mother, from whom we get our bones, and flesh, and blood,
and marrow. "I die daily" is true of all that live. . . . Man walks,
then, not only in a vain show, but wrapped in an uncelestial aureole
of his own material exhalations. A great mist of gases and of vapor
rises day and night from the whole realm of living nature.*

— Dr. O. W. Holmes, *Atlantic Almanac*, 1869

November 1994. I am in the pulmonary clinic of a New York hospital,
hunched over a white plastic breathing tube around which a Chinese
technician is molding my lips with cool, kind hands. (How easily he
could take advantage of my vulnerability, simply by dampening his
kindness, which, because he is tender and efficient, exposes his sensibility to shocks, and bruises him; he does not.) It is a measure of the
anxiety I hide behind a façade of cheerfulness and careless optimism
that I do not entirely understand the function of the test I am about
to take in this buzzing cell of machines and computers — though the
technician painstakingly explains, and not as if I were an idiot. In and
out, in and out. *Whoosh.* "Very good effort," he says, his earnest, gentle
brown eyes urging me on, his own thin, white-jacketed chest rising and

falling as if to provide me with a good example of how to live; but how can this be true? To say "it is as normal as breathing" to me is to say precisely nothing, to offer me only jagged images of the past. With occasional brief respites, breathing, for the last decade or so, has been for me a matter of monitored calculation and labor, and frequently of panic verging on terror. (Do you know what keeps the perception of terror at a bearable remove? The obligatory rigorous absorption in the awful sensation of the moment; one is too busy dealing with the ins and outs of breathing to place oneself in dangerous existential space. And when the struggle verges on being lost, one simply lacks the requisite energy to care; one allows oneself almost sweetly to rest on benevolent chance.)

Very good effort. But my head is doing the work my lungs should be doing (my husband, Mr. Harrison, used frequently to call me a calculating bitch; and these words come back to me, a strangely timed bubble of amusement); nothing's coming naturally. I cannot for the life of me — for the life of me — determine from what area breath arises, or whether to breathe from areas I vaguely define as throat, neck, chest, diaphragm. (I have forgotten where my diaphragm is. My body can't locate its own muscles.)

I am in the sixtieth year of my life.

I hate to fail at tests.

I can see by the worried faces around me that I am failing these. I have precious little oxygen in my blood (a small black cap attached to my index finger relays this information to a computer as I force my body to move up and down a stair); my body's ability to diffuse the oxygen is limited.

I wait for my breath to return, giving (I know) all the appearance of struggle and exertion . . . whereas in fact I feel myself simply to be a waiting emptiness; and I am visited by flash memories: Swings — flying into the playground air, into the sky (once with viral pneumonia, the giddiness of that flight unalloyed by rational fear), accompanied by the reassuring grating squeak of the chains that anchored one to proximate earth. And monkey bars, jungle gyms: I never quite made it to the thronelike top of those steel climbing-bars-cum-labyrinths (my Tower of Babel) — one didn't tempt the gods, I learned this lesson early at my mother's knee. (Well, at any rate, at her feet. Her feet that walked in decorous insanity and piety.) And roller-skating on dark Brooklyn streets under the maple trees, the street lamps casting splotchy puddles of light through veined green leaves; and, for the happy hell of it, green seed pods from the maple trees split and attached to my nose with spit. I was weightless then, and safe, agile, and accomplished. Free. Skating came to me as easily as breathing, I could start on a wish and stop on a dime and nobody could catch me, nobody could find me in the raggy liquescent light. And double-dutch jump rope, *A my name is Anna, my husband's name is Al.*

Hide and seek.

I am bemused to notice that I am not apologizing to anybody in the white room for my very poor effort. When after a car wreck I was carried to a hospital emergency room on a gurney, I apologized to the emergency medical technicians for their having to hoist my weight. I spend a great deal of time apologizing for not being able to breathe, in the act of contrition being profligate of breath, casting on air words that serve no function but to exasperate my friends. But the solicitude of friends notwithstanding, I know there are acquaintances and even friends who regard me with contained reproach — one *should*, after all, be able to breathe, should one not? The defect must lie in my character, must it not, or in a history I have cunningly manipulated with this (however unconscious) precise objective in mind? And then there are the people who hate my apologizing because they see it as an act of aggression: it is tantamount to an accusation that they are lacking in empathy and forbearance. And this is an altogether tiresome thing for all concerned.

Three times my lungs suffered grievous assault: ten years ago, in India, when white fungus bloomed like vanilla cotton candy on moldy hotel walls; and twelve years ago, in what was once a Utopian community called New Harmony, in a charming guest cottage called Orchard House, where sealed windows kept inside the scented dust of corn hair from the fields below.

(It was out of season in New Harmony; on the floor below, two photographers with whom I was traveling, he pretending to be Stanley, she Blanche, breathed the sweet fresh air of the courtyard while they played their silly, dangerous games.)

Two years ago, an Indian demon seized me by the throat in Varanasi; I could feel the exact moment of the attack of the viral microbe. (At times like this it is easy to adopt a Jain-like cosmology and to believe that all of life, including microscopic life, is equal to one's own in unalterable combination of volition and fate.) I had come to India at the dribble end of monsoon. In Delhi the hot dry weather, after torrential downpours provided relief almost as illusory as it was temporary, was replaced by hot humid weather; my lungs burst from the inability to absorb sticky air.

(The Indians personalize air, and another element they call ether, a vibrant, radiant matter that fills what would otherwise be empty space, of which Indians cannot conceive. It is tempting to believe that geography defines belief, and to agree with Kipling that heat is the central fact of Indian life. Here is what a nineteenth-century Englishman wrote about the aggressive air: "When it stopped raining the vapour used to rise out of the ground up to a height of about a foot and remain static. I saw a chap get a shovel and stick it into one of these banks of vapour, and it stayed on the shovel when he picked it up." I believe this story.)

The malicious demon accompanied me as I wove a woozy way down a stinking alley lined with small three-, five-, and seven-story houses leaning together on lanes so threadlike the sun seemed never to have penetrated them, their overhanging lintels casting deeper shadow on shadow. I passed bright, naive paintings of gods in their benevolent and hideously malevolent aspects on whitewashed mildewed walls. Bony pye-dogs rooted in the decomposing organic slime. Motor scooters skipped through water-filled potholes, splattering cows, whose flanks I brushed (an astonishing intimacy). Bursts of color punctuated the way: bolts of silk — indigo, emerald, yellow, purple, crimson, pink — lean against the leaning houses in the narrow alleys; and in spite of my vertigo, or perhaps because of it, I am enchanted. Catherine wheels go off in my head. Stepping in ordure and in piss, through a gauze of sweat I see gold and silver and bras and saris and icons of Hanuman the monkey god and Ganesh the elephant god in stalls illuminated by naked light bulbs. Drying cow-dung patties bloom like brown fungus on the narrow houses. At the end of the shadowed alleys enormous temples are held tight in crowded space: immensity contained in smallness.

By the time I reach my hotel, the virus has migrated from my throat to my intestines; and for two days the cool marble bathroom of my hotel room effectively becomes my headquarters and my home.

English tourists, having been bitten by the same bug, left the hotel in droves, their nascent nostalgia for the Raj aborted. I stayed on; I had lived in India after all for four years (thirty years ago) without having had a single stomachache, I'd be damned, my vanity was involved, also the travel essay I had embarked upon. After two days the Thing rejected the reluctant hospitality of my guts and entered my lungs; shrapnel pierced me, bombs detonated, mines exploded every time I coughed. Vanity, arrogance, and what I deemed to be necessity upheld me. In the company of a woman whose manner was both nannylike and Delphic, fiercely efficient and undemonstratively loving, I made my way, by plane and Ambassador car, to the hill station of Ootacamund, just as a health-imperiled woman of the Raj might have done -- Ooty being, in any case, on our itinerary.

My companion, whom I have settled upon calling Mrs. God, establishes us in adjoining cottages — mine called Lovedale Valley — that have the perversely reassuring English smell of chintz and mutton, porridge, mold, and damp.

Bearers come and light wood fires in my cottage three times every day and bring hot-water bottles and rice gruel, from which I graduate to kedgeree — rice gruel and dhal.

A black spider big as a soup plate dangles four inches from my nose. *What am I doing in this country of heat and damp and dust and mud where everything is trying to kill me?* This country that I love.

A doctor leaves his golf game at the Wellington to take care of me. A bearer brings me roses, lavender and red and yellow and pink and golden orange. Mrs. God inveigles an invitation to the snooty Ooty Club, where I drink brandy, sugar syrup, lime, and hot water under the neutral gaze of stuffed tiger and bison heads. Everyone is kind. Little, since the Raj, has changed: leek soup, baked fish, roast beef with horseradish sauce — four courses, 45 rupees. Little has changed except that the natty club members who look like Lord Peter Wimsey dressed for a country weekend have brown faces.

When I am sufficiently recovered I find immaculate beauty amidst waterfalls and precipices and winding ridges, near and distant hills dressed in every possible shade of blue, sheltering boulders and fantastic rocks that fall off into breathtaking purple voids, and the crowding beauty of trees — silver oak and blue gum trees and rosewood trees a hundred feet high. Tribals call these hills, the Nilgiris, "butterfly country." Like Lady Lawrence, who loved so much the land her forebears and her husband served and ruled, "I walk in overwhelming glory." Albeit tremblingly.

Ooty's bazaar, with its smells of incense and pungent human flesh and eucalyptus oil (vaguely medicinal, vaguely erotic), its neon colors and its kerosene flares and sticky sweets and pots of boiling peppery food, was forbidden territory to British children; and some of them dreamed of it all their lives thereafter, in exile, in the dull suburbs of "home."

It is called Charing Cross. It is, like every Indian bazaar, an illustration and embodiment of Indian metaphysics: it is a cosmos in a microcosm.

I forget my self.

I returned to New York by way of Rome, where I met my children and interviewed Mussolini's granddaughter, a woman capable of alarming mischief (and quite stupid). When we went to the Vatican Museums my children popped me into a wheelchair and we found secret shortcuts and elevators and gallant uniformed men. It *was* nice, like going behind the cupboard door to the magic garden . . .

This is what I think about gardens (about Paradise): the amazing thing is not that we lost the Garden; the miracle is that we are so often able to find it again.

And in New York, my deceptively unsentimental friend Alice Turner popped me into a wheelchair to see the Matisse exhibit at the Modern, and I was no more than a hand's length away from each cleanly voluptuous canvas, feeling myself to be contained and held fast in light, swimming in Matisse, immersed in Matisse, bliss.

Two weeks ago the Thing came back. I recognized it, a Familiar. (I think it will choose to visit me from time to time. Perhaps it has taken up residence in my body; who knows whose restless black ashes I inhaled in Varanasi amidst fires and burning corpses?) I prayed that this time it would be good enough to give my poor lungs a break and remain in nether regions; it did not. Shrapnel and bombs and fireworks.

I am on the phone with my doctor and with preternatural calm and clarity see the receiver slipping from my hand. I have not passed out, nor have I fainted; I hear every word my doctor calls out, I observe myself holding on to the bars of my brass bed, I float above this ludicrous body, which belongs, I know, to me, but which feels very much as if it belongs to another. I find this (as my son, Joshua, said when he was beaten up by thugs, his painter's eye cut by brass rings) interesting. In a detached kind of way. (The English word *thug* comes from the Hindi word *thugee*, a professional roadside assassin who killed his victims by strangulation. My throat.) Anna, my daughter, says with a trace of envy that this episode, which was in fact caused by oxygen deprivation, is a state the medieval mystics she adores longed to achieve, a prelude to union with God. Fuck that, I say, I'll settle for a tidy flat in Purgatory.

So now I am in the hospital being armed with medicines, vapors, inhalers, pills, having my immediate future arranged for me, portable oxygen carriers and an oxygen supply for sleep. (Will it interfere with my dreams? Alas, it will; and I will be left to wonder if what passes for memory and illumination in the dreams I court and savor is carbon dioxide poisoning.) And I am enjoined to lose weight. Perhaps I will choose to see the humor in this: my breasts, I am told, are too big; my lungs are like an accordion that cannot expand. Oh for Christ's sake. My *tits* are too big! So my disease is a result both of restriction and of obstruction. For years I have been treated for chronic organic pulmonary disease, a combination of emphysema and, it now seems, bra-cup size. Oh. And tissue damage, scars, from a childhood bronchial pneumonia — red expressionist flowers of blood blooming on white sheets — which my mother regarded casually.

Perhaps I have been right all along to apologize. For years I smoked six packs of Carltons a day. (I started smoking when I took up with my Jazzman lover; try to imagine listening to Ben Webster at Minton's without a cigarette in one's twenty-two-year-old hand.) I have not had a cigarette for eight years, but I have allowed myself to grow fat. And

I thought — what *can* I so foolishly have thought? — that it was the
better part of grace to shroud my reclusiveness with affable lies (I do
not know in what part my reclusiveness was chosen or in what part
enforced); that's what I thought if I thought at all. It became a family
joke that I couldn't get myself to the post office or to a dinner party
across the street but that I could fly to Afghanistan on ten minutes'
notice. I lived my writing-traveling life, dissimulating, accepting the
kindness of strangers (and taking frequent stops for coffee, shots of
whiskey, and feigned interest in window displays); and all in all I had a
good, indeed a blessed life . . . which sounds valedictory.

I do not feel valedictory.

I have spent whole mornings in the Pantheon regarding clouds
drifting over the oculus, the world contained in an eye, the eye like the
eye of God. I have seen the sun rise over the Ganges and milky
moonlight shining on the Ganges and little paper boats carrying candles and marigolds floated on its waters in the first dark (I have also
seen turtles, bred for the purpose, eating decomposing human flesh on
that river). I have sat, half in shadow, half in sun, among palm trees
and yellow butterflies and geraniums in Sicily, my breath keeping
unconscious rhythm with the obsessively unselfconscious breathing of
the sea. I have shared physical love with geniuses of physical love. I
have been soothed and excited by the deceitful calm of Guatemala's
volcanic Lake Atitlán, which the Maya believe is bottomless and inhabited by pernicious, capricious spirits (and on the shores of which a
parrot always greeted me with the caw *ma-ma*, which pleased me). I
have eaten a sun-warmed peach in the snowy mountains of Abruzzo
and a dewy morning mango from my very own Hyderabadi mango tree,
the shadow of a great Deccan rock gentling all weariness. I have been
loved. I have seen wild blue men dance in a pre-Islamic oasis in the
Sahara and Maya dancing in the Guatemalan highlands wearing inquisitors' masks. I have met an Anglo-Indian woman with green eyes
and rings on the toes of her stockinged feet, and I have met a one-hun-
dred-year-old nut-brown Indian Lady whose mother was the Plague
Inspector for the port of Bombay and a maharajah who aspired to
sainthood and my cousin from Venafro del Noci who speaks Esperanto
and writes sonnets, and Mario Cuomo and Louis Armstrong, several

guerrillas, a murderer or two and Eleanor Roosevelt and Esther Williams and hundreds and hundreds of people with stories to tell (I have sat on Frank Sinatra's lap). At an Indian wedding my throat has been anointed with ocher, my head with vermilion, the air around me haloed with attar of roses and startled with horn and drum. I have eaten risotto with porcini and truffles and I have dined under tents on gold plates, fanned by peacock feathers; and I have eaten the body of God. I have held a newborn lamb in my arms in the red mountains of Morocco. I have gone to sleep in a villa at the source of the Arno and smelled the brown river waters mingling with the cinnamony scent of red roses and the sweeter fragrance of new-mown hay (elms and acacias cast lacy shadows on my bedroom wall).

Gardens and bazaars.

My children.

"In every kind of adversity, the bitterest part of a man's affliction is to remember that he was once happy," St. Boethius says. I call that blasphemy. And untrue.

I can remember — of late the weight of my life has expressed itself in the weight of my body — the times when I shed that weight; I learned to ride a bicycle in Prospect Park when I was thirty-six; I circled around the trees that ringed the bandstand and felt more beautiful than Greta Garbo.

Only two years ago I walked from Central Park West to Fifth Avenue across Central Park.

I want to do that again as much as I want to do anything again . . . as much as I want to dance with Jazzman, whom I have left (or who has left me — who cares, and what possible difference does it make who left whom?).

I am cranky at this moment, and incoherently trying to decipher and sort out blame; but in the car coming back from the hospital with Jan, my friend of great goodwill and visceral optimism, I felt liberated — I would breathe again, with artificial help, but without calibrating and without force and without deception and without the exhausting use of ameliorating charm to prevent people from seeing my short(breathing)comings. (I have, now, by various measures, twenty-five to fifty percent of normal lung capacity; in time I may regain twenty-five percent more, which will serve.) I want to dance with Jazzman before I die.

Before he died, the first man I ever loved, my English teacher Arnold Horowitz, wrote to me that the secret of growing old successfully was to require less and less of life, his glibness a sign of acedia and terminal ennui. (I read that letter beneath a lemon tree in my garden in Tripoli; and I never saw Arnold again — except in dreams.) I, on the other hand, want more and more: I want to walk across Central Park. In the snow. In the rain.

*
> *I fear that I shall journey alone, that the way will be dark; I fear the unknown land, the presence of my King and the sentence of my judge.*
>
> — Saint Brendan, exile and sailor

Here is a secret. I apologize excessively. But I am not so un-self-regarding as that might lead the unwary to suspect. This is the curative knowledge that sustains me: I do not fear death. Perhaps I would be wise to fear that compulsory journey, as I do believe in Judgment; but I have been on so many journeys, I have been born again so many times, life has offered me so many delicious chances among the indispensable sorrows (and I grab, I grab); I will be born again. I am unafraid of death and I want very much to live, and this combination — a matter of temperament or of God's grace — works for me. In the dark. When the breathing machine sighs.

I have been born again so many times. (I will tell you all about it. I will be Scheherazade. Not now. Later.)

"Let me ax you something," says the man with dreadlocks in the thrift shop, where I am glancing covetously at a 1920s hexagonal blue mirror I know I will not be able to resist, "has you excaped from the hospital?" I am carrying a portable oxygen cylinder, and there are plastic tubes in my nose (bright lipstick on my lips . . . shall I color my hair aubergine? bright cherry, I think, threaded with plum). I want to tell him I have escaped from a hospital for the criminally insane.

The first time I went out with my portable cylinder, my daughter, Anna, came with me. We went to Balducci's, where we bought lemon curd and truffle oil and pork sausage with parsley and cheese, and French country bread and Camembert and goat cheese and Parmigiano Reggiano and prosciutto and veal cutlets and Scottish salmon and roast duckling and baby greens and edible flowers and out-of-season cherries ($9 a pound!) and blood oranges from Sicily and figs and the pasta Anna calls "fat worms."

The manager of Balducci's patted me on the head, a gesture I would, in the ordinary way, have regarded as condescending. I liked it, and him. People smiled. The woman behind the *tavola* who has asked me every week for years how I feel (every week I answer, "*Meno male,*" less bad, a colloquialism designed to blind the evil eye), burst into tears. Most people smiled. They are used to freaks in the Village, I said to Anna, meaning no disparagement and no disrespect (pain eventually makes freaks of us all). But one woman instructed her children to avert their eyes. "She shouldn't let herself be seen like that," another woman said.

Why, I wonder.

"It's good for them to see people in your condition," Anna said; I didn't have to ask her what she meant.

In my building, which is down the street from the Flatiron Building (one of New York's most sensible, original, and beautiful buildings — admit), people are tactful and plainly solicitous and sometimes both. When I walk around my neighborhood with my tank I get looks that range from piteous to contemptuous to scared, and working people who wear the dreariness of their work on their tired faces are least likely of all to smile or to acknowledge me, most likely to cut me a very wide swath.

Perhaps I will conduct a demographic survey. I will become a surveyor of facial emotions as I swing the elegant cane I intend to buy while I bridge this time into a less encumbered future. I like in any case to use a cane. It provides me with the requisite illusion that I can control my environment; I endow it with a kind of intelligence: it guides and leads me, and it anchors me. I suffer from vertigo; I feel as if the earth cannot be relied upon not to fling me into space. . . . I trust canes, extensions of my body, which I do not trust, except —

and how lucky this is — when I am making love. A cane is a strong prop.

> *The wood of the cross is mine for my eternal salvation. . . . I am strengthened by its roots, I lie down under its branches, I fill my nostrils with its savor as with a sweet breeze. . . . The immortal plant, it stands midway between heaven and earth, a strong prop for the universe, binding all things together, supporting the whole inhabited earth, a cosmic interlacing which embraces the motley of humanity; the Spirit holds it firm with invisible nails so that its contact with God may never be loosened, as it touches heaven with its peak, keeps its base firmly on earth, and embraces all the atmosphere with its measureless arms.*
>
> — Saint Hippolytus

Monday. Today the fridge broke down, the compressor burned out. When I woke up the fridge was burning hot to the touch and I vexed a morning away compulsively imagining the immolation I would have suffered if fire had attacked the oxygen supply (an utterly improbable scenario).

Tuesday. Today I was reading the daily lesson from my daughter's collection of the sayings of (erotic, neurotic, contentious, bold, mystical) saints, at the same time breathing medicine through a nebulizer. I never feel that the vapors are getting to my lungs, where they are supposed to go. I instruct myself with every breath, and I am a lousy learner. I was greatly surprised to find, after I'd read the words of Christ to the Benedictine Saint Mechthild, "the nightingale of Christ," who was gentled into sleep by angels chanting the psalms and urged by her Lord to seek him through her five senses, that breathing had come naturally to me. I had not once stopped to question the idiot workings of my recalcitrant body. This is what I read:

> *You shall take your mother only in me, and my love shall be your mother, and as children feed at their mother's breasts, so shall you feed of love as of your mother's inward comfort and the softness which may not be showed in speech. And that mother shall give you food and drink, and she shall clothe you, and in all your needs shall procure*

for you. And she shall help you and comfort you as a loving mother helps and comforts her daughter in time of need.

Encouraged, I went on to read the words of Saint Luke, the physician, patron saint of medicine: "Stay quiet with God." Mmmm. Yes. Lovely. I am bound to say, however, that I once rubbed the nose of a statue of the patron saint of medicine ("His words be medicine unto a sick soul"); and the next day my children came down with measles.

Life is never boring. I used to say this to my children when they were young: Life itself is never boring, I said, though one may through dereliction be bored. It is to their very great credit that they did not find me insufferable.

I am a walking *memento mori*. I remind people that someday they too will cease to breathe. I am the skeleton at the feast. Nonsense, my friend Anne Tabachnick says. Tabachnick is a painter, she sees surfaces profoundly: "It's just that they've never seen an oxygen tank outside a hospital. They've seen crutches and wheelchairs, they're used to them. You look funny to them, you look strange." Like a woman with a beard would look to a child.

(What is the thing people say when they find it distasteful to visit their relatives in intensive care units? "I couldn't bear to see her with tubes coming out of her," they say, feigning a delicacy they no doubt believe they own.)

"It isn't any of that," a friendly editor says to me. "It's that they're afraid" — her pragmatism comforts me (and life is never boring) — "that they might be called upon to *do* something."

In St. Croix with my friend Suzanne, before the acute stage of this illness, I got stuck in a sand trap from which I couldn't extricate one leg, and the blue-green waters of Sue's beach buffeted me. I couldn't at all breathe, slammed by all that lovely liquid this way and that. Caught in seaweed, I was torn between the necessity to relax and the necessity to energize so as to free myself. Suzanne put her strong brown arms around me and with utter unselfconsciousness breathed into my mouth. "Do you suppose," I asked Sue, sitting on her terrace that night, "that life is a matter of swinging from one polar opposite to another and of achieving balance through grace? In this case through your grace, perhaps through the grace of God — the breath of God?"

"Oh you silly," she said, and swung her legs over the rail.

What if the panic attacks that governed my life were nothing but (immensely) a lack of oxygen? What if, when the ground refused to meet my feet, the trouble was in my lungs and in my blood and not in the chemistry of my brain or in the revealed secrets of the past?

It is an upsetting and invigorating thought.

I wake up in northern light; the sky is full of wheeling birds tracing their runic calligraphy, their flawless choreography proof . . . proof of what? I ask myself drowsily. The machine hums. I turn toward the cool and elegant light.

November, the week before Thanksgiving. "You are better, you are so much better," my lung doctor says. "When you were here ten days ago you were blue-gray. You were suffocating to death."

How odd. How very odd. How odd to have walked so close to that formal dividing line and not to have surmised it.

At midnight my daughter calls, her conversation in part scholarly, in part giggly, until: "Don't die, Mommy," she cries.

There is no remedy for death.

My son wants pasta with fresh tuna for Thanksgiving.

I plan the Thanksgiving menu: *Antipasti:* roast peppers, orange, yellow, red, green, with garlic and olive oil; mixed mushrooms sliced and sautéed in truffle oil; *bruschetta* with olive paste. *Pasta:* spaghetti with tuna and mint in tomato sauce. *Sorbetto.* Roast pork with spices and herbs and pear sauce; *soubise.* Roast duckling with mixed baby lettuces. Cheese. Fruit tart. Chocolates.

I say the Jesus Prayer — "Sweet Lord Jesus, Son of God, have mercy upon us" — and breathe.

I go on my way rejoicing, bearing in mind the words of Cellini (who professed himself — his true suffering and his boys' comics picaresque adventures notwithstanding — to be sound as a roach): Content with what God and the world allow me to have, I go on my way rejoicing.

Torn, of course, between necessary laughter and tears. Here am I, a woman near the close of the twentieth century, reading, by happenstance, the late-nineteenth-century words of the Beecher sisters, Catharine Beecher and Harriet Beecher Stowe (the words make my oxygen-thin blood dance a little jig, they are like lines of archaic poetry, a map of an unknown country in an unknown language): "In a full-grown man weighing one hundred and fifty-four pounds, one hundred and eleven pounds consists of oxygen. . . . Every grown person receives, each day, thirty-three hogsheads of air [63 gallons] into the lungs to nourish and vitalize every part of the body. . . . The right side of the heart receives the dark and impure blood, which is loaded with carbonic acid. . . . Every time we think or feel, this mental action dissolves some particles of the brain and nerves, which pass into the blood to be thrown out of the body through the lungs and skin. . . . In the skin of every adult there are no less than seven million minute perspirating tubes, each one a fourth of an inch long. If all these were united in one length, they would extend twenty-eight miles." What dear affection I feel for this body, my dissolving human brain and nerves, my dark and impure blood, this meaty perishable renewable Atlantis.

2

FOOD, FLESH, AND FASHION

I LOVE FOOD. I also see it as the agent of my destruction.

When my lover and I separated I bought a bread-making machine. It was such a comfort to me, having something I could feed and control so that it would feed me, knowing that if I pushed all the right buttons I would get all the right results.

Food is good, the source of immediate sensual pleasure, gratification, gain . . . which is what makes it bad: food is bad, it's the source of gain. Fat. Which we all hate.

But it's perfectly possible to hate one's fat and to love one's body at the same time. I'm fat. I love my body when I'm having sex, nice body, so obedient, so capable . . . I rise, like yeast . . . so beautifully able to give and to take.

I don't think I know a single woman who knows what she looks like.

Mirrors notwithstanding, and in spite of the fact that we're invited, from the time we approach puberty, to take stock of our physical assets (and maximize them), and of our deficiencies (so as to minimize or mask them), I can't think of anybody who sees her body in a clear and dispassionate light, of anyone who doesn't center her anguished attention on an imperceptible flaw, or, on the other hand, perversely see as lovely that which others perceive to be flawed and love herself exactly for those physical attributes others have chosen tactfully to overlook. Make the most of what you've got, Mama says; but she looks so hopeless and sounds so exasperated when she says it ("your *hair*, dear . . ."), preparing us all for lives of trembling narcissism.

I thought I was fat when I was in junior high school. I wasn't fat. My breasts were developed — my first bra was size 32B. I didn't wear the trainer bras girls wore in those days, the point of which eludes me: Were they meant to coax nonexistent breasts into being? buds into flower? Were they supposed to make girls feel that they were northerly endowed so as to reduce the envy they presumably felt for their southerly endowed brothers? Were they a way (like dollhouse tea parties) to ape Mommy? Were they a transition between playing dress-up and being real women?

So much attention given to what wasn't there. In my case, however, what wasn't there *was* there, prematurely. I was unconcerned until Aunt Angie presented me with that size 32B from Macy's, to the accompaniment of female family laughter; and after that I was painfully aware of my breasts when I played punchball in the school gym in my horrid pea-green standard-issue middy suit, unable to absorb the principle of running around bases, so terrified was I of exposing my busty difference. I was more keenly aware of them when I was issued a freshman's drab tank swim suit in New Utrecht High School. (Every week I told the phys ed teacher I had my period, so as not to have to get into that suit; it was months before it dawned on her that if I were telling the truth, I was a medical anomaly if not a freak.) I was the champion roller skater of West Ninth Street because skating was something you could do alone, in the dark, with no one to regard your breasts jumping up and down like independent creatures. Skating was like levitating, almost: one flew, and executed daring turns and stops, and, in the swimmy light of street lamps filtered through maple leaves, one imagined one had auburn hair and green eyes. Nobody could touch me then.

"Barbara is water-retentive," my mother said (it was one of her ritual proclamations), as if I needed any more proof that I was fat. Which I was not.

When I was seventeen I sat with my teacher Arnold Horowitz (the thrilling proximity of beloved flesh!) on the window seat of his living room (the gross inadequacy of my flesh!) regarding, with the heart-stopping mingled terror and joy of first love, the winy maple tree that perfumed his room; we listened to a record of Kathleen Ferrier singing a folksong one line of which was about the "soft brown down" on someone's white arms in the moonlight. I took that as a coded direction to visit the electrologist. Can you imagine? I peer at my arms now and wonder what I could have been thinking of, what I could have been agonizing over. What on earth, except a totally crazy relationship to my own body, could have caused me to regard the hair (such as it was) on my body as a problem? In fact (I know now) I had beautiful hair, and negligible body hair. One school day when I was fifteen, teaching us to parse a sentence, Arnold wrote on the blackboard *The girl with hair the color of sun-warmed wheat* . . . , and then he passed my desk and smiled and mouthed *you*. What, I wonder now, would it have taken to reconcile me to myself in those sad and tingling days?

. . . In those days when I had gonorrhea. How I might have gotten a venereal disease was a mystery to me, but I had learned, from reading *Dr. Fishbein's Medical Home Examiner*, a staple tome in those households for which I baby-sat, that a spur on the heel was an indication of that disease. I also had, according to the evidentiary tables of *Dr. Fishbein's Medical Home Examiner*, pleurisy and rheumatic fever; but I chose, not insignificantly or inconsequentially, to worry only about gonorrhea. I didn't wear sandals for years.

Whenever I see and am tempted to envy a pretty teenager striding along in apparent possession of her beauty and in disregard of approval or condemnation, I remind myself to think: The chances are she hates her flesh.

Once from the window of a moving car I saw a young girl sitting at a soda counter, penny loafers dangling from her toes. For a long time I saw her image — her bare feet, the daring of exposure — as the perfect image of freedom.

I despised my fat. I weighed 110 pounds; I was five foot two ("Short legs, dear, are not American" — guess who said that).

I was thinking about this the other day as I ate the fruit-jelly slices I'd ordered from the Vermont Country Store catalogue. I was eating the sugared fruit-jelly slices — semicircles of lime green and orange and lemon yellow and pink with crescent candied rinds marginally more chewy than the jellied flesh of the sugared fruit — because I wanted to eat the sugared fruit-jelly slices, in defiance of the fact that I am fat. (Perhaps this doesn't explain why I ate two pounds of them. Moderation was another of those Mama-speak virtues I seemed incapable of exercising.) I happened to be nostalgic for jelly slices (also for sourballs) at the time I ordered; how was I to know that my latest diet would coincide with their arrival?

Nostalgia, for me, often takes the shape of food. When I think of my old neighborhood, I think of the corner candy store: jelly beans in a sack, and "dots" — little sugary pastilles of pale yellow and pink and blue, stuck on long strips of virginal white paper; black and red licorice sticks, and jawbreakers and candied "lips" — rubbery gummy things you attached to your own lips and ate from the inside out (a satisfying sort of cannibalism); and malted-milk balls and sugar babies and candy cigarettes, red at the tip. I think of the ice cream truck: it had a little picket-fence swinging door and a gabled roof with fake windows, so sweet and small-town-like — Icicles and Fudgsicles and Creamsicles and chocolate-almond bars, Dixie cups and sugar cones and plain cones: abundance. If you were good, your mother let you have one. (But it had to be from the Good Humor man; the other brands were, in some indecipherable way, bad for you.) Lemon and chocolate ices from the Italian bakery, charlotte russes — goodness, I long for them — in summer season: sponge cake in a ruffled paper cup and a layer of mashed fresh strawberries and whipped cream with a cherry on top, the bliss. When I think of home I think of Grandma cooking the Sunday gravy — the tomato sauce for "macaronies" — on the big black stove in the kitchen. When I was a good girl, Grandma let me dip a piece of bread in the thick sauce, which bubbled for hours.

I can't remember a time when the words *good* and *bad* didn't attach to food.

Mangia, mangia, it's good for you. . . . Don't eat that, you naughty girl, it's bad for you.

I went with Grandma to the kosher livestock market and watched chickens being ritually slaughtered, blooded, their necks slashed. Grandma collected the blood in a tin bucket, and she went home and made blood pudding of it, blood thickened with sugar and flour, blood punctuated by raisins. . . . I went home and sat beneath the mulberry tree, which formed a circle around me, hiding me, protecting me; I ate the ripe purple berries, staining my lips, my face, my hands, my starched white blouse with the blood of the sweet and delicate fruit. . . . When

I lived in India with Mr. Harrison for four years, I missed (in addition to the love I did not feel for my husband) only one thing: dark red cherries.

I measure generosity and I measure meanness in terms of food. "The kind of woman your mother is," my Uncle Pat once said to me, "is the kind of woman who serves one pork chop per customer for dinner." This was a summary of her character as far as he was concerned, and with it I secretly concurred.

"Barbara has a weight problem," my mother used to say, a kind of mantra when she was mad at me. I wouldn't have minded so much except that she said it in front of my beaus, or, lacking that opportunity, when she was in the process of devouring a whole huckleberry pie and (life being unfair) not gaining an ounce as a consequence. "Barbara is water-retentive." Jesus, what a judgment.

I was a slender young woman. Sometime in my late twenties (when my poor grandmother, who regarded me as maritally retarded, was making novenas for me to marry) I grew, imperceptibly to me, into my early image of myself: I became slightly overweight . . . and, later — now — frankly fat. ("Why are you fat?" a colleague asks. "Don't you like men?" People are idiots.)

Once, in Libya, the sheik of a pre-Islamic oasis called Gadames told me Sophia Loren had slept in the bed I was about to sleep in (the sheets, apparently, hadn't been changed since she made a moving picture in the hotel four years earlier); he told me I was more beautiful than she, and I allowed myself to feel flattered until he added this codicil: "Because you're fatter." (He'd weighed me on the barley scale.)

The miraculous meal we had that night had been prepared by a Neapolitan couple who led an odd kind of improvised life in the desert, this little patch of which they had made to blossom like the rose . . . and the fig tree, and the mulberry tree. They squabbled incessantly — their contentious syllables the music of their lost home. The old man shot pigeons for us and cooked them; we had rough red wine of his making; and his wife served the olives she had cured, and the pasta she made, and a sauce composed of tinned tomatoes and fresh cactus pulp. The sheik, as we stood on a windswept dune surrounded by oceans of sand where Tunisia, Libya, and Algeria conjoined (and where French military planes swooped like desert hawks), told us he'd met Josephine Baker once in Paris, and spoke of steak and pommes frites as if they were foods fit for gods; he was sad and glad in equal measure — glad because he had seen the wide world, and sad because he never would again. (He didn't whine.) There were seashells buried in that sand — and water nowhere to be seen. In that surreal wilderness of stingy sand, only the food was real.

I have given much thought to food, and to the flesh in which I live, and have entertained much conjecture on the subject of fat. I have learned that almost anybody can sound authoritative on this subject, in spite of the fact that the theories, the analyses, the prescriptions are mutually contradictory. It's almost as if anything one says about food and flesh is capable of reflecting truth — or the truth of the moment.

Is overindulgence a form of self-medication for pain or a frank urge to self-destruction? Is it neither? Is it sensuality pure and simple? Is fat a matter of genes, or of character and will, of discipline and sloth? of mommies? Is gluttony a mortal sin or is overeating a disease or disorder? And do the answers lie in our culture or in our poor selves (if indeed there are any definitive answers)?

When I am at the supermarket, are people "reading" my food cart in order to read my character?

Sometimes I want a boy's body — I want, when I swim, to enter the water like a sword. I do not want the impediments of breasts.

Do we really look to drag queens the way they look to us?

What has happened to the civilized, simple pleasures of the table?

In 1936, the satirical essayist Rose Macaulay was able to speak of food as pleasure and perishable art: "Here is a wonderful and delightful thing, that we should have furnished ourselves with orifices, with traps that open and shut, through which to push and pour alien objects that give us such pleasurable, such delicious sensations, and at the same time sustain us. A simple pleasure."

A simple pleasure, however, that led to the downfall of the human race ("every pleasure has also its reverse side, in brief, its pain . . . [all pleasures have] the little flavor of bitterness, the flaw in their perfections . . . which tang their sweetness and remind us of their mortality and our own, and that nothing in this world is perfect"): "The vice of gluttony was in Paradise, most deplorably mistimed." It was through gluttony "that our first parents fell." Macaulay took the fruit-and-downfall business with a dollop of wit: "The only fruit that has ever seemed to me to be worthy of the magnificently inebriating effects wrought by its consumption on both our parents is the mango. [How many calories in a mango, I wonder.] When I have eaten mangoes, I have felt like Eve."

Somehow one knew Eve, mother and sister of us all, ultimate troublemaker, twin and dangerous friend, was at the bottom of all this. Haven't we always been told so?

"It scarcely bears thinking about, the time and labour that man and womankind has devoted to the preparation of dishes that are to melt and vanish in a moment like smoke or a dream, like a shadow, . . . and afterwards no sign where they went is to be found."

Oh yes, there's a sign. The stigmata we bear are called cellulite.

Even Macaulay, frank and free in her appetites, expressed a degree of aristocratic disgust for food: Bread, sausage, jam, veal, "Better see no food prepared. Close the eyes, open the mouth, and say a grace that you were not there at the making of the pleasant finished product that slips so agreeably down your throat and into your system. And, if you come to that, what would your system look like, do you suppose, if you should have the misfortune to see *that*? It ill behooves us, with our insides, to be dainty about looking upon the manufacture of anything that goes into them; at its worst stage the object to be consumed can scarcely have presented so ill an appearance as does the place prepared for its reception."

Poor Macaulay, she starts off singing the uncomplicated praise of food and winds up describing the human body that consumes it as a sewer.

I read Sartre in my late teens and made the mistake of taking him seriously. He told me that if one really loved another human being, one had to set oneself the imaginative task of loving every orifice, every inch of intestine, everything the loved body contained, enveloped, or expelled: gall and mucus, shit and spit. I gave this imperative grave consideration, never for a moment understanding that Sartre might have loathed flesh — particularly if it was female flesh — and was himself incapable of human love. . . . Men are afraid of women's bodies (their secret interior plumbing); women exude so much, not the least of which is blood. (Unclean! An Arab text tells us that breast milk is menstrual blood "twice-boiled.") Men are bound both to love and to hate the bodies they exited from and from which they must separate so completely in order to be distinguishably male. And women read men's self-centered words and wonder why the world seems off center. We are both erotic and motherly, and as a consequence, alas, threatening. We don't mind nearly as much as they do that men, who have exited from us, also enter us. We don't mind at all.

We are heir to the imperatives and the contradictions of decades, of centuries. A less kind way of saying this is that we are slaves of fashion. (The first time I saw the expression *fashion slaves* was in 1983, in the window of Milan's Rinascente: stylishly dressed mannequins held the banner — FASHION SLAVES — aloft. The Milanese are a realistic people and are capable of singing in their chains.)

In the fifteenth century the ideal beauty had narrow shoulders, small breasts, a large rounded belly, wide hips, great big thighs, short legs, and a small head — she was a perfect embodied Botticelli. (Also she wore a permanent half-smile akin to a simper.) In the 1880s women were obliged to have hourglass figures to satisfy the demands of fashion, the ideal measurements being 38-18-38, which means that their waists were smaller, even, than Scarlett O'Hara's, around which Rhett Butler could join his two hands. In the 1920s fashion dictated no tits, no hips; women were fashionable ironing boards around which to drape cloth. The 1940s were complicated, as, from my mother's wardrobe, I remember: Women worked in war factories, so they had to look strong and capable; they also, poor things, had to look soft (like Betty Grable), as if on call for the men who flew the planes they built. They had somehow to give the illusion that if you ripped off their clothes you'd find pink candy underneath. Stand-ins for the men at the front, they had to be women (unmanned) underneath. I rather like the fashions of the forties, and I do think women have a shoulder-pad fantasy — *undress me and I'm ready to service and to serve.* In the fifties, when I grew up, a moderate hourglass figure was called for, à la Monroe and Loren. Simultaneously, adorable Audrey Hepburn, coltish and elegant, offered us fashion lessons (as if anyone in the world could ever look like more than a pale caricature of her, so *sui generis* was she; an actress who worked with Hepburn told me that during the filming of *A Nun's Story* she lived on apples, mineral water, and vitamin shots, a penance worse than that which the nun suffered).

Women are offered alternative visions or versions of beauty upon which to model themselves. Paradoxically, the fact that idealization of female beauty takes different forms results not in the perception of choice but in a multiplication of bondage. "Throughout the nineteenth century," writes Lawrence Venuti, the translator of I. U. Tarchetti's nineteenth-century novel *Passion* (which provided the inspiration for Sondheim's musical), "romantic writers and painters challenged the dominant concept of female beauty by associating the erotic with illness. In opposition to the fleshy, salubrious ideal of femininity that characterized bourgeois culture, a consumptive thinness was construed as the sign of a heightened sensibility, both passionate and spiritual. The title character of Jules Barbey d'Aurevilly's *Lea* (1832) possesses a more than angelic beauty precisely because she suffers from tuberculosis. Her lover, Reginald, waxes rhapsodic: 'You are the most beautiful woman in creation! I shall never give you up, not you, nor your sunken eyes, your pallor, your sick body.' Their first kiss turns out to be their last. At that very moment she succumbs to the disease, and love and death are grotesquely linked in her bloody vomit: 'Her heart's blood flooded her lungs and rose to her mouth,' leaving her 'no more than a corpse.'" In *Passion*, the hero's carnal infatuation with a woman of abundant physical charms is revivifying; his later obsession with the tubercular Fosca, on the other hand, "is marked by a rapid physical decline that implicitly depicts her as a vampire-like femme fatale, sustaining her own life at the expense of her lover's."

. . . I am hopelessly retro, I love the fifties. . . . I am strolling down a Brooklyn street; honeysuckle; and I am holding Arnold Horowitz's hand. I am dressed in a flared, quilted skirt, bright flowers splashed on a field of black satin, that reaches in provocative waves to my calves, and a silky wraparound black blouse, and black Capezio ballet slippers,

I am wearing Shalimar because it smells like vanilla and Arnold loves it. I am loving myself, feet skimming the ground, loving the way I look. . . .

A brown shirtwaist dress with faint yellow and orange stripes and pearly buttons that emphasized my hourglass à la mode figure; a body-clinging dress of lamb's wool, soft as a cloud, for which my own curves provided the only ornamentation; an olive-green dress, black checks, high at the neck, tight to the waist, flared in inverted pleats to midcalf; a shaggy pink angora sweater that cinched my waist and a thin black silk moiré skirt — how I loved those clothes. Why did I abandon the body I loved, the clothes I loved? By insidious degrees. And sometimes I allow myself to think that this body, which, after all, men have loved, is fine, capable, and beautiful. The theories I entertain are contradictory; so are my own.

Toward the end of the fifties, lots of us who believed ourselves to be free spirits took to wearing a beatnik-type uniform: black. Black skirt, black blouse, black leotards. The head of the secretarial pool at Macmillan, where I worked, sent out memo after memo: Wear nylons! she said. We ignored her. (She was Steichen's daughter and Sandburg's niece — *and don't you forget it!*) We thought she was old. Old and fey. We knew we'd get old someday, but we didn't *know* we'd get old. (It's interesting how knowing one will die — and I did know that — is quite different from knowing that one will grow old.) Dan Wakefield asked me to go with him to a fashion show given by Jimmy Baldwin's sister. "I can't go," I said, "I've been wearing the same black blouse and skirt all summer." "All the more reason," he said. "Anyway, I'm getting married that day," I said. Which was true. I curled my hair for my wedding; I cut my long brown hair and curled it. I agonized over whether to wear gloves. I carried white gloves. I didn't wear them. I couldn't decide whether to let the neckline of my hastily bought white dress plummet to reveal the curve of my breasts, or to modify the neckline with a pin. At this time I weighed 130 pounds and considered myself — except when making love (but not to my future husband) — grotesque. I was not grotesque. I was not skinny, either. I'm fatter now.

I do not think of fat and food all the time. Only when I think about fat and food.

Sometimes I allow myself to wonder if my fat is a costume, if I am acting out a female version of "Beauty and the Beast." My fat is a kind of test: if he loves me in spite of it, he will be my lord, my knight proper, my love.

In *The Physiology of Taste*, written in 1825 and translated and annotated by M. F. K. Fisher, Brillat-Savarin celebrates "the [instinctive] leanings of the fair sex toward gourmandism. . . . A tempting diet, dainty and well prepared, holds off for a long time the exterior signs of old age.

"It adds brilliancy to the eyes, freshness to the skin, and more firmness to all the muscles; and just as it is certain, in physiology, that it is the sagging of these muscles which causes wrinkles, beauty's fiercest enemy, so it is equally correct to say that, other things being equal, the ladies who know how to eat are comparatively ten years younger than those to whom this science is a stranger.

"Painters and sculptors have long recognized this truth, and they never portray subjects who, through choice or duty, practice abstinence, such as anchorites or misers, without giving them the pallor of illness, the wasted scrawniness of poverty, and the deep wrinkles of enfeebled sanity."

At a dinner party Brillat-Savarin sat across from an exquisite creature who ate lightly during the first two courses, which disturbed his equilibrium, as it upset his theories. "Finally the dessert arrived, a dessert as impressive as it was generous. . . . Not only did she eat everything that was offered to her, but she even asked for portions from those plates which were farthest from her. Finally she had tasted every one; and my neighbor confessed his astonishment that this little belly could hold so many things," and Brillat-Savarin's sensibilities triumphed: he needed women to be well fed, pink, and plump.

Today — when illness is regarded as a crime, and crime is regarded as illness — food is a substance to be controlled, like a dangerous drug. Imagine if someone today behaved as Brillat-Savarin's young woman did; one's friends practically tear the food out of one's mouth if one is fat (or, alternatively, tell you that you are beautiful just as you are, which means you are not. . . . I once traveled to Sicily with an Armani-skinny-and-elegant American resident of Rome. She wouldn't let me eat Sicilian pastries, and she made a little moue every time she saw me lusting after one. By the second month of our trip she'd recognized defeat and was telling me I was beautiful just as I was, which meant I was not).

Brillat-Savarin met his dessert-loving beauty again two years after their first encounter; she was seventeen, and married. Her charms were unveiled "to the last permissible limits of fashion," and she was "truly ravishing." Her husband, like a "certain ventriloquist who knew how to laugh with one side of his face and weep with the other, . . . seemed delighted to have his wife admired, but . . . as soon as he felt the admiration too pressing he was wracked with a shudder of very obvious jealousy," and "took his wife off to a distant province, and as far as I know that is the end of the story," a story which, to our ears, sounds like a fairy tale.

"A married couple who enjoy the pleasures of the table have, at least once a day, a pleasant opportunity to be together; for even those who do not sleep in the same bed (and there are many such) at least eat at the same table; they have a subject of conversation which is ever new; they can talk not only of what they are eating, but also of what they have eaten, what they will eat, and what they have noticed at other tables; they can discuss fashionable dishes, new recipes, and so on and so on; and of course it is well known that intimate table talk is full of its own charm. . . . A shared necessity summons a conjugal pair to the table, and the same thing keeps them there; they feel as a matter of course countless little wishes to please each other, and the way in which meals are enjoyed is very important to the happiness of life."

I call that sweet.

It was during the first year of my marriage that I fashioned a rule: never leave the house without a paperback to read. Because my husband and I, no matter how exotic our surroundings, never had anything to say to each other over meals. (One of our great fights occurred when I picked a black olive off his plate.) The Duke and Duchess of Windsor, having little to say to each other in public, I am told, recited fairy tales in French when they dined out alone.

How lovely when all appetites are mingled. How delicious when, in *Tom Jones*, before the lovers bedded each other, seducer and willing seducee shared a meal before they shared each other, consuming flesh and fruit, tearing meat from bones, sucking sweet meat from claws of fish, in preparation and titillation (hot and practically growling) for the meal their bodies would soon make of each other. "In the anguish of the repose of the madness of love," the thirteenth-century poet Hadewijch wrote, "the heart of each devours the other's heart." Hadewijch was writing of the love of women for Christ — "He eats us; we . . . eat him" — but the principle remains: classically food was not only a spur to love and a metaphor for erotic love but an intrinsic part of love, as, in the act of love, we are all cannibals. "As soon as Love . . . touches the soul, / She eats its flesh and drinks its blood." I love you so much I could eat you up, we say; and we do. Love is a feast. From the Song of Songs: "As the apple tree among the trees of the wood, so is my beloved among the sons. I sat down under his shadow with great delight, and his fruit was sweet to my taste. . . . Thy lips, O my spouse, drop as the honeycomb: honey and milk are under thy tongue; and the smell of thy garments is like the smell of Lebanon. . . . And the roof of thy mouth [is] like the best wine for my beloved, that goeth down sweetly, causing the lips of those that are asleep to speak. I am my beloved's, and his desire is toward me."

"Women whom Nature has afflicted" with "long faces, noses, and eyes [and] no matter what their height . . . a general air of elongation . . . have flat dark hair and above all lack healthy weight; it is undoubtedly they who invented trousers, to hide their thin shanks." Without healthy attitudes women, miserable, are "scrawny, and bored at table, and exist only for cards and sly gossip," says Brillat-Savarin.

My hero, the mystery writer and theologian Dorothy L. Sayers, who in middle age became enormously fat (and in the process mannish-looking), called gluttony one of the "warm," large-hearted sins — as opposed, for example, to envy, a cold, pinched, mean sin. Nice. But in the Middle Ages it was gluttony, not abstention, that was regarded as the midwife of gossip, scurrility, and loquacity. Food, no matter what our emphasis, is central to our ideas of ourselves.

"Thinness is a horrible calamity for a woman. . . . As for women who are born thin and whose digestion is good, we cannot see why they should be any more difficult to fatten than young hens; and if it takes a little more time than with poultry, it is because human fe-

male stomachs are comparatively smaller, and cannot be submitted as
are those devoted barnyard creatures, to the same rigorous and punc-
tually followed diet." Brillat-Savarin was convinced that "every thin
woman wants to grow plump," and in his time — when skinniness
suggested tuberculosis, poverty, and/or approaching death — every
bourgeois woman probably did; and he incited women to the kind of
sensuality that would be seen today as torpor: "Before eight o'clock in
the morning, and in bed if that seems best, drink a bowl of soup
thickened with bread or noodles; . . . or, if you wish, take a cup of good
chocolate." At eleven A.M. they were to eat "eggs scrambled or fried in
butter, little meat pies, chops." Then they were to take a little exercise,
which he defined as shopping or leaving calling cards at the houses of
friends. Dinner was to consist of "soup, meat and fish, as much as you
wish; but add to them dishes made with rice or macaroni, frosted
pastries, sweet custards, creamy puddings, . . . Savoy biscuits, babas,
and other concoctions which are made of flour, eggs, and sugar." They
were to drink beer or Bordeaux wine, to avoid acids, to sweeten fruit
— and they were not to tire themselves by too much dancing.

(This is more or less the program followed in Montecatini-Terme,
in Tuscany. One is spoiled and pampered at grand hotels, fed such
lovely things as *la risotta* (when the cooked arborio rice is liquid and
creamy, it is assigned the feminine form) and anthropomorphized pas-
tas the names of which translate as "little cupids," "clowns' hats,"
"priests' hats" — sometimes served with a sausage that is called "the
priest"; and the tubular "grooved bridegrooms" (ziti with ridges) and
"husky bridegrooms" (zitoni — larger ziti), served with silky sauces and
ragùs. One sleeps well after such meals and the mind-clearing *digestivi*
and espresso that follow them. In the early morning, one walks leisurely to a gilded and tiled art nouveau spa, an architectural folly and
extravaganza; and, to the accompaniment of the music of a string
quartet, partakes of various foul-tasting mineral waters from brass pipes
and spigots; and then rushes back to the hotel in time for the waters
to have worked their bubbly magic on the organs — but not, one hopes,
a moment too late — and eliminates, before breakfast, the excessive
amount of food one consumed from the groaning board the night
before — a benign binge-purge process for which there is sanction.)

Imagine believing that women's stomachs are smaller than chickens'!

On the one hand, one wishes to kiss Brillat-Savarin on both cheeks; on the other, one finds him appalling, as he speaks of women as if they were somewhere on the food chain between barnyard and swamp creatures: "Sheep, calves, oxen, poultry, carp, crayfish, and oysters: Everything that eats can grow fat."

His idea of exercise is the idea of exercise I held dear for years: lie down as soon as you feel the urge. (Walking and swimming and making love seemed to me perfectly adequate uses to which to put one's body.) Arnold used to say — in the high school days when the world was divided into jocks and intellectuals and each scorned the other — that exercise disturbed the balance of toxins in one's body, and I was inclined to agree. Brillat-Savarin called exercise "horribly tiring, and the perspiration it brings out places one in grave danger of . . . pleurisy; dust ruins the stockings; stones wear out the soles of dainty slippers, and the whole business is hopelessly boring. Finally if, after these various attempts, a tiny headache is felt, or an almost invisible spot shows itself on the skin, the whole system of exercise is blamed and abandoned, and the doctor fumes helplessly."

In spite of this retrospectively quaint advice, and in spite of the fact that he well understood that "as long as appetite lasts, one mouthful leads to another with irresistible attraction," he had vast distaste for obesity — however he defined it: "Very well then; eat! Get fat! Become ugly, and thick, and asthmatic, and finally die in your own melted grease."

Melted grease: medical students call fat cadavers "squirters."

Brillat-Savarin — like a nanny, like a mother, and like contemporary weight-loss gurus who insist on showing you disgusting globs of yellow rosin to represent fat, each glistening globule a reproach — offers reward and punishment, compassion and contempt in one breath: "It takes real courage either to lose weight or to keep from gaining it," he says; but then he talks of melted grease.

Brillat-Savarin's idea of an "anti-fat" diet rests on the presumption that "it is only because of grains and starches that fatty congestion can occur, . . . [which is demonstrated by the feeding of] fattened beasts. . . . A more or less rigid abstinence from everything that is starchy or floury will lead to the lessening of weight." He advises, for the obese, soups, roasts, leafy vegetables, salads, "a chocolate custard or the jellies made with wine." Also liqueur, and veal and poultry, and, every summer, thirty bottles of seltzer. He disagreed with the belief, widely held in his day, that acids — including both vinegar and sweetened lemonade — prevented obesity. He suggested quinine instead. And he advocated the use of something called an anti-fat belt, to be worn day and night to support and confine the belly, so that "excess weights which the intestines acquire" would not drag "on the various envelopes which make up the walls of the belly."

We laugh; but none of this is much more preposterous than the grapefruit diets and Jell-O diets and oat bran and banana diets and the eat-dessert-before-the-main-course diets I have in my lifetime seen prescribed. The diets of my youth prescribed endless protein (including eggs), green stuff, and no carbohydrates. I lost tons; I also lost any realistic view of what I looked like.

How is it possible to look at our bodies objectively (and with love)? How can we not feel that what enters our bodies is either ambrosia or razor blades and sometimes both at once? Why has eating, an act of animal survival civilized by ritual and refinement, become more complicated than quantum physics?

The other day in the changing room of my apartment building's rooftop swimming pool I saw two bare-chested models: breasts like tulips, curved and pert and ample for hors d'oeuvres if not for a meal. And you could play spoons on their ribs and place clothes hangers on their collarbones. By what miracle does this happen? Am I supposed to look like this?

I was with an overweight swimming companion at the time. She informed me, in tones of infinite yearning, that there is a small town north of Milan where, as a result of centuries of inbreeding, a gene has mutated so that fat will not stick to the bones of the villagers, who can, and probably do, eat whipped cream and drink wine all day long without fear of cholesterol. (Why not me, Lord?) She also, being clever, said, as the jets in the hot-water tub soothed our troubled flesh, "*Everyone* owns our problem. It belongs to everyone who sees it." Yes; there is a way in which our weight is a conversation with the world, as the Scarlet Letter was; character defects can be hidden or disguised; our weight is, literally, writ large.

I started this by saying that American women didn't know, couldn't know, what they looked like. Italian girls grow into their beauty very early. They seem to have a sense of style and self-possession that begins before they menstruate and never deserts them (whereas puberty is just about the time American girls lose any body confidence they ever might have had). My Roman friend Kiki, a great beauty, told me she looked with deep concentration in the mirror when she was twelve years old and from then on knew — by what sublime process she was quite unable to tell me — exactly how to dress, how to *be* in her body. And you can see them, on the squares of Italy, women like Kiki, supremely casual and triumphant in their flyaway beauty, their bodies both relaxed and tensile and hot and cool, everything perfect . . . and you couldn't duplicate it, nobody could; why? What's more remarkable is that it all comes off looking so effortless. It is not accompanied by Fear of Food; and it applies from their First Communion to their burial shroud.

It is true that Italians have been known to go on diets that one would be hard put not to call strange. In 1930, rebelling against all classical forms of art, the Futurist Marinetti, a Milanese whom the moron Mussolini counted as a friend, proposed combinations of food that wildly prefigured the excesses of zealous *cuisine nouvelle:* pineapple with sardines, salami in black coffee with an infusion of eau de cologne, Strega with eggs and red pepper (an aphrodisiac); needless to say the stuff never caught on. Italians are given occasionally to indulging in "white" diets, which include the pounded white meat of chicken and exclude red meat but include white wine. They do this out of respect for their *fegatos,* their livers, which frequently after a great meal they swathe, using blankets like cummerbunds; they diet periodically and with gusto, just as they periodically "purge" themselves with gusto — which means they drink lots of mineral water and eat boiled vegetables until the mood passes — but on a day-to-day basis they are remarkably sane about food. Perhaps they had enough of endless dieting and manipulation of food in the fifteenth century, when the monk Savonarola, the "gravedigger of Florence," established Sumptuary Laws, disallowing Florentines from having more than two meals a day, and those only three courses each. Italians managed, of course, to circumvent the law (a matter in which they have no equals): one of the courses was likely to be a "roast with pie," which might include pork and songbirds

— larks covered by their own tongues, chickens, ham, eggs, dates, capers, almonds, flour, spices, sugar, saffron. . . . *Four and twenty black-birds baked in a pie.*

Italians' "deep contentment with the accustomed bespeaks an atti-tude toward a meal that makes of it a daily *festa*" (and not a test), Kate Simon writes; "many of the lovely words that purl out of Italian mouths, you will notice, deal with eating: *'Ha mangiato bene?' 'Sì, mangia bene.' 'Che mangiamo oggi?' 'Dove mangiamo?'* All are invitations to long, animated discussions [and not about calories or fat grams]. Should you be on an Italian excursion bus that takes off at, let us say, 8 A.M., the exchange of greetings and autobiography will last until about 9:00, to be followed — first from one quarter, then another and soon burbling through the bus — by requests for a coffee stop, which will include a nibble of cake [a *cornetto*] or a small sandwich. At 10:30 paper parcels will unfold and chunks of bread, slices of prosciutto and medi-cine bottles full of wine come into action. From that time on, until the lunch stop at 1:30, lascivious fantasies are exchanged about delicious possibilities: pasta, chicken or veal, salad, fruit and wine, always familiar, always a promise of pleasure. . . . The pace of an authentically Italian meal is distinctly musical. The first movement, the pasta or soup, is a *presto agitato*, fast and eager. The meat is cut, lifted and chewed in a calmer *allegro*, while the fruit introduces a stately *adagio* of slow, careful selection, aristocratic discarding, exquisite peeling with knife and fork, the deliberate, slow jaws returned to serenity. We have now reached the interminable *lento*. Although your bread, wine and first course were brought with the speed that accompanies emergencies — a hungry man is a man in serious trouble — the waiter, having fed you, turns to more urgent matters." The waiter is performing a kind of triage, and catering to another raging hunger.

At this very moment I am daydreaming of a perfect *bollito misto*.

Why am I always looking for the illusive perfect Italian restaurant in New York? I know at least six restaurants in Rome I consider perfect, including one that is in what amounts to a parking lot behind the Pantheon. I love that restaurant so much . . . "You have ordered well, signora," the waiter says, as if choosing perfection from a perfect menu were clever of me; to celebrate my perfection, he brings me a glass of

Averna (the *digestivo* that, in perfect Italian fashion — and like coffee, which is said both to stimulate and to pacify — arouses the appetite before the meal and calms the full stomach after the meal). I love that restaurant so much I didn't allow my eye to see that our *al fresco* was being shared by at least six Vespas and five Cinquecentos. I was happy to regard the carved wooden doors of the thin houses that leaned toward us on the narrow cobblestone street, the cheerful pots of flowers. "Barbara," my friend Alice informed me, strands of spaghetti *carbonara* curled lustrously around her fork, "we're eating in a parking lot!" "Yes, but such a lovely parking lot," I said, "a *Roman* parking lot"; and Alice agreed. (And how can one not regard as perfect a restaurant where a waiter greets you with open arms, asks you where you have been and how your Uncle Carmine is — after an absence of five years, during which time you have gained twenty pounds.)

So Kate Simon is right: "The passion for Italian food is less a need for veal in six styles or chicken in three than a yearning for Italianness. So, even if your diet forbids you . . . you will eat pasta because you see it eaten with a total joy, a concentration of pleasure, as if it were a rare Lucullan dish rather than the habitual staple served at least once a day. You will plunge and wallow in the manipulating, slurping, moistly shining, sexy happiness, not so much to eat as to share the buoyant Italian greed for experiencing deeply, everything, from roaring in a winner at the races to the wash of peach juice in the mouth."

On great, and sometimes not so great, occasions in the Abruzzi it is not uncommon for a meal — a *panarda* — to last as long as six hours. "Each time you think you have reached the end of the meal," Waverly Root says, "it starts all over again." Traditionally a proper *panarda* had no fewer than thirty courses. Root details a memorable *panarda* served in 1962: "three fish dishes; mountain ham, country bread and mountain butter; double consomme; and boiled meats. . . . Mortadella . . . guitar macarone, fritters in celery sauce, grilled trout, roast kid, potato omelet, and artichokes fried with *scamorza* cheese. . . . Sausages, cardoon soup, veal rolls with beans, eel country style and grilled mutton with salad rich in mountain herbs, . . . baked artichoke hearts, broccoli in sauce, galantine of chicken in jelly, pickles and artichokes in olive oil, deep-fried brains and utility meats, veal with tuna sauce and capers, chicken

hunter's style, and lamb chops. . . . Pig's liver, kidneys, rock partridge
with ham, veal scaloppine with truffles, and peas with ham. . . . Toasted
scamorza cheese, pecorino cheese, . . . dry and fresh fruits, cake, cook-
ies," and confetti. Twenty years later, in the little town of Avezzano, in
Abruzzo, I went to a First Communion celebration at which two
hundred guests consumed melon and prosciutto, stracciatelle, lasagne
with bechamel and meat sauce, spaghetti with shellfish, fish fry, quail
with potatoes, green salad, *vitello tonnato*, spinach in olive oil, ices, fruit
and cheese, gelato, fruitcake with white frosting, and coffee, wines, and
liqueurs. Afterward, family and close friends and constituents went back
to the mayor's house (it was he whose child, Angelo, had received his
First Communion) and consumed *digestivi*, marzipan fruits, and pastry
puffs colored and shaped like peaches, pink and green and pale yellow,
drenched in peach liqueur, split open to reveal a chocolate pit; and,
with midnight drawing near, open sandwiches of caviar, of butter and
walnuts, and of prosciutto. In the morning, to keep up our strength,
we ate beefsteak, spinach, strawberries and coffee.

I also remember a single succulent peach, one my friend Laura ate,
tears running down her face: "Ah," she said (on her first visit to
L'Aquila, from which her people came), "this is the first peach I have
ever eaten." I remember the way my throat ached from the trickling
sweetness of the cherries I bought on the Piazza Sonino in Rome; and
I remember the joy with which a Venetian woman, stealing days in
Sicily with her married lover, drank *orzato*, an almond drink, "like liquid
pearls," she sighed, her words interwoven with the suspiration of the
sea. I remember the way the smell of ripe peaches mingled with the
brown river smell of the Arno in a farmhouse in Tuscany, and how the
moonlight accentuated the heavenly fragrance.

One of the things that makes the terrible melancholy of Giuseppe
di Lampedusa's wise and beautiful novel *The Leopard* bearable is his
sensual evocation of the delights of the table: the "monumental dishes
of macaroni, . . . the burnished gold of the crusts, the fragrance of sugar
and cinnamon they exuded, were but preludes to the delights released
from the interior when the knife broke the crust; first came a mist laden
with aromas, then chicken livers, hard-boiled eggs, sliced ham, chicken,
and truffles in masses of piping-hot, glistening macaroni, to which the

meat juice gave an exquisite hue of suede . . . huge blond *babas, Mont Blancs* snowy with whipped cream, cakes speckled with white almonds and green pistachio nuts, hillocks of chocolate-covered pastry, brown and rich as the topsoil of the Catanian plain from which . . . they had come, pink ices, champagne ices, coffee ices, all *parfaits*, which fell apart with a squelch as the knife cleft them, melody in major of crystallized cherries, acid notes of yellow pineapple, and those cakes called 'triumphs of gluttony' filled with green pistachio paste, and shameless 'virgins' cakes' shaped like breasts." Lampedusa's Don Fabrizio uses food to comment upon his world: "Don Fabrizio asked for [virgins' cakes], and as he held them in his plate looked like a profane caricature of St. Agatha. 'Why ever didn't the Holy Office forbid these cakes when it had the chance? St. Agatha's sliced-off breasts sold by convents, devoured at dances! Well, well!'" And: "All Sicilian expression, even the most violent, is really wish-fulfillment: our sensuality is a hankering for oblivion, our shooting and knifing a hankering for death; our laziness, our spiced and drugged sherbets, a hankering for voluptuous immobility, that is, for death again." Death, and life: when the Sicilian prince smells a fresh peach — "big, velvety, luscious-looking; yellowish, with a faint flush of rosy pink on the cheeks, like those of Chinese girls, . . . products of love, of coupling" — he thinks of the inside of a dancer's thighs. . . . The sad and lonely old man, his world lost to him, is recalled to it by food, food that is oblivion and memory, life and death.

I attribute the "buoyant Italian greed for experiencing deeply, everything," to the fact that Italians know they will one day die, knowledge bred deep in their bone and marrow, knowledge denied us, in our Puritan zeal for moderation. (Is it any accident that that super-Puritan, quintessential Calvinist Ralph Nader, when he decided to address himself to food-consumers' issues, began with the hot dogs that vendors sell at baseball parks? He deluded himself into thinking sports spectators the continent over would rise up in protest against the unwholesomeness of stadium franks. Whereas everybody knows that no hot dog in the whole world ever tastes as good as the one you're eating when your team is winning on a summer day; and who cares what's in it?)

Knowing that you will die is salutary — good for the liver and skin and heart, a tranquilizer for that desperate fear of age that we are cursed with. Calvin believed money and property accrued to those God deemed virtuous. The contemporary version of Calvinism is that the virtuous are rewarded with healthy bodies — and perhaps with immortality, secularly attained.

Ancient Romans had picnics on tombs. They communicated with their dead and rejoiced in the company of the living. We store our dead on ice, waiting for a Great Unfreezing Day when secular magic will cure what killed us.

What underlies our confusions — our dieting and our compulsions and our ludicrous conversations (do you want to be told how many fat grams are in the bean dip when you go to a party?), our queasy and rabid fear of deterioration — is that we are fundamentally uncertain of the nature of our bodies.

Are we our bodies? Is the body the source of personhood? I once remarked to the wife of a governor that her husband was a very handsome man, as indeed he was; she replied, rather primly and with what I suppose is a form of political correctness (but so *boring*, and so banal), "It's what's inside that counts." Fiddle-de-dee.

The medievalist Caroline Walker Bynum writes, in *Fragmentation and Redemption*, that there is in Western culture a "duality . . . more profound even than gender: a tension between body as locus of pain and limitation, and body as locus not merely of pleasure but of personhood itself."

Women who perceive themselves to be oppressed by a double sexual standard are accustomed, when thinking of these matters, to focus on the dichotomy between virgin (the paradigm for whom is Mary) and whore (the paradigms for whom are Eve and Mary Magdalene), a distinction, basically, between spirit and matter, (pure) soul and (nagging, demanding, vociferous) flesh. The truth of Western culture is rather more complicated than that. Historically the flesh was seen as greedy and lustful and flawed and subject to putrefaction *and* as holy, worthy of resurrection. In Christian theology God became flesh, enfleshed by Mary's human flesh; flesh is good. Our poor bodies are arenas for mystical encounters *and* for temptation. "Medieval piety," Bynum says, "did not dismiss flesh — even female flesh — as polluting.

Rather, it saw flesh as fertile and vulnerable; and it saw enfleshing —
the enfleshing of God and of us all — as the occasion for salvation."

It is fair to say, however, that female flesh was regarded with more
suspicion than was male flesh — for one thing, there was more *fleshiness*
to female flesh than to male flesh. Women are more their bodies than
men are.

Men are able to separate their minds from their bodies in a way that
is alien to most women. When Senator Bob Packwood was alleged to
have sexually harassed God knows how many women, the immediate
defense his supporters put up was: But he's so good on women's issues!
As if his testes were in one place and his brain on a distant continent.
This is the Gary Hart syndrome, the "good" man whose "only" pec-
cadillos are sexual, the fragmented man who disengages body from soul
and mind. ("It is *only* a crime of passion," William Kunstler said when
seeking reinstatement to the bar of an attorney who had hired thugs
to throw acid in his girlfriend's face, blinding and disfiguring her . . .
and, Kunstler said years later, of the murders allegedly committed by
O. J. Simpson, it was "merely" a crime of passion, and so should not
be considered murder in the first degree.)

Women are the caretakers of the flesh: their flesh gives birth to flesh;
they attend to the flesh from birth to death — they care for the newborn and the young and the sick and the dying. It is natural for a woman
to see her body as her *self*. Think of the paradigms: Eve's *body* was the
arena and origin of temptation and sin; Mary's *body* — which gave flesh
to God — was the arena of redemption, the source of her personhood
and her saintliness.

So are we our bodies? "My body is the one part of me that is always,
undeniably, here," writes Sallie Tisdale, leaving unanswered whether
the body is merely discardable housing for the soul. We may pooh-pooh
the notion of owning a soul (an encumbrance as embarrassing to some
as fat); but few of us would deny being in possession of "hearts" and
minds and spirits. And where exactly, in what physical organs, do we
locate these objects or attitudes or states of being? "Theorists in the
high Middle Ages did not see body primarily as the enemy of soul, the
container of soul, or the servant of soul; rather they saw the person as
a psychosomatic unity, as body and soul together," Bynum writes. How
nice for them. And Saint Thomas Aquinas, so maddening to women

on many other counts, writes that the nature of resurrection is that the soul survives death, "but the full person does not exist until body (matter) is restored to its form at the end of time." Body and soul, according to Dominicans and Franciscans, yearn for each other after death — a pretty fancy. The body, according to Saint Bonaventure, is a composite of spirit and matter.

But it is by matter that we are most often judged — by others, and by ourselves.

"With few exceptions," says Sallie Tisdale, "to diet is to put image — *surface* — before kindness, wisdom, and joy. We diet to be thin, not to be healthy. . . . Hatred of female bodies is deep within us, surely. But even deeper is a fear of all bodies, of the imperfect and unpredictable flesh itself."

When I walk into a room I absolutely know that the first thing anybody will think about me is: She is fat. How fat she is. Yuuch. This may not be true. I *know* it nonetheless. And I know women who are a perfect size 8, and they know it too — they know that everybody in the room has a kind of radar that will allow them to know they've gained a pound and a half.

One solution to this problem is not to walk into a room unless you have good reason to believe it is one in which you will be perfectly safe and completely loved by all therein. How many rooms does that make available to you?

It is better not to have an opinion — any opinion — if you are fat; it is certainly better not to voice an opinion if you own one. After all, anyone can dispute you: What do you know? they'll say; you're fat. I am not alone (did you think I was?) in this fear. Erica Jong, righteously inveighing against the fact that weight is perceived as *will*, says, "I've even had my weight attacked in purported reviews of my books." What is being judged is not one's metabolism or one's flesh-and-only-one's-flesh; what is being judged is one's character: you are slothful, you are given to instant gratification (Fool! Don't you have any decent long-range goals?); you are acting like low-class trailer trash: SHAPE UP. (As for your wisdom, your generosity, your wit, your kindness, your goodness, do they announce and declare themselves when you walk into a room?)

A famous feminist, svelte, who on occasion could be heard to moan that there was a fat lady in her skinny skinny body hammering to be let out, was once, in my presence, shown a portrait of a gorgeous woman who'd had nine kids: "Yeah," she said, "but what does she look like below the neck?" "*Jesus*, Gloria," I said; whereupon she attacked me for not being understanding of her problem — her problem being invisible fat.

Another Spokesperson, whom I interviewed when I was five or ten pounds overweight and she, an occasional actress and producer, was concentration-camp weight, allowed as how men's perceived superiority resided in their large size: "You, for example," said the fragile (but tough as nails) lady, "could, for instance, knock me over with your weight — with one finger." And how I wish I had.

Well; but anger isn't usually the response to casual cruelty. Hurt is. I'll never know why those kids on the Grand Canal in Venice laughed at me when I passed them by; but I'm willing to bet — even though there is no evidence for it — that it was my girth; and it poisoned a summer day.

Once I was invited to give a speech at a college where a stringy cousin of mine worked. She saw fit not to pass the invitation along, seeing as how it would embarrass her for her colleagues to know she had a relative who wasn't thin.

I have a friend who weighs over three hundred pounds. She is magnificent. She is a gifted teacher of young children. She is funny. She is loyal. She is smart. But she is F A T. And that, so far as the world is concerned, is her only identity. I realized this when she was my guest at a California restaurant. You'd have thought I'd brought a serial killer to dinner. I'd cased the joint ahead of time, and her arrival disturbed no one's arrangements; but people made it appallingly clear that they were repulsed and disgusted — put off their food, poor dieting things — by her weight. She gave every appearance of sailing above it all, so as — kind creature — not to upset me; but of course it hurt. (How do you think it would feel to be obliged to ask for a seat-belt extender on an airplane? For the unfashionably bulgy, life is a series of small humiliations.)

. . . Patricia Neal says to Roddy McDowall, What would you rather be, fat or dead? Dead, says Mr. McDowall; and Ms. Neal agrees. On a

TV talk show Cloris Leachman says, "Fat people should kill themselves so the rest of us don't have to see them." Just chitchat, meant-to-be-clever talk, small talk — unless, of course, you happen to be fat. . . . Woody Allen in a Woody Allen movie sees a rotund lady jogging around the Central Park reservoir in a red (bless her) sweat suit; "Jesus," he says, "why doesn't she just put her fat in a little red wagon and pull it behind her?" (And he isn't remotely pretty.)

. . . At the MacDowell Colony, a communal residence for artists, I have unwittingly made an enemy of a young woman in a wheelchair. Her disability is the result of bone cancer; I have, in the course of private conversation, used the word *malignant* to describe someone or something in the news, I forget now what. She spins around to confront me and orders me never ever to use the word *malignant* again, it causes her pain. (Long ago I was bitten by a mad dog, twelve anti-rabies needles in my stomach; I do not as a consequence seek to exorcise the word *rabid* from human speech.) She speechifies all the time, her wheelchair her pulpit; she monitors what we watch on television, judging most of it to be racist, ageist, sexist, -ist, -ist, -ist (Linda Bloodworth Thomason's *Designing Women*). Then, exhausted from speechifying and edifying, she says, "Oh why is it always me? Why do I have to always be the conscience of the group? Why do I always have to raise everybody's consciousness?" "Perhaps you don't," I say. "Why don't you give yourself a vacation, perhaps we can get along without you, think how pleasant that would be for you." She shoots a malignant glance at me. So later she takes her revenge. We are — ten or twelve of us, painters, writers, musicians — in a cabin deep in piny woods; my friend Bill McBrian is playing Cole Porter music on the grand piano; we sing along. The conjunction of sophistication and rural woodsy simplicity amounts to a kind of innocence that delights us all. She has been waiting for her moment. We pause to catch our breath; and, her clear high voice occupying all of space and demanding everyone's attention, "I've always thought," she says, "that fat people were subjected to the most awful unacknowledged oppression." She says this apropos of absolutely nothing; and she folds her thin lips in a little smile, and she sighs, and we are meant to interpret her sigh as one of compassion, which it is not.

. . . I am waiting in the lobby for my doorman to find a package UPS has left for me. A young woman, slender, skin the color of cinnamon toast, green eyes, masses of crinkly braided yellow hair and crinkly braided black hair, strides to the elevator. The doorman bars her path and questions her identity (she works at our health club, and I vouch for her). "How could you forget anyone so beautiful?" I ask the doorman, who, after a slight pause, during which he can practically be seen to be organizing his thoughts, says, "*You're* beautiful, Mrs. Harrison," which I take to mean I am not. "Everyone is beautiful in their own way," he embellishes, by which I understand that he believes I am ugly. "As a friend of mine says," he rolls on, "beauty is in the eye of the beholder," which I interpret to mean he pities me. As I step into the elevator, "Remember," he says, "beauty comes from within." It's funny, of course — *he's* funny — but I want to savage him. . . . I am at a party. An editor of a newsweekly asks me, by way of greeting, if I have ever been to bed with Warren Beatty. I have not. Susan Sontag has, he ventures. Have you? I ask. Prompted, perhaps, by this unhappy beginning, he asks me how it feels to be a "large" woman in a world of thin women — this world, the world of this party, is thin/rich/famous — and I reply brightly, "Fine, as long as men keep falling in love with me." But I am smarting and hurting and I harbor a grudge.

Sometimes I wonder if all the reasons (intricate and casual) I give for not going to parties are lies; sometimes I wonder if my not going to parties (my Prozac-controlled inclination to agoraphobia, my acute panic attacks) is all about weight, about boundaries: terror. I wonder if the flesh I have added to my skeleton is designed to hide the fear (to shelter a fragile psyche), or whether the flesh has caused the fear and resulted in psychic fragility. . . . Our bodies are drama and stage both; and the drama is incomprehensible to us, to be apprehended only dimly and by intuition. Our bodies are drama and stage, and we are also the audience.

To escape humiliation, we diet.

Oh. There are things one wants to keep even from oneself. When I first met my lover Jazzman thirty years (and several marriages) ago, he used to make a fine meal of my breasts: "I want to see if I can get a whole one in my mouth," he said once. Oh. Now (we have had a return engagement), this man, the best lover I have ever known, the only man with whom I have ever been fully orgasmic (I love him; he was my first lover; he is my history, and, sometimes I think, my doom), says, "I may smother if I go down on you." I know this to be physiologically impossible. He may mean one of several things (he is old): he may mean that he can't sustain an erection if he pleasures me orally first; he may mean he finds it aesthetically unpleasing to be surrounded by too much soft white flesh. But that's not what he says. I am in possession of conflicting evidence: I know that the minute he sees me, he gets hard; we cannot share the same bed without his getting an erection; he has been "abstinent" (by which I tend to believe he means impotent) for six years; I have aroused the beast. I know these things. What do they matter? I am fat. He is cruel. Sadistic? Inarticulate? Cruel. He knows that I know a terrible thing: his mother was the madam of a brothel; she initiated him. Smother=mother. He is afraid to be sucked back in. There is too much enfolding flesh there. He is a prudent man, he says. He means he is afraid.

But I am fat.

(I once got down on all fours to confer with my cats: "Do you love me even though I'm fat?" I asked them.)

To escape humiliation, we go on diets.

"The six most important necessities which the Creator has imposed on mankind are to be born, to move about, to eat, to sleep, to procreate, and to die," Brillat-Savarin says. Such blessed matter-of-factness . . . whereas we are nervous about everything. And no more so than when we diet — an obsessive activity that focuses on exactly that which you wish to dismiss from a ravening consciousness: food.

My own attempts at dieting have been farcical — anguished, too. I discount the times I've dieted successfully; one diet supersedes another as I gain back the weight I lost — one everlasting failure in a long series of punctuated failures.

Once I went to "Fat School," doctor-supervised weekly meetings at St. Luke's Hospital. We made charts and kept records of every morsel of food we ate every day and what mood we were in when we ate it (angry, tired, bored, happy, etc.); I was always in the same mood: hungry. I am always hungry. I do not know when I am satiated, the word means nothing to me. We recorded with whom we ate and under what circumstances and where. I had visible evidence before me that I often eat alone. But I like to be alone, I am never bored, I am excessively fond of my own company. I like also to eat with people. It is next to impossible for me to understand how people can get together without sharing food . . . which encourages conviviality, "brings together from day to day differing kinds of people, melts them into a whole, animates their conversation, and softens the sharp corners of the conventional inequalities of position and breeding" (Brillat-Savarin).

"Why do people always have to *masticate* together?" asks a cranky friend of mine, a Texan who sleeps with a loaded revolver, *The Book of Common Prayer,* and the *Social Register* next to his bed. (Our fledgling romance did not prosper.)

But: while I have happily and lustily shared meals with other lovers, I was never able to eat when I was in the sole company of Jazzman, whose flesh I first loved and whose flesh first loved mine, and made a meal of it. I shopped for him and with him for the old-fashioned status food he craved — steak and lobster and littleneck clams; I listened patiently to the redundant cooking advice he proffered, and indulged the food rituals he adhered to, garnered, for the most part, from his mother. I watched him ruining perfectly good steak, simultaneously burning and steaming it on tinfoil, thinking how adorable he was; I cut the lemons and the tomatoes exactly the way his mama did; and I never put food in my mouth (I was satiated). M. F. K. Fisher says that "love has a thinning effect upon most female silhouettes, when it is unrequited (as opposed to the fullness of its satisfaction!)." I have not found this to be true.

Our group counselor at St. Luke's Hospital checked our charts and our records — *H* for Happy, *B* for Bored, 759 calories for half a broiled chicken . . . and the charts and the records reminded me of the records I kept when I was a child evangelist and noted the dispositions of people I encountered when I went from door to door with *The Watchtower* and *Awake!* — *I* for Interested, *NI* for Not Interested, *GW* for Good Will, *S* for Sheep (bought literature), *G* for Goat (displayed antagonism or opposition). These records provided the basis for return visits, known as back-calls, and I hated them; I hated keeping them; I hated going from door to door; I was singular and a freak, a Jehovah's Witness (but slender at the time), and for a while I reveled in my singularity, and later, when I met Arnold Horowitz, I was ambivalent about it, and later still I hated it like nothing else and wanted, more than anything else in the world, to be ordinary.

We kept records, at Fat School, of one entire week of daily activities. Minute by minute. I had a terrible report card: SEDENTARY!!! the counselor scribbled — incised, actually — on my chart, though I'd made an effort (hoping at least for "Respects the Rights of Others," which, in elementary school, meant you didn't throw spitballs — we didn't have guns in those days).

Once I stole a look at the hospital records of my physical exam: "Heel calluses." Back to the wilting guilt of gonorrhea for one vertiginous moment. I slammed the record book shut.

I want a silver scissors with which to cut the bloody umbilical cord to the past. The farcical and terrible past.

After Fat School sessions we repaired to the Hungarian pastry shop across the street — whipped cream and lard and cherry confections — and ate and ate and ate.

The trouble was, of course, we all knew how to diet; our counselor's pre-Passover advice on alternatives to matzo balls and suchlike made us giggle. (There is no "alternative" to cranberry cream, to Indian milk-sweets, to thick pork chops cooked in tomato and sage and butter; no alternative to buffalo mozzarella with truffle oil, no alternative to dark chocolate — which, we are told, replicates the emotional high of requited romantic love.) We knew how to diet; what we didn't know was how to transfer that knowledge from our brains to our stomachs, our emotions, our genes, our will. I know rationally that the chocolate mousse I long for is not the only, the last, the best chocolate mousse in the world . . . but what if it is? I want it now. Maybe an air conditioner will fall on my head on the way home from this restaurant and I will die not having had the only last best chocolate mousse in the world.

The tyranny of scales. When I am dieting, that moment in the morning when I weigh myself determines the cast of my day. Perhaps if I move the scale a little to the left, a little to the right . . .

When my children and I lived together I would sometimes bribe them from the bed in which I lay: $20 to go down the hill and buy me a pint of dark chocolate ice cream. I had no takers. (Dieting, I am an invalid.)

I went to one meeting of Overeaters Anonymous. Everyone else there was bulimic or anorexic; I was the only one who was fat. I was the only one there whose secret was visible: lazy, overflowing flesh. The meeting was in the basement of a church: lazy flesh *and* spiritual sloth? In *The Sayings of the* [Church] *Fathers* it is written, "As the body waxes fat, the soul grows thin; and as the body grows thin, the soul by so much waxes fat." Muriel Spark, whom I love and adore in spite of it, equates fat with venality and stupidity. She characterizes one of her notorious villains — a woman who disappears when there is no one in a room to see her — as one whose poundage outweighs her intelligence. (Oh. And I am afraid that I am fatter than I am good, fatter than I am smart.) Spark's bête noir is the "English rose," plump and pink and soft and ripe, bullying and vapid.

Here is a *Newsweek* cartoon by Lynda Barry: "What happened to the Women's Movement?" In separate panels, different women answer: "too hairy, radical, lesbian, poor; too many rules; way too p.c.; no jokes; lame music and boring sex; too anti-male, middle-class, caucasian-centric; bad clothes, bad hair, totally anti-breast implant, anti-Republican, fat; anti-baby, anti-housewife, anti-husband; no profit motive; they tricked me!" Which, of all these many pejorative words, is underlined twice, despised twice over? The question answers itself: FAT. There is nothing worse than fat.

So I sit in a church basement surrounded by anorexics and bulimics, and I am as unempathic as a toad. Hot and cold and clutching tranquilizers, I huddle there in the mink coat I bought to counteract the ice that surrounded my heart when my father died.

When I was young and slender I had a bright red sweater with a cluster of embroidered flowers on the left shoulder. I felt pretty and bold. I had a shiny nylon blouse with diagonal pleats that narrowed from bust to waist; the white straps of my bra and my slip were plainly visible; and I wore the blouse with a black grosgrain ribbon around the high chaste neckline; and I felt like a virginal vamp.

I have closets full of clothes. During my fat periods I become infatuated with designer labels. Ah! In a boutique on the Piazza di Spagna I have found a yellow-on-yellow Krizia that fits! I wear it to a wedding on the Sorrentino Peninsula; a member of the aristocratic Gonzaga family — sweet and tall and thin and kind — wears the same dress. I console myself with *calzone* and pigs' feet and Château d'Yquem. This is Italy, after all, where consolations proliferate and abide.

Fat is a matter of class. Fat people are poor people. The mind makes that equation, though it is untrue. So I armor myself with designer fabric and cloth — a Fendi bag, a Nicole Fahri creamy silk tunic. (Size 8! Ridiculous. Ms. Fahri has a genius for making her customers feel loved.) Donna Karan and Robert Clergerie shoes. Armani shawls. Voluminous silk chenille tunics from pricey boutiques and sand-washed silk pants (imagine fat *and* polyester). Salwar camises of Tassah silk from Bombay. They reassure me.

I keep a file of clothes, pictures of clothes, that have only one thing in common: they are all pinstriped. A pinstriped Edwardian tunic from the Valentino boutique; pinstriped pants of black worsted wool (a fly, suspenders); a Nicole Miller pinstriped jacket and long skirt, wool; Ralph Lauren jacket and trousers, pinstriped, wool blend; a Ralph Lauren pinstriped jacket, beaded and sequined (so sexy: *bang* goes my heart); a pinstriped Margiela jacket worn over a flowered skirt; a pinstriped jumpsuit with white piping; Princess Diana wearing a miniskirt (pinstriped) and double-breasted deep-necked pinstriped jacket; a Bill Blass pinstriped chiffon evening dress (*bang bang*); a pinstriped Jil Sander suit (combines "the most severe tailoring with subtle fluidity," says the *New York Times* — a bipolar suit, and absolutely dreamy); pinstriped baseball shirts; a jacket of Bengal silk pinstripes; a pinstriped silk sarong; Katie Couric in a pinstriped suit and pearls; a chocolate wool pinstriped pantsuit; Escada's double-breasted cutaway jacket and multilayered skirt, charcoal; Donna Karan's dark blue pinstriped coat dress with an asymmetrical skirt (worn with dark blue tights); a white Richard Tyler pinstriped dress with bra halter top. . . . PINSTRIPES BORROWED FROM THE BOYS! a catalogue says. I see Diana Rigg on *Mystery* wearing a pinstriped suit, and her sexiness, her radical femininity, makes me cuckoo with delight. What does this say about me? I am the least likely candidate for androgyny you are likely to meet. Anne Taylor Fleming, describing the outfit Barbra Streisand wore at the presidential inauguration gala, calls it "a three-piece pinstriped male power suit, with a feminine touch. Instead of pants, she wore a skirt that was slit from ankle to thigh, while above a definite hint of cleavage poked over the form-fitting vest." She calls this "cross-dressing," and writes, "What the slit says is: We may imitate your wardrobe and ask to be let into your male-only chambers, but, rest assured, underneath, we are still your centerfolds, your MTV dream girls. . . . Calvin Klein takes it a step further: In his ad, a pouty-lipped, pinstriped beauty seems naked under her suit jacket." My friend Anne sees a "dual apology" in these garments: "an apology for being strong, assertive and achievement-oriented, [and] an apology for robust, straight-out female sexuality. . . . They exemplify society's effort to keep women off balance, to keep them beholden to the new sex-object imagery: male on top, seductress underneath." Oh dear. I think that is making too much of a good (and playful) thing; the message is in the eye of the beholder — and of the wearer. And if we didn't want to exchange ambiguous messages, we'd walk around naked or draped in blankets. It *is* sexy (as it was in the forties) for women to play at being two things . . . though why assertiveness and sexuality are supposed to be mutually exclusive I am sure I don't know. There isn't a woman in the world who doesn't understand what's going on when a woman takes her hair down — her bunned or braided, constricted hair — before a man; the gesture is perfectly seductive. And nice.

For a long time I didn't know why I was collecting these pictures. I understand now that pinstripes for me represent a happy combination of sexiness and moderation (a combination I am unlikely to achieve in life); they are about skinniness and competence; they belong to the world of boundaries and manageability; there is nothing extravagant about them; they are (superficially) all business; they signal the opposite of "wanting minor pleasure now instead of major pleasure later. Fat is not believing in a future, which is why you want the minor pleasure now. (A candy in the hand is better than true love round the corner.) Fat is also honoring the pleasures of the day: living now, not later. . . . Fat is heart attacks, bad knees, and a self-perpetuating low self-image.

Fat is all kinds of things, but one thing it's not is thin. Another thing it's not is beautiful. Fat is disgusting." Fay Weldon wrote that. It confirms my worst fears: When I walk into a room people say, Here is a woman courting a heart attack; let's not court *her*. Here is a woman with "low self-image."

Once I had a sleeveless shift, cut above the knees. It was banker's gray and pinstriped, and I felt sexier in that dress than I have ever felt in any dress before or since.

Fay Weldon also wrote: "Once, the rumor that you'd lost your virginity was what ruined your life, destroyed your prospects, as the stuff of fiction. Now it's the accusation of fatness."

Weldon says that overeating is succumbing to "mere gratification." I want of course to kill her — what's "mere" about gratification? But I am cowed all the same by her words, which I choose, in a charitable mood, to invest with irony. It cannot be true that "fat is depression. Fat is a dulling wall between you and the pain of reality; fat is a comfort, an excuse, and an escape from sex. Fat is yours to control. Fat is transformation; fat hurts and humiliates. Fat is how you lose the little girl in the fullness of the woman. . . . Lucky the thin. . . . Society's approval shines on them. Weak and unlucky the fat, who because they refuse to see it will go on trying forever to change the world rather than themselves, crying 'It isn't fair' all the way to their extra-size coffins. Anything, anything except get thin. There is a nobility in it." Maybe what Weldon says is true, but it can't be *all* true. No single motive can account for a cluster of actions, for knotted, clotted, gene-driven, past-driven, pleasure-driven, pain-driven, appetite-driven behavior, behavior both sensual and flagellating deriving from motives rational and irrational. It is equally true and false to say, as some feminists have said, that getting fat is the way one asserts oneself and claims one's space; food, regarded in this light, is an instrument of rebellion. ("Do you always see both sides of a question, Barbara?" my shrink asks. "Yes and no," I say. "This isn't Monty Python!" the good man says. But it is, it is. It's absurd.)

Is fat mine to control? Because, as Tisdale says, "our size must be in some way voluntary, or else it wouldn't be subject to change," a fat person is given to feeling like a bad person, a person who will not exercise control. There are no happy homosexuals, Tennessee Williams said; might he have said it of fat people? Is it true that "fat is how you lose the little girl in the fullness of the woman"? I doubt that anything so epigrammatically glib could be more than a shadow of the truth. I consider myself a sufficiently happy person, grateful for the life I have been given (like Benvenuto Cellini, I try to accept that which the world and God allow me to have, and quite frequently succeed; I go on my way rejoicing); but it is clear to me that, however large a component joy is in my life, there clings to my happiness (tainting it) the conviction that fat is (absolutely) bad, and skinny is (absolutely) good.

I go to my doctor, who oversees my diet (I am sure to wear light-weight clothes so as not to disturb the scales I wish I could levitate over). "I've been bad," I say, by which I mean that I have not lost weight this week. His nurse, Giselle, walks in: "Have you been good?" she asks. My doctor, Mitch, who is my friend, assures me that *good* and *bad* are words that do not apply. He is beautifully kind. But on weeks that I haven't lost weight, I break my appointment with him.

Women are nervous when they are preparing food, and women are nervous when they are eating food.

Food is enemy and food is savior. Frankfurters cause cancer and whipped cream causes senility and green tea prevents cancer of the esophagus; we are bombarded with statistics purporting to prove the goodness of some foods and the harmfulness of other foods. We believe exaggerated claims because we wish to — because we wish not to die. In fact, statistics are seldom rational (I could show you statistics, I reckon, that prove men who wear blue bow ties have fewer strokes than men who wear blue socks); statistics are mystical. "Statistics show that of those who contract the habit of eating, very few ever survive" (William Wallace Irvin).

Is food "a dulling wall between [me] and the pain of reality . . . a comfort, an excuse, and an escape from sex"? Yes and no. Either I am vastly deceived or I like my reality; and if I were in the business of dulling or avoiding reality, would I be exposing myself this way?

Of course it might be true that I am choosing pain in order to avoid pain. I bear this in mind. I have a friend — the author of *Nine and a Half Weeks*, a classic of sadomasochism — who says she would take physical humiliation and pain over subtle emotional manipulation and pain anytime. I bear this in mind. I have, once or twice in my life, when emotional pain was literally unbearable, seen the point of flagellating oneself with a whip — to distract one from pain. I have understood that food is an escape from the pain of living — until it adds to the pain of living.

I have wondered if I were using food, the barrier of flesh, to put space between me and my always-encroaching, ever-too-hungry-for-me father. I have wondered if I were not using food to please my mother — I have given her a measure by which she can prove that what she predicted has come to pass: "Barbara will have a terrible life."

Food, like God, can be put to many uses.

In both the Moslem and the Christian traditions there is a ritualistic way to renounce food, which seems infinitely more dignified than my fevered attempts to diet. Moslems do not eat from sunup till sundown during the month of Ramadan. Catholics traditionally gave up meat for the forty days of Lent. Now Catholics are frequently instructed not to give up anything but rather to add to their religious lives — add service to the poor, add acts of mercy and charity. One sees the point. . . . Did my Aunt Betty truly think God would spare my Aunt Lee from cancer if Betty gave up Fannie Farmer chocolates for the rest of her life? . . . The proper theological answer is that God rejects no gift; and no sacrifice offered to Him in faith is lost (as was once said of an eighty-five-year-old who renounced sex). One sees and applauds the point, but one sees also the point, charming and formal, of the old ways. Here is Brillat-Savarin, two of whose great-uncles swooned with delight when, after the deprivations of Lent, they watched the carving of a ham, the breaking of a pie crust: During Lent, he says, "neither butter nor eggs, nor anything that had once lived and breathed, could be served. Our forefathers, as a result, had to satisfy themselves with salads, preserves, and fruit, dishes, alas, which are far from sustaining; but the faithful suffered patiently for the love of God." Strict observance — "collation severely apostolic" — created one pleasure, "which is unknown to us today: the end of fasting, the de-lenting, at the first meal of Easter. . . . If we look closely, . . . we see that our pleasures are based on the difficulties, privations, and yearnings we suffer to attain them. All of this was apparent in the act which broke the Lenten abstinence." We live in a time largely devoid of ritual; dieting is the ritual of the secular cult of fitness. It has this disadvantage: it has no end.

By and large, men fast for political purposes. Women renounce food for spiritual/religious or cosmetic purposes, or for what they imagine to be health purposes. In times past, people who traded in the supernatural saw evidence of divine or demonic intervention in women's food disorders; now we assign psychological or biochemical reasons to the phenomena. Fat is attacked every which way — behaviorally, psychologically, chemically — and it remains intractable.

Should I blame it on my mother? She's no longer here to take the rap; and perhaps it is true that I grew into her picture of me (it is certainly true that she did not willingly offer her body for food).

"In a family," says the Italian novelist Elias Canetti, "the husband contributes food and the wife prepares it for him. The fact that he habitually eats what she has prepared constitutes the strongest link between them.

"The mother . . . is the core and very heart of this institution. A mother is one who gives her own body to be eaten. She first nourishes the child in her womb and then gives it her milk. This activity continues in a less concentrated form throughout many years. . . . Her passion is to give food."

No such passion moved my mother, who fed me, I was given to know, every four hours when I was a baby, regular as clockwork, no matter whether I'd screamed with hunger for hours or violently shoved food aside. This was a source of pride to her, perhaps not unnaturally, as it was her practice to refer to herself as "Barbara's relative," never "Barbara's mother," so little did she relish the maternal, nurturing role. (I was obliged to call her Connie.) This history is not in my conscious mind when I am eating smoked salmon and caviar, and I feel quite safe in assuming that it isn't pushing the molecules of my unconscious around either. (And what if it were? I am a civilized adult and ought, I suppose, to know how much salmon and caviar I should eat . . . I suppose.)

Women are obsessed with food. "The 20th-century Western craze for female dieting," Caroline Walker Bynum says, "may owe something to [the medieval] assumption that women prepare food and men eat it. . . . Food is particularly a woman-controlled resource. . . . Although the first cookbooks were written by men and the job of chef in the wealthiest households went to males [a fact that mothers, in order to bolster their sons' egos and to assure them implicitly that any urge they might feel toward cookery is not a sign of homosexuality, are pleased to stress], everyone agreed that the basic social responsibility for food preparation was woman's."

Poison is a woman's murder weapon. "Cooking was so much a woman's role that it appeared, to men, not merely arcane but threatening. When medieval men projected their hostility toward women into suspicion of what went on in the women's quarters, they frequently spoke of women's control of food."

To consider how much women were and are subjected to criticism and reproach, judgment and scorn, both for their culinary efforts and for the shape of their bodies, is to understand how limited this "control" is. Do our troubles stem from the fact that we are unable fully to control that which we are given control of?

Having obliged them to stay in the kitchen, men nevertheless saw "women's power to feed . . . as domination." They believed that women increased or decreased the sexual ardor of their husbands "by adding to [their] food such things as menstrual blood, semen, or dough kneaded with a woman's buttocks."

"Gather ye rosebuds while ye may," said Robert Herrick, so prettily, so extravagantly. He also said, exhorting us to an unnatural frugality, "A little meat best fits a little belly." Women's little bellies have — against all evidence — been seen as fit containers for what the Victorians called "dainty" fare (now the tendency is, if we are seen in public, to eat salads and fruit — the food that used to be Lenten fare); whereas men, "in part because meat had, for a thousand years, been seen as an aggravator of lust," Bynum says, were thought to be naturally carnivorous. "Cookbooks came increasingly to suggest that women . . . hardly needed to eat at all."

I happened, the last time I was in Italy, to find myself in Siena during the week of the counter-Palio. This is the week after the great horse race — the medieval equivalent of the World Cup soccer games — in which members of each Sienese district vie, in splendid medieval trappings, for glorious victory (after which each neighborhood, or *rione*, has its separate feast). Now, where men with banners on horseback had ridden to sweaty, heaving triumph, I saw, parading around the piazza, victorious horsemen dressed as foolish women and helpless babies; and bearded men sat in baby carriages sucking oversized pacifiers, a disconcerting sight. I understood it to mean that the victors were deliberately humbling themselves so as not to incur the evil eye or the wrath of the losers. And what better way to become weak in the sight of your enemies than to reduce yourself to the status of vulnerable women and children?

(When biological males become transsexuals, they espouse flouncy weakness and renounce privilege. Radical role reversal is almost entirely an option men choose to avail themselves of.)

What better way for men to become the meek who inherit the earth than to renounce their maleness? Women renounced what was available to them — not property, which they didn't own, and not maleness, which was not theirs to renounce: they renounced food. "Women," Bynum says, "tend to manipulate their bodies whereas men manipulate their environments. . . . Eating, feeding, and not eating enabled [women] to control their bodies and their world [by] voluntary starvation, charitable food distribution, and eucharistic devotion."

Is the message to be gleaned from this that while successful dieting may be impossible, renunciation is de rigueur?

I read in a fashionable paper that socialites chew and ingest toilet tissue before going to parties. The toilet paper ensures the easy evacuation of whatever little bitty bites of food the rich skinnies do allow themselves to consume; and they are, with one action, controlling intake and output. (Do we laugh or cry?) We may think the relationship of medieval women to their bodies was strange — starving themselves and licking lepers' pus, willing themselves into trances and levitating and having ecstatic nosebleeds and receiving the stigmata — but surely the dietary practices of the upper classes today are strange too?

But it is not becoming for me to laugh at the foibles of others. When I was a Jehovah's Witness kid, I held the belief that the patriarchs and prophets — Abraham, Isaac, Jacob, Zedekiah, et al. — would make an appearance on earth in our lifetimes, before the end of the world. I used to wonder if these "faithful men of old," as we insisted upon calling them in the lunatic jargon of fancy religions, would shit; I had a hard time associating holiness with excrement and filth. I used to wonder, too, what we'd feed David and Jonathan when they came to eat at our house in Bensonhurst — a question inspired by my mother's being a foul and perverse cook (beef heart stew, slow-simmered beef liver, chicken feet soup with escarole, mackerel baked with catsup) as well as a stingy one ("one pork chop per customer"). My obsession with food was total.

Renunciation and penitential asceticism were not, as one might be forgiven for supposing, indications that women were lacking in "a sense of self-worth." Food, Bynum says, was a means toward "fusion with Christ, with his suffering. . . . To soar toward Christ as lover and bride, to sink into the stench and torment of the crucifixion, to eat God [at the Eucharist], was for the woman only to give religious significance to what she already was. . . . Women reached God not by reversing what they were [as did men, who became like women in an attempt to achieve intimacy with God], but by sinking more fully into it."

Fasting was a means for women to achieve power. (Catherine of Siena starved herself to death — but she bullied popes and directed papal politics.) Fasting "was a way of implicitly disputing the misogynist clerical view that they were not created in God's image," a way of achieving union with God without clerical intervention or mediation.

Dieting is a means — though clearly not always an efficacious one and sometimes a self-destructive one — of achieving power, the power that accrues to those who embody the norm. (Slender women are chosen women.)

In the past, women fasted "not to eradicate body but to merge their own humiliating and painful flesh with [Christ's] flesh, whose 'chosen agony' was salvation." Fasting was a way to join ecstasy to agony. The face of Bernini's *Saint Teresa in Ecstasy* (which was the master's favorite of his works) has often been described — sometimes in derision, sometimes in assumed moral indignation — as orgasmic; but it could have been called, with equal authority, *Saint Teresa in Agony*. Mystical Saint

Teresa of Avila felt God in her body — which was the body of her soul. She mingled ecstasy with agony. . . . I often wonder if when Christ called out, on the Cross, "My God, my God, why hast thou forsaken me?" there wasn't an element of rapture in that cry, as well as the utter despair, the desolation, of abandonment. That is what we experience in orgasm — "the little death" — rapture and desolation. . . . There was a sensual, erotic, even an orgasmic component to renunciation of food; fasting prepared the way to a swooning bodily union with the Beloved.

There was a class component in this, too: Women's radical asceticism was, Bynum said, "a rejection of a Church which, as it touched more and more of life and provided ordinary folk with appropriate ways to be religious, seemed a threat as well as an opportunity to those pious women who wanted, without compromise or moderation, to imitate Christ." Ordinary folk — peasants — could not afford to renounce food, which they had little enough of to begin with; they could not sacrifice to God what they didn't have.

To fast was a way to become physically unattractive so as to avoid marriage, a way to reproach and embarrass and thumb one's nose at one's family. It was a way to rebel and to escape what the world required of one. It was a way to run away from home — from the kitchen and the nursery — without literally running away from home. Women who began at puberty to renounce food often became "healers, teachers, and savers. . . .

"By their very extravagance, audacity and majesty, they rejected the success of the late medieval church, rejected — for a wider, more soaring vision — an institution that made a tidy, moderate, decent, second-rate place for women and the laity. . . . Women often expressed their dissatisfaction with what they saw as their religion's worldliness and compromise not by leaving the institution but by fulfilling its precepts with a vehemence that frightened and titillated its leaders."

Women were and are immoderate creatures, immoderate in love, immoderate as to bodies and diet. If men prefer the kind of women we call bimbos it is because "real" women are immoderate, vehement; they are as immoderate as their mothers, who gave their sons their life's blood/milk. The extravagance of women embarrasses men. (In real life, and sometimes in films, too — Anna Magnani is the victim of her lyrical excesses — women larger than life do not find it easy to mate conventionally.) Mistresses are extravagant, wives are not.

Women themselves fear their inclination to extravagance — extravagance that leads to recklessness in love; and dieting (I think) is partly a response to that fear. Women diet apparently to have bodies that will please men; but also (I think) to have bodies that won't scare *themselves* — bodies that won't make visible their tremendous appetites.

One might say that. One might also say that to indulge one's appetites — to forgo dieting — is to create space, the space in which to assert one's abandon and desire. I return to my initial premise: practically everything that can be said about food, the flesh, bodies, and eating has an element of truth — because nothing looms much larger in a woman's life.

"To eat," Bynum says of her medieval women, was "to consume, to take in, to become God. And to eat was also to rend and tear God [in the Host]. Eating was a horribly audacious act." And Sallie Tisdale, a contemporary writer with a contemporary sensibility who has decided never again to diet, says much the same thing: "To like myself means to be, literally, shameless, to be wanton in the pleasures of being inside a body. I feel loose this way, a little abandoned, a little dangerous" — the way a child feels when he's fingerpainting with his excrement. "I sense a cornucopia of flesh. In the midst of it I am a little capacious and unruly."

What is a girl entering puberty to think when she sees nude models clutching teddy bears to their bosoms? when she sees Madonna photographed in the innocent colors of the nursery, pale blue and bubble-gum pink, a bare-assed pink Madonna astride a baby-blue inflatable dolphin; the prophet of polymorphous perversity parading around in saddle shoes and ruffled bikini bottoms; the woman who says "my pussy is the complete summation of my life" sucking her thumb? Does she think it's hot stuff to grow up? or better to stay in the pastel world of childhood? Here the irony is that to be a "real woman," one must remain a little girl.

What are women to think when they see, on magazine covers, women cup their breasts in their hands, or (Sharon Stone, bellybutton winking out from chiffon) actresses holding their breasts in their own hands. Are they wondering, Could I cup mine? Could he cup mine? What size cup? For never did there live a woman who thought her breasts were made to order.

In matters of diet, rebellion and compliance are braided. To diet is to conform to societal norms and/or to exercise individual control. To diet immoderately, excessively, extravagantly — as an anorexic does — may be seen as a willed act of rebellion against a controlling parent or a cultural imperative, or as an act of control born of desperation, or as an act of self-loathing. It may be regarded as biologically determined or as psychologically determined; but the one unyielding fact is that ninety percent of anorexics and bulimics are women (just as, in the Middle Ages, it was women who received in their bodies the stigmata). We are accustomed, by menstruation and by childbirth, to regard suffering in our bodies as "natural."

Anorexia has been seen also as an act of secular saintliness. On TV (the *Sally Jessy Raphael* show), a woman who has a London clinic for anorexics says, "Only the nicest people get this disease. They feel they are not worthy in a suffering world to be full, satiated." Women, she implies, carry the wounds of the world in their bodies — as Simone Weil did when she starved herself, during World War II, because she could afford to eat while others, in the camps, were dying of starvation. And as the thirteenth-century Saint Margaret of Cortona did: "I want to die of starvation to satiate the poor."

Princess Diana called anorexia "our shameful friend."

As far as I can see, there exists no single explanation — individual or societal, psychological or social — for any diet-related, flesh-obsessed phenomenon.

Bynum makes the point that there are ties that bind contemporary women to medieval women in spite of apparently completely different values and norms. Anorexia nervosa typically takes place at puberty, at the onset of menstruation: "Refusal to eat [like binge eating, or bulimia] is a way of asserting power over a body that appears to have slipped away from control into painful or embarrassing excretions, and over a family or a society that is rushing the girl headlong into an adult female role she does not choose — one that promises less freedom than did childhood. . . . Medieval women . . . show striking parallels to the modern syndrome [which includes insomnia and hyperactivity and the "grossly distorted sense perception" that so many women, as regards their bodies, suffer]. In some female mystics, disgust at all . . . food becomes an involuntary physiological reaction. The vomiting out of unconsecrated hosts, for example, was sometimes part of a general revulsion at food, especially meat. . . . Refusal to eat ordinary food was often accompanied, as it is in modern anorectics, by frenetic attention to feeding others. . . . As in modern anorexia, 'control' was a basic issue to medieval women who adopted relentless fasting as a kind of self-definition."

Whatever the permutations of eating, not eating, dieting, not dieting, food is one of the means by which women attempt to become fully human, to become visible as multidimensional human creatures. The attempt may look frivolous and may inspire derision and contempt, depending on the form it takes (it may also look noble and inspire envy or sympathetic regard); but if this is a game we are playing, it is a game in dead earnest. It is the game of self-definition; it is the drama of self.

In the continuing drama, black comedy insinuates itself:

The first real "date" I had with Arnold Horowitz was at Chop Suey Heaven, under the elevated train line on Bay Parkway in Brooklyn. I made the mistake of ordering soft-shell crabs. That was forty-five years ago; and I am still unable to forget my addled inability to discern how to eat the things, which I buried under a mound of wilted lettuce. Nothing, you say, to get fussed about? It was shame. How could he love me? The first time I had drinks with Arnold's family, I was completely tongue-tied, unable to say what beverage I wanted. Choice — the act of imbibing a beverage of my own selection — was inimical to the dependency I felt.

When my mother died, I forgot how to eat. In the mornings I woke up, during the days of her dying and our deathwatch, and found myself crawling on my hands and knees, groaning and keening. I was an animal. I was a baby. And when we went out at odd hours for the odd meals that punctuated our bedside vigil, I gorged; I gorged and I dribbled, I spilled food all over myself. I behaved as if eating were an activity I had yet to master. (At the funeral dinner, my brother told me a private joke inspired by a clap of thunder: "That's Ma going up to heaven and finding Pop there," my brother said. Lightning struck a tree nearby: "That's Pop clapping eyes on Ma and thinking he's been demoted to hell." It wasn't howlingly funny — unless you happened to have been brought up in that house in Bensonhurst; but it was, after days spent in subterranean underwatery gloom and mystery and misery, a relief to laugh. I wet my pants, the assembled uncles and aunts made prune faces, and my brother and I laughed harder and harder, we couldn't contain ourselves.)

I loved being thin — silk caressed me more sensuously, perfume seemed to me more delicious, and the most unlikely men, who had never before seen the point of me, flirted. But there were times when I had contempt for the whole enterprise: I am a member of a literary panel. A playwright-cartoonist says, his words projectiles, hardly calculated: "I always knew you were brilliant. I didn't know you were glamorous." (Black silk tunic with a cowl neck, and tapered black silk pants, and the red nail polish and lipstick I never apply when I am fat.) "Will you come to us at the Vineyard?" I am flattered, pissed, pleased, deeply disturbed — I am me, the old me, the same me, am I not? Am I? Being thin changes things. . . . Who was my contempt for? Him, or myself? Both? And if I did so much enjoy being thin, why did I allow myself to get fat again?

I have used food to get blotto, to stuff the emptiness: chocolate ice cream instead of sleeping pills. Sometimes I use food to goad my senses on; and to satisfy one appetite, in the latter case, is to arouse the whole menagerie. Nice; the purposeful use of a drug. Food is my drug of choice. But sometimes I eat with the unselfconscious pleasure I think we were created to eat with. I eat because food is good and because my body is good (I am good). Wheat is good and grapevines (which, in medieval iconography, grew from the wounds on the Cross) are good, and loaves and fishes and wine are good.

Yes; but I wish I didn't understand my daughter when she told me that she used, years ago, in her most fervently food-obsessed days (puberty), to look strangers — female strangers — up and down on the street, a commentary forming in her head: "I'm not as bad as she is" / "She's not as bad as I am." And sometimes — working with the indigent, plucking lice from their hair — "The hell with it. Why should I think it's important to be pretty, this woman's sores stink." Or, at a party: "The hell with it. I'll never be as thin and pretty as the rest of them." The pity of it all is that she was (and is) thin, and beautiful; and she is good.

In the thirteenth century, Chamseddine Mohamed el Hassan el Baghdadi wrote: "The joys of the table are superior to all other pleasures, notably those of personal adornment, of drinking and of love, and those procured by perfumes and by music."

I want everything — candlelight and music, soft fabric and strong hands caressing me, perfume and wine, love, sex, food, joy, the dance of the blood, and the unselfconsciousness that is the gift of angels. I want *always* and consistently to love my lovable body, which has given and received so much pleasure — and I don't know how. I want to be like the saint who saw, written on the flowering branches of her self, the names of the five senses: sight, hearing, taste, smell, and touch. I want to be as accepting of flesh as I am of water and air.

In the meantime, I peruse a catalogue from my favorite gourmet food store: "silky-soft small, tasty, tender calamari," pork chops stuffed with sautéed apples and onions, shell steak stuffed with mushrooms and red peppers, Parmigiano Reggiano, wild mushroom ravioli, basil baguette loaves and herb and cheese loaves, smoked Scotch salmon, prosciutto di Parma, arancini, broccoli di rape, "chocolate-covered cheesecake — super rich, creamy inside covered with fine bittersweet chocolate," "Chocolatissimo cake, called 'the world's richest, densest, darkest chocolate cake.'" "VERY SATISFYING." Pornography. Then I read the I. Magnin's catalogue that has come in the same mail: mortification. A battle between pleasure and pain, devils and angels . . . and the terminal inability to identify which is which and who is who.

I fantasize about a tawny-gold dress of crushed silk velvet (and one of purple, and one of black), Indian pearls and Rajput enamel around my neck. I dream of a dress of sheer wool bouclé with a cowl neckline, bittersweet-chocolate brown. I think of a dress I have kept for twenty years, as if it were a destination I would someday return to — the River Jordan of dresses: a slender column of black Fortuny silk, Alcenon lace at the square neck and at the wrists. These are waking dreams. At night

I dream of white thighs; and I dream of a man in golden tights, who loves me. I wake up caught in a web of conflicting impulses and desires. Exposure, and defense. Hiding, and revelation. I decide to go on a diet. In earnest. For real. Redoubling all past efforts. I mean it this time. I mean it every time. I float above my body, regarding myself from a great height; I regard this body with pity, amusement, weariness, and love.

☙ 3

HOME
ECONOMICS

Every woman should imbibe, from early youth, the impression that she is in training for the discharge of the most important, the most difficult, and the most sacred and interesting duties that can possibly employ the highest intellect. . . . Her station and responsibilities in the great drama of life are second to none. . . . She is the sovereign of an empire.

> — Catharine E. Beecher and Harriet Beecher Stowe,
> *The American Woman's Home, or, Principles of Domestic Science,* 1869

We study [domestic science] in order to prevent the work of housekeeping — which, however we may hate to admit it, is the basis of our civilization — from blighting the things that are the flower of our civilization. . . . The modern home is but a cell in the social body.

> — Martha Bensley Bruere and Robert W. Bruere,
> *Increasing Home Efficiency,* 1911

THE BEESWAXED DOOR of varnished golden oak at the end of the long hall smelled good and was satin to the touch. From the doorpanes of vinegar-washed glass, lozenges of oblong amber light, thrown on the polished wooden floor, formed a kind of entryway into that spotless white kitchen, which like all good kitchens was always sunny, a laboratory and a shrine. In that room where we learned to make cocoa and oatmeal porridge and were instructed in the care of the fine china and silver that few of our families owned, housekeeping — which was referred to always as "homemaking" — was presented to us, by pretty Miss Plum, as sacrament and science; and, stirring our pots in the gleam and gloss, laboring prettily in the pretty aprons we had sewn (I felt like Meg in *Little Women*), having left the ardors and the arduousness and the competition of the classroom — and the boys — behind, we were all prepared to believe this; which was odd. At home, after all, one's mother stood scowling and scary over a washboard in stained striped pajamas, doing the family wash in a double-tubbed sink, her chestnut-colored hair limp, her lips moving soundlessly, her charm placed where it was always placed when there was no handsome young man hovering in sight of her immense and immensely blue eyes — in hibernation, like a beast that needed masculine warmth. At home, roaches flew out of the oven when the stove was lit on those rare occasions when a roast was deemed a necessity. One couldn't imagine a roach daring to enter the vicinity of little Miss Plum, our home economics and hygiene instructor in sixth grade. There wasn't much going on in Miss Plum's head (which, however, was crowned by an electric aureole of red hair); but she gave off the scent of soap and the aura of goodness, even when she was telling us that if we bit our nails we would never become high-fashion models and that to look at a strawberry bush when we were "carrying child" was to ensure that the child would be born with a strawberry mark on his skin. . . . Where would we have seen a strawberry bush? . . . And even Rischa, the class terror, born to tyrannize and pout, wasn't arrogant enough to think she'd be a model. Miss Plum played a record of Frank Sinatra singing "What Is America to Me?" ("The house I live in, the church, the store, the street . . ."), and her hazel eyes filled with tears. "Oh, my dears!" she'd cry, furthering in me the illusion that I was in a tableau from *Little Women*, and causing us all — even hard-hearted Rischa — to wonder what Aurora Goldshitz called "Miss Plum's secret sorrow" was.

The boys were off doing something called vocational. Something with wood.

I do find it odd to have lived long enough to have been taught the stuff and nonsense Miss Plum, the addled sweetie pie, taught, and then — just last night — to have seen on television Surgeon General Joycelyn Elders suggesting public school children be taught masturbation. . . . I find myself on the threshold of queasiness just putting the word *masturbation* in the same sentence with Miss Plum, whose tinkly voice I often hear reproaching me when I pile unscraped china into the dishwasher ("Never boil your best dishes, girls"). . . . It being public-access television, there followed, after this sound bite, a hazy image of a man masturbating. . . . If I were to commit suicide (which my religion disallows), I would do it by the simple expedient of watching public-access television all day and all night long, after which I would surely die of boredom if not of horror.

I cannot for the life of me think of another thing I learned in home ec or hygiene. In civics, we learned how to fold and crease the *New York Times* so as to be able to read it on the subway in the rush hour, standing up or sitting down. (All our parents read the *Daily News* . . . and my father, who worked nights in any case, never had trouble securing a seat. He chewed a whole head of garlic before he entered the subway car, nobody wanted to be near him.)

Thinking of these things, I feel great affection for the days when we were allowed to sing "Abide with Me" in the school auditorium. "Abide with me! Fast falls the eventide; / The darkness deepens; Lord with me abide! / When other helpers fail and comforts flee, / Help of the helpless, oh, abide with me!" Sweet.

Perhaps I am getting those days mixed up with other days — we moved so often; I have iconized an image of my father kneeling to mix turps and paint, a ritual of our nomadic peregrinations. We moved, but always within a circumscribed area. If the BMT — the Culver Line train or the West End train or the Sea Beach train — didn't go there, we didn't move there. . . . Now the trains don't have names, they have numbers and letters, which strikes me as appropriate in a city that doesn't allow its children to sing "Abide with Me." I wish you could have seen those trains. They had waxed yellow basket-woven wicker seats and white enamel poles to hang on to and to swing around, a constant source of irritation, the swinging, to parents, and a constant source of dizzy delight to children. (The Crazy Lady, an enormous black woman with many skirts and petticoats and no underpants and a

distinctly funky aroma, used frequently to do a jig around those poles
on the West End, Sea Beach, and Culver Line trains, flinging her raggy
garments over her head; and, when I was old enough to date, I prayed
she wouldn't be on the train we were on because her unseemliness
seemed to tarnish me, it made it impossible for me to look the boy I
was out with in the eyes; I feared the diffusion of disapprobation. And
I, in her precincts, felt crazy.) And the stations had great big black iron
potbelly stoves; the stink of rain-wet wool if one stood close enough
to get warm!

This isn't a digression. In memory, which is not hierarchical, there
are no digressions. And in fact all these things coexisted — my father,
who tried to kill me once, he who in photograph and memory humbly
kneels at tins of paint; the subway, where a man once pretended to be
removing grit from my eye while his own hot eyes devoured me and
his restless hands roamed — and my father, sitting on the other side of
me, watched, his breath coming hard and fast; and my mother, sitting
across the aisle, compressed her lips into a thin line and kept her eyes
glued to the New World Translation of the Holy Bible. They are all
together in my life with Miss Plum and "Abide with Me" and they are
all together in my memory.

In one of the houses in which we briefly lived, we occupied the parlor
floor, and our landlord, a sour-smelling old man, lived in the basement
with his sour-smelling, greasy daughters. Here is our room plan, back
to front: a generous sunny kitchen, off of which was the bathroom; a
small bedroom with no windows and room only for my parents' double
bed; and a living room that served also as a bedroom for my brother
and me — a railroad flat we called it, a shotgun flat, rooms all in a line,
one room opening onto another with no doors between. Two daybeds
covered in deco chartreuse and lime and dusty rose and gray leaves and
flowers lined one living room wall, and in those beds my brother and
I slept head to head; I found bed bugs in my bed one day, a fact I was
imprudent enough to announce when we had a visitor. They were
potato bugs, my mother said. They were bed bugs, however; they had
migrated from the landlord's apartment below. My mother told me to
instruct the landlord's daughters, to give them Bible lessons (she and
I were Jehovah's Witnesses then); so I did. I read to them from Watch

Tower books that an increase in wars, pestilence, and rape was a sign of the end of the world (Matthew 24); and one of the greasy girls asked, What's rape? I hadn't the slightest idea. But I did have an idea that there was something unclean in the relationship of the motherless girls to their father . . . my unconscious drank in parallels. On a street near this narrow squalid limestone house a man in a car hailed me one day as I walked home from school swinging my book bag. "Do you know where Ellen lives?" he asked. "I'm sorry, no," I said, docility operating in me reflexively and defensively. "Too bad," he said, "I wanted to suck her pussy." "I'm sorry, I don't know where she lives," I said, genuinely distressed at my inability to please, the meaning of his words not having made their way to my brain. "So have you ever been laid in the back seat of a car?" he asked. Whereupon I ran as if a viper were gouging my heels. Home to my mother — to whom of course I could not tell this story, for two reasons: she might have said, "Don't tell me that, I'm too sensitive to hear it"; she might have seen the serpent coiled in my soul. I saw this man again in our local cleaners, and he said to the clerk with bleached ratty hair, "Did you see an eel last night?" and she, raising her chin in my direction as if to impose discretion on him, answered in pig Latin, which she should have known I'd understand: "Es-yay e-hay ame-kay" (Yes, he came). And I saw him one last time on an alternate route we took from school, a route that took us by the cemetery over which the elevated train rumbled. He was parked in his car holding a doll to his hairy chest and looking at all the young girls, just looking.

I haven't been in a subway for years, I wonder if they still have No Spitting signs.

I've lived long enough to see housekeeping turned into a political issue, reviled as drudgery and grind and instrument of female oppression, and semirehabilitated as (shared male-and-female) necessary evil. Can one depoliticize what has once been politicized? I've lived long enough to have seen the sunlight at the end of that school corridor as balm — the pure white kitchen as *sanctum sanctorum* — and subsequently to have been obliged to wonder if the light at the end of that tunnel wasn't the light of an oncoming train.

I am so much more interested in memory and in the improbable juxtapositions of circumstances that make up the warp and woof of natural history than I am in ideology, which wearies me.

I did not learn in home economics that one day — today, this morning — my entire happiness would depend on a pot of paper-white tulips and a spray of white orchids leaning (it seems to me as, supine, I regard the blue enamel sky from my bed) in sweet amazing juxtaposition against the sun-struck Empire State Building.

The spice rack in my mother's kitchen held dried oregano, basil, and bay leaves. It would never have occurred to me — I lacked the vocabulary — as I stirred porridge with girls who lived in apartment buildings that smelled of chicken fat or pork-and-beefy tomato "gravy," that one day — yesterday — I would serve my children orichietti with porcini sautéed in truffle oil and sweet butter. . . . Yet it is true that no dessert ever tastes so good to me as the chocolate pudding, hot from the pot (which I was allowed to lick), my mother made. Especially good before the skin formed.

In the next room the woman who cleans my house is applying lemon oil to rosewood. Her name is Mimi.

In Tripoli our servant was called Mohammed. We were amply fond of each other. He had a small farm near Wheelus Air Force Base and King Idris's palace. He saved my life when a kerosene fire I accidentally set in the garage spread out of control; he saved my cats' lives, too. So now does he love Qaddafi? Is he still alive? How does he remember me?

Can one deromanticize what has once been romanticized?

We reinvent the world by housecleaning, that's what's nice about it.

And some of the words for the acts are so lovely. If one could only hold them in mind, the grimy acts themselves might be transformed (from the book by the Beecher sisters: "The wood-work of the house, for doors, windows, etc., should be oiled chestnut, butternut, white-wood, and pine").

Dollhouses are nice, too — small, manageable, orderly worlds.

When we were public school children at least once a term we were taken to see a gabled house in Gravesend said to be one of the first houses built by the Dutch settlers of Brooklyn. (It was across the street from the local public library, the smell of which — glue and rubber-stamp pads and old magazines turning into yellow ash and old leather and the clean smell of new print — was my favorite in the world . . . next to honeysuckle, which bloomed in secret Brooklyn places.) The Dutch house looked like every other house on the block: it had been sided with ugly asphalt shingles and aluminum, and large bay windows had been inserted in its weary façade, and there was a plaster Madonna in a barren rock garden on the lawn. Who cared about the dopey old house? (But we took our egg-salad sandwiches and our containers of warm and slightly rancid milk into the library, adding to the familiar smell, which I perceived to be the fragrance of goodness.)

It was the full-scale-model Dutch house (Delft blue) at the Brooklyn Museum that captured my heart. All the better that I found myself there always alone. It was there that I formed the belief that life was simpler, less cluttered, and therefore both more romantic and more pure — and easier — when women churned their own butter and baked their own bread and made their own candles and addressed themselves to unquestionably basic and immovable necessities with neither the luxury nor the curse of choice. This idea exercised the pull of strong charm for me; it is still difficult for me not to succumb to it.

I close my eyes and an image comes to me: dough rising on a windowsill in the shadow of a pomegranate tree. And another: I am sitting in a Land Rover, my lap full of Berber cloth, sewing café curtains from the beautiful woven stuff while my husband talks to the village sheik, whom I may not approach; this is in the Sahara and the wind and sand wash my cheek. . . . I love these images and I hoard them, but I did not love my life then; the images are like snapshots of a solitary tree left standing in the wake of a natural disaster; they are like a pot of geraniums in a bombed-out building. . . . Outside the dining room windows where the café curtains hung were a trellis and grapevines, and the garden I had planted profligately without rhyme or reason — petunias behind sunflowers (a garden that, like memory, recognized no hierarchy and no conventional priorities) . . . and spilling over the tall whitewashed

mud walls, framing the massive green wooden doors, purple bougain-
villea . . . and in that garden date palms, too (male and female), and a
tree that bore strange, misshapen pocked fruit, neither grapefruit nor
oranges, and deformed.

> *All houses wherein men have lived and died are haunted houses.*
>
> — Longfellow

> *Only the dead know Brooklyn.*
>
> — Thomas Wolfe

For three years I was a housekeeper in the mansion Henry Ward
Beecher built for himself at 124 Columbia Heights on the Brooklyn
waterfront. The man Sinclair Lewis called a combination of Saint
Augustine, P. T. Barnum, and John Barrymore had moved from Indiana
— for financial gain, it was said — and exercised his duties as pastor in
Brooklyn for forty-three years. By those who didn't love him, his
sermons were called "Sunday Harlequinades." (Sinclair Lewis said, "He
came out for the right side of every question — always a little too late.")
John Brown's rifles were called Beecher Bibles; the flamboyant aboli-
tionist-suffragist preacher thundered from the pulpit of nearby Plymouth Church. He wore a slouch hat and a blue velvet cloak and carried
loose gems in his pocket, fingering them lovingly as boys finger marbles.

I never saw his ghost.

I was ignorant of history (in junior high school we studied the War
of the Roses, to what possible end I cannot imagine — we did not study
the history of immigration, of which we were part); I shouldn't think
my ignorance of Beecher would keep his ghost from appearing if it had
a mind to, though; I was kept ignorant of history by the masters I served
in Beecher's old house. . . . I do wish he'd chosen to show himself.
When we lived on West Ninth Street in Bensonhurst, a potty old man
lived next door, and he appeared at his front door to bang a pair of his
old shoes together and bellow imprecations whenever a kid dared to
sit on his stoop or to play skelzies in its vicinity or even to look as if
he might be entertaining the idea of playing stoopball on the old man's
steps. It always gave the day some oomph to think of him, peeking out

from behind the curtains, monitoring us, waiting to make his boisterous appearance. We really were quite fond of him — he made us feel consequential — although we pretended to be afraid. I would have gotten lots of oomph from Henry Ward Beecher.

In 1871 Beecher was sued for adultery by his erstwhile friend Theodore Tilton, a newspaper reporter and editorial writer active in Plymouth Church (which was later bought by the Watch Tower Bible and Tract Society, the legal arm of Jehovah's Witnesses, into which fire-and-ice religion my mother plunged me when I was nine years old). Tilton's wife, Libby, was an invalid who had spells and vapors; she would frequently lie prostrate trumpeting her imminent death and calling for Henry Ward Beecher (a handsome fellow) to give her final unction. Tilton indulged his wife; and he was pleased to see that Beecher's "unctions" inevitably resulted in Libby's getting better immediately after his departure. Mrs. Henry Ward Beecher, Eunice (called by those who didn't fancy her, whose number were legion, "the Griffin"), found her husband and Libby Tilton in flagrante delicto. Whereupon Mr. Tilton sued Henry Beecher for damages in the amount of $100,000 for alienation of affection. Beecher's wife, the Griffin, stood by her husband at the time (one doesn't know what punishment she exacted for that perverse act of fealty; perhaps Beecher had Eunice in mind when he said, "'I can forgive, but I cannot forget' is only another way of saying, 'I cannot forgive.'"). He was canny; he insisted that no fault attached to Libby — thus tying his lawyer's hands; a jury found for the courtly gentleman by a vote of nine to three (a vote with which history does not concur).

The man who was the star and subject of what was known variously as "The Great Brooklyn Romance" or "The Great Scandal," depending on his contemporaries' point of view, had in the drawing room of his mansion — so unapologetically did he love color and opulence and sensual fittings — Persian rugs strewn all over, three deep, one atop the other. When he owned that house it had window awnings, marquees and eaves; its greatest feature was a view of the Manhattan harbor. (And it was across the street from the house where John Roebling lived — 110 Columbia Heights — when, incapacitated by the bends, he supervised the engineering of the Brooklyn Bridge from his window with a telescope. This house was later razed to make way for an undistinguished Watchtower building . . . undistinguished is putting it kindly.)

In 1927 the Watch Tower built an addition to the Beecher house, and in 1950 another, destroying forever the graciousness of the original structure. No more Persian carpets. By the time I went to live and work there, no more anything beautiful, opulent, sensual.

Henry Ward Beecher immersed himself in the great issues of the day. It was the distinguishing purpose of Charles Taze Russell — who founded the Society of Bible Students, later called Jehovah's Witnesses — to secede from the world, the great issues of the day meaning little to him except as he could mesh them with Bible prophecy. (Indeed, newspapers reported that on the night when Russell and his followers celebrated the death (not the resurrection) of Christ in 1878, he was found on Pittsburgh's Sixth Street Bridge dressed in a white gown, waiting to be wafted to heaven.) But — while Beecher concerned himself with women's rights and the abolition of slavery and Russell frenziedly consulted Bible prophecies and convoluted chronologies and the Great Pyramid ("God's Stone Witness") in order to determine the date of the end of the world — there are parallels between the two men. Both married strong-willed women and lived to regret it; both were sexually and sensationally peccant, as a result of which they found themselves in courts of law; both were charged with financial finagling. (In 1912 the national Presbyterian weekly called Russell "the cleverest propagandist of the age, a man before whom Mary Baker Eddy, Madame Blavatsky, . . . and Joseph Smith pale into puerile ineffectiveness.") And the parallels amuse me all the more because I served in the house of the one, at the will of a successor to the other. At the time, aflame with religious zeal that coexisted with coruscating doubt, I allowed myself to know nothing about their feverish eccentricities, upon which lives depended and found their meaning. (I was far too concerned with the state of my own trembling soul and furthermore not allowed to read any but prescribed books.)

I was nineteen when I was chosen to serve at 124 Columbia Heights. My father, who seemed unable to understand that every act had consequences, had bought a *Watchtower* magazine on a street corner from one Mario Brigande, a random act that changed our lives forever. "Brother" Brigande came to our house to conduct a home Bible study. My mother seemed to grow more beautiful and visibly more vital by the minute as she drank in the opaque, hallucinatory poetry of a religion drenched in apocalyptic images and driven by a hatred of sinful flesh. She blazed. My father asked impolite questions; soon we were calling him, in Witness parlance, "a goat . . . an opposer." The world was divided into sheep and goats, and we were sheep; my mother was more comfortable with this singularity than I was, she rejoiced in it — I equated exclusivity and rarity with freakishness and loneliness (which became my portion); but I was irrevocably attracted to it, too. I was swept along by her passion and by my need to hear her say that I was good. *You are a good girl, Bobbie.* . . . Sometimes I fancy she did say those words to me once, but I can never be sure.

Over the years my brother, furiously charming, lived more on the streets than at home. My father packed his suitcases to leave us. Over and over. And over and over he came back. We rode the subways — the Sea Beach and the West End and the Culver Line — hoping for a glimpse of him. My brother and I packed his suitcase for him once, unasked, when we were very young — at this time my brother had sores on his head and he lisped and he fell over his own feet, and one time he soiled his pants at school and had to wear a sign saying I AM A DIRTY BOY until my mother came to school (reluctantly). He packed Daddy's suitcase and we hugged each other and curled up together in a big old chair and cried, snot and tears all over our faces. . . . I went along with Witness propaganda for another reason, too, besides the newness and the excitement of difference: now I had a sanctioned reason to have contempt for my father, and I was supported in that contempt, that rich loathing, by my mother — he was an enemy of God. Before that I couldn't allow myself to hate him — his hands, his tongue, his hot wet voice at my ear. . . . I preached the gospel of doom from door to door. I was tired for so many years.

This is what I read, a nine-year-old, my first lesson:

As the earth rotated on its axis . . . thrown-off matter gradually formed into great rings about the earth at its equator, where the centrifugal force of the spinning earth was most powerful. . . . According to the density and specific gravity of the materials thrown off from the molten earth, they formed into rings of water mixed with mineral substance, the densest and heaviest being nearest the earth-core, the next heavy being immediately next out beyond it, and so on, the lightest being thrown out farthest and being almost wholly a water ring. Thus an annular or ring system existed, and the appearance to the eye of God was like that of a great wheel, with wheels within wheels, and with the molten earth itself as the spherical hub of them. (*The Truth Shall Make You Free*)

I flattered myself that I saw the world through the eye of God. Meanwhile, my classmates were learning that the principal export of Bolivia was tin. And I wanted to be their friend; but they were "of this world," and I couldn't be their friend, even if they had wanted me, which they did not, and who could blame them? strange, unplaceable girl that I was, unnaturally good, forbidden to salute the flag, unable to celebrate birthdays or "demonic" holidays, to rejoice in Allied victories or support the Red Cross or make aluminum-foil balls and rubber-band balls to support the war effort . . . and yet, in spite of it all, unable to hide at school my starved love of learning, my adoration of the word. Teacher's pet. Outsider. Poison.

And images of babies and horses swimming in blood at Armageddon, and birds picking out the eyes of the wicked whom Jehovah would destroy at Armageddon — I read all this too; and I read that the Roman Catholic Church was the "scarlet whore of Babylon," "the abomination of abominations."

I was afraid for many years; I masked my fears with what must have looked like — and very possibly was — smugness. In the strange gardens of our souls, flowers and rank weeds grow together, a crazy quilt.

I earned an appearance of righteousness by door-to-door preaching and eager responsiveness at dreary meeting places called Kingdom Halls, always waving my hand in the air to provide rote answers to rhetorical questions — which made it hard for the Witness girls to like me, too; they thought (and perhaps they were right) that I was showing off. I never could learn how to behave. I was deflated by the notion that all one had to do, to gain popularity, was to be one's natural self.

I hadn't an idea what that self was, so I impersonated; I impersonated myself by impersonating other people who appeared to have selves; and this was the way to social ruin. I tried to be like everybody else, which had the unfortunate consequence of making me different from everybody else, and isolated. And I wanted — at the same time I dreadfully wanted companionship — to be alone with that self I was unacquainted with but which I had dim and rather terrifying but also tantalizing glimpses of from time to time.

At 124 Columbia Heights (known as "Bethel," or house of God), I cleaned fifteen double rooms on the first floor of the old Beecher house daily, and two more rooms on the second floor (the lower you were in the overseers' estimation, the lower the floor you cleaned — they were anything but subtle; one was meant to accept in all humility one's weaknesses, which were never, however, clearly articulated; one knew only that one was not best loved). Once in a while one of the "brothers" who worked in the offices would come and massage my back — in which I chose to see nothing untoward although my skin felt like electricity. Sometimes one of the other girls visited me; and the conversation we had seemed charged and odd, I didn't understand why it made me uneasy: Brooke sat on a twin bed while I was making its mate and told me how women in jails played "boy and girl," husband and wife. I did not consciously allow myself to understand the sexual content of this; it was gratifying for me to believe that Brooke, who on all other occasions spurned me, thought enough of me to visit me, and that overwhelmed all other considerations (Brooke was popular and pretty).

The bells rang at six for us to rise and shower in the communal bathrooms (my shared room was in the 1950 addition), as his — Henry Ward Beecher's — had rung every morning at six. Breakfast and a discussion of a Bible text with all the members of the "family" was at six-thirty, and we were at work by seven-thirty. We worked six days a week. On Monday nights we had a "family" reading of *The Watchtower*; on Tuesday nights we were expected to attend a local Bible study group; on Wednesday nights we were supposed to make "back-calls," or return visits to people with whom we had placed Witness literature on Sundays; on Thursday nights we went to something called the Theocratic

Ministry School, where we learned to be more perfect; and on Sunday nights we studied *The Watchtower* again, with a Brooklyn congregation.

Perhaps things are different for the women there now. I hope they are.

The thirty-four beds I made every day were smelly. Once a week I changed the linens. Each room had a sink and a mirror, which I cleaned. I vacuumed the hall and dusted and vacuumed each room each day, and every day washed three floors. Every day I scrubbed the tub that thirty men used. Once a week I sorted linen in the laundry room under the aegis of a white-haired "sister" who wore purple and mauve and lavender and told me not to try too hard to be liked.

I wanted only to be liked.

Sometimes the families of the "brothers" whose rooms we cleaned would send them cakes, which they would place high in their closets (which we brush-scrubbed every six months with strong detergent). Sometimes I would dig my fingers into their cakes and smash the resulting moist mess against and into my mouth as if I were under great compulsion. Sometimes I would peel — lick — all the icing off. And afterward I denied that I had.

No doors were locked.

Don't live in the past, my brother says, get on with your life. How do I tell him that I am contained in my past (and my past is contained in me)? Can I explain to him that the past is not a place I revisit, but my present and future home? "If the past and the future exist," Augustine said, "where are they?" At this very moment, this instant — which is over the moment I call its name — I am incorporating the past (which includes this moment) into the present; and the present has become part of my future — which is also meaningless, because it has already begun, and is therefore Now; and the past and the future and the moment are one.

You will understand why I gave so much thought to domesticity: I worked in the way I have described in the Beecher house for three troubled years. Long before the women's liberation movement gave issue to consciousness-raising groups and the discussion of the politics of housework, I thought about the meaning of housework (sacrament or science); and this was the meat of the thinking of Harriet Beecher, Henry Ward Beecher's sister, the author of *Uncle Tom's Cabin* (whom Sinclair Lewis called "a ruthlessly humanitarian woman," more disastrous than a hurricane, and whom Henry James savaged as well).

She was the most celebrated woman author of her time. I tell you that Uncle Tom — gentle, forbearing, submissive, pious, "the sunshine of [his] circle," addicted to self-denial — was really a white woman, a white housekeeper, in blackface and drag.

Henry Ward Beecher's father was a Calvinist, a missionary to the Wild West. Charles Taze Russell's father was a Presbyterian haberdasher. As an adolescent, Russell had written Bible texts in chalk in front of whorehouses and saloons, warning men against courting eternal damnation; before he was twenty-five he had founded a Bible class, become coeditor and financial backer of a periodical called *The Herald of the Morning*, sold out his business interests, and began — as "Pastor" Russell — to travel from city to city sermonizing. His writings tend toward the conclusion that he believed himself to be a second Napoleon, come to plague and eviscerate the Roman Catholic Church.

Russell, the president of what was then called Zion's Watch Tower Tract Society, began in 1889 to amass property in Pennsylvania. With the accrual of property came charges of financial flimflammery — and discord with his wife, the coeditor of the *Herald:*

"I can show you a thousand women that would be glad to be in your place and that would know my wishes and do them. . . . I can show you a thousand women that if I would say, 'I want sweet potatoes,' sweet potatoes would be there. If I wanted pumpkin pie, pumpkin pie would be there." So said Charles Taze Russell, according to his wife, Maria Frances Ackley Russell, in the Superior Court of Pennsylvania.

"I am like a jellyfish; I float around here and there. I touch this one and that one, and if she responds I take her to me, and if not I float on to others." So said Pastor Russell, according to his wife, in Pennsylvania's Court of Common Pleas.

In 1897, after eighteen years of marriage, Maria Frances Ackley Russell — who for years had preserved her husband's reputation, defending him against charges by Bible students that he was aberrant and autocratic, sinful, a traitor, a liar — left her husband, fleeing to relatives in Chicago to gain protection from the man she claimed was committing gross improprieties with other women and who, furthermore, was conspiring to have her incarcerated in a lunatic asylum.

In 1903 she filed for legal separation in the Court of Common Pleas at Pittsburgh. The lurid case was resolved in Mrs. Russell's favor. Russell fought his wife's demands for separation and alimony for five years, initiating libel suits against newspapers and a minister along the way. In 1908 Mrs. Russell was granted a divorce. In 1909 she appealed for an increase in alimony, and Russell moved out of the jurisdiction of the Pittsburgh courts, transferred his assets to the Watch Tower Society, declared himself penniless, and moved his staff and his operations to Brooklyn to avoid being jailed for failure to pay alimony. (A justice of the Superior Court of Pennsylvania delivered himself of the opinion that Russell's "course of conduct toward his wife evidenced . . . insistent egotism and extravagant self-praise [and] continual arrogant domination.")

Russell complained of a female conspiracy against God — and against his person. He blamed "Women's Rights" for the pickle he found himself in: "Ah, it is really too bad. Because before she became a suffragist she was an ideal wife. I might say she was as perfect as it is possible for anyone to be." He entered a caveat: "It is a great mistake for strong-minded men and women to marry. If they will marry, the strong-minded had far better marry such as are not too intellectual and high-spirited, for there never can, in the nature of things, be peace . . . where the two are on an equality." He never denied that she was "a woman of high intellectual qualities and perfect moral character"; he only called her cuckoo.

This is an excerpt from the brief by Congressman Stephen Porter, attorney for Maria Russell:

The apartments in which the Russells lived were on the fourth floor of a business house on Arch Street, Allegheny, Pa. There was no neighbor within calling distance at night. . . . Shortly after respondent had started . . . reports about his wife's sanity, all of the employees were removed from the building, leaving Mrs. Russell, in case her husband was absent, alone.

Utter desolation. . . . What must have been the feelings of this woman after . . . years of indignities? . . .

While living alone with his wife in this large building, he prepares a cunningly worded letter to the effect that they have reconciled their differences, and then on Friday evening of that week he presents it to his wife for her signature, and all night long he follows her about from room to room, urging, coaxing, pleading and threatening until her head is in a whirl of doubts and fears, and thus forces her to sign the letter under protest. . . .

A few days after this, [Russell] telephoned a message to his wife that he was going out of the city, he did not say where or what for.

The wife drew her own conclusions about his intentions. He then wittily circulated false reports of her mental derangement, and all this maneuvering to completely isolate her from all society and that of her own family, the withdrawal at night of all employees of the Watch Tower from the building which she lived, and the utter desolation of her home and the withdrawal of all support, to her mind pointed to one conclusion, namely, that he proposed to deal with her upon the pretext of insanity, and that his unrevealed errand that night might be for such purpose. [Mrs. Russell] left the building and took a train for Chicago to seek the protection and counsel of her brother.

While poor Mrs. Russell was sick with erysipelas, a febrile streptococcal infection of the skin and subcutaneous tissue, the Pastor conveyed messages to the sickroom by way of one Rose Ball, whom, according to Mrs. Russell, he frequently "kissed and fondled." Among the messages he conveyed was that his wife's sickness was a judgment from God. He called her "weak-minded, mind-poisoned, [under] Satanic hypnotic influence." Satan, he said, took the form of her sister — his own father's second wife, i.e., his own stepmother. (Isn't it tempting to think there's a tasty Oedipal conundrum here?)

Mrs. Russell accused her husband of "improprieties" with Rose Ball, an orphan whom the Russells had taken into their home in 1888 — seventeen years after Beecher had been sued for adultery (or for what he called administering "final unction"). Pastor Russell admitted he had gone into Rose Ball's room at night — but only, he said, "to minister to the sick." Miss Ball, whom he admitted fondling and kissing and dandling on his knee — to administer "spiritual tonic" — was "an adopted child of the family in short dresses."

So in 1909 Russell and his entourage moved to Brooklyn; he purchased Beecher's 1868 Plymouth Church; he bought Beecher's four-story brownstone parsonage on Columbia Heights as well.

Still, although he removed himself from the jurisdiction of the Pittsburgh courts, he found himself continuing to be plagued by "fallen angels," in the shape of pubescent girls. He had one of them, sixteen-year-old Sophie Hassan (who insisted upon calling Russell her "bridegroom"), carted off by the cops to the Kings Park Asylum for observation — his standard way of beating off demons ("all men are more or less influenced by a pretty woman's charms").

To all who would listen, he swore: "I did not leave [Pittsburgh] because I was afraid to be put in jail." He left because God, in whose interests he was acting, had revealed to him that there were "hundreds of thousands of very very intelligent people in Brooklyn."

He shored up his own vanity at every possible opportunity: "If I were to die tomorrow, I think my former wife would soon follow me, for she could not live unless she had me to nag."

When sex paled, money continued to exert its charms. In 1911 a member of his flock donated to the Watch Tower Society something called "miracle wheat." Russell's followers were encouraged to believe that the wheat — which was sold for $60 a bushel, or $1 a pound at Russell's Hicks Street Tabernacle, the old Plymouth Church — yielded as much as one and one half to two times as much wheat as ordinary grain, the market price for which was 59 cents to $1 a bushel. The press had a field day. So did the Department of Postal Inspection and the Department of Agriculture. General counsel for the Watch Tower Society issued disclaimers that can only be admired for their nice slitheriness: "The advertisement in *The Watch Tower* does not say that miracle wheat is worth $1 a pound. It says simply that [we are] willing to sell it at that price. . . . I might place high value upon worthless furniture if I wished to, and if people wanted to buy at the price I named they could do so, if they wished, though I made no claims that the furniture had any real value beyond that of ordinary furniture."

Russell claimed to have been smitten by the devil in the form of the *Brooklyn Eagle*, which he sued, unsuccessfully, for libel; for his failure to prevail he blamed the "seven Catholics on the jury," a statement he amended to include "the Protestants on the jury [who] were led to hope for escape from eternal torment . . . for giving the *Eagle* the verdict."

The last words the old scoundrel uttered before his death on a moving train were: "Bring me a toga."

(Fifteen years ago a nonagenarian Brooklyn Heights doctor, who had come to hear me lecture at the Montauk Club, told me that when he was a young practicing physician, Russell — who had vehemently protested to the *Eagle* that Bethel was not "a harem" — presented himself to him with syphilis. I have no way of knowing whether this is true.)

> *Woman is merely a lowly creature whom God created for man as man's helper.*
>
> — *Let God Be True*, Watch Tower Bible and Tract Society, 1946

I knew none of this penny-dreadful, demoralizing stuff when I worked at Bethel. But the air was heavy with misogyny and masked carnality that no amount of lemon oil or bleach could erase. And I felt all the time a little crazy; under obligation to be submissive and subservient and charming, too, but not too charming, I hid even from myself the fact that I was "intellectual and high-spirited"; but my dissimulation just made me feel fake, to myself and to others.

What I mean by "charming" is that you were supposed to have something called a "personality." I didn't. I tried to invent one; it didn't work.

. . . I keep thinking of the Culver Line train. My mother and I would ride to Witness meetings on the Culver Line train, she in her ocelot-trimmed winter coat, her lustrous hair in a snood, radiant in her chosen martyrdom. Sometimes her friend Diana rode with us, and I would hear snatches of conversation: "It doesn't matter, he still has that *thing* in his pants." "Don't you know nuns do it with statues of Jesus before they're accepted into the convent?" I pressed my nose against the window. (*"Shhh!"*) My calves were scorched by the heat blasting from the screened radiators beneath the wicker seats. Around this time a

Mad Bomber with a gripe against Con Ed set off bombs on subways; and I used to wonder, riding with my mother and Diana, what it would be like to splinter into a thousand pieces; I hurt my stomach thinking of this, thinking of being separated from myself and flying through a void, my disintegrated flesh missiles hurtling through space, my flesh my enemy. . . . And when they weren't talking about the vileness of men and the salaciousness of nuns and the imminence of the end of the world, they were all the time talking, it seemed to me, about organ meats: Diana said they were bad for you, all the collected poisons of the animal were there; my mother, who cooked heart stew and simmered livers — but never in aluminum pots, which the Witnesses said contained poison — said that that was where all the potency was.

How they feared and hated men.

My mother spent most of her daytime hours going from door to door. She left the routine housework — the washing of the dishes, the centering of the doilies, the dusting of the old mahogany furniture — to me. I did not undertake these repetitive tasks with gladness, nor was I, in any way I could understand, rewarded for doing them.

She had little regard for my school homework, which was the work of the "devilish world."

Yet I was required to "give a witness" at school by being good at my studies. The bind this placed us both in was similar to the one implicit in the words of the Beecher sisters ("ruthless humanitarians," indeed): "A common precocity in children is usually the result of an unhealthy state of the brain. . . . The wonderful child should be deprived of all books and study, and turned to play out in the fresh air." On the other hand, "Inactivity of intellect and of feeling is a very frequent predisposing cause of every form of nervous disease." How did we walk such tightropes as these? Were we mad? *Don't use your brain too much and don't use your brain too little. Don't allow yourself to feel too much; don't allow yourself to feel too little.* Told to resist, as were the Beechers' acolytes, both "apathy" and "a restless longing for excitement," enjoined from "a craving for unattainable good and dissatisfaction with the world," but forbidden to seek "alleviation in exciting amusements," we must surely, on that moral seesaw, have been so vertiginous as to have been mad.

We had furthermore never to forget — if we wished to use the path of fantasy for escape from impossible demands — that "Castle-building . . . undermines the vigor of the nervous system." I remember the exact spot — which, as it happened, was in front of the house on Seventy-fifth Street where Francis Ford Coppola's parents lived — where I promised God I would never fantasize again, fantasizing being a form, we were told, of "idol worship."

The only thing that saves one from complete screaming lunacy when one is trying to follow these impossible deformative demands is to adhere even more closely to that which gave them issue — the religious organization that required them of you in the first place. You had, I discovered, no peace unless you allowed yourself to be chewed alive, swallowed whole.

The one regret my mother expressed before she died was her insistence upon my centering the doilies with an almost scientific precision. "If I had another life to live," she said — when I asked her to forgive me — "I wouldn't punish you for the doilies again." The doilies were dipped in sugar water to stiffen them; and when I see her anxious white hands fluttering over their placement in the bedroom my brother and my father shared, when I hear her high harried voice ask me if I *intended* to do things wrong to hurt her, I see all her vast discontent, her frustration, her inability to find joy in any object animate or inanimate, her belief that objects, and people, existed in order to hurt her, her inability to attach her love to anyone or anything but a demented punitive Jehovah . . . who loved her.

When I asked her to forgive me, for unspecified sins, for having hurt her — which God knows I must have done — I wanted, really, I know, for her to ask me to forgive her, or, barring that, for her to say she loved me. Would my life be different today if she had said "Forgive me"?

"How can housework be made into a creative activity?" Gaston Bachelard asks. And he answers: "The minute we apply a glimmer of consciousness to a mechanical gesture, . . . we sense new impressions come into being beneath this familiar domestic duty. For consciousness rejuvenates everything, giving a quality of beginning to the most everyday actions. . . . When a poet rubs a piece of furniture — even vicariously — when he puts a little fragrant wax on his table with the woolen cloth that lends warmth to everything it touches, he creates a new object; he increases the object's human dignity; he registers this object officially as a member of the human household. . . . Objects that are cherished . . . are born of an intimate light, and they attain to a higher degree of reality than indifferent objects. . . . From one object in a room to another, housewifely care weaves the ties that unite a very ancient past to the new epoch. The housewife awakens furniture that was asleep. . . . A house that shines from the care it receives appears to have been rebuilt from the inside; it is as though it were new inside. In the intimate harmony of walls and furniture, it may be said that we become conscious of a house that is built by women, since men only know how to build a house from the outside, and they know little or nothing of the 'wax' civilization. . . . No one has written better of this integration . . . of our vastest dreams into the humblest of occupations, than Henri Bosco, in his description of the old faithful servant, Sidoine: '. . . When she washed a sheet or a table cloth, when she polished a brass candlestick, little movements of joy mounted from the depths of her heart, enlivening her household tasks. She did not wait to finish these tasks before withdrawing into herself, where she could contemplate to her heart's content the supernatural images that dwelt there. Indeed, figures from this land appeared to her familiarly, however commonplace the work she was doing, and without in the least seeming to dream, she washed, dusted, and swept in the company of the angels.' . . . Through housewifely care a house recovers not so much its originality as its origin. . . . A dreamer can reconstruct the world from an object that he transforms magically through his care of it. . . . Rilke writes . . . that in the absence of his cleaning woman, he had been polishing his furniture. 'I was . . . magnificently alone. . . . I was an emperor washing the feet of the poor, or Saint Bonaventure, washing dishes in his convent.' . . . Alone, as we are at the origin of all real action that we are not 'obliged' to perform. And the marvelous thing about easy actions is that they do, in fact, place us at the origin of action."

Advertising directed at women — women purring at their Maytags, women singing paeans of praise to furniture wax, women becoming orgasmic over the properties of the latest detergent, women making icons of their pink or avocado or stainless steel appliances, fifties love-ads to Proctor's dual-automatic toaster: "love, honor . . . and *crisper* toast" — is brilliant to the extent that it is a perverse embodiment of Bachelard's sentiments, which are profoundly true. True for the poet, who is not "obliged" to dust every day. True on those days when organizing drawers and closets, nice in itself, becomes a meditative metaphor for an impossible organization of the self. True when one handles and cleans and rearranges beloved artifacts so that the loved thing becomes, not only precious in itself, but part of a drama of inanimate things — a perfect arrangement unlike (and an antidote to) the unruly arrangements of one's lived emotional life. Not true, one must believe, for the cleaning woman whose absence provided Rilke (who wore a "big apron and little washable suede gloves" to polish his big black piano) with his epiphany.

The romance of the trousseau is real. Brides don't want *things* because brides are unimaginative and crassly materialistic. A house all shiny and new from the inside out is the gift a bride offers her husband. It isn't a negligible gift, or an undignified one. But the moment house-keeping is perceived as a futile exercise in chaos control, a thing in and of its boring self to be done over and over forever and ever — not an animistic love of objects nor a duty offered up in praise, nor a conscious rejuvenation, nor a dreamy way into memory and order — it ceases to become hallowed and becomes drudgery, a cause and manifestation of panic, a Sisyphean task.

Nuns are waxing the altar in the church of Santa Cecilia in Trastevere, scrubbing the tile floors of the Renaissance Cosmati brothers. "Look at that!" says my friend Judita, married to a dull tyrant. "Of course they like *their* husband," their husband being the Lord Jesus. Judita is an opera singer. She comes to hear the nuns sing, and to hear the nuns' silence. Silence. And cycles of praise and labor, contemplation and service. Part of the romance of being a nun is beeswax and lemon oil. For Judita, who doesn't like her tedious husband, housekeeping is a thankless grind, her home not a cloister but a prison.

In his lyrical poem "Love Calls Us to the Things of This World,"

Richard Wilbur's image of nuns rosy with the steamy ardors of washing clothes and hanging billowing garments to dry ("maintaining a difficult balance") is beautifully true — every bit as "true" as my mother's slack, bitter resentment over the scrub board.

"The morning air is all awash with angels." The exotic fact that there is holiness in daily living, the astounded recognition of the beatitudes of the quotidian, can be sweetly and immensely liberating; and it can be the tool with which to keep woman in her place. Only work that is chosen is beautiful. Not all of us can say (of anything) what Saint Joan of Arc, burned for her troubles, said of her unique calling: "I was born to do this." But for those of us who can, those blessed with a vocation, there is no way to escape the vocation that does not lead to a slow dying or to despair, or perversion. "The glory of God is a person fully alive," wrote Saint Irenaeus, the father of Christian theology; a person fully alive, fully human (it cannot be said too often), is a person with work in the world.

"Work, even the most simple, performed with constant perfection in the midst of inevitable difficulties, spells heroism." Such heroic resignation to simple tasks as Pope Benedict XV spoke of is the product of cultivated love — it cannot be engendered by fiat. And even the saints allowed themselves to be querulous when their temperaments did not suit their work. Beloved Maria Rafaela Porras, who, with her sister, Dolores, fled from her community to escape the harsh imposition of Church rule, founded the Congregation of the Handmaids of the Sacred Heart and was elected its mother general. But she was replaced by Dolores. And for the rest of her life she did housework: "How patient we have to be to live in this world!" Maria bemoaned, sounding not patient at all — and quite eager for greener pastures.

Late-nineteenth- and early-twentieth-century books about housekeeping have one of two conflicting messages, both designed to reconcile middle-class women to homemaking. Either — as in the case of the Beecher sisters — they reinforce the notion that housekeeping is sacred or — as in the case of Mr. and Mrs. Bruere — they seek to disabuse their (women) readers of the notion that sanctity has any part in the running of a household and to replace piety with science ("ordered knowledge"), so as to subordinate "the work of housekeeping [to] the business of living." (The books — one of which I read because of my time-attenuated relationship to the Beechers, the other because a recipe for coddled eggs caught my fancy — have in common, besides the inflation of necessity by romance or by contrived science, one thing: the fanciful and rather endearing notion that canned soup would make the revolutionary difference between happy orderliness and drudgery.)

The illustrations of Catharine E. Beecher and Harriet Beecher Stowe's book on domestic science (subtitled *A Guide to the Formation and Maintenance of Economical, Healthful, Beautiful, and Christian Homes,* and dedicated to "the women of America, in whose hands rest the real destinies of the Republic") are (as Norman Rockwell's illustrations were later to be) so sentimental as to provoke simultaneous nostalgia and exasperation. In these idealized representations of family life, three generations gather in the light of lamps in a cottage room bathed in soft moonlight to play with simple toys and read edifying (to judge from their size) tomes. The cottage, a shrine to innocence, shares a country road with an unintimidating white gingerbread church framed by hanging moss and old oak trees. (Like the head of the baby Jesus in paintings of the Old Masters, the children's heads are so oversized they hardly look like children at all, more like dwarfs.)

In any community, including a family, the most prized commodity is privacy. (I was twenty-two before I had a room of my own.) So I was interested to see that an important feature of the Beechers' architectural drawings were arched recesses in every room — recesses for busts and flowers and umbrellas and for what the sisters called "statuettes." But I think these were symbolic crawl spaces: I think the sisters must in their heart of hearts have wanted to pull the walls in around them and retire from good works and communal evenings. I think they had a healthy instinct, which they unhealthily denied, to hide, to preserve themselves, to find themselves . . . alone. For the record they urged the use of movable screens to replace walls (were all those dwarfy children supposed to watch their parents in the act of love?); one screen in a large room was to be moved according to the time of day, so that the room might serve as sleeping room, sitting room, breakfast room, parlor and sewing or "retiring room"; this would enable a 25 x 16 room to serve, at any hour, two functions. For the system to work, all members of the family were obliged to act in preordained synchronicity

— otherwise there would be no purpose to the moving and shifting of a screen (the back of which formed a built-in cupboard complete with shelf-boxes and washing pitcher and slops).

There is something of the child's fascination with dollhouses in this scheme, and — with its pleased insistence on little cubbies and little boxes ("cheaper and better than drawers and much preferred by those using them") — something of the romance of miniatures that informs fairy tales, where a world springs from a bean shoot and the universe is contained in a snowflake. For women who possess little but their wits, the appeal of miniaturization is self-evident. (I have a friend, tall, with big teeth and big ideas and big bones, who surrounds her person and her life with miniatures — miniature jewelry, miniature *objets;* even her voice is (unsettlingly) small, squeaky, like the voice of a miniature person. This is the way she appeases and apologizes to the world for taking up room in it.) To miniaturize the world is also a way to possess it, to tame outer and inner jungles (which is part of what *The Glass Menagerie* is about). But the danger is that one loses what one gains: the Beechers' plans for busy, screened Christian living is a Calvinist nod to the apprehension that in privacy, where leisure flourishes, art — and vice — flourish too; and art and vice are dangerous if one is in the business of curbing human nature and taming human instincts and subordinating all to a religious exercise of benevolence and duty.

Daddy works at night. He sleeps ten feet from the television set. "Lower the television!" he yells from his bed. My brother turns it lower . . . lower . . . "Lower the television!" At last my father, naked except for boxer shorts, enters the living room, holding closed the fly of his shorts. "I told you to lower the television!" But by this time my brother and I have shut the television off, we are waiting (why?) for him to make his nightly accusatory appearance. Holding his fly. We turn blank faces to his face, which is ruddy with wrath. He reenters the bedroom he shares with my brother and slams the door; we hear him muttering and turning in bed. We are held captive in the living room by some force we do not understand. Until his room is silent we cannot move. We look at each other, each of us hugging our knees. We turn the television on without sound.

Sometimes Daddy watches television with me. His face is in my face, watching my every reaction. I can't bear this scrutiny; I can't release myself from it. I try to make my face a mask. His breath is hot. Occasionally he is rewarded with my tears.

One day the field mike was left open at Ebbets Field and Leo Durocher, the Dodgers' manager, was heard to say, during a baseball game we watched, "Shit" (to an umpire); "fuck you." I feel, when I hear these words in my father's presence, the way I feel when I see the Crazy Lady on the BMT line: I feel crazy, I want to die.

> *No statesman, at the head of a nation's affairs, has more frequent calls for wisdom, firmness, tact, discrimination, prudence, and versatility of talent than . . . a well-educated and pious woman. She has a husband, to whose peculiar tastes and habits she must accommodate herself; she has children whose health she must guard, whose physical constitutions she must study and develop, whose temper and habits she must regulate, whose principles she must form, whose pursuits she must guide. She has constantly changing domestics. . . . The mere gratification of [her own] appetite is to be placed last.*
>
> — *The American Woman's Home*

For the Beechers' middle-class homemakers there were the deserving poor to relieve, benevolent societies and schools to aid, these tasks to be performed in "the leisure of two evenings," and — a sop — "the leisure of two other days might be devoted to intellectual improvement, and the pursuits of taste." In order for this call to women's assumed higher nature to cohere, work must be made to sound like pleasure (just as pleasure must be made to sound like work).

If there were no poor, "there would be no chance to gain that noblest of all attainments, a habit of self-denying benevolence which toils for the good of others, and takes from one's own store to increase the enjoyments of another." What after all could these servanted women do if they were denied the means "to relieve and instruct the suffering, ignorant, and poor. . . . Even among the most wealthy, abundant modes of self-denying benevolence may be found where there is a heart to seek them."

"The family state" is literally heaven on earth — "the aptest earthly illustration of the heavenly kingdom, and in it woman is its chief minister. Her great mission is self-denial. . . . To man is appointed the out-door labor [which includes] civil, municipal and state affairs, and the heavy work, which, most of the day, excludes him from the comforts of home." She who is "chief minister" must be "habitually gentle, sympathizing, forbearing, and cheerful; [she will] carry an atmosphere about her which imparts a soothing and sustaining influence, [rendering] it easier for all to do right, under her administration, than in any other situation." She must be "the sunshine of the circle around her. . . .

"When the family is instituted by marriage, it is man who is the head and chief magistrate. As Christ loved the Church," so the husband must "'suffer' for her, if need be, in order to support and elevate and ennoble her. . . . Any discussion of the equality of the sexes, as to intellectual capacity, seems frivolous and useless, both because it can never be decided, and because there would be no possible advantage in the decision."

If there was ever a time that my mother regarded my father as "head and chief magistrate" and herself as "chief minister," that time passed before I was born. I am tempted to wonder if it was not the fact of my birth that destroyed the illusions upon which her happiness was based. In pictures of them before I was born they look so happy, so congruent. (These are pictures I have rescued from my aunts; my mother made a bonfire of her snapshots — the past was her enemy.) She gave no evidence of ever having felt herself to have been elevated or ennobled by him.

> *The fable of Juno hanging in the air with a rope around her neck and her hands tied by another rope and with two heavy stones tied to her feet . . . signified the sanctity of marriage. Juno . . . had a rope about her neck to recall the violence used by the giants on the first wives. Her hands were bound in token of the subjection of wives to their husbands, later represented among all nations by the more refined symbol of the wedding ring. The heavy stones tied to her feet denoted the stability of marriage. . . . [Among] the earliest barbarous peoples, wives were maintained as a necessity of nature for the procreation of children. In other respects they were treated as slaves, as is still the custom of nations.*
>
> — Giambattista Vico

We were on our way to a Kingdom Hall meeting when my mother, suddenly and without word or warning, removed her wedding ring and threw it on the train tracks. Thereafter, whenever she had a family wedding to attend, she went to the five-and-ten-cent store to buy a fake wedding band; these excursions appeared to give her pleasure.

What would have been her fate, I wonder, if there had been a women's movement during her lifetime.

She was a woman in search of a cause, a vehicle for her intelligence, her passion, and her punishing need to see the punishing world punished. Her sorrow — which was indistinguishable from her gladness — swung on a strange axis: when, so ardently, she took up with a totalitarian religion that explicitly defined itself as a "theocratic organization," she — who had never before had a community, only two wrangling families, his and hers — "toiled for the good of others" by preaching an apocalyptic message of doom. (Benevolence to the poor was satisfied by preaching to them.) So far, so good; she could do that — and in the process exercise a kind of authority. But she was obliged, by *The Watchtower,* to regard her religious leaders in the same light as the Beechers exhorted women to regard their husbands. The catch was that she had also to regard her husband as her "head," she had to see herself, in relation to him, as "the weaker vessel." And she despised him.

A comedy — a tragedy — of errors. When we first became Jehovah's Witnesses she would rush breathlessly to Kingdom Hall meetings with tales of his having "persecuted" her, of his having spoken of Jehovah and "His organization" in vile and violent ways. But then, at the very utterance of her words and as sympathy began to flow toward her, making her radiant, he would appear casually at the Kingdom Hall, smiling, cheerful, amiable to all.

This put her in terrible danger. She saw herself regarded without trust by her coreligionists. The ground of her happiness was swept from under her feet. Perhaps it was when it was made clear to him (by me, whom she required to be her deputy and spokesperson) that she would no longer sleep with him, ever, that he stopped all pretense of friendliness and relished his role of "goat," "opposer," "persecutor." Damned.

To her beauty was added the incense of martyrdom.

I often wonder if my mother ever read a book before she became a

Jehovah's Witness. Afterward she was permitted to read nothing but Watch Tower literature.

Her religion had delivered her from the fate she feared: she was no longer a cipher. She no longer bore any resemblance to her own mother. She had escaped the claustrophobia of Main Street and the activities she found idiotic for the glories of a theocracy.

But — oh my poor mother! — this road was not safe for her either. All roads led, for her, to the home of her hoarded sorrow and her contained rage. Her beauty and her fervor and the haze of martyrdom that surrounded her made at least one man mad. And he placed her in profound danger (no net). This is what happened:

It is evening in Brooklyn (there is honeysuckle in the air, and a light fog rolling in from the ocean), and I am going from door to door with Chas, whose dynamism has made him the object of many girls' desire. He is a young man with blunt features, a blunt manner, flying hair, and a bullish passion for proselytizing equal to my mother's own vampish/vampira passion; her enticing passion runs parallel with and at last crazily headlong into his virile passion. Chas had recently been released from prison, where, as a "minister," he had spent the duration of World War II, an incarceration that seemed glamorous and dazzled gaggles of girls. In a moment of silliness (it was hard to be a pretend grown-up all the time) I asked him who, of all the girls, he "liked." "Don't ask me that, it's too painful," he said. (I was used to people's emotions being painful; emotions didn't seem to be good for anything *but* pain.) No alarm bells went off in my head, for in spite of the fact that I was unnaturally good and serious, I was a child.

One night soon after, at dinner, very calmly under the circumstances, Daddy says to Mother — in Italian dialect, which I am not expected to understand, but which I do — that his mother saw Chas and my mother walking *mano a mano*, hand in hand, on Sixty-sixth Street, where the two were preaching door to door. An intake of breath. Mine? Hers? I do not remember what she said, if she said anything at all. I was suspended in his terrifying calm. I remember a laugh, I don't remember whose. Not mine. (Mrs. Rochester's laugh.) I believe it was soon after this that he tried to kill me, I was insufficient to his needs. Whatever happened around that table (about which I am quasi-amnesiac), it seemed in some odd way to release them both to act out their cherished fantasies. (He tried to kill me.) Soon Chas appeared in our sunny kitchen almost every day when Daddy was at work. He knelt at her feet and polished her toenails red. They studied the Bible together, their heads and hands touching. Sometimes they danced; she was surprisingly clumsy, she danced with grim flat-footed determination as if dancing were something over which to gain dominion and control. (She hated it that I danced; and when I danced in the kitchen with a girlfriend she insisted I scrub the floor with bleach, to remove the skid marks our heels made. . . . I love to dance still; I dance well.)

Chas said to me, "I am your real father. You must obey me." My response to this was to give my brother a vicious pinch and to exercise a kind of tyranny over the little boy.

He followed behind me on the way to school, poor little boy, his crayons and pencils dribbling from his clutch, his orthopedically shod feet making heavy weather of it. I sprinted ahead, at school I was a star; I disregarded my little brother (storing up guilt).

I hated Chas.

When I approached the thought of the danger my mother had placed herself in, I swooned; the world fell away from me. I did not know how to guarantee her safety; I sensed, through a scrim of inarticulate denial, that her peril jeopardized whatever security I had.

I hated my father.

One day I found, in the book bag that my mother carried her Watch Tower literature in, the Bible she and Chas consulted. There was a long letter from Chas in it, which I read. It was a doctrinal thesis: They were married in fact and in the eyes of God if not in law, he wrote (citing Scripture to prove his arcane point); they were affianced — which was tantamount to marriage; and their marriage would be fully consummated after Armageddon, after birds had plucked the eyes from my father's ruined body. In the meantime, they would spiritually love . . . and love . . . and love. And hold hands.

I ask you to believe that I wanted to protect her. I had no one else to protect me. I wanted to protect myself.

I told Diana's sister Olga about the letter I had found, it burned a hole in my mind. I don't know why I chose Olga, who was eight years my senior. Perhaps she invited confidence. She "liked" Chas. And my father hated her — he hated her because she was such a small woman (it seemed at the time a strange reason to dislike a woman), "small as a kid," he said, his hands trembling. (His hands trembled when he spoke of Teddy, too. Teddy was a polio-crippled, deformed young woman, also slight — my height and size — who was entertaining the idea of marriage: "Who would marry her? Why? Bastard," he would rage at dinner, the point of his disapproval lost on me.)

Just before he died, my father raised his scrawny frame from the bed where he watched shadows collecting in the corners and he said, "But who is that other guy? The guy that looks just like me, since I was born — the guy that does terrible things? The guy that did terrible things all my life." "You never did terrible things, Daddy," I said. Then he said, "Don't trust Barbara, she lies."

It was a relief to have told Olga. It did not occur to me that I was being disloyal. I wanted with all my heart to save the woman who had sacrificed me to unhealthy appetites and unhappy days; I loved her.

Weeks passed. My mother was summoned to the house of another Witness woman, who gave her to understand that the matter was grave. Witnesses lived in those days (as I did for years thereafter) with the threat of disfellowshiping — excommunication — controlling our thoughts, blanketing our doubts, informing every action; every questionable word or deed was reported. I felt a premonition of disaster, fear for her, my maternal love for her aroused. Late at night my mother returned from her call. I leaned over the banister and called out, "Mommy, Mommy, what did she say, are you all right?" My mother said, her words black with bile, "She asked me if I trusted my children. She asked me if I trusted you." It had happened. I had fallen off the face of the world. "Olga told her about the letter." She said this to me without looking at me. I don't think she ever again looked me straight in the eyes. She smiled, a twisted smile of justification that seemed to say, *I have been right all along. The world — my own daughter — exists to harm me.*

Chas never came to our house again. I think the woman who issued the summons must not have reported my mother to the overseers; I think she used her knowledge to torment my mother, for whom Chas's departure was not the end of trouble. Her beauty — and her record number of conversions to "the Truth" — maddened women, too, but not as they had maddened him. They reported her for overstepping herself, for volunteering too many answers at Kingdom Hall meetings, for vanity and pride. She endured this calumny with silent suffering, until her season of condemnation passed. I understood nothing. I practiced my faith ever more zealously . . . and lived a parallel life: I was in love with my English teacher, Arnold Horowitz, I dreamed of converting him . . . and alternately of dying with him at Armageddon.

She hated Arnold Horowitz.

(He belongs later in this story; and in any case, my mind and my emotions skitter: I am feeling so crowded with love and pain and an ancient bewilderment I cannot write of it now.)

Why, when I asked her to forgive me — before her liver burst and her blue eyes closed for the last time — could she not have said yes. "If I had another life to live, I would not punish you for the doilies again." I kissed her spongy cheek. But her flesh had long since become morbidly repugnant to me, as intolerable as the touch of a succubus. It is also true that I loved her.

I had thought, until now, that she was very very dead. She is not. The love and the pain are alive inside of me — she remains. My Mother.

I have had a life that has included vast tracts of joy. I could at this moment, if I wished, simply close my eyes and remember a melting light bathing an ancient landscape; a riotous food bazaar in a Renaissance cloister; a yacht at night cradled in silken waters — an Aeolian volcano performing its nightly magic of fireworks; a piazzetta in Rome where I sit in a sienna-colored coffee bar covered with wisteria, watching all of life come and go — the piazzetta a perfect skin for my skin (and the delicious splendor of knowing a painting by Rafaelo is only yards away); a corner stall in southern India where nothing happens and everything happens — a cosmos in a microcosm (the vast held fast in the small). I can remember the small of Jazzman's back. His tongue. But (just as there is a tendency to interpret an affair in the light of its sad ending) excavating for memory often results in the disproportionate release of distilled poisons — and this is not fair.

It's not fair to forget coziness. Missionaries would visit us in the house we lived in on Seventy-fifth Street — two sisters, one pretty, one plain, who had returned from Guatemala, which they were unable to love (because they were allowed only to give — to improve sinners — and not to receive; they suffered from the fact that receiving gladly, a form of generosity, was one which, in their determination to uplift sinners and bind up the brokenhearted, they were trained not to avail themselves of; it was inconceivable to them that their potential Guatemalan converts might have something with which to nourish *them*; the grace to receive had been bred out of them). On Saturday nights we sat, Jane and Ruby and I, huddled together in the recess that held the big radio, and listened to *Lux Radio Theatre*, and surrendered ourselves to soapy make-believe. Then we gave one another oatmeal facials. That was nice.

(This was the same radio on which my brother and I heard Red Barber, a free-form poet, broadcast the play-by-play doings of the boys of summer, the Brooklyn Dodgers, whom we loved . . . as we loved Red Barber, his honied Southern voice, his ironies, his folksy homilies and his gift for the universal metaphor and his effervescent praise of the natural world, the body, and God — all disguised as play-by-play baseball announcing.)

My mother and Diana listened to the nutritional guru Dr. Carlton Fredericks *(Living Should Be Fun)*. Sometimes, when he was still persona grata, horrible Chas joined them, and he and Diana vied for my mother's attention and admiration.

Fredericks's 1965 cookbook, *Food Facts and Fantasies*, was dedicated "to the apostles of conformity — without whose punitive implementation of their determined opposition to freedom of thought in science, this text would never have been written." The dedicatory page included an excerpt from Bertrand Russell's Nobel Prize acceptance speech: "The wise herd does not too severely punish its deviants — they are idiots, criminals, prophets, and discoverers."

These words explain the whole of Fredericks's appeal to my mother. She and her religious brothers and sisters were also escapees from conformity who took delight in such "persecution" as came their way, regarding it as liberating stigmata. Fredericks too was an outsider; he inveighed against "medical scientists"; my mother questioned — indeed dismissed — anyone whose wisdom did not issue from *The Watch-tower* (and therefore held in contempt pretty much the whole wide world), but she was able to make an exception for Fredericks because he heaped scorn and dripped contempt on "worldly authorities." In his books he never uses the word *authority* without putting it in quotes (he also attributed his fringe position to "a conspiracy of silence," something the Witnesses also complained of). And Bertrand Russell's words were tailored for her — she had chosen a way out of the herd; her deviance was of course apparent to her (she was crazy, not stupid); but she was able to regard it as the privileged deviance of the prophet and the discoverer.

She accepted her religion's imperatives against blood transfusions without hesitation; she embraced her differences.

(There were times when the recognition of my mother's deviance hit me like a blow in the stomach. Uncle Pat, the brother she loved, cooled toward her and she flung herself into a frenzy, her arms twirling like a windmill, and said, "Why, why? Am I a harlot that you treat me like this?" I doubt that Uncle Pat had ever heard the word *harlot* uttered in a living room before. Who for that matter had? . . . Another time I came home from school to find fire engines outside our Seventy-fifth Street house: she was rolling her head from side to side on a pillow resting on a windowsill, her chestnut hair fanned out, her eyes open and staring at the sun, as if in a kind of fit or a prelude to self-destruction. In fact she was following the instructions of some quack eye doctor who had confiscated her glasses and prescribed this exercise to correct her myopia. . . . She had fantasies about marrying Nelson Eddy in the New World after Armageddon, it having been rumored that he had once given the Witnesses a financial contribution. *Sweetheart, sweetheart, sweetheart / Will you love me ever?* The New World was a very Victor Herbert kind of place, an endless operetta, all swooning kisses and cherry blossoms, no sex.

. . . Are you withdrawing your sympathy from me and giving it to her? I don't mind, I see the point.)

Psychiatrists, as far as the Witnesses were concerned, were the devil's propagandists; Witnesses found an ally in Fredericks: "We, unlike some psychiatrists, do not wish you to adjust to the mediocre, or to the world as it now exists. We want to develop *true* revolutionaries in the ultimate sense, clear-eyed and healthy, who will overthrow the old concept of medicine. . . . Once you become an informed, zealous revolutionary, you will find the real reality is not mediocre and that the battle *is* worth fighting."

They were searching for the "real reality"; they were fugitives from "the world as it now exists."

My mother believed in everlasting life on a cleansed and pretty and perfect earth; and Fredericks, who offered a variation of everlasting life, must have made her feel less freakish (or more deviant — it is hard to know which might have pleased her more): "We like to see healthy people around us who really don't believe they should surrender to their so-called allotted life spans, [people] who deny the calendar and the clock. . . . A hundred years of good health should be man's natural birthright provided he follow certain simple rules of living. . . . If such an assertion annoys you, *you are sick*." Fredericks contended — and this pleased her too, for she believed the world was plunging toward perdition — that progress was illusory: "Our life span has not actually increased very much when we recognize that the number of babies, children and young adults who died by the million before the advent of antiseptic medicine and antibiotics now live, and live long enough to raise the total statistic of the 'average man.' . . . Life expectancy has not materially been increased for adults forty-five years of age or older." This might have been lifted straight from *The Watchtower* (or vice versa), and why it should give anyone great pleasure to believe that the life span was unlikely to exceed forty-five is perplexing.

My mother was not quite nineteen when she married, and not quite twenty when I was born.

Wheat germ and blackstrap molasses and brewer's yeast and chiropractors and stainless-steel pressure cookers were good; carbohydrates caused periodontal disease; fluoridated water "represent[ed] enforced conformity inflicted on bodies"; and milk cartons conveyed poisons into milk.

Having settled the meaning of human history and the chronology of "the end times," the meaning of life and the reason for evil, the nature of God and the origin, destiny, and nature of man, and having furthermore separated the world into "sheep and goats," thus obviating the need for cultural or character study and for poetry (and all this in a six-month Bible study), my mother and Diana had the rest of their lives to live. And what — given that artistic or entertaining pursuits were denied them, and that gossip, while seductive and fruitful terrain (endless talk of the "imperfections" of their brothers and sisters), was also perilous terrain (for once the deadly stuff of slander, clothed in "theocratic" language, began to unravel, who knew who might be snagged and snarled, subject to condemnatory examination and the inquisition?) — what was there to talk about? Their trials and tribulations with their husbands — with sex, that is — and with their children; their converts; and sweetbreads and tripe and brewer's yeast, food being both a refuge for the sick of heart and morality made flesh.

Fredericks provided recipes for brain "oysters," brains à la king, brainburgers, brain soufflé, brain canapés, sweet-and-sour beef heart stuffed with brown rice. Adele Davis (the nutritionist whom Diana preferred to Fredericks, a difference between the women that engendered discussions good for hours), steamed hearts with parsley and herbs, and stuffed peppers with shredded hearts, and had recipes for liver dumplings and liver in sweet-and-sour sauce and creamed brains and baked brains in bacon rings. It was Davis's idea that the favorite meat of infants was raw calves' brains: "It is uncanny how a child whose appetite is not perverted by sweets will select foods of outstanding nutritive value." Diana's conversion had been delayed by my mother's infatuation with glands and organ meats; it took Adele Davis, in 1947, to bring Diana around: the functions of glands and organs, Davis said, "is to carry on vital life processes; therefore they contain proteins of the most superior quality and larger quantities of many vitamins and minerals."

(Giambattista Vico, the eighteenth-century father of the social sciences, called the liver man's "blood factory.")

You have to understand that they were talking not so much about food as about morality, duty, and goodness: "If a mother fails to buy a ten-cent vegetable peeler which would ensure thin parings, she probably removes so much of the iron stored near the surface of many vegetables that she produces anemia in herself and her children. . . .

She may be responsible for grandmother's cataracts if she cooks food containing B_2 in glass utensils."

Wheat-germ oil lurked in everything we ate — in salad dressings, boiled escarole, and in my mother's watery lentil soup; brewer's yeast supplanted the "liquid sunshine" — cod-liver oil — I'd choked on in our Sanitexed kitchen, finding its way into milk and fruit juice.

She made smashing good things, too: the family foods of poverty that her memories could not subordinate to the imperatives of Fredericks and Davis — grilled pork livers (much more delicate than you'd imagine, and never slimy) covered in fragrant bay leaves and wrapped in meltable membrane, and a peasant soup of spare ribs (and sometimes pigs' feet) with potatoes and cabbage. And we had Italian whole wheat bread from the corner grocery, and fish from the fish man who parked his truck under the maple tree outside my window (I thought, when I first moved to that house on Seventy-fifth Street, it was the ocean I smelled). We had huckleberry pie and blackout cake and crumb cake from Ebinger's — a bakery so loved in Brooklyn that, its German origins notwithstanding, it neither closed nor changed its name during World War II. When our Jewish neighbors went to visit their relatives in Florida they carried boxes and boxes of Ebinger's cakes with them. Green boxes, tied in brown and white string with the aid of a clattering, cunning thread dispenser that is part of the music of a Brooklyn childhood. Every Saturday the line for Ebinger's stretched around the block. Oh. And the softest lightest airiest angel food cake, with a hard bittersweet-chocolate glaze.

In those days milk was still delivered in horse-drawn carriages; I loved the crisp clip-clop of horses' hoofs in the first morning light.

She prayed before we ate, which gave my father the opportunity to take the largest helping.

One day I arrived home to find Diana and my mother on the kitchen floor; they were following Davis's instructions to "get down on all fours, imagine you are a steer, try to imitate the movements a steer would make, and notice which muscles you use. The lean meat of the frequently used muscles will have the most flavor; the least used will be the most tender. . . . Chew cud . . . wiggle your ears. . . . You may now lie down in a shady spot and ponder morbidly over how you will be butchered. . . . The front of your chest, from your neck to just above your waist and from the cut along your breastbone to your shoulders, is the *brisket*."

They were meat. And they were alchemists. They disguised tuna by rinsing off the oil and cooking it with chicken fat. They followed Davis's instructions to change the flavor of any meat by removing its fat and preparing the meat with the fat of another species.

They placed their faith in so many promises. They believed they would live forever. My mother believed she survived her first operations for cancer — which she talked herself into believing was rheumatoid arthritis — without having had a blood transfusion; in fact my father had acceded to doctors' requests to transfuse blood. My mother believed she would find love in the New World — preferably not messy sexual love, but if there were to be sex, God would see to it that she'd manage, though she couldn't imagine how, to enjoy it — if not with Chas or Nelson Eddy, then with Wily Vernon, a man whose ugliness in some way quieted and consoled her, and whose deep baritone voice caressed her, and whose hands caressed the flesh of little Witness girls, including my own. He married (amazing how, sooner or later, most perverts do), and I remember his wife, the pretty widow of a police officer, sitting on the swing of a playground we passed in our door-to-door work, swinging and crying, crying because he didn't make love to her, she didn't know why. I knew why.

For a while — until evidence to the contrary became overwhelming — Mother and Diana believed the promises of Adele Davis that if they cooked right the result would be "beauty, clear thinking, co-operativeness, cheerfulness, and freedom from bickering and quarreling, as well as freedom from illnesses and infections. When [the housewife] hears her physician praise the beauty of her children, when she sees her husband, young beyond his years, succeeding because of his energies, when she feels the surge of vibrant health in her own body, she will realize that she is largely responsible. She has shouldered her tasks and has seen to it that good health has come from good cooking."

She could have done, of course — and did do — without my father's energies.

It came to nothing, all of this. The end was death and disillusionment.

But she cherished the thought, my mother did, until the day she died, that she was interesting. She fought so hard against being commonplace. The nurses like me, she said, because of the interesting way I tie my sweater around my neck.

Women's rage must, I sometimes think, by now be coded genetically — how can women not have tantrums when they are treated like idiot children? In Fredericks's *Cook Book for Good Nutrition*, women, whose attention span he must have assumed to be that of a gnat, are told how to make housekeeping a "game." For the delectation of their families they are instructed to make "Purple Cows" — grape juice, milk, egg yolk, honey, brown sugar, lemon or lime juice; if they substitute cranberry, raspberry, or strawberry juice, they may call it a "Pink Piglet." (Reason enough for a man to take a mistress.)

I find it hard to believe that rage does not accompany the impulse (expressed and acted upon by my aunts) to "tidy up the forest" behind their country house, or to clean the oven so as not to give the neighbors occasion to criticize if they died overnight.

When a neighbor died, her death was labeled "undignified . . . her living room was clean but her bedroom was a mess." (The goodness of one's death, Muriel Spark wrote, resides not in the dignity of one's bearing but in the disposition of one's soul — a far cry from being told to wear clean underwear in case you were to get hit by a truck.)

The stern Protestantism, the saccharine calls to piety, of proselytizers like the Beecher sisters, have, sub rosa, the kind of rage that frightened me in my mother and Diana — precisely because I didn't recognize it as rage. Times, of course, change; but some kinds of poison have a half-life that enables them to circulate in the collective unconscious for generations. These poisonous droppings are like the bits of scattered space vehicles littering up the skies. The same rigid pioneer Protestant ethos that inspired the Beechers inspired the Witnesses (I do not think I am stretching the point); from 1869, when *The American Woman's Home* was published, to 1934, when I was born, how much basically had changed? The same blend of piety and pragmatism (the equation necessary for hypocrisy) was at work. And so was an inarticulate rage.

The Beechers, as sweetly as possible, without any heated manifestation of rage, issued little sallies against the tight dresses women of their time were obliged to wear, costumes that placed "pressure of the upper interior organs upon the lower ones. . . . Corsets [press] upon the hips and abdomen, and . . . throw out of use and thus weaken the most important supporting muscles of the abdomen, and impede abdominal breathing." There's a terrifying "Christian" calm in so matter-of-factly reporting one's inability to breathe. (What would happen "if one woman told the truth about her life? / The world would split open," Muriel Rukeyser wrote.) "When these muscles are thrown out of use, they lose their power, the whole system of organs mainly resting on them for support can not continue in their naturally snug, compact and rounded form, but become separated, elongated, and unsupported. . . . This . . . causes dull and wandering pains, a sense of pulling at the centre of the chest, and a drawing downward at the pit of the stomach. Then as the support beneath is really *gone*, there is what is often called 'a feeling of *goneness.*' This is sometimes relieved by food."

Dull and wandering pains and a feeling of goneness that is sometimes relieved by food: rage has been transmuted into blank despair. ("I am disappeared," a friend of mine said when she thought she was dying — gone, a feeling of goneness, resulting in panic and a sense of pulling at the center of the chest, as if one's heart were literally breaking.) I know that feeling of goneness. It is sometimes relieved by food.

"The *heart* also feels the evil. . . . Dreadful ulcers and cancers" result from these "internal displacements."

But these are "troubles that must be concealed" — one didn't speak of them in polite society, in large part because "nothing that the public can be made to believe . . . will ever equal the reality" of borne pain.

I look for clues wherever I can find them. My mother did not spring like Topsy from the ether. She was, however singular, a product of a context and a time.

She was practiced in denial. "What do I do to get well?" she asked when she was dying. "There is nothing you can do," the Indian resident said. "Oh, I see," my mother said, "if I eat well and keep my strength up, I'll be better."

God.

One concealed even from oneself exactly what one was speaking of;

unspecified horrors abounded: "There frequently is a horrible extremity of suffering in certain forms of . . . evil," the Beechers said, "which no woman of feeble constitution can ever be certain may not be her doom. . . . If one must choose . . . the horrible torments inflicted by savage Indians or cruel Inquisitors on their victims, or . . . the protracted agonies that result from such deformities and displacements" — tell me they weren't talking about more than corsets — "sometimes the former would be a merciful exchange. . . . If the facts and details could be presented, they would send a groan of terror all over the land.

"As if these dreadful ills were not enough, there have been added methods of medical treatment at once useless, torturing to the mind, and involving great liability to immoralities."

I lived between and behind the ellipses of words like this.

I sometimes think my mother's exhibitionism — she paced the house naked, all the lights on, when she thought I was asleep; she sat in the bathroom with her legs up on a chair, in full sight of workmen on the roof next door — was her only way to break her silence . . . in those days when cancer was "a sin," and one didn't, even with one's husband, openly speak of birth control.

What do women want? They want to breathe. The Beechers' solution to restraints and constraints — they were talking of corsets, ostensibly — was a jacket covered by a kind of chemise "so loose that a full breath can be inspired . . . while in a sitting position." Not much to ask for.

The author of *Uncle Tom's Cabin*, tortured and breathless, transposed her suffering onto Uncle Tom. Well; at least she put it to reasonably good purpose. I cannot think what purpose my mother's suffering served, except to add to the weight of the world.

(C. S. Lewis, the Catholic apologist, advanced the argument that every stroke of pain is caused by the chisel of the Creator to make humans complete. I am not happy to regard God as a chiseler — though in all fairness to C. S. Lewis, he made his rhetorical point before he fell in love, before the woman he loved died, before he experienced the most profound depths of suffering.)

My mother developed genuine affection for her converts — whom, taking her words from Saint Paul, she described as her "letters of recommendation to God" — but the amelioration of suffering she sought, as she went from door to door, was not theirs but her own. Her apparent self-denial, her exhausted efforts to save the world, were a form of self-affirmation.

She had a carelessly dynamic insensitivity that amounted to brutality. When the husband of her very good friend Alice died — a man even my mother could not despise, he was so trustfully loving — she said, as Alice was contemplating funeral arrangements: "Not burial. Cremation. All those worms. His eyes and nose. Ears. *The worms crawl in, the worms crawl out*," she sang, slapping her thighs in accompaniment. It was an astonishing moment. Another time, as we sat in a hospital corridor, she bent forward eagerly and asked a stranger, the wife of a man who was closeted with doctors (and audibly drowning in his own blood): "Is he dying?" drawing out the syllables with a kind of sigh that seemed almost like contentment; "Is he dying *now?*" "*Mother!*" "I'm only trying to take an intelligent interest," she said, genuinely offended.

There were two American Indians — sisters — who turned up at local conventions; everybody was vaguely embarrassed by them. There was one black family in our South Brooklyn congregation; my mother invited them to dinner only, in the course of twenty years, one time. If sex were filthy with a white man, to what horrors of degradation would it sink with a black man? When she deduced that I had lost my virginity (after I had lost my Witness faith) to a black man, I think the sin was quite literally black in her eyes. ("You say terrible things in your sleep," she said to me the morning after; she had kept vigil at my bedside to monitor my sleeping speech; I found an apartment of my own the next week.) Her piety was contaminated with a racism she would most vehemently have denied. As was Harriet Beecher Stowe's: the "matter of lightness is the distinctive line between savage and civilized bread. The savage mixes simple flour and water into balls of paste, which he throws into boiling water, and which come out solid, glutinous masses, of which his common saying is, 'Man eat dis, he no die,' which a facetious traveler who was obliged to subsist on it interpreted to mean, 'Dis no kill you, nothing will.'"

One doesn't wish to say that Stowe's opposition to slavery wasn't principled — any more than I wish to deny the authenticity of my mother's commitment to winning souls for Jehovah; but Stowe's visceral opposition to slavery stemmed in some part "from a love of thoroughness and well-doing which despised the rude, unskilled work of barbarians. People, having once felt the thorough neatness and beauty of execution which came of free, educated, and thoughtful labor, could not tolerate the clumsiness of slavery." Implicitly she believed in the unalterable alienness and irredeemability of the black man (as my mother believed in the irredeemability of the given alien world). She dreamily idealized the eighteenth century, when "there were few servants, in the European sense of the word; there was a society of educated workers, where all were *practically* equal" (italics mine).

In her small world, masters were Protestants and servants were Catholics: "The old New-England motto, *Get your work done up in the forenoon,* applied to an amount of work which would keep a common Irish servant . . . a raw creature of immense bone and muscle, but of heavy, unawakened brain — toiling from daylight to sunset. . . .

"Old world servants . . . come here feeling that this is somehow a land of liberty, and with very dim and confused notions of what liberty is. They are very extensively the raw, untrained Irish peasantry, and the wonder is, that with all the unreasoning heats and prejudices of the Celtic blood, all the necessary ignorance and rawness, there should be the measure of comfort and success there is in our domestic arrangements."

It followed quite consistently that she should set herself against the suffragist movement: "There has been a great deal of crude, disagreeable talk in these conventions, and too great tendency . . . to make the education of woman anti-domestic. . . . Our common-school system now rejects sewing from the education of girls, which very properly used to occupy many hours daily in school a generation ago. The daughters of laborers and artisans are put through algebra, geometry, trigonometry, and the higher maths, to the entire neglect of that learning which belongs distinctively to woman."

Even in solitude and without being aware of the sin or the danger, children may inflict evils on themselves, which not infrequently ter-

minate in disease, delirium, and death. There is no necessity for explanations on this point any farther than this; that certain parts of the body are not to be touched except for purposes of cleanliness, and that the most dreadful suffering comes from disobeying these commands. . . . The wise parent will say that this is what children cannot understand, and about which they must not talk or ask questions. . . . Disclosing details of wrong-doing to young and curious children, often leads to the very evils feared . . . paralysis, mania, death.

— *The American Woman's Home*

My mother extended this principle to menstruation. What little I knew I managed to find out myself from twilight "dirty talk" on Brooklyn stoops. I told Olga (who told my mother), "I know what Kotex is." I was nine. This served as an excuse for my mother to burn my "worldly" books — *Heidi* and *Gone with the Wind*, *War and Peace* and *The Black Hole*, a pornographic book that had been lent to me innocently by my downstairs neighbor when I was waiting, on the back steps of Seventy-fifth Street, for my mother to come home from her preaching work. When, soon after this, I got my first period in my aunts' country house, I scandalized myself. Afraid to say the words, I left my soiled panties in full view on the bathroom floor; and then I listened to the aunts saying — biting off their words — "Call her mother. It isn't our business." When I arrived home, "Why does God let such terrible things happen to women?" my father said, addressing his words to my mother, who assumed her mask of ice. I have tried on and off for years to figure out what he had in mind — he spoke as if monthly bleeding came to him as news; memory and reason hit the blank wall of my past shame and my lasting incomprehension.

Up until then, my association with blood was the war effort: before we became Jehovah's Witnesses, my mother announced to my Aunt Anne with a kind of excitement I had never heard in her voice before that she was going to give blood. She said this almost as if giving blood were illicit. (And, in fact, Red Barber — my darling hero — told me, years later, that the word *blood* had not been used on the radio until he called for contributions of blood on his Ebbets Field radio show.) My mother never did give blood; but I remember feeling distinctly American the day she announced her intention; and I remember thinking that my mother was in some way attached to the larger world, which thought had never before occurred to me.

After that, my own blood, dark and salty, became fascinating to me. I smelled it and I took pleasure in its rank smell. I read my runic Kotex pads. When I rang doorbells in the door-to-door work I slipped my hand underneath my underpants and played with the beads of blood that formed on my pubic hair. I loved my blood. (For the rest of my life I loved getting my period — as I loved going to the supermarket to shop when my children were young; it provided me with proof absolute that the moon was in the sky and all was as it should be and I was a natural woman.)

One day I dropped red nail polish down the toilet bowl and my mother screamed, "They'll think it's blood!" and accused me of sabotaging her life, Chas was coming over that evening.

"Like Gavelle water?" Gavelle water was a bleach, carried to Brooklyn's Italian families, by way of a horse-and-cart shuttle, in refillable ten-gallon glass bottles. My mother was conducting a home Bible study with a recent convert, and I was awakened from a little daydream (based on my secret, under-the-table perusal of the Song of Songs), by this conversation: Mother: "We are saved by the blood of the lamb, washed clean." Millie-the-convert's husband: "Like-a Gavelle-a water?" No joke intended. Mother: *"Eeek."* My mother was fond of remarking that she was too sensitive for this world, certainly too sensitive to tolerate an old man's comparing the blood of the lamb with Gavelle water, especially when he was rubbing my Aunt Anne's foot with his own at the time.

My mother never for a moment surrendered to the idea that the house — any of her rented houses — was her natural stage, the scene for the drama of her life, her opportunity to exercise the pale glamour of piety, the setting for her sacred duties.

Few women did. Appended to the Beecher sisters' *American Home* was "An Appeal to American Women by the Senior Author of This Volume" — a frank and forlorn acknowledgment of failure (self-pitying and grandiose):

My Honored Countrywomen: It is now over forty years that I have been seeking to elevate the character and condition of our sex. . . . I am sorrowful at results that have followed these and similar efforts, and ask your sympathy and aid. . . . Latin, Geometry, and Algebra, . . . intellectual excitement exhausted the nervous fountain. The next attempt was to introduce Domestic Economy as a science to be studied in schools for girls. . . . Ere long [it] was crowded out by Political Economy and many other economies, except those most needed to prepare a woman for her difficult and sacred duties. . . . It came to pass that the older States teemed with educated women. . . . Meantime the intellectual taxation in both private and public schools, the want of proper ventilation in both families and schools, the want of domestic exercise which is so valuable to the feminine constitution, the pernicious modes of dress, and the prevailing neglect of the laws of health, resulted in the general decay of health among women.

Catharine Beecher, the founder of the Hartford Seminary for Women, gave her life to the education of women, and blamed herself for the continuing malaise of women . . . who were suffocating, and were dying, but not for lack of proper ventilation or domestic exercise or "the disagreeable effluvia of close sleeping rooms" thrown off by "the air from the skins and lungs," or by "the strong and healthy husband, feeling the want of pure air in the night [who] keeps windows open and makes such draughts that the wife, who lives all day in a close room and thus is low in vitality, can not bear the change, has colds and sometimes perishes a victim."

The overworking of the brain and nerves . . . resulted in a deficiency of mental development which is very marked. . . . Young women, at this day, are decidedly inferior in mental power to those of an earlier period [before she began instructing them], notwithstanding their increased advantages [which she helped to provide]. . . .

Alarmed at the dangerous tendencies of female education, I made another appeal to my sex, which resulted in the organization of the American Woman's Education Association, the object being to establish *endowed* professional schools, in connection with literary institutions, in which woman's profession should be honored and taught as are the professions of men, and where woman should be trained for some self-supporting business.

The organization and endowment of the professional schools is yet incomplete from many combining impediments, the chief being a want of appreciation of woman's profession, and of the *science* and *training* which its high and sacred duties require.

What man would not be tempted to escape the ministrations of the Beecher women and their like, so intent upon improving one and all? What man — what human being — wants to be another human being's "job"?

What *is* a woman's "profession"? The question is absurd: "A woman is just as much an ordinary human being as a man, with the same individual preferences, and with just as much right to the tastes and preferences of an individual. What is repugnant to every human being is to be reckoned always as a member of a class and not as an individual person. . . . What form the occupation, the pleasures and the emotion may take, depends entirely upon the individual" (Dorothy L. Sayers, *Are Women Human?*).

> *Multitudes of intelligent and conscientious persons, in private and by the press, unaware of the penalties of violating nature, openly impugn the inspired declaration, "children are a heritage of the Lord."*
>
> — *An American Woman's Home*

"Put me in a box," my mother said when she thought she was pregnant for the third time. It was after this that I was delegated to tell my father that she would be sleeping in my bedroom from then on. "Put me in a box," she said to Aunt Anne, to whom she further reported that he had said, "But we were careful, weren't we, Connie?" "He said *that?*" Aunt Anne asked, appalled; as if the only thing worse than sex itself was talking about sex.

Domestic service, disgraced, on one side by the stigma of our late slavery and, on the other, by the influx into our kitchens of the uncleanly and ignorant, is shunned by the self-respecting and well-educated, many of whom prefer either a miserable pittance or the career of vice to this fancied degradation. Thus comes the overcrowding in all avenues of woman's work, and the consequent lowering of wages to starvation prices for long protracted toils.

None of these evils had to do with unrestrained capitalism and an unacknowledged class system, of course; all vices — including *the* vice — owed their existence to women's reluctance to regard their houses (and all the children God saw fit to send them) as their destinies, their jobs, and their opportunity to improve others. Women were so stupid — after all those years of Beecherizing! — as not to understand the sacred nature of their toil. . . . If only they had movable screens. Or earth-closets in lieu of the water closets that flushed human excrement by way of sewers into the sea. The Beecher sisters rested fond hopes upon earth-closets, invented by an English vicar; these things consisted, "essentially, of a mechanical contrivance (attached to the ordinary seat) for measuring out and discharging into the vault or pan below a sufficient quantity of sifted dry earth to entirely cover the solid ordure and to absorb the urine. [Like a kitty-litter box.] The discharge of earth is effected by an ordinary pull-up similar to that used in the water-closet, or (in the self-acting apparatus) by the rising of the seat when the weight of the person is removed. The vault or pan under the seat is so arranged that the accumulation may be removed at pleasure. [Dear God, *whose* pleasure?] When the ordure is completely dried and decomposed, it has not only lost its odor, but it has become, like all decomposed organic matter, an excellent disinfectant." And the excellent result would be that this night soil could be used, as it was in China (and, even today, in India), to refertilize the earth, so that "not a particle of manure is wasted." The Beecher sisters did not approve of waste.

The earth-closet was the only mechanical contrivance the Beechers — as addled as Miss Plum was and, in this regard, more dangerously eccentric — gave their seal of approval to; in other regards they had (depending upon how charitably one wishes to judge them) a romanticized notion of household drudgery (provided it was performed by someone other than they), or a demented fear of technology:

"The sewing-machine, hailed as a blessing, has proved a curse to the poor; for it takes away profits from needlewomen; women who use this machine for steady work, in two years or less become hopelessly diseased and can rear no children. . . .

"Thus it is that the controlling political majority of New England is passing from the educated to the children of ignorant foreigners."

(Foreigners, one supposes, like the women of my immigrant family, many of whom worked in sweatshops.)

"Add to these disastrous influences, the teachings of 'free love'; the baneful influence of spiritualism so called, the fascinations of the *demimonde*; the poverty of thousands of women, who, but for desperate temptations, would be pure — all the malign influences are sapping the foundations of the family state. . . . Many intelligent and benevolent persons imagine that the grand remedy for the heavy evils that oppress our sex is to introduce woman to political power and office, to make her a party in primary political meetings, in political caucuses, and in the scramble and fight for political offices; thus bringing into this dangerous *melee* the distinctive tempting power of her sex. Who can look at this new danger without dismay?"

(And who would not be "pure" were it not for temptation?)

Poor played-out, disappointed, idealistic lady. One hears a dim echo of her song, on the one hand, from such successors to the spiritual hucksters Madame Blavatsky and Indian child-guru Krishnamurti as Marianne Williamson, Clare Prophet, and adrenalized purveyors of self-love, and from messianic talk-show hosts ecstatically hawking "self-esteem"; and on the other hand, from neoconservatives and the religious far right. We seem always to be marching to the same drummer in different makeup and to the same rhythms; the tunes vary slightly and superficially; the battleground never changes.

(Marianne Williamson advised the president of the United States that the solution to any problem was "Do it kindly." The thing about fancy religions is that they are always simple-minded.)

"Marriage, as all statesmen agree, is the seed-plot of the family, as the family is the seed-plot of the commonwealth. . . . Marriage is . . . 'the sharing of every divine and human right,' and . . . citizenship itself is nought else. . . . Since all nations began with the cult of some divinity, in the family-state the fathers must have been the sages in auspicial divinity, the priests who sacrificed to take the auguries or to make sure of their meaning, and the kings who brought the divine laws to their families." It is difficult to quarrel with Giambattista Vico's poetic premises . . . one wonders: is the notion that one person is another person's "job," or the fiat that the man is the unchallenged "head" of the family, a perversion of Vico or an inevitable consequence of his thinking? I cannot abort my love for him, or for Augustine or Saint Paul, who wrote like angels — which is perhaps why I so much love these words of Auden's: "Time . . . worships language and forgives / Everyone by whom it lives; / Pardons cowardice, conceit, / Lays its honors at their feet. / Time that with this strange excuse / Pardoned Kipling and his views, / And will pardon Paul Claudel, / Pardons him for writing well."

I remember these things:

The stoop, under the el, where I sat when an upstairs neighbor girl told me there was no Santa Claus. I remember this with photographic precision (why?); the el train rumbles overhead. I am wearing a plum-colored snowsuit. The snow on the stoop is covered with a crust of soot.

Waiting near the window for my father to come home. When. When. When. "Don't let him know you saw me do this," my mother says. She is nursing my brother. *When.*

She is bathing. I am sitting on the toilet bowl, a tapeworm is making its way out of my body; I ask her — not knowing what the strange thing is — if I have "piles," which I have heard grown-ups discuss, perhaps the thing (which looks like a buckled snake, a checkered ribbon, a flat serpent) is piles (which I dimly perceive it is not). "Yes," she says, lifting a soapy shapely leg and smiling. Imagine. My body is inhabited.

A friend rings the doorbell. I have heard her spoken of as Mary the Spick. I yell, "Mary Spick is here!" Mary Spick turns away and my mother rushes toward me, lunging at my hair.

In the corner of the living room, weeks before Christmas, is a solid object covered with a sheet. My mother is visibly, immensely pregnant. I never ask her what her stomach hides; I never lift the sheet . . . under which is a child's desk, my Christmas present.

I am alone in the weedy garden. A man passes by doing a goose step. This frightens me. I play animals. He is a giraffe with a great slack jaw. Kind Mrs. Schultzie from next door passes by, balancing grocery bags, swinging from side to side. I call out, "Mrs. Schultzie, you are an ele-phant." I go to bed without my dinner for having called Mrs. Schultzie a fat elephant, which I did not. I don't understand. Nobody believes that I saw a man doing a goose step. I wear my Dick Tracy watch and look for Japanese airplanes.

Alone in the weedy garden I see, at the end of the street, three crones dressed in black pushing baby carriages up a long hill, silhouetted against a bleached abyss. I see them now: anomie, blank loneliness, aridity; I enter weedy halls of fear.

Uncle Pat is home from the war. He is yelling at my father because no one has taught me how to ride a bike or to swim. I am at the top of the stairs with the turkey roast we are supposed, on this occasion, to share. During the war Aunt Mary lived downstairs. Aunt Mary and my mother are screaming now: "She's crazy," Aunt Mary says, "your sister is crazy, Pat." I am told to carry the roasting pan and the turkey downstairs. I am paralyzed at the top of the stairs, without volition, my legs jelly. "Go! Go!" I do, hugging the wall. "You poor kid," Uncle Pat says. I am trembling and splattered with hot grease.

My brother and I play with Dolores down the street; she is the first "best friend" I have ever had. On Avenue S we jump from roof to roof, spanning a two-foot space, four stories yawning below. We put my brother in the dumbwaiter in Dolores's apartment and haul him up and down. There is always laundry hanging in Dolores's kitchen. She is very ugly.

On the way to school we pass a haunted house. In front of it there is a raised slab of blue slate inscribed with letters no one can read. Sometimes I step on it.

Arbor Day, dancing around a Maypole.

A grade school teacher takes my hand and says, "Never be like me."

There is a mezuzah on the front door of our Seventy-fifth Street house. I play handball on the garage doors and listen to the neighbors: I need to hear how people live.

Aunt Angie entertains young men from Watch Tower headquarters. *I want them to love me* (I am twelve). I forget how to handle a soup spoon and dribble liquid on my blouse. Angie glares. I forget how to walk. I leave Angie's bedroom door open when I go to sleep so the young men will see copies of *Seventeen* magazine and *Girl of the Limberlost* and know that I am grown up.

Uncle Tony is home from the war. I save the hair from my hairbrush and put it in his pockets.

I remember a dog — a collie, my brother's — given away under cover of night when he was sleeping.

And a piano (mine) which, after I spent a weekend away from home, was no longer there.

As resistant to technology as the Beechers were, they perceived, how-ever reluctantly, that if "science" was not enlisted in the service of the housewife, their cause would be certifiably dead; they surrendered to an inevitability that achieved fruition in the early twentieth century (when everybody believed in progress) by such writers as the Brueres, secular religionists whose belief in progress was pathetic and madden-ing (mad): "No girl who has once made an omelette can ever be afraid of an egg" (*Increasing Home Efficiency*).

Bruere and Bruere changed the terms, but not the substance, of the discourse. For *sanctity* and *piety* they substituted *efficiency* and *machinery*, *production* and *consumption*: "Isn't this what the home is for . . . to produce something more valuable than it consumes? . . . The home is properly a machine to make something with, not a self-sufficient, disassociated fact. It is efficient not through its own internal harmony, but through its ability to produce something socially valuable." The end result was to be the same, however, as that advocated by the sanctimony school of homemaking — an abundance of children: "The home which does not give to the community its complement of chil-dren is inefficient. . . . Back somewhere in the minds of us all is the conviction that homes that have not produced these things have not given to the community all it has a right to expect of them." Things? Children are *things?* "The modern housekeeper is in the throes of metamorphosis from producer to consumer. . . . To live is to consume."

The Brueres delivered themselves of the fantastic opinion that a woman "can rest from the cook-stove and broom by taking care of the baby." This corresponds to nothing whatsoever in real life.

I remember, before my son was born, making satisfying tables and lists of how, between feedings and diaper foldings, I would spend the extraordinary amount of free time I thought I would have. And then a real person imposed his needy and imperious bawling self on this schedule, which had seemed so measured and reasonable; and he was the center of my world; he controlled me . . . which is as it should have been, for an infant is entitled absolutely to absolute and entire and all-time-eclipsing love. But that love can coexist with frustration and irritation; I shouldn't call being emotionally and physically available twenty-four hours a day restful, quite. . . . Not restful; but when your baby is at your breast, his whole being dependent upon your own, and (this is the only time one is regarded with such tenacity and simplicity and purity and guilelessness) when his gaze fixes yours until he abandons himself trustfully to sleep — bliss of an order that cannot otherwise be known.

"Mrs. Allison brews and bakes, and sews and gardens, and runs the whirligig of her little household in accord with the dancing of the happy world about the sun." Mrs. Allison tap-dances so prettily in her sunny cosmos because she budgets and uses labor-saving devices and because she does what would today be called prioritizing (horrid word; and one of the good things babies do is to instruct one in humility by asserting their own priorities above one's own, a very useful thing; it is not entirely healthy to live without having to care for another living thing — a cat will do).

The Brueres believed nothing but good would issue from conventional marriage if one would only manipulate one's resources scientifically; they collected testimonials to this effect: "'We used to have a woman come in by the day. When she stopped coming, we just purchased a vacuum cleaner for a hundred and twenty dollars [out of an annual income of $3,000] which the women folk now prefer to outside help. . . . We have also a motor-operated washing machine, two electric sad-irons, and one gas iron.'" How simple it was going to be, this march to progress! (What the womenfolk themselves had to say about all this is not noted.) An "ex–domestic science teacher . . . had four years of special training, followed by five years of teaching, and now her seven-room servantless house and her two small daughters are no weight on her spirits. Food comes and goes on her table without anxiety, a vegetable garden seems automatically to produce green things, and it is as though the house cleaned itself. The work of housekeeping is well subordinated to the business of living. It is a desirable condition based on knowledge of housekeeping — ordered knowledge, . . . in startling contrast to the wisdom of 'mother,' who was equipped . . . with nothing better than tradition, devotion to her home, humility [and] a firm and disastrous conviction that her own experience, however limited, was an infallible guide."

I know of no house that cleans itself, no vegetables that walk unac-companied to the dining room table. I know of no system ever created by man or woman that frees us from the tyranny of muddle. . . . And I wonder if there would have been a women's liberation movement if these utopian notions had had any basis in life as life was truly lived.

"Consumption is our one universal function, and through it we have power and happiness and progress, or retrogression and spiritual and bodily death. . . . Children . . . are the most valuable crop of all, . . . not only the greatest good to the individual but the most valuable gift to the State."

The Brueres refer to children as little units of consumption . . . things, as they say on Rodeo Drive now, that are delightful to "acces-sorize." I refuse to see my children as gifts to the State (or, for that matter, as units of rebellion against the State), though I am able to regard them, when it is possible for me to regard them abstractly at all, as hostages to the future — beloved hostages, gifts to the future; and I choose not to accept the utilitarian proposition that "consumption is our one universal function," but instead to believe that our universal functions derive from and are implicit in the ideas articulated by Saint Paul, who knew better than the Brueres what constituted the stuff and "all-ness" of life: "There remaineth faith, hope, and charity, and the greatest of these is charity." Misogynist Paul may arguably have been . . . I say arguably, because it was also Paul — so virile, young, and beautiful in Caravaggio's luminous oil in Santa Maria del Popolo at the moment of his blinding epiphany that to see the painting is to be terminally unable to hate him — who said, with breathtaking inclusiv-ity: "In Christ there is no male, no female, no slave, no freedman, no Jew, no Gentile."

Insofar as "spiritual death [or life]" is concerned, orthodox theology instructs us that the only form of consumerism that is necessary to our perpetual spiritual nourishment is the eating of the body of Christ (an idea the materialistic Brueres would, I suppose, have found repellent — what would they have made of Beloved Ida of Louvain, on her merry eager way to Holy Communion: "Let us go devour God"?).

Christ, as Dorothy Sayers exults, neither rebuked women for being female nor urged them to be "feminine." As for the vulgarly pietistic Beechers and the consummately materialistic Brueres, what would they have made of those women, honored in Scripture and legend, who refused to regard themselves as breeders bequeathing a "crop" to the Nation? What in the world would they have made of the fourth-century saint, Paula, who sailed from her homeland with one daughter, leaving two children behind, to establish hospices and monasteries for men and women in Jerusalem? (and was celebrated in a thirteenth-century poem:

> The children remain on the shore.
> The son outstretches his arms and cries,
> While Rufina weeps, begging
> Her mother and asking her
> To stay and tend to her grief.
> But the mother does not listen.
> To the outsider, it seems
> That Paula is pitiless and without feeling,
> She seems to lack compassion,
> In thus rejecting everything,
> Her own children, her domain,
> And her country. But in fact, she does have feeling,
> One that has inspired her trust in God.
> She cares for nothing else.
> This feeling extinguishes the others,
> And pity is vanquished by faith.
> She is indeed fighting her own sorrow.
> For great is her grief, and the struggle within her.
> For on the one hand, she cannot help but remember
> That she is a mother; but on the other, she is more determined
> To serve the Lord God.)

Whether it is Ingrid Bergman or Saint Paula, when a woman follows her nature, she is reviled. (And I do not pretend I find Saint Paula easy to comprehend, I am vastly disquieted, in the light of my own history, by women who desert their children, my tolerance is not inclusive. . . . Saint Paula is the patron saint of widows; in the absence of other proof, I take this to mean that Rome has a sense of humor.)

At the Housekeeping Experiment Station in Darien, Connecticut, elaborate time- and motion-saving studies taught women how to husband their resources: "Take for instance the cooking of the matutinal egg: This is their chart for the cooking of three eggs. In the first case the eggs were boiled with the comparatively inefficient utensils, stove, saucepan, spoon, etc. In the second case they were coddled with the efficient fireless coddler."

Ah, if a fireless coddler could save us from endless battles over "family values"! The Brueres were of a mind to believe that upon such minutiae rested the future of the race, no less than the success and happiness of a woman's life: "If three women can do the work of five households sufficiently well, can society afford to take five women to do it in a world that still needs so much to be done — it being remembered always that the home is not a thing to be produced regardless of cost or consequences, but a means to civilization?"

COOKING WITHOUT A FIRELESS CODDLER

1. Place three eggs in boiling water.
2. Watch the clock. After three minutes,
3. Take serving dish in left, (3a) spoon in right hand.
4. Lift one egg out of water.
5. Place in serving dish.
6. Place spoon on stove.
7. Carry service dish to breakfast room.
8. Place egg in cup before right person.
9. Return to stove.

COOKING WITH A FIRELESS CODDLER
[*whatever that is*]:

1. With the right hand lift the cover from the coddler.
2. Omit.
3. Place cover on table.
4. With left lift kettle of hot water at same time.
5. Lift egg rack from coddler with right hand.
6. Pour a little hot water into the coddler.
7. Omit.
8. Omit.
9. Omit.
10. Omit.

10. Place serving dish on stove.
11. Look at clock. After one minute,
12. Lift second egg from water with spoon, with same motions as 3, 4, 5, and 6.
13. Repeat No. 7.
14. Repeat No. 8.
15. Repeat No. 9.
16. Repeat No. 10.
17. Look at clock. After one minute,
18. Repeat 3, 4, 5, 6, 7.
19. Repeat No. 8.
20. Return to kitchen.
21.
22.

TOTAL MOTIONS, 27.
Trips to breakfast room, 3.
Time, six minutes.

11. Omit.
12. Rinse out coddler. Pour water in sink.
13. Return coddler to table.
14. With right hand place eggs in rack.
15. Place rack in coddler.
16. With left hand lift kettle. Fill coddler to three-egg mark.
17. Omit.
18. Place kettle on stove.
19. With right hand put cover on coddler.
20. Carry coddler to breakfast table.
21. Place before mistress.
22. Return to kitchen.

TOTAL MOTIONS, 15.
Trips to breakfast room, 1.
Time, 50 seconds.

I have questions left unanswered by the Brueres: How can a three-minute egg take fifty seconds? What use would the housekeeper make of the five minutes and ten seconds she saved by using a fireless coddler?

> Can you brew, can you bake,
> Good bread and cake?
> Before my love I utter.
>
> Can you sew a seam?
> Can you churn the cream?
> And bring the golden butter?
> What use is refraction,
> Chemical reaction, biologic protoplasm,
> Psychologic microcosm?
>
> Would you be my weal,
> You must cook the meal, —
>
> You shake your head, —

You I'll not wed, —
And so, Farewell!

— Vassar College, c. 1895

The Brueres decried "striving to dignify useless work through the introduction of various and sundry complications. . . . All the flutteration to put hand sewing, and home-baking, and preserving, and the making of Christmas mincemeat on a plane of what might be called moral elegance is just a bracing back against tomorrow. . . . To make jelly is ceasing to be an important part of housekeeping — to eat jelly is, let us hope, the unending privilege of us all."

Every generation reinvents the wheel, and the essential nature of the wheel remains unchanged. Now, of course, in the era of Martha Stewart and food boutiques, it would be difficult to find a proper-thinking young woman who would not happily hand the vacuum cleaner (and the egg coddler) over to someone else, so as to enjoy the comely — and status-accruing — pleasures of quilting and fancy baking and gourmet cooking and preserving. (I do not exclude myself; I am sixty and will never make another bed without grumbling, I have made enough beds for a lifetime; I am, now, making collages from silk swatches; I bake bread and make eight-course Christmas dinners and I can't remember the last time I scrubbed a bathtub, thank God.)

Bruere and Bruere express sadness for "Gorgon[s] of thrift," for the housewife who triumphs in "the things she is learning to do without. . . . 'Homekeeping,'" one of the respondents to their questionnaires says, "'means more than a matter of endless contriving and economy. . . . Suppose I do throw away the meat bones without making a delicious soup of them. I am ready to slip into a fresh gown before dinner, to pick a posey for the table, to tell the baby a story, to read with my husband, and to go to bed with a clear conscience and a quiet mind.' The middle-class housewife, . . . bound by the romantic tradition of the 'Proper sphere of woman,' and terrified at the indelicate possibility of appearing unwomanly, flutters ineptly on her threshold."

"Rose Perniola," my mother says, "uses *heavy cream*. She uses *Kleenex* to mop up spills." (Translation: Rose Perniola has a serious character defect.)

"Your mother," Rose Perniola says, "spends five hours looking for the store where a pound of macaroni costs two pennies less and then she complains because she is tired."

"Don't buy two-ply toilet paper, Bobbie," my mother says — the whole of her prenuptial advice to me — "people will use just as much and one-ply is cheaper."

These conversations, the secondary stuff of their lives, made me grind my teeth with wild exasperation. Years later in my consciousness-raising group I experienced the same active weariness when women complained about the tiresome minutiae of their lives. One woman took at least a half hour to describe a ten-minute drive over the Brooklyn Bridge during the course of which her baby threw milk up on her. *So what?* I wanted to scream. A baby spits up on you! *So what!* What life is altogether pretty? *Who cares?* But perhaps what I thought was a justifiable aversion to whining was simply my unwillingness to entertain another's obsession or compulsion.

. . . My compulsion, this very moment, being to want, God help me — just as if I were sitting in my kitchen waiting for my children to come home from nursery school — to make a case for soup made of leftovers. Junk soup. I experienced the perfection of intent every time I made good use of leftovers, and few things matched the satisfaction of seeing what my children called junk soup simmering on the stove. Recycling icebox detritus into goodness. It went too far, this urge: when my children wouldn't eat overripe bananas I used them to make banana bread, and when they made it clear that they hated banana bread I turned that into banana-bread pudding, which of course they didn't eat. . . . But (I admit) I still think my efforts at economy, however farcical at times, were better than whining about the Brooklyn-Bridge-spit-up trip; in some regards I find myself more lovable than others.

I still love junk soup.

. . . It has just now occurred to me to wonder what has happened to moths — the ones that ate our woolens in the summertime. I never see those small white moths now. I used to love the smell of mothballs. Mothballs smelled clean. . . .

Every generation reinvents the wheel — and in the process it often adds to rather than subtracts from a woman's burdens. The Brueres wanted, for example, to change Vassar's ditty, in keeping with the spirit of the times:

> Are you up on the pure food laws affecting the manufacture of canned soup?
> Can you assure me that you know the conditions governing the sanitary production of pastry?
> Can you bring enough influence to bear on public opinion so that the family clothing will not have to be made in a sweat shop?
> Do you know how to get honest government inspectors appointed, to assure me of the purity of the milk and meat and butter you promise to serve me?

There were times when I used actually to like cleaning floors and scrubbing and stuff, music blasting, the mindlessness of the task a kind of soporific, an antidote to the seesawing of my emotional life, my marriage. And those days were followed by days when I felt like a gerbil in a cage, chained to the wheel day after day. Both — the pleasure and the grind — are true facts of life, the enemies of which are stasis and generalities.

It's the perpetually unfinished quality of housework that makes it oppressive — it never ends, like bad psychoanalysis, or a dream interrupted. It is paradoxically true that it is exactly this daily re-creation of the world that lends housekeeping its nobility and romance.

Has anyone ever done for women what Charlie Chaplin did for the men on automobile production lines?

"We have reached the Civilization of a Surplus now." That is the premise upon which the Brueres built their "scientific" twaddle.

They wrote this in 1911. My mother was born in 1914. Certainly some of the attitudes they introduced must have filtered down to her; I know they did, in the form of the notion that one needed only to systematize to ensure efficiency and order and happiness. She hemmed herself in with so many rules. (Is there a universally correct way to iron a man's shirt? I could do it today, her way, blindfolded; and in fact ironing — perhaps because clean clothes smell so good and because the results are not so ephemeral as those of other household tasks, so that one has a genuine feeling of accomplishment, and because I listened to Red Barber and to the *Hit Parade* while I ironed — remains a household chore I willingly do.) This is the way you fold the garbage bag, this is the way you dry the dishes, this is the way you make the bed. These self-imposed imperatives brought her nothing in the way of happiness or household beauty . . . and then she joined Jehovah's "Theocratic Organization," the "New System" (which would crush "this Old System of Things"), the "New World Order"; and to the minute and all-encompassing regulations of this system she surrendered herself with every ounce of her being. The payoff would be consumerism on a monumental scale: eternal life on a cleansed and perfect earth (after the vultures had picked the flesh from my father's bones).

. . . I do remember my mother's having told me I was good: someone, in our presence, said, "Cleanliness is next to godliness," and I, insufferable child that I was (smug and scared, believing and fissured with doubt), rejoined, "Cleanliness is part of godliness." How tiresome I was. But she called me good.

"We have reached the Civilization of a Surplus now." This was written only one year after the Great Immigration from Western Europe, one year after my paternal grandparents arrived in America. My father, when they wrote this, was ten years old, without language or moorings in a Mulberry Street cold-water tenement flat with a tub in the kitchen and an outhouse in the stinking alley. He got his first pair of shoes when a bicycle he swiped (and didn't know how to ride) hit another kid and he was hauled off to court and a kindly judge issued him a pair of shoes. He got his first suit a couple of years later when he had to appear in court for a stabbing incident in which he and a friend — exploring the underground passages used, in Little Italy and Chinatown, by the Tongs for internecine warfare — were implicated. Several years later he boxed at Madison Square Garden in the amateur Golden Gloves meets; when my grandmother found out about it, she chased him down Hester Street and Mott Street and Mulberry Street with a knife (this was a protective gesture). He didn't box again till he ran away to California, where, after he was arrested for vagrancy and after he picked bushels of apples for chump change, he taught a rich man's kid how to fight. He had run away because my grandfather told him: Go out and find your brother Lennie and don't come back until you do. He didn't find his brother Lennie. So he didn't come back for two years. He was a wiper on a freighter, that's how he got to California — by way of the Panama Canal. What did the Brueres know of lives like this? My father and his brother Lennie went down to the produce markets early in the morning and speared fruits and vegetables that fell off trucks with a homemade stick and spike. My grandfather was a mason and a carpenter (Bruno Hauptmann, the convicted killer of the Lindbergh baby, was his friend, a fact that terrified me when I was growing up); and he brought me chicken livers from the hospital he worked in, to build up my strength and keep me from scarlet fever. My grandmother had twelve children, of whom five survived into adulthood; my Aunt Louise died when she was twenty-three, before the universal use of antibiotics. Of a rheumatic heart brought on by scarlet fever. When she wasn't looking after her brood and moderating the temper of her husband, Grandma made intricate lace to sell (nearly blinding herself in the process — paper flowers, too); and this was not, for them and for hundreds of thousands of immigrants, a Civilization of Surplus.

It's amazing, actually, for the Brueres and people like them were well meaning and even — if you exclude the fact that they seemed not to know how real people really lived — progressive and charitable (perhaps I mean the people who were real to me: first- and second-generation Italians). It was clear to the Brueres that the very sense of security that Americans tried to create by saving was destroyed by the necessity of saving, which necessity the Brueres sought to eliminate by social programs: to scrimp and save for the future, and for the education of one's children, was to "torment all our productive years with the fear of a helpless old age and dependency." They believed in universal free education and adult "university extension schemes" and labor-saving devices that would permit women to go to concerts and lectures and devote their social services to the community; they urged communal action "to force money from the state"; and, in a departure from Puritanism and Calvinism, they urged the state to provide old-age pensions, which would free Americans from the slavery of saving and

enable them, with the money thus withheld from insurance compa-
nies, to take up intellectual pursuits and improve their minds. They
advocated "a universal system of scientifically administered insurance
against sickness, unemployment, and old age. . . . For even if people
have not saved money during their youth, it is idle to say that they have
not contributed to the wealth of the State. . . . If a man takes out an
insurance policy, he merely turns over to a private corporation certain
sums of money which . . . [the corporation] uses . . . to its own very
considerable profit. . . . He should be free to turn over to the community an equivalent in brain and muscle. . . .

"It is for us as an organized community to say whether we shall have
savings with fear, or freedom with efficiency." (It would be fun — or
perhaps it would not — to hear these arguments advanced on the floor
of the House today.)

People like my maternal and paternal grandparents had very little of
either — little savings and little freedom. All this progressive advice was
for the benefit of the middle class.

The Brueres have nothing but a kind of Ayn Rand–like contempt for
sad-sack altruists who "go without" for the sake of their children, with
the result that the "ugly fear" of a penniless old age "steals their chances
of present efficiency and looks mealy-mouthed and virtuous while it
does it."

. . . Oh how I wish I were rich so as not to have boring money
arguments with myself. When I have money I spend it. I live profligately and generously and I love it. When I had no money I slept and
worked and cooked and ate and entertained in one room (my children
slept in a big bedroom, separated from each other by an arched doorway). Today I found out that the maximum benefit extended me by an
insurance policy I took out twenty years ago, when it seemed impossible
to me that I should ever require surgery, is $1,400 — which, if I needed
brain surgery, would probably be sufficient to pay the surgeon for the
insertion of an ice pick in my worried brain, but would not be sufficient
to pay the anesthesiologist. If I manage to live four more years I will
qualify for Medicare — not a thrilling reason to stay alive. So I will
have to take practical steps to change this state of affairs — after all, I
am sixty, and everything removable is still inside of me, waiting to be

removed when need be. I will hate every minute of my practical en-
deavors, I will approach panic; my son used to say that he could smell
me (when we were poor) when I was making out checks or paying taxes;
I was feral, like an animal, full of crazy fear. Now I live in an apartment
building with a swimming pool. I am motivated more by the joy and
the physical well-being I feel when I swim than by the potential demands of my gallbladder or the possibility of milky cataracts; and only
time will tell how foolish I am.

My last home — before I entered that beautiful period of my life when
I lived alone in an apartment I loved, in a neighborhood I loved, making
a life I loved, and in the process discovering the evolving self, the
identity, the personality that had for so long eluded me — was the
Watch Tower's Bethel. I went there when I was nineteen (my mother's
age when she got married). My father drove me there as if he were
handing me over to a groom; he sat so meekly in the lounge overlooking the New York harbor and skyline, so meekly in that room of
mismatched blond furniture and six (never-played) grand pianos. A
terrible blank, supercilious room. Hunched up, he sat there as if he
were staring his own demise in the face.

There I was, in a house that grew like a barnacle out of the old
Beecher house, overwhelming it in the process; and it occurs to me
now that our otherworldly existence in that house (there were close to
five hundred of us, only twelve of us female) was a variation of the kind
of commune that the Beechers yearningly envisioned (a strange fulfillment): "a colony of . . . Christian people . . . with a central church and
schoolroom, library, hall for sports, and a common laundry. Suppose
each family to train the children to labor with the hands as healthful
and honorable duty; suppose all this, which is perfectly practicable,
would not the enjoyment of this life be increased, and also abundant
treasures be laid up in heaven, by using the wealth thus economized in
diffusing similar enjoyments and culture among the poor, ignorant, and
neglected ones in desolated sections where many now are perishing for
want of such Christian example and influences?"

We were not the "cultivated" Christians of "abundant wealth" the
Beecher ladies foresaw; and we diffused not culture but revelations of

doom to those we judged "poor, ignorant, and neglected" (never food, never clothing, never shelter, just husks, dry words); and we had no hall of sports . . . but, governed by faceless men, we were, for all the world, children.

Sometimes I think of men and women who slept two to a room for over fifty years — like my dear roommate Mary Hannan (who had gone to Normal School and who knelt at her bed to pray every night in her flannel nightgown with the Peter Pan collar and said what a bother it must be to have a boyfriend, all that bathing and attention to oneself on Saturday night), her bright blue eyes innocent in their nest of wrinkles, her parchment skin, her dry kindness — I think of men and women who for so many years were denied the pleasure of sleeping alone in a room without the censoring presence of another consciousness; and I wonder how they did not all go mad. Mary is dead now. They didn't tell me when she died, I was by that time long gone; and Mary — who loved me well — had not been allowed to maintain her friendship with me.

Mary, more than forty years my senior, never condescended to me, but she kept an eagle eye on me:

The overseer of housework — a man with a harelip who was related to Theodore Dreiser and to the Cold War congressman Martin Dies — scolded me one day (a scolding was likely to turn into a reproach of your "Theocratic spirit," and did); he scolded because he'd found dust in a stairwell I'd been assigned to clean. I retreated to the broom closet (we called it the hopper) where I kept my cleaning supplies; and I cried. Then Evie Sullivan, whose husband was an overseer of house-to-house preaching, accused me vitriolically of using the vacuum cleaner on the one day she needed it to perform her not-exhausting job of vacuuming the barbershop; so I cried some more. And more. (Poor dim Evie; she was old and fuddled; why did she have to work at all?) Ernie Talarico passed by and saw me crying. Ernie Talarico, smart and engaging and aquiver with a scarcely contained randiness, was a waiter in the communal dining room, although he had been at Bethel for almost twenty years, having offended whoever it was who had the power to give him a job suited to his talents. He was short and dark and walked very fast and his straight black hair flew back behind him and remained in an almost horizontal position till he came to rest. Everyone — except for those who had power over him — liked him. He had a beautiful speaking voice and a beautiful singing voice, and listened to classical music, and (because of whatever murky misdemeanor or offense he had committed) he was not given one of the prime rooms offered to Bethel veterans, but shared his cramped room for many many years. He was both bitter (but not brittle) and kind, an attractive combination, if a potentially lethal one. The day he spied me crying, he left a dozen red roses outside the door of the room I shared with Mary Hannan.

Oh, Mary Hannan was intrigued. If you wear one rose to the dining room it will mean you accept his intentions, she said. So I did not, reluctant to make a display of myself, not knowing to what I might be committing myself. I do wonder what my life would have been had I worn a red rose to the dining room, he was kind.

Ernie Talarico is dead now, too.

Sometimes I snuck away to a guest room — maintained for the occasional use of Bethelites' relatives, at the discretion of the overseers — to read "worldly" books (*Franny and Zooey*, Emily Dickinson). I was scared to be caught out, but too scared to lock the door, which would have ensured me a tenuous privacy. . . . The Beechers' contention that worldly novels "tend to throw the allurements of taste and genius around vice and crime" might have come straight from a *Watchtower* magazine.

One day I found in a waste-disposal room a whole cache of pornographic magazines and books on the third floor, where Bethel women and girls lived. For days after that (word got around), we cast wary looks at one another; sometimes our mutual frightened suspicion splintered into giggles.

I have compared the Brueres, in their contemptuous dismissal of altruism, to Ayn Rand. They were pre-Skinnerians, too, so ruthlessly pragmatic, so relentlessly utilitarian as to be able to suggest that "a man's choice of profession is not his own business. It is a social question. . . . Inclinations" toward one kind of job — one kind of life — or other are insufficient reason to pursue that job, that life. "The idea that a child's career *must* lie in the direction of its inclination [is] only a fraction of the truth. . . . What's the use of being able to do something superlatively well if society doesn't need to have that particular thing done at all?" In vain might one have protested among the Witnesses that society "needed" a poet, "needed" a lunatic van Gogh (who, it could be argued, set an awfully bad example for the children). . . . My friend Walter, who was at Bethel when I was (and who made his escape shortly after I did), remembers that on his first day of entering headquarters he saw a "brother" — an old man — on a scaffold washing walls; he asked the man how long he'd been doing this. Twenty years, the man answered; and Walter's stomach dropped precipitously; he prayed that night that he would not be assigned the job of washing walls — anything but, he prayed. He was assigned to wash walls.

The Brueres argued against "the social calamity" of parents' scrimping to send children to college — "splendid parental force wasted." While they were willing to go so far as to say that unemployment was the "parent" of "juvenile delinquency, crime, and prostitution," their draconian — and tragicomic — solution was an analysis of "whether the product is needed or not. . . . We do not know either what the community needs in the way of applied middle-class brains or what it is willing to pay for."

This is what happens when vulgar pieties like those of the Beechers are replaced by authoritarian materialism: people are reduced to units of consumption and production (even when what is being consumed is, as in the case of Jehovah's Witnesses, something fancy like "the Truth").

This is what happened to Witness children: we were not allowed to go to college.

I call this sinful. A child, the *Bhagavad-Gita* says, is a guest in the house, to be loved and protected but never possessed.

This is what happened at Bethel: our inclinations, like those of children, were regarded as frivolous: "The failure of any one individual [is] a social waste for which we and our children must pay!" The "Nation" — or in our case, our leaders at Bethel — must decide our proper jobs. This was true whether or not one worked at headquarters. I had a friend who played first violin for Stokowski; he left that job because music — "worldly" music — was regarded as a doorway to the enchantments of sin; he became a furniture salesman so that his children could labor at the preaching work full time. I knew another man, also a violinist, who became a presser in a dry-cleaning shop for the same life-denying reasons.

"It is idle to call channeling young people into useful jobs an unwarranted interference with personal liberty. What personal liberty have the hungry? At such a time academic discussion becomes both inhuman and unpatriotic; what we need is an enlightened statesmanship [and] market regulation of the need for plumbers, teachers, bricklayers and doctors. . . . A man's choice of profession is not his own business. It is a social question."

This poison pill — the inability to choose the gratifying work to which one's talents and instincts and intuition guided one — was sugarcoated: The eyes of a young man dedicated to knowledge gave out, the Brueres fabulously tell us, in the course of his studies at a seminary. Dispirited, he hired out to a chicken farmer and eventually became "the best poultryman in America." And the moral is: "His life came near being wrecked because he was educated merely in the line of his inclinations."

God grants us free will; the Brueres do not.

Both vulgar pieties and materialistic imperatives have been used to keep women and men in their place, depending on what "society" required of them at the time.

What we ask — to be fully human — is to find satisfaction in chosen work. If man is subordinated to something abstract called economics, man becomes part of a machine, Dorothy Sayers remarked. "'God created.' The characteristic common to God and man is apparently that: the desire and ability to make things," she wrote. Imagine if someone had advised Newton not to waste his time observing apples. Think if our Creator had thwarted His own impulse to create — truly an unthinkable thought: He would have imploded. Active negation of Energy is unimaginable. A life without chosen work is a life without the possibility of felicity. And work chosen only because of the material advantages it will bring will not be very good work: the cabbie who told me he was studying oncology because cancer "was big now" will not be a very good doctor. Pity his patients.

To work is to pray, the saints say; to waste one's natural talents is, the saints say, to sin against God. That is the sin of Onan.

> Fireflies
> are daughters to the stars
> and go in the countryside to catch the scent of hay
> which is the scent of God
> because it smells of work.

> — Giovanni Cerri (translated by Luigi Bonaffini)

We are called to be cocreators of the Kingdom of God.

> For everything to which one is enclin'd
> Doth best become and greatest grace doth gaine.

After several years of housekeeping at Bethel, I was reassigned by the president of the Watch Tower Society to the proofreading department — a transfer, he let on (with some satisfaction), that was densely dangerous to my salvation, as, if I didn't watch it, I might begin to think I was equal to the men in the department, and if, as appeared likely, my intelligence, thus rewarded, were to pick a quarrel with my faith.

My intelligence, that unruly beast, had already turned against me, with fairly devastating consequences to my psychic equilibrium; and my love — for Arnold Horowitz, for the whole of the splendid pulsating world — had done me in: I could no more imagine Arnold swimming in the blood of unbelievers at Armageddon than I could imagine a day when the New York skyline, which I saw from my blond bed, in the room I shared with dear Mary Hannan, would no longer be there, stern and resplendent, full of that good so intimately braided with evil that is the very stuff of precious liberty and life.

But each morning I rose to my tasks with "the women [who resembled] 4-H Club beauty queens in simple cotton dresses," grave, decorous, pretty, unobtrusive (as Richard Harris, a *New Yorker* writer who came to Bethel to write about us, said); until that day, that moment, when I knew it was finished and I would rise no longer in the service of a vicious god whose compassion was not equal to my niggardly own.

Blossoms in the dust: in the dark places of my soul, my doubts — and God's grace — had been operating for years; it only seemed sudden, my conversion to unbelief; it had made its ineluctable way in the dark through eons of pain.

They sent the doctor — the wheezy chiropractor — to my room. He brought three cans of Campbell's tomato soup and told me to stay in bed.

If I leave this place, I asked myself, what is the worst thing that can happen to me? And the answer was — for I had utterly ceased to believe — I will live a mediocre life. That did not seem terrible to me; mediocrity was preferable to being chosen in the killing ways I had been marked and chosen, it appeared to me in the guise of calm. (I worship normality; I reverence ordinariness — it is a kind of heresy, it amounts to idolatry.)

My mother.

What would I do? I was her stand-in there; she wanted me there.

But I knew, with all the force of my being, that if I did not leave I would die. I was already dying, in pieces. Some days, when I tried to go from door to door, I could not talk, and some days, going from door to door, my legs refused to work (I spent half a night, once, on a subway platform, unable to walk six feet to passing trains — so scared). I saw things — I saw black clouds in sunny skies; but through the terror, I heard the faint sound of trumpets, I felt the hook of God, the tentacles of joy.

I called a cab and left that place, its ghosts, its hypocrisies.

I moved into a new world that trembled in its shining and in its brooding, a sentient weariness the buffer between me and the restless avidity coiled within me, my voraciousness to know the unknowable world equaled by my sense that God's world itself longed, with great and beautiful poignancy, to be known . . . and to be loved. I had left the measly pieties behind; I had left the crushing machine behind. With me remained the conviction, a renewable source of joy, that the world waits for us to redeem it.

I never looked back. Pratfalls, night terrors, panic, broken bones and a broken heart, humiliations, failures, rejections, sadness, grief, horror, weariness, shock, poverty, illness, betrayal — nothing I experienced changed that overwhelming fact: I never looked back; I never needed to look back.

My mother never asked me why I left. The word *God* was never exchanged between us. The word *sex* was never exchanged between us. Nor was the word *love*.

Often I think of those days, a lifetime ago, when evil (as the Shadow and the Watch Tower knew) lurked everywhere. Sometimes it takes very little to set me off, very little for me to remember the palpable quality of that evil that I had been warned, all my young life, against — the evil (I was taught) that was within me, the devil who was in the wicked world waiting to pounce, to eat me up and vomit me out. The warnings had been gratuitous; I had always known evil — I had, in my innocence, not known its name; I had not greeted and embraced it. In the home of my family, where I was not safe and never inviolate, where I was prey to predators hungry and wretched, insatiable and profane, I had looked at evil but not known it by its name; and I have, since the day I left Bethel and the day I left the house I called home, encountered evil in its purest form; but the fear of evil no longer obliterates the sun.

There is God, a God born into a world waiting to be born.

Sometimes it takes very little to set me off: "The water in which the potato . . . a family connection of the deadly nightshade, . . . is boiled is to be feared, because the water is the element into which . . . the evil principle is drawn off, by which we are all in danger of suffocating and of being poisoned." I read that nervous, impenetrable sentence in the Beechers' book. It set me off.

It made me laugh and it made me cry.

There is no remedy for suffering.

I go on my way rejoicing.

4

LOOT
AND LISTS AND
LUST (AND THINGS)

The miser may hoard his money. What is it after all — so much silver and gold. Any man can work and accumulate money; but where is the man with another string of Persian enamel beads such as these?

— Anonymous

The eye does not see things but images of things that mean other things.

— Italo Calvino

A LATE-SUMMER afternoon. I am sitting at Bailey's Beach in Newport eating a slightly rancid egg-salad sandwich in the company of the doyenne of Newport society and the father of a director of one of the world's great art museums and various other bungalow owners, rich but not well fed. Fortunately there is so little actual matter between the two slices of bread (dry as old crumbs on the outside and moist — gluey wet — on the inside) that I am not likely to suffer food poisoning. Look, after all, at how long these people live. Yesterday afternoon I went, with the grand Newport lady, to pay a courtesy call on Douglas Fairbanks, Jr. The butler asked if I'd like some iced tea. Water, I said, thank you. Twenty minutes later he reappeared with a glass of tap water in a Waterford crystal glass on an ornate silver salver. That evening the

Newport lady (who is kind enough to allow herself to be interviewed on the Klaus von Bülow matter) promised her grandchildren a special treat for dinner — SpaghettiOs, poor dears.

Now the father of the museum director is regaling us with stories of how his son, of whom he is bantamly proud, managed to get this art treasure, that art treasure from this "little Turk," that "little Greek," one "little Wop," some "little Jew." The word *Jew* provokes a collective intake of breath. A nod in my direction. What has gone around the circle very quickly, I surmise, is the communal conjecture that as I am a New York writer, I must, ipso facto, be a Jew, some little Jew. Not to worry. The old man (his feet are so long, so white) casts a meaningful look at the crucifix I wear around my neck and mouths *She's OK*, as if for all the world I were not present. My stomach lurches, nothing to do with egg salad (these are people who also collect other people, Klaus von Bülow, for example).

> *We are but dust and shadow. The years as they pass plunder us of one thing and another.*
>
> — Horace

No morality attaches to the acquisition of things. An absolutely exquisite object may be the heart's desire of an absolute vulgarian. (A vulgar object may be acquired, on the other hand, with beautiful motives by the pure of heart.) For the distinguished old-fashioned Americans gathered that day at Bailey's Beach, beautiful objects were insurance against the depredations of time, talismans against barbarians howling at the gate.

. . . My son and my daughter are on their way to Peshawar to visit their father. Bring me back something beautiful, I say (I always say). My son brings me a heavy fabric vertically striped, a domestic room divider (a woven wall), vegetable-dyed indigo, purple, beet red, ivory, fawn, black. Of two pieces, it is sewn together in large, irregular, crude stitches and bound at its edges with cheap commercial fabric. I am as moved by these added, adaptive homely imperfections as I am by the assured perfection of the weaving, the inarguable logic of its colors, earthy and serene. My son cannot look at it without being reminded that it is loot, spoils of war, the Afghan war, sold to him at the border bazaar for the price of a bowl of rice. He loves it nevertheless; and I sense in him a slight, contained regret that he has yielded the object to me. Sometimes I think he believes I am incapable of assigning values and perfectly loving things. . . .

I read about collecting as a means to distinction in a book called *Lock, Stock, and Barrel* by Douglas and Elizabeth Rigby, published in 1944, during the war — manufactured under government regulations for saving metal and paper (and because it was published during World War II, probably largely unread, which is a great pity).

I found this book — it sprang to my attention, it leapt to my hand — when I was thinking about collecting and gathering and accreting and things; I found it in a secondhand bookstore.

What you desire you call into being; for a collector the chief, perhaps the only, virtue is patience.

When I looked for a birthday present for Jazzman, I found, in a flea market, a pair of 1930s cufflinks with a golfing motif (strange as it seems to me, the man I love is a golfer); I had never before seen such objects and never again have I seen similar objects, nor have I seen that particular vendor again.

Lock, Stock, and Barrel tells me that collecting provides for the specialist "the rich harvest that springs from knowing more than one's neighbors": "The African hunter wears about his neck the tusks of wild boars, the teeth of lions and leopards he has slain; and the more he can exhibit, the prouder and happier he is. . . . The true collector is a transformed hunter."

We hunt for things and experiences, for states of grace, satiety, security, self-definition, immortality; we hunt out of love and lovingly, and for motives of snobbery; we hunt with graceful intuition, perception and integrity, and with an urge to cherish and preserve; we hunt out of avarice, greed, lust, hunger, fear, boredom, restlessness; we hunt, like the Bailey's Beachers, out of a simple sense of entitlement; and we hunt because it both soothes and excites us — it combines, as Increase Mather said, "the ardor of pursuit with the serener rapture of possession." We hunt with what Henry James (who deprecated his own "handful of feeble relics") called the "avid and gluttonous eye." We hunt and we gather — as I did, when my children were very young and I was poor, of necessity mated with cunning. I shoplifted, belts and ties and socks and scarves. . . . Necessity, cunning, a cheap thrill and a *frisson* of terror, a profound satisfaction. We hunt and treasure so as to feel a sense of continuity — of circularity — with the past; we honor the mind and the hand of the maker in each object we ardently pursue. We collect to survive; our survival depends in part on our ability to classify and codify and catalogue: we hunt and choose in order to tame chaos, to bring order to a world too full of being, too full of things. We hunt and gather and collect and accrete for the reason we do everything else: we die. We die due to reasons beyond our control. Over our possessions, we allow ourselves to believe, we have control. With our possessions we weave our shrouds. Everything we collect is a *memento mori.*

In Bali I bought a primitive carving of a monkey — a loom shuttle in the shape of a monkey, which fit sweetly in my hand. My monkey, which is a little more than a foot tall, has a hole in the middle of its stomach, and one in its side, to accommodate (I suppose) the woof thread — these holes are utilitarian (but spooky for all that).

I say I bought a carving of a monkey. I mean I bought a monkey.

The monkey has high breasts, widely spaced on her chest, small but pendulous; she wears her hair in a topknot; she has nicely set ears, and a nose that has suffered some injury over time, which makes her look like a leper. One of her arms is longer than the other — it appears to be reaching for the hole in her belly. She has an expressive coconut-shaped face that narrows to a skewed and sly monkey grin. Her asymmetrical eyes — two holes of unequal circumference — look inhabited. They remind me of the iridescent pictures of Jesus with those eyes that follow you around.

You can see the hand of the maker — the mark of the chisel — on the wood.

The day after I bought the monkey from an Arab trader in Manggis, I went to a sacred monkey grove with my guide, Akhee, who uncharacteristically tried to hold me back — "It is enough, madam" — after I stopped to peer down a long avenue of lacy trees (my feet quite longed to march down that avenue, to feel beneath my sandals the protruding roots of trees under a thin cover of slippery, sun-splashed black dirt; I wanted the lacy net canopy of leaves over my head). It was very hot.

"*Akhee!!!*" A big brazen monkey has scratched her way up my leg and my skirt and resting for a while on my head has chattered her way down my arm and grabbed my purse and run away with it into the green-gold gloom. "*Akhee!!!*" Six thousand dollars in traveler's checks, $700 in cash, two pairs of glasses, a gold-filled amulet calligraphically engraved that I bought from the Arab trader (the Arabic letters probably read *Eat me*), my passport, an Atrovent inhaler, and one hundred Xanax are in my purse, gone forever in the sacred gloom. "*Akhee!!!*" I need my Xanax. Well; what to do. I don't know. I am rooted. Hostile mocking monkeys, hundreds, all around me. Akhee appears with a bunch of bananas. Yes, but all monkeys look alike, he will never find my mugger; look at all the ravening, filthy, nattering things. Swinging sedately from side to side, breasts flopping as she coolly walks toward Akhee and his bananas, the monkey who has chosen me glances at the remaining pair of glasses on my nose, the gold glittering at my throat, and, after a quiet moment of reflection, releases my purse and opts for the bananas. How can this be? How can she — I have been in a kind of blackout — of all the monkeys in the grove, have answered Akhee's appeal? Everything in my purse is intact. Well, everything but my medical bottle of Xanax, which the bold monkey holds with one prehensile thumb, a banana in the other. She bites the (childproof) bottle with fearsome teeth and apparently inhales the drug.

Akhee says she has taken vengeance for my having bought her ancestor, the monkey with the hole in her belly.

I kept my monkey, trying not to feel revulsion for it, on a bookcase for some time.

Later that year, on a trip to a game preserve in southern India, monkeys — horrid, unblinking, and kept from us by a ring of fragrant fire — eyed the mutton curry and the saffron rice pudding we ate in a thatched hut on the sacred Cauvery River. Hundreds of flying foxes — fruit-eating bats with pterodactyl wings two feet long and clever rats' faces — hung upside down from trees in repulsive repose, and the forest was alive with elephants, lions, atavistic wild dogs (the forest was as alert as we); but it was only the monkeys I feared. On Chamundi Hill in Mysore, where Durga, the wife of Shiva (in her malevolent aspect), slew the buffalo-demon king, pilgrims climb a thousand stairs to the temple on the summit of the hill. We take the macadam road that serves cars wherein are less ascetically inclined pilgrims; it is lined with monkeys, forward and social and talkative; I will not get out of the stuffy little Ambassador car.

When I kept my monkey on a table surface, it used occasionally, in the night, to change position; and I would see it in the morning staring in a direction opposite the one I had last seen it in.

I am fully aware of the fact that there are no inanimate objects.

Tired of the monkey's willfulness, I hung it on a wall, where now it seems content to be.

My monkey shares a room with a three-inch crystal figure I bought at the Taj Mahal Hotel in Bombay. A few gold lines sketch in the folds of a country woman's sari. Around her bare upper arms are tiny jewels — diamonds, emeralds, rubies — set in 18-carat gold. One of her legs, unclothed, undraped, is bent as if by rickets. Her crystal hair is waved and gathered in a bun; her likable features are clearly articulated; her breasts are full and high, her belly round.

Tonight I left the monkey and the glass woman next to my computer. I wanted to see if they would have turned around during the night. They did not. I can only suppose they like the company they keep — two smiling naked fat white porcelain babies with pouty red lips and jet black hair, bought in Bombay's Chor Bazaar, provenance unknown; a Byzantine ivory figure of Christ of astonishing beauty, traded for several gold rings in Chor Bazaar. (I had two of these ivory figures once; I gave one of them as a house gift to a friend, a Texas millionaire. What else do you give a man who has everything but happiness? He put it in his safe-deposit box, which I consider treachery, false imprisonment.)

In my hallway I have a three-foot wooden statue of Saint Luke, bought from an antiques dealer in Antigua, Guatemala, a quarter of a century ago and said to have come from a deconsecrated church, though it is not unlikely that it was the antiques dealer who deconsecrated it, a thought I keep firmly trapped in the back of my brain. Traces of the gilt and rose and blue paint that once made it gorgeous remain.

Luke, the patron saint of medicine, has a lovely planed and sculpted nose; I rubbed it when I got it, and the next day my children had the measles. Now he is draped with all my necklaces, crystal and gold and silver and lozenges of glass, amethyst and coral and turquoise, and plastic gaud and flash and pearls and ivory; and lately I have taken to putting my glasses on his nose — at last I always know where to find them. He is a happy saint, I think; his glitter greets me at night, delights my cats, and, like "The Purloined Letter," will, I trust, deceive burglars — if any can get into the pleasant fortress I live in, which I do not think they can.

It is amazing the things people collect — teeth and toupees, skulls and chamber pots, trolley-car transfers, hair and fans and kites and forceps, dogs and coins, canes, canaries, facts, data on Siamese twins or the Dionne quintuplets, Presley stuff and Beatles stuff and buttons and fans and bones, hat pins and forged signatures and first editions — and how devoted their proprietorship is.

In the orchard of her house near Cambridge, Germaine Greer plants apple trees collected and secured from an apple archivist; she says she hangs her jewels out on their branches when she prays for rain, and then the orchard sparkles with shooting lights. Witchy.

Harry Elkins Widener jumped into the Atlantic from the *Titanic* with a rare edition of Bacon's essays, calling out (it is said) as the waters seethed over his head: "Little Bacon goes with me."

Stanley Baldwin made it a practice to take one of the stuffed owls he collected with him on weekends away from home.

Julius Caesar could not bear to be parted from his mosaic tables, which he took with him on campaign. (I have a rosewood campaign chest, rescued from Chor Bazaar when Indians, in the sixties, were still intent upon relieving themselves of physical reminders of the Raj; it is a neutral object — it might have been carried by coolies to the hill stations in the blistering Indian summers; it might have seen battle. I have not been able to attach a story to it, which is just as well: I love it for itself alone.)

A Russian countess paid extravagant sums for bedpans that had belonged to famous or notorious people.

Baron Lionel Walter Rothschild collected albino animals and birds; N. C. Rothschild collected fleas — thousands of them — preserved in spirits in individual vials, marked with the place of origin and with the name of the host, animal or human, on which the flea had been found.

From the *New York Times*, July 9, 1994: Dr. John K. Lattimer, the eighty-year-old head of the urology department of Columbia-Presbyterian Medical Center, has in his collection W. C. Fields's top hat, Hermann Göring's heavy gold ring on which is embossed Göring's crest, and a case made from a cartridge shell in which Göring kept the cyanide he used to kill himself two hours before he was to be hanged. "I like little things you can carry around," Dr. Lattimer says; "I found they made me an appreciated dinner guest." He has a sword that belonged to George Washington; ten cases of Lincoln assassination memorabilia, including the key to box number 7 at Ford's Theater, where the president was shot; casts of dinosaur footprints, the skull of a saber-toothed tiger and bones of the woolly mammoth; J. Robert Oppenheimer's porkpie hat.

There appears to be no intrinsic logic to this eclectic collection. In fact there is. The Göring *objets* can be explained by the fact that Dr. Lattimer's job, after World War II, was to guard the Nazi defendants at Nuremberg so that they would not commit suicide. Every collection reveals the logic of the sensibility — more or less accessible — of the collector. A friend of his father's brought him a bayonet, a souvenir of World War I; and that started Dr. Lattimer off.

There is no telling why some people cannot be separated from their path, once started, and others veer, and shunt their attention from one type of object to another. I have a friend who bought a house in order to keep in it the artifacts of the fifties and forties she compulsively collects. She started with a chenille bedspread and now has dozens. (I have the ur–chenille bathmat, flea-market, vintage 1940, $12; delighted to have it, I am equally delighted now to leave the genre alone.) The friend of whom I speak bought one set of Fiesta ware at auction years ago for a pittance, and now her kitchen has shelves and shelves of the stuff; and if she is unable to complete a set, she is near to grief, for the relief of which price is no object. In her house everything is of the same vintage — flashlights and the working vacuum cleaner, the records and the record player, magazines and books; the swimming pool is Hollywood-fifties kidney-shaped. Her identity is severely threatened if her objects — the very stuff of her life — are not in place and admired; her love for them magnifies the value of the objects; and the objects magnify her.

I am a magpie. If I were given the bare facts of my life and asked to guess what I collect, I would say subway memorabilia and baseball memorabilia — Brooklyn Dodgers baseball memorabilia; in fact I collect neither.

I collect because an object has associations for me, it speaks directly to my nature and to my past, to my needs, and to my embrace of magic. (Look: there is magic and magic. There is sleight of hand and there is the Resurrection, and there is much in between.) And I collect for simple aesthetic satisfaction — for what Keats called "luxuries bright, milky, soft and rosy." Diderot says these motives are entwined: "The aesthetic experience is dependent on a wealth of associations, analogy, and associative memory." Yes.

But I am told by the Rigbys that "the true collector . . . has nothing but scorn for the simple gatherer. . . . In an era of growing enlightenment and adulthood the magpies are recruited chiefly either from the ranks of children and simpletons, or from the abnormal misers and hoarders, although we must include those who are adult except in their childish collecting habits. . . . An accumulation may not properly be called a collection when the assembled objects bear no intelligible relationship to each other. The man who piles his house with junk of every description owns, in this sense, not a collection but a congeries." The Rigbys have on their side the snobbery of Edith Wharton, who, in *The Decoration of Houses* (1902), professed herself horrified that anyone should buy "trash" because of the associations it evoked, and condemned anyone who did so ("a vacuous mind obeying a sad compulsion").

One man's trash is another man's treasure.

Louisine Havemeyer, whose husband made a fortune in sugar refining, has been called the owner of "the best and wisest collection in America," a felicitous encomium, bestowed retrospectively. (In portraits, Mr. Havemeyer looks like a solid burgher. . . . I always think it's best, if one wishes to maintain a good opinion of another, not to inquire too deeply into the source of his wealth.) When the contents of her rooms at 1 East Sixty-sixth Street went on auction in 1929 — rooms created by Louis Comfort Tiffany and Samuel Colman — what has been called Tiffany's most important interior was regarded as in large part junk. The Metropolitan Museum was the recipient of French impressionist paintings and Oriental ceramics and Japanese armor, but Tiffany's adornments went unremarked upon. How wonderful these large rooms must have been a 1993 exhibit at the Metropolitan — "Splendid Legacy: The Havemeyer Collection" — allowed us to see. Of all the wonders, the most wonderful perhaps was a suspended stairway — an unanchored, floating stairway — that hung like a fili-greed crystal-trimmed balcony over a two-story velvet-draped gallery where Rembrandts lived beneath a ceiling quilted with Japanese silk brocades; in this rosy splendor children — her thirteen grandchildren — romped. Except for one panel, the flying staircase is lost; and Tif-fany's windows are lost, and a peacock mosaic by Tiffany — who drew inspiration for the Havemeyer rooms from Japanese, Chinese, Islamic, Byzantine, and Celtic sources — is lost.

Here is a list of things that Louisine Havemeyer collected. (I give the list in vertical form, which seems to me the natural form a list should take.):

Persian rugs on gilded, overstuffed couches (redundant, delicious)
Tiffany leaded-glass windows, mosaics, lighting fixtures, chairs,
          balustrades — "in any place that provided a rationale,
          lights sparkle[d]"
Favrile glass, opalescent glass
Amethyst- and opal-glass fire screens
Quilted silks and textiles in tawny gold (the color of burnt sugar)
Goyas and El Grecos (including *Toledo*), Vermeer's *Women Weighing
          Pearls*
Chaise longues (so romantic; Dickens suffered his fatal brain hemor-
          rhage on a chaise covered in green velvet, in the dining
          room of his house in Kent)
Japanese *Noh* robes
Islamic tiles of that astonishing piercing blue and that unparalleled
          tranquilizing blue
Monets that shimmered like her Favrile glass; Cézanne's *Bridges*

> An indoor fountain, a visible reminder that that which is given replen-
> ishes and becomes that which is received: a self-renewing
> resource, the watery apogee of urban abundance

So can it be said that these "assembled objects bear no intelligible relationship to each other"? They were joined in her imagination; her nourished sensibility was the unifying force. (Louisine Havemeyer's friend Mary Cassatt, about whom Havemeyer made speeches, guided her purchases; she bought her first Degas when she was twenty-two. She was a militant suffragist who placed Cassatt's paintings at the service of the movement. She said "it was very easy to talk about the emancipation of women, but art was a very different and difficult subject." She was a moving force in the American Women's War Relief Fund and the Belgian Relief Fund. She was pretty and plump and the recipient of the French Legion of Honor. The various aspects of her life apparently worked together as well as the objects of her collection did. She lived inside a prism of her own making.)

The three-story turreted Havemeyer mansion, with its treasures behind locked doors, in closets, and in servants' rooms, was torn down in 1930, a year after Louisine Havemeyer died; no voices were heard in protest.

As to Dr. Lattimer, he bought the knife used to attack William H. Seward the night Lincoln was shot, and one thing led to another, in his case Lincoln memorabilia. He has the prostate of Nicolas Murray Butler, late president of Columbia University, in a bottle. He owns Napoleon's penis, which he refers to fastidiously as "the urological relic"; he bought it from the family of the man who performed the autopsy. He won't let it be photographed.

The thirteenth-century Japanese regent Takotoki collected as many as five thousand dogs, "developing such a predilection for them that he would accept them in payment of taxes. He fed them on fish and fowl, and carried them in palanquins on their daily outings, and provided for their accommodation kennels with gold and silver decorations."

Cardinal Ippolito, Jacob Burkhardt says, "kept at his strange court a troop of barbarians who talked no less than twenty different languages, and who were all of them perfect specimens of their races."

Don Ferrante (1423–1494), king of Naples, "after executing his defeated enemies, [had] them carefully embalmed, dressed again in their best clothing, and collected in a special room in his palace, there triumphantly displayed, making, in effect, a museum of contemporary mummies whose faces were still poignantly familiar to whatever audience might be forced to look upon them."

(The inclination to collect people, both dead and alive, and to collect bodies, both juicy and desiccated, finds prettier expression in the baroque church of Gesu Nuovo in Naples. Set in the golden side altars are rectangular boxes in which are wooden busts of saints; separating the boxes are vertical rows of glass drawers full of skulls and bones. Boxes, honeycombs, nests: the receptacles recede into the dimness of the ceiling; the bones of the dead look like children's playthings.)

In a coffee-and-tea shop in Brooklyn Heights I found an old tea box. Black letters on a faded green and tangerine background: CHOICE NEW SEASON TEA, VIA SUEZ CANAL. A painting of faded green mountains; and, bigger than the mountains, flamingos on a faded orange pond; and, bigger than the flamingos, a duck; lotuses and a palm tree and a stunted fir. On yellowed stickers in an elegant hand: *1890 ld & 50; John Davis, Gaspe Basin, per Admiral.* Stylized Chinese lettering on orange medallions. I found this object intensely romantic and runic (and perfectly box-sized, one square foot). I bought it for $40 and brought it home. Eventually, years later, the box fulfilled its destined function — now it houses silk poppies, bent and hidden, that remind me of all that I loved (which was precious little) about Morocco . . . where poppies and wheat grow together, the exotic and the domestic combined.

I lived in a house on Sackett Street, in Brooklyn, that figures in my dreams as an unplundered (unsacked?) treasure house, a place of squandered opportunities. My children, Mr. Harrison, and me. When we moved in, the abandoned house, a four-story brownstone of noble proportions that had housed for her entire life the ancient lady who died there, had become the clubhouse of neighborhood boys, who were not wicked (only deficient). The upright piano was damaged beyond repair, its ivory keys like rotten teeth. But there was a 1920s walnut table and sideboard (scarred), and there were drawers and cupboards full of magical things (old buttons and egg beaters, cracked china cups and iron cooking vessels and pine boxes with sturdy iron hinges). That house was so nicely fitted with cupboards and drawers suggestive of good things kept in reserve, abundance encapsulated, that one could dream about it forever. ("And to add fantasy linen is to draw a picture, by means of a volute of words, of all the superabundant blessings that lie folded in piles between the flanks of an abandoned wardrobe. How big, how enveloping, is an old sheet when we unfold it. And how white the old tablecloth was, white as the moon on the wintry meadow!" — Gaston Bachelard) But I was blindly practical at the time, and turned my attention to things like termites and the washing machine and the oil burner; and (my marriage was in ruins) as far as my imagination was concerned, those little Edenic containers might just as well have housed snakes and spiders as lavender-scented sheets. I threw the old precious stuff out.

Now I often visit Sackett Street in my dreams. The house, in my dreams, is vastly enlarged — it has a glass conservatory and almost as many parlors as drawers, and in each of them are treasures: pink marble tables with ebony filigreed wood, plantation chairs and chaises of colonial cane, Victorian slipper chairs, and walking sticks and marquetry tables and Ming vases and an emerald Buddha and Lucknow tiles and silver tea strainers and crazy quilts and Jaipur enamels and watered-silk wall hangings and refectory tables and ivory caskets and mirrored cloth and shrines made of piqué assiette, and Pieros and a Matisse, silver peacocks and golden bowls, old leather safari chairs, sable throws, sea glass, dancing Shivas, velvet shawls, Bedouin rugs, marbles and mosaics and precious rosy seashells, a jade prayer wheel, lace ribbons and smoky gilded mirrors, diamonds from Golconda casually disposed, dragonflies and butterflies and yellow hummingbirds and pomegranates. I wander through those rooms full of longing.

I threw the buttons and all the old things out; I concentrated on making curtains for the children's rooms.

After the divorce we moved to Washington Avenue, across the street from the Brooklyn Botanic Gardens (shootings on the avenue, cherry blossoms in the gardens). Very old people lived in that apartment building. Nice for them, because they took their shriveled bodies across the street to sit on benches under lilac trees; bad for them, because the gunshots were moving ineluctably closer. One old lady implored my children not to ride their bicycles in the marble lobby because her baby hated noise. Her baby was forty-five, he had a tin plate in his head, she said. She said she worked for Helen Hayes. "Who's Hell?" my children said: "She says she works for Hell and Hayes. . . . Who's Hayes?" My daughter swallowed a cherry pit and the old lady told her that a tree would grow inside of her. So Anna hated her. Once the old lady baby-sat for my children, and when I didn't come home by three she called my parents, and my father and my Aunt Lee came in just in time to find me kissing a black man in civil rights overalls goodnight. So I hated her too.

In the basement of this building full of very old people were storage cubicles, open, unlocked, disregarded. I never looked very close. I saw shadows in the dark, lumpy humped shapes: tables, chairs, cartons, boxes, lamps, dusty heaps. It is inexplicable to me now that I did not investigate (and help myself to abandoned treasure); the windows of the basement were black with cobwebs and grime; I was not a hunter then. . . . I too was afraid of the gunshots, of the violence, of the crazy lady who worked for Hell and Hayes.

My narrow focus dampened fantasy: I threw a Tuareg rug down the incinerator because cat hair was all over it; I had forgotten rugs could be cleaned. I left Renaissance goblets of green incised glass — given to me by a courtier of the Nizam of Hyderabad — around on kitchen windowsills (they broke); nobody is brave enough to survive a divorce intact, appearances notwithstanding.

In an old book, I see a photograph (circa 1944) of the contents of a ten-year-old boy's pockets: marbles, a slingshot, a fountain pen, an Indian arrowhead, a model of a Flying Tigers plane, a battery, a patch of sergeant's stripes, a toy sword, a Dick Tracy ring, a roller-skate key, several old coins, a compass, a miniature horseshoe, a toy soldier, bottle caps (including one Coca-Cola and one pineapple soda cap), a crayon, a ball of rubber bands. His father took this picture; perhaps he was prescient; perhaps he knew that the innocence this collection represents was soon to vanish from the world.

. . . In 1944 schoolchildren collected aluminum foil from gum wrappers and rubber bands and made the rubber and the foil into balls for the war effort. I didn't, I couldn't, my religion didn't allow it; we were "not of this world." But my love affair with the world had already begun. I loved these tangible objects; unbeautiful in themselves, they had a kind of mystical significance for me, they spoke to me of everything I was not. They still do. . . .

In the same book I find a photograph grotesquely inimical to innocence. In November 1937 Göring organized an international competitive display of hunting trophies; almost every country in Europe sent exhibits, and sportsmen from all over the world heeded the pathological call. The photograph is of thousands of square feet of stags' antlers, serving no purpose aesthetic or utilitarian, only emblematic of a decadent's wish to gather and control, surrogate objects prefiguring the heads, skulls, scalps, hair, ears, hands, and phalli that are among the spoils of war.

Saint Anne, the mother of the mother of God, was raised by stags on flowers and fruit.

When my Uncle Tony went to fight in Burma, I asked him to send me the ear of a dead Jap. Why an ear, I wonder, and why such a bloody request? I didn't even like the word *Jap*, I thought it was discourteous, and it offended me, although, like everyone else, I sang "Whistle while you work. Hitler is a jerk. Mussolini is a meanie and the Japs are worse" (an adaptive survival strategy on my part; it is very tiresome to be singular, to be a freak).

Why an ear? Pre-Confucian Chinese punished rebels by cutting off their ears, which became trophies and were collected. In the sixteenth century the Japanese collected and buried thirty-eight thousand pairs of ears and the same number of noses from Korean enemies, and then erected a monument — the Mimidzuka or Ear Mound — to celebrate and mark the spot.

> *Beautiful things from all over the country were gathered together thick as clouds.*
>
> — Yen Yüan

In Hyderabad we sat on a white sheet on the ground of the dealer's dark inner courtyard — the *talma* — and the antique-wallah brought us bounty tied in red cloth. The rhythms were slow and complex, a game with serious purpose, leisurely and thrilling, of show and tell and touch. Children and women (their faces half covered with black scarves) peered out from behind doors, giggling. Once he brought out, wrapped in white cloth, an entire suit of armor; in the hot dimness of the courtyard I thought at first it was a corpse. And we gathered, we gathered; and so many of those beautiful things we treated in the nature of souvenirs — Rajput paintings and bronze caskets, brass lotuses that unfolded at the touch of a secret spring, Hyderabadi perfume bottles of amber glass and brass, intricate brass ropes, stone Divali oil-wick holders; we brought them home to friends. I want them back, I want to recall them and to give them the love I (arrogantly) think I am singularly suited to bestow.

In the old city famous for its pearls we sat on tattered rugs in terraced, crumbling, narrow tenements and leaned against bolsters and pillows and watched Indian ladies buy their daughters' dowries. From rusted petrol tins the jewel dealer spilled diamonds and rubies and emeralds onto muslin-covered rugs . . . and these riches were so much outside one's experience one thought: How lovely these candies are, they look like jewels.

Somewhere in southern India, we came upon a ruined palace the grounds of which were used for the town council and elementary school. (Mr. Harrison was delivering chemical manure.) The ground was strewn with chunks of amethysts, as if the dusty unforgiving soil in a fit of generosity had yielded purple crystalline flowers.

I filled the Land Rover with this loot (under the approving eyes of the villagers and the baleful eye of Mr. Harrison, who was, in many matters, more fastidious than he needed to be). Lovely, like Lady Christmas, to give the things away. ("Look like purple plantar warts," said a man who had made my going to bed with him a two-year project. . . . He disliked me.)

There is a banyan tree in southern India that covers three acres. Its branches drop shoots to the ground, and these take root and support the parent branches. One tree is a forest: children play hide and seek among its trunks and branches (there is no distinguishable difference between trunk and branch). Conceivably one tree can go on and on forever. The mother tree of this banyan is dead; I see a metaphor in this: life goes on. And on. And it is folly to try to separate what is dead from what is alive in the soul — the past and the present meld; the past is understood by the works of the present; and the present by the works of the past. I feel united to history when I touch the Indian things I possess — my own history, and that of the subcontinent, which I love. Collecting unites the past with the present as the branches of the banyan tree commune with the root. The leaves know what the branches know and the roots know what the sap and the branches know. . . . And collecting is like this — the past and the present unite in one object, and all is seen and known; the object becomes the vehicle through which one communes with the past and interprets the present.

> *Collecting is a world habit. Collectors practise it consciously and with a definite, recognized aim. The rest of us practise it more or less unconsciously.*
>
> — Arnold Bennett

Jeffrey Dahmer was a collector.

Polygamists are collectors. Womanizers are collectors (and invariably melancholy). We live in units — in tribes and clans and families, and city-states and nations — that are collections of individuals — because we feel safer together than alone. The earliest material collected was food. The hunger of a womanizer, who collects women as automatically as plants and animals collect food, is never satisfied; he never achieves satiety — "how beautiful they all are," said the nicest womanizer I know; we were seated at a window table in a restaurant and the girls in their summer dresses were passing by and he didn't even know he'd said it, sweet sad man — and that's why they are melancholy. His hunger is always renewed, his security always threatened. The femme fatale is a collector who is in turn collected. . . . Once one man deems her necessary for the survival of his notable pleasure, she seems necessary for the survival of all members of the tribe, she facilitates a primitive male bonding, she herself almost always experiences a surprising loneliness.

The dead are gathered together and buried in cemeteries so that they and their survivors do not have the despair of loneliness.

God destroyed the Tower of Babel and confounded man's language to reproach us for believing that loneliness could ever be assuaged without Him, and for thinking that a collection of individuals could order society and achieve security without reference and deference to Him.

About an hour's drive east of Tripoli, there is an ancient Roman city, founded by the Phoenicians, on the sea — a ghost town, in the 1960s, when I lived in Libya, untouristed. Imagine being unhappily married and walking through room after ruined room paved with splendid and witty mosaics veiled with a thin layer of fine gritty sand (and listening to the commiseration of the sea, the manic howling of the hot dry *ghibli* winds). Serpents and winged horses. I wanted — it would have been very easy — to plunder, to pick up and hold in my hand and own one bit of ancient Rome. King Idris wouldn't have minded; the Italian ambassador — who led me once, through tunnels of sand, to the excavation site of a colosseum on the seashore — would have been disapproving but understanding in that tolerant Italian way (a shrug). No one need have known. Mr. Harrison wouldn't let me do it, of course. I have forgotten what the mosaics look like now; I consigned them to forgetfulness when I was denied ownership. (And does Qaddafi care about them now, I wonder.) The city was untouristed but not unpopulated. I was never alone, I walked in the company of ghosts. The objects were possessed. No one would have minded; and I would have owned Rome.

There is a collector, a novelist, who understands the mystical connection that unites the collector with the object and the past, the fetishistic, animistic elements of collecting; her name is Susanna Moore (I read about her in the *Times*). She grew up in Hawaii, and her avidity was inspired by photographs of plantation workers sent to relatives and marriage brokers in Japan. She started to collect black-and-white stills taken by the newspaper photographer Weegee. She collected hair ornaments ("jade hairpins and the quivering gold wands decorated with knobs of carnelian peacock feathers worn by concubines") and textiles ("Tahitian pareus from the 1940s, black lace mantillas from the Philippines, the size of bed sheets, and silk and brocade obis") that she "found in curio shops on disreputable streets in downtown Honolulu." She collects shoes — "turquoise silk slippers from the court of the last Empress of China, Ci Xi, bought from a profligate cousin of Chiang Kai-shek, . . . 19th-century red Chinese shoes embroidered with the forbidden stitch, their half-inch soles made from 22 layers of un-bleached linen" (the forbidden stitch and 22 layers of unbleached linen make my heart beat faster) . . . 1990 Manolo Blahnik clear plastic mules covered in pastel seashells — "mules possessed of a gold heel that is so elegant, so disdainful that it can only be called withering." She calls these things her totems; and she says her intention was "never to honor their esthetic value but to make an ordered whole out of a confluence of details. A collection is imbued with information about the collector — information that, I suspect, is the very purpose of the display."

(We tempt people to read us, we invite them to consider our objects so we see ourselves reflected in their eyes; this is a test — it says something about them; and it proves our worth to us.)

"Within its own systematic universe, a collection represents the not-unhappy conflict between past and present," Susanna Moore says; "and the collector is given the chance to incorporate himself into that universe. . . . He is obliged to participate in the game of history." In fact, collecting makes history — the accumulated sorrow of the world — bearable.

One tends to think of collecting as a means of preserving; Moore suggests that collecting may also be a form of nihilism: "Nothing is really beautiful except that which is good for nothing." Her love of adornments and shoes derives from their ultimate valuelessness (she is pleased to have a friend, a heterosexual man, who likes to try on high heels with their seductive "swan of an arch," and in particular black-and-white satin evening sandals copied from a pair made for Marilyn Monroe). "It is that very valuelessness that I prize — once used they are lessened in value." Collecting is "an extremely specific, extremely subjective gesture that is so eccentrically individualistic, so embedded in the unconscious as to be almost irrational."

I love her musings so much more — it isn't a question of agreeing or disagreeing — than the rigid "psychological perspectives" of Werner Muensterberger, who, in *Collecting: An Unruly Passion*, says that "an object . . . is meant to undo the trauma of aloneness when the infant discovers mother's absence," and that collecting is "a tendency which derives from a not immediately discernible sense memory of deprivation or loss or vulnerability and a subsequent longing for substitution, closely allied with moodiness and depressive leanings." Yes, well, but so what? Aren't we all a bit wacky, after all? I'll give Muensterberger this, though: I have never once gone to a garage sale or an antiques show and not heard someone talk about her mother's attic. . . . To say that collecting "reduces . . . the tension between id and ego" and to babble about "phallic-narcissistic" personalities does nothing for me. "The reason [collectors] themselves give for their infatuation, their taste, and their personal preferences are, needless to say, subjective, and, considering the unavoidable self-consciousness of collectors I have interviewed, I tend to question the validity of the various conscious explanations they give in this regard." Fiddle-de-dee. Bunkum and arrogance. Muensterberger tediously compares the relic or cherished object to an infant's comforter or a toy dog — "a technical device for those in need of tangible support [in] existential crises." There may be truth in the coldness and sterility of his arguments, but I so much prefer the reason John Steinbeck gave for collecting: "I guess the truth is that I simply like junk."

Collecting, Susanna Moore says, "is information made intimate." That is because there are no inanimate objects; nothing that tells a story can be said to be inanimate. Here is a fabulous story, by way of Calvino, that Marco Polo tells to Kublai Khan:

"'Your chessboard, sire, is inlaid with two woods: ebony and maple. The square on which your enlightened gaze is fixed was cut from the ring of a trunk that grew in a year of drought: you see how its fibers are arranged? Here a barely hinted knot can be made out: a bud tried to burgeon on a premature spring day, but the night's frost forced it to desist. . . .

"'Here is a thicker pore: perhaps it was a larvum's nest; not a wood-worm, because, once born, it would have begun to dig, but a caterpillar that gnawed the leaves and was the cause of the tree's being chosen for chopping down.'

"The quantity of things that could be read in a little piece of smooth and empty wood overwhelmed Kublai; Polo was already talking about ebony forests, about rafts laden with logs that come down the rivers, of docks, of women at the windows. . . ." And we feel a whole new story is about to begin: "Women at the Windows."

One hears it said that *things* do not bring happiness; in fact they do. I have an Indian telephone from the 1940s in my living room; when my American-made phones have gone silent after I hang up, this extension gives a sharp little *ping!* and this gives me an instant of complete gratification, and warmth. That little sound encapsulates all of India for me (a cosmos in a microcosm).

When my mother entered the hospital to die, I rooted around in her maniacally tidy closets (my mother wrapped her garbage so as "to make the garbageman's job nicer, dear") and came away with eight frosted highball glasses, green gazelles leaping over tall marsh grass. I didn't need to be told that what I was doing wasn't nice. When the predictably meager spoils were divided after she died, I went straight for the bureau that doubled as a desk in her terrifyingly clean three-room apartment. (Just weeks before, she'd been on her knees, under the kitchen table, wiping the floor around our gathered feet with a washrag before we'd even finished dinner.) But nothing she'd ever written, and nothing that had ever been written to her, remained. For forty years she had read nothing but religious literature, read it and underlined it with a soft red pencil and a ruler; and all of that was gone, too. Think of the riddles I might have been able to solve. My daughter took a plastic orange drinking container with a green straw that my mother — whom Anna loved — bought for Anna when she was a baby to drink her orange juice from. (Anna found this fifty-cent container witty and enchanting, associations with my mother — whom Anna loved — aside.)

A man I have held in my heart for many years had a stroke; and he remembered my name. I flew to London to be with him. I spent the hours I was away from him in a kind of frenzied drift through London's markets; my desire attached itself to two Clarice Cliff candlesticks that I could not afford and that I bought. His beauty, for which he had been famous and adored — beauty that I had hungered to be the proprietary owner of, beauty that seemed so identical to virtue as to rule out the possibility of evil happenstance — was ravaged. Imagine! so many years of love, more on my side than on his (he says: *different* on your side), and so many years of deadly jousting and high-wire verbal acrobatics, and also prayer; and it was I he remembered and I he called after he was released from the hospital. (I was in San Francisco when he called; and when I collected my phone calls I could not understand the bleat that was Salim saying his name and calling mine.) I bought two Clarice Cliff candlesticks that I could not afford because I felt rich (richly rewarded) and I felt sad. His flesh had changed; even his kiss had changed, it was flaccid now.

At Swaine & Adeney, Her Majesty's whip and leather makers, the Queen Mother's umbrella makers (185 Piccadilly), "Listen, madam, hear it rustle, listen, hear it rustle," Mr. Johnson says. Sibilant and reverent, Mr. Johnson of Swaine & Adeney opens and closes a black silk taffeta umbrella, hand stitched, with a rosewood handle (£500); he caresses umbrellas with ostrich handles and umbrellas with pigskin handles, umbrellas with crocodile handles and snakeskin handles, umbrellas of Malacca, birch, and ash, and one umbrella ("The King's Umbrella") with bands of gold and silver and the royal insignia, and a handle of ivory ("*Indian* ivory," Mr. Johnson says; he is beautifully precise) that sells for £1,000. But I want a walking stick for our walks — Salim's and mine — in Queensgate Gardens in southwest Ken. He shows me one with a handle of Indian *bidri* work — silver set into a black alloy metal (£1,240 alas); and one made of apple wood from a two-hundred-year-old tree felled in the hurricane of 1987; and ivory walking sticks and sticks with pugs' faces on their handles, and sticks of silver and bone, sticks that sheathe daggers and sticks hollowed out to contain spirits of the drinkable kind. I buy a stick of light wood with a carved wooden serpent twisted about it in relief, and zigzag geometric carving near the handle, which is silver and floral (£90). What I think about this stick is that it once belonged to a witch doctor and that a Victorian gentleman attached the silver handle. (All Mr. Johnson can tell me is that it comes from West Africa; he wanted me to buy the stick of English apple wood, which was for him the epitome of romance.)

I lost that stick in a cab in Rome — when I used it to flag down cabs my daughter called me the Dowager, she did not approve; I left it somewhere near the Piazza del Popolo.

I have never seriously considered collecting walking sticks, though I feel bereft when I think of my lovely snaky one.

King Tutankhamen was a collector of walking sticks and staves, which went with him into the antechamber and the burial chamber of his tomb.

(I never saw much to love in Egyptian art, its monumentality and humorlessness exhausted me; but to learn that in King Tut's tomb was a toy chest containing samples of minerals that he'd evidently gathered — as kids everywhere, in a less dreadful time than ours, did — humanizes him for me, it scales him down.)

When I left Jazzman (or he left me; it comes to the same thing, and our life together has been a series of departures), I bought a Clarice Cliff vase that I could not afford. I bought it because I felt impoverished . . . salvage from the ruins.

My three-tiered candlesticks and my vase are part of a line of Clarice Cliff's pottery produced in 1929 called Inspiration, which had what she called Egyptian Scarab Blue glazes (made with raw oxides of copper, cobalt, and iron). On a field of mottled turquoise, there are, in abstract fluid forms, cobalt blues, Persian blues, Prussian blues, gray and white and aqua and streaky mauve. The vase, fourteen inches high, and the three-and-a-half-inch candle holders visually anchor one part of my long and narrow living room (which looks to me, in my most self-censuring moods, like a waiting room in a bus station). There is a handwritten mark on the vase and on the candlesticks; and after I learned that the writing on the Inspiration line was nearly always that of a young woman called Ellen Browne I loved them even more — I saw the hand of the maker. Cliff called her work "bizarre" and called her workers the Bizarre Girls. In *The Bizarre Affair* (a book by Leonard Griffin, Louis K. Meisel, and Susan Pear Meisel), there are pictures of young women working at the pottery, shoulder to shoulder, smiling, their hair shining; they have old-fashioned names like Ivy and Sadie and Elsie and Lily and Winnie.

I first came upon Cliff's pottery in an otherwise prosaic shop on Fulham Road ten years before her canonization at a Christie's auction in 1983. I felt the thrilling reward of a race I hadn't known I'd entered: in the dim shop her pottery shone like jewels in Aladdin's cave.

Cliff's girls produced sugar sifters; salt and pepper shakers; vases; teapots; jugs; hexagonal, octagonal, conical, tiered, globe-shaped candlesticks, cookie jars, plates, bowls and honey pots; flower pots decorated with red-roofed houses like a child's first drawing of a house. Her pieces were painted with cypresses like black fire; yearning lilac trees with jet-black trunks; black-and-green tree trunks as sinuous as cobras; trees with globby orange leaves (like cotton candy or balloons); good-natured shapes with painted forms that resemble melted ice cream; feminine and conventional-looking cherries and nasturtiums painted on a tea set the design of which was radically geometric — triangular handles and spouts and feet. Fluid color patterns within a rigid geometric shape. The working-class Cliff, who designed for the market (and consequently produced her share of instant kitsch), made strong, assured cubist glazed ceramics that were whimsically but accurately decorated (in harmony with fairy tales and dreams) with Hansel and Gretel cottages (one window, orange smoke); Japanese-inspired sweet bridges and pagodas; delphiniums, crocuses — English flowers as seen in a distinctly non-English dream; masks (which she called wall medallions), screechy and grotesque, savage, ugly (but then I have never seen a mask I liked).

There are collectors to whom it would be thrilling to have one of every pattern and shape Cliff — who considered herself a commercial artist — designed; I don't collect this way (and would therefore, by a purist, be disdained). I love the Cliffs I have because they are beautiful; nothing in the world could convince me to buy a mask, or a teacup that felt awkward in my hand.

For a while I collected American art pottery — the shapes pleased me, and the colors; and it was at the time cheap (and I was poor). There is an art potter much admired now, as he was in his lifetime, called George Ohr. (He posted this belligerent sign outside his works: "the Greatest Potter on earth 'you' prove the contrary" [sic].) Nothing in the world could convince me to buy the souvenirs he sold at fairs in the early 1900s: miniature chamber pots filled with ceramic turds.

Cliff had a line called Limberlost, from the book *Girl of the Limberlost*, which I bought, when I was ten or twelve, in a five-and-dime. (I was simultaneously reading *War and Peace*, which I have never, I say without pride, read again.) In *Girl of the Limberlost* an embittered mother, in an unaccustomed demonstration of natural affection, starts to brush her daughter's hair . . . but when the hair clings electrically to her skin she drops the brush as if she were burned, leaving the girl of the Limberlost to wonder wherein lay her sin. (This is the only part of the book I remember.)

My mother, who slept in my bedroom in one of the twin maple beds, could not bear to touch my flesh. . . . Isn't it strange how objects and books call to one? . . . In dreams she holds me in a terrible embrace.

Musings on the Industrial Revolution from the mythical city of Leonia, which accretes: "You begin to wonder if Leonia's true passion is really, as they say, the enjoyment of new and different things, and not, instead, the joy of expelling, discarding, cleansing itself of a recurrent impurity. . . .

"This is the result: the more Leonia expels goods, the more it accumulates them; the scales of its past are soldered into a cuirass that cannot be removed. As the city is renewed each day, it preserves all of itself in its only definitive form: yesterday's sweepings piled up on the sweepings of the day before yesterday and all its days and years and decades. . . . Perhaps the whole world, beyond Leonia's boundaries, is covered by craters of rubbish, each surrounding a metropolis in constant eruption. The boundaries between the alien, hostile cities are infected ramparts where the detritus of both support each other, overlap, mingle" (Italo Calvino, *Invisible Cities*).

The apartment we moved to after we left the unexplored basement-cave of Washington Avenue was blocks away from a barnlike Salvation Army shop, where women poorer than I from across the urban divide of the Gowanus Canal searched, among the heterogeneous smells and dander of other people's discarded garments, for usable clothes. It was dark and very cool in there, as treasure houses should be; and, as an anodyne to restlessness (and to fill up the empty places), I went there, first in a dilatory way and then more and more often and more and more purposefully, as I found objects that might have come from my own childhood, and objects so exotic they might have come from another planet. It soothed and excited me, I was on a dig. (I never found any of my brownstone-renovating neighbors dallying there; I never found any of my Italian-American neighbors there — they would just as soon have rummaged through the city dump.) In this cornucopia, I found Depression glass, a Stickley desk, a jelly pantry. (When I'd stripped the layers and layers of paint, I found, under layers and layers of old newspaper, slips of paper on pine shelves in spidery faded lavender handwriting: "peach preserves, 1798." I felt overwhelming affection — the kind one feels for an unselfconscious animal — for the cupboard, a shrine to life that could never be lost so long as someone was alive to love it.)

In the Salvation Army I found the pacifying distraction I'd found in the bazaars of Tripoli, where, under grape arbors in narrow alleys and amidst sun-dappled whitewashed walls and Tuareg rugs and cups of sweet tea, I understood that to enter the labyrinth of things is to suspend disbelief in the world's goodness; when the world is alive with things that layers and layers of experience have gathered around, sadness and bounty may coexist.

> *The difference between the factory hand and the craftsman is that the craftsman lives to do the work he loves; but the factory hand lives by doing the work he despises. . . . The characteristic common to God and man is . . . the desire and the ability to make things. . . . Between the mind of the maker and the Mind of the Maker [there is] a difference, not of category, but only of degree.*
>
> — Dorothy L. Sayers, *The Whimsical Christian*

Collecting is like sex; satisfaction renews and creates new appetites.

From the Salvation Army I moved to flea markets and antiques exhibits — sideshows of things and people (if I ever went to a spring or autumn exhibit at the three piers on the East River in New York without seeing the turbaned woman — who is perhaps a man — dressed in layers of white chenille and heavy makeup and fifties costume jewelry, I would feel cheated and deprived of luck).

My last great find is a vaguely ecclesiastical-looking runner of linen and silk, its fringed ends bordered with block-printed vegetable-dyed tawny and sage-green stylized flowers outlined in raised stitches of yellow silk. The happiness an object like this inspires (the tiny knots in the stitches on the underside are living things) could not possibly be derived from a machine-made thing.

"Any decoration is futile if it does not remind you of something beyond itself, craftsmanship involving not only the mastery of technique, but the evocation of the spiritual qualities of breadth, imagination, and order," wrote William Morris, who deplored the "masses of sordidness, filth and squalor," the "pompous and vulgar hideousness" of the Industrial Revolution ("Shoddy is king"). Like his near contemporary Dorothy L. Sayers, Morris, the great and prolix designer of the Arts and Crafts movement (paintings, tiles, tapestries, carpets, stained glass, wallpaper, books, furniture), honored and drew his inspiration from the severity, honesty, and integrity of the craftsmanship of the Middle Ages, which Bachelard called the "great age of solitary patience [which] we have only to imagine . . . for our souls to be bathed in peace."

Morris's wall hangings were embroidered by his wife, Jane (a Pre-Raphaelite beauty with whom Rossetti was madly in love); Morris taught her medieval techniques that he had learned by unpicking the stitches of medieval cloth, no mean task but a humble one.

The sage green of my runner is the color of the velvet medieval gowns the women of the Pre-Raphaelite circle wore. The runner provides me with fantasy; and — "my work is the embodiment of dreams in one form or another," Morris said — it is the stuff of dreams . . . once someone else's dreams, now my dreams (there are no inanimate objects).

> *It was once the custom for kings and citizens of high estate to make dedicatory and votive offerings to the gods — statues, vases, jewels, or symbolic objects of various sorts. Once made, the offerings became holy in themselves and were never destroyed.*
>
> — Douglas and Elizabeth Rigby, *Lock, Stock, and Barrel*

On my runner is a vase, 13½ inches tall, at its most bulbous 17½ inches in circumference, and at its most narrow 2¼ inches in circumference; its long and narrow (swanlike) neck widens slightly before it culminates in a 3½-inch circular flat lip. It would be impossible for this elegant object to share space with another object; it must, like the ark of the covenant, exist in splendid isolation. It is of a color that used to be called *eau de Nil;* and at its base there is an elliptical puddle of darker, denser green. It is like the grapes in certain fourteenth-century Italian still lifes: light seems to shine through it and from it. Sometimes it appears to be crystalline, and sometimes satin, and sometimes smoky. It gives and receives light. It fades sometimes to a numinous gentle gray; and sometimes it turns into a fresh, almost electric green. It can do no wrong. My virtuous vase. . . . "The work becomes daemonic and through it the collector feels that he stands face to face with the artist himself."

Marie Antoinette collected goldsmiths' work of the Italian Renaissance and Chinese peach-bloom porcelain, the very name of which is exquisite and could make one love her.

I cannot resist peaches, or, indeed, anything with the word *peach* in it. At Balducci's I found a funny peach, round and flat with a depression in the middle (a navel), which came to two rounded points (its flesh was ivory). What kind of peach is this? I asked. A *donna* peach (a *lady* peach), the greengrocer answered (in fact it looked like the reproductive organs of a small, happy animal). How adorable the Italians are, I thought, anthropomorphizing food. In fact he had said *donought*, not *donna* — and indeed the peach, which was a peento peach, did resemble a donought.

The day after I saw the peach for the first time, I read about it in the *New York Times.* (This is what I mean about things coming to you if you want them enough, one has only to be patient and to believe in synchronicity.) It was said to be the descendant of a Chinese peach, brought to England by way of Java, and to America by way of a Georgian.

In *The Leopard*, the Prince enters a Sicilian garden; he pauses, gazes, remembers, regrets: "A vigorous smiling Neptune was embracing a willing Amphitrite; her navel, wet with spray and gleaming in the sun, would be the nest, shortly, for hidden kisses in subaqueous shade." He visits the garden — from which "emanated a promise of pleasure that would never turn to pain" — expressly to see "the foreign peaches . . . big, velvety, luscious-looking; yellowish, with a faint flush of rosy pinks on the cheeks, like those of Chinese girls." ("The Prince gave them a gentle squeeze with his delicate fleshy fingers. 'They seem quite ripe,'" he says, his knowledge coming from long experience.)

At the time of my divorce it fell to me to divide the household goods; this proved to be a clever move on Mr. Harrison's part — I allotted to him the Chinese bronze teapot that would have secured my financial future, right or wrong having nothing to do, so far as the constitution of my character is concerned, with guilt or the absence thereof.

On the morning after my (one) adulterous night in India, the man with whom I shared a bed (he of the plantar warts) sent my husband a box of duty-free Scotch; this, presumably, was my price. . . . The trader rat always leaves something in place of the objects he appropriates ("he has been known to exchange toadstools for a bunch of silver spoons, a rabbit's skull for a kitchen clock"). This characteristic has variously been described as a "carrying mania" and a "moral sense."

I bought a pink Lalique brooch in New Harmony, the nineteenth-century secular Utopia in Posey County, Indiana, that Texas oil heiress Jane Blaffer Owen was trying to refurbish and revivify. (Her husband's forebear, Welsh-born Robert Owen, had established it.) The lady in the artsy shop who sold it to me for $8 said it looked to her like a frog. The night I bought it I slept on fine creamy linens in a serpentine-poster bed. Vases of apricot- and peach-colored roses cast refined reflections on oiled and polished surfaces. A Mantegna oil of the Crucifixion hung above my bed. The uncovered windows looked out onto a walled garden in which everything that bloomed was white; in the moonlight the birch trees' silvery glow illuminated my tidy parlor, and I ate the pear preserves Jane Blaffer Owen made with my fingers as I regarded the Crucifixion; I submerged myself in the lazy leisure I suspect God of enjoying when he is not regarding us.

> *This — all this — was in the olden*
> *Time long ago.*
> — Edgar Allan Poe

Henry James loved things. He was unable to compose on any machine other than his Remington typewriter.

. . . In the cellar we had a typewriter belonging to Theodore Roosevelt, and a sword belonging to him too. My grandfather was said to be a mercenary. I do not know which of these facts is true, or where any of these things is now. We had a ladder, in the country house, that Bruno Hauptmann, the kidnapper of the Lindbergh baby, built. My grandfather was his friend. This is true. The ladder inspired me with visceral and intellectual revulsion. . . . We had a pearl-handled revolver, too. . . .

James's Isabel Gardner leaned against the stones of the Pantheon and "envied the security of valuable 'pieces' which change by no hair's breadth, only grow in value, while their owners lose inch by inch youth, happiness, beauty." One needs to place oneself in familiar and sincere relation to enduring time. . . . The first time I saw the Aurelian Wall in Rome I felt a kind of vertigo, a compulsion to touch it. . . . When I touch my cool, pale blue settlement vase I feel kinship with the woman (the girl) who made it, an immigrant, or a sanitarium patient.

So many of James's characters reveal themselves in relation to *things*. Here is poor Mr. Rosier, who loves with all his heart Isabel's pretty little convent-bred stepdaughter, Pansy Osmond, a sweet nosegay of a girl without a flaw in her composition, "admirably finished . . . really a consummate piece. He thought of her in amorous meditation a good deal as he might have thought of a Dresden-china shepherdess. Miss Osmond, indeed, in the bloom of her juvenility, had a hint of the rococo which Rosier, whose taste was predominantly for that manner, could not fail to appreciate. . . . 'I love my things,'" says Mr. Rosier — his little bits of Louis Quatorze, his simple and pretty faience, as simple and pretty as Pansy, passive, docile, limited, dear, a rosebud who "ought never to wear anything but muslin" — but "I care more for Miss Osmond than for all the *bibelots in Europe!*" he cries.

Poor limited Rosier, of whom Isabel says, "he has about the extent of one's pocket-handkerchief — the small ones with lace borders," is admirably suited to Pansy; kind and honest and innocent in his affections, his appreciation for the unspoiled girl is "based partly on his eye for decorative character, his instinct for authenticity; but also on a sense for uncatalogued values, for that secret of a 'lustre' beyond any recorded losing or rediscovering, which his devotion to brittle wares had still not disqualified him to recognize."

Alas, Rosier's bits and pieces are despised by Gilbert Osmond: "I don't care a fig for Capo di Monte! . . . old pots and plates." Gilbert has the real thing: his daughter, Pansy.

Mr. Rosier, with the tremulous optimism of the simple-hearted, sells all his bibelots at auction for $50,000. "I couldn't stop for the sale; I couldn't have seen them going off; I think it would have killed me. . . . I should tell you," he informs Isabel, "I have kept my enamels. Now I have the money in my pocket, and [Gilbert] can't say I'm poor?"

Gilbert can say he is a fool. . . . And we are left to imagine what Rosier, without his sweet Pansy, will become, how brittle, and how, without the humanizing beauty of her exquisite, lustrous flesh and blood, effete.

In December of 1939, loot from the estate of William Randolph Hearst was sold at Marshall Field's in Chicago, and in a St. Louis department store, and in a Seattle department store. In 1941 the larger share of his possessions — everything from tiny carved cats alleged to have belonged to Cleopatra to paneled European rooms, *objets d'art* and hallowed junk — was installed in Gimbel's (where objects started for sale at 35 cents) and at Saks Fifth Avenue.

Saks sent out 100,000 engraved invitations, to foreign ambassadors and to charge-account customers; the sale, which was promoted as if it were a rare and novel (chichi) art event, was less than highly successful. Gimbel's, which in its greater wisdom turned its sale into a populist circus and employed conventional merchandising methods, did very well: customers were encouraged to avail themselves of Gimbel's Easy Payment Plan for purchases of $23 and over — "just as we should if you bought a refrigerator."

"Gimbel's is selling acres of art to museums and millionaires — but Gimbel's is also selling acres of art to Flatbush, Montclair, Peoria, and points west. . . . You don't have to be the Countess G. to cherish an exquisite little Ch'ien-lung jade Kuan-Yin. . . . You can live in Flatbush and love Reynolds. You can live in Montclair and worship Ingres. . . . You can ride the 7th avenue subway and carry home a pair of dainty earrings that belonged to Martha Washington.

"We're a plain store for plain people. We don't have any chi-chi, we don't have any frozen-faced footmen. Plain ordinary people want waterless cookers, window ventilators, new hats. We have them. Plain, ordinary people love hand-blown early Jersey glass, old wrought iron, portraits by Gainsborough, rooms from the Duke of Hamilton's palace, 17th century Dutch flower tiles. We have them. It's all as simple as that. . . .

"Have you always wanted an ancestral portrait? We have some. . . . Do you want to touch, every day of your life, a silky satinwood table that Hepplewhite made? We have it."

Turner watercolors were priced from $6.75 to $298.50. A del Sarto sold for $7,980. It is said that one Mrs. Klotz of the Bronx requested "a Benvenuto Cellini bowl to go with a blue dining room."

Who wouldn't want to touch a silky satinwood table that bore the mark of the maker?

What brilliant marketing — to compare a waterless cooker to a Gainsborough and to put both in the realm of possibility and necessity.

I think this demotic fairy tale, which really happened, is more romantic than "Rosebud."

For my thirtieth birthday a courtier of the Nizam of Hyderabad gave me a string of carved, unpolished Mogul emeralds. Nobody knows what they are — what treasure they are — when I wear them. I know.

I have a silver Victorian reliquary that I wear around my neck together with a silver cross and a graceful gold image of the Madonna, lilies in her arms and under her innocent feet. I bought the reliquary, which has a stylized art nouveau cross on it, after I was very nearly struck by a car. I popped into the nearest antiques shop, and (how is it possible to believe in accidents?) my friend the dealer handed me this lacy pendant, which I bought. Something is inside it, a shadowy presence dimly visible through silver lace. It would have to be taken apart for me to see what is inside, and that would destroy it. A jeweler held his glass to it and said it was an angel, with clearly articulated wings and lovely (his word) wavy hair. Detail increases an object's stature, as the *Dictionary of Christian Botany* remarks of the periwinkle.

I gave my lover a gold chain and a cross made by the sculptor Germano, which I bought in Florence. I clasped it around his neck, my naked breasts against his naked satin-smooth back. Don't take it off, I said, heart in my throat (giving it to him meant: I love you forever, there is no turning back). Never in this life, he said. But he has taken it off, he put it around his granddaughter's neck in a moment that combined flamboyance with generosity toward her and a perverse wish to hurt me and to separate himself from me and to be seen to separate himself from me; and, responding with a miserable pettiness to his betrayal, which sprang from his fear, I demanded it back, for which I hate myself. Bartering with Christ.

> *Granary, bin and cellar are village prototypes of library, archive, museum, and vault.*
>
> — Lewis Mumford

In seventeenth-century France, the words *cabinet, closet,* and *museum* were used for the room in which a collection was displayed, or for the collection itself. (Museums are curio cabinets, some — like the Victoria and Albert — more than others.)

In the Imperial Library in Vienna, large birds — pelicans — were trained to pluck books from the upper shelves (are you giddy with delight?).

I actually like hodgepodgy museums, museums where things are jumbled and not discretely organized and where apparently unrelated objects — swords, carved thimbles, desiccated frogs, jade figurines, snake skins, musical instruments — are gathered capriciously; these museums (which exist in backwater cities of Third World countries) force the mind to unify and tidy and classify all by itself, without the assistance of a curator.

The mind is a curio cabinet made up of cubicles in which there are rare and lovely things and unnatural things, flowers and monsters and moss and voluptuous ruins, pearls of great price, stuff and ideas and colored experiences and animate notions.

Touch them.

Items gathered in one place give us the illusion, and sometimes the actuality, of security. Vision is a search and an embrace. We find things and things find us. "Classification is," for the Rigbys, "nothing more nor less than a tool for creating order, a means for arriving at valid interpretations."

(The urge to tidy the world is what leads people to interpret experience by means of a puerile and artificial division of generations — baby boomers and generation X; and "the sixties," "the seventies," "the eighties," "the nineties" — as if each were a totally discrete entity, which it is not.)

I used sometimes to watch Untouchable ragpickers near the train tracks of Secunderabad. From piles and piles of colored cloth some hanks would be rejected, some selected — and for the life of me I could see no discernible principle at work. It was like a game of chess where pieces were moved about at random. We don't know why a little boy picks up certain items from the gutter and discards others; we only know he does. We don't know why, on the seashore, we discard certain shells and keep others — the logic of the moment eludes us; we only know that we do. The mind's propensity to discriminate and organize and define and choose will not be denied, no matter how unpromising the raw material.

(Untouchables are now called *harijans*, children of God. The caste system is another way, far less benign than collecting, of organizing the world.)

For the purpose of establishing form, order, and hierarchies of value, a list will do as well as a collection. In fact some lists are themselves worthy of collection:

Michele Gaillard de Longjumeau, the wife of Florimond Robertet, minister of finance under Charles VIII, Louis XII, and Francis I, is revered for having compiled a catalogue of the couple's "paintings, bronzes, marbles, ivories and alabasters, the Chinese porcelains, goldsmiths' work, silverware and jewelry, the tapestries, Venetian glass, French faience, Italian, German, Flemish, English and Spanish pottery, church ornaments and books." This was not an inventory but "a little masterpiece, drawn up lovingly, giving details of the provenance, use, form, location and associations of most of the items, taking one into the Robertet family circle, showing a couple of lovers and amateurs."

The lady's catalogue was a kind of autobiography: ". . . twenty-three rings on a little gold chain, in each one of which there is a diamond worth two or three hundred francs. Their number is that of the years of my marriage, and I have taken pleasure in collecting them so that every time I look into my cabinet I may be reminded how long I enjoyed happiness."

To bring order into my life I make grocery lists and Filofax to-do lists (I lose them); and I once made lists of Reasons to Divorce or Not to Divorce Mr. Harrison, a device that enabled me to pretend that chaos could be forced to give birth to order.

(On the other hand, when I make columnar lists of the Good Points and the Bad Points of the man I love, items have a tendency to snake, apparently of their own will, across to the opposite column — Good so often masquerading as Bad and vice versa, I wonder at my own absurdity.)

I collect lists.

In the seventeenth century, John Tradescant classified and catalogued his garden, all the shell creatures, insects, minerals, "outlandish-Fruits and the like," therein; "Utensils, a catalogue of his Benefactors as well as an enumeration of his Plants, Shrubs and Trees both in English and in Latin"; he also classified and catalogued events and relics: "Blood that rained in the Isle of Wight, attested by Sir. J. Oglander; . . . Henry the 8 his Stirrups, Haukes-hoods, gloves." In his possession was "An Umbrella" — the only one in seventeenth-century England; a stone circumcision knife; and a "Brazen-bull to warm the Nunnes hands; Casava Bread, 2 sorts; Divers sorts of Ambers with Flyes, Spiders, natural; A Dodo Bird; A Bird sitting on a pearch naturall; Divers things cut on Plum-stones; Chirugeons Instruments framed upon the points of needles; Half a Hasle-nut with 70 pieces of houshold stuffe in it."

Sir Edwin Lutyens, the architect of New Delhi, collected jokes and counted among his list of "pet hates," we are told in *Madame Blavatsky's Baboon*, "long-stemmed glasses, fish-knives, cut flowers, silk lampshades, pile carpets, the seaside, statistics, painted nails, the diagonal placing of furniture — and . . . religious enthusiasm."

In the nineteenth century the young and gluttonous Sultan Moulay Abd el Aziz of Morocco collected (without understanding the madness of his heterogeneous enthusiasms and his undiscriminating infatuation with the West) "gramophones, toy railways, typewriters, musical stuffed birds and a great host of clockwork toys, ... miniature rifle ranges, balloons and fireworks, [and] even though there was no road in all Morocco, a scarlet state coach . . . from London." A billiard table reached him on the back of a camel (while his people starved). "A British bulldog with false teeth" was sold to him for $40,000 by an American crook; a motorboat "occupied a room to itself in the palace and was tended by a German engineer, though there was never any suggestion of the vessel putting to sea. . . . Grand pianos and kitchen-ranges; automobiles and immense cases of corsets; wild animals in cages, and boxes of strange theatrical uniforms; barrel-organs and han-som-cabs; a passenger lift capable of rising to dizzy altitudes, destined for a one-storied palace; false hair; cameras of gold and of silver with jeweled buttons; carved marble lions and living macaw parrots; jewels, real and false; steam-launches and fireworks; ladies' underclothing from Paris, and saddlery from Mexico; trees for gardens that were never planted, or, if planted, were never watered; printing-presses and fire-balloons — an infinity of all that was grotesque, useless, and in bad taste" — all these were seriously described, by the British press, as "evidences of Christian civilization at Fez" (Gavin Maxwell, *Lords of the Atlas*).

I am perhaps overly fond of this list, which, in the service of a presumed higher cause, unites things that to the unindoctrinated eye have no bearing one upon the other; it is offered, in a book called *Thy Kingdom Come*, published in 1874, to establish proof that in our time the world will end: "Discoveries and inventions, etc., pave the way to the coming Millennium . . . , making ready the mechanical devices which will economize labor, and provide the world in general with time and conveniences [which will ultimately] result in the uprising of the masses and the overthrow of corporative Trusts. . . . 'Seal the book, even to the time of the end: many shall run to and fro. . . .' The predicted running to and fro — much rapid travelling — also confirms [the end], steamboat, steam-car, telegraphy . . . all belong to the Time of the End. . . . Today thousands of mammoth cars and steamships are carrying multitudes hither and thither, 'to and fro.'" Class warfare and steam engines=the time of the end; our search to impose meaning on disparate phenomena is silly and sad.

And here is the most beautiful of lists, Gerard Manley Hopkins's:

> Glory be to God for dappled things —
>   For skies of couple-colour as a brinded cow;
>   For rose-moles all in stipple upon trout that swim;
> Fresh-firecoal chestnut-falls; finches' wings;
>   Landscape plotted and pieced — fold, fallow, and plough;
>   And áll trádes, their gear and tackle and trim.
> All things counter, original, spare, strange;
>   Whatever is fickle, freckled (who knows how?)
>   With swift, slow; sweet, sour; adazzle, dim;
> He fathers-forth whose beauty is past change:
>   Praise him.

Every Saturday in the cold walled town of Arezzo, old gynecological instruments — not unlike torture instruments — are put up for sale. They are covered with rubber sheeting.

Dante hated Arezzo.

> *The work becomes daemonic and through it the collector feels that he stands face to face with the artist himself. [In] the copy the daemonic quality is lacking; . . . [it is] a mirrored figure, and one cannot commune with a man in a mirror.*
>
> *— Lock, Stock, and Barrel*

New ivories boiled in black tea achieve the crackle and the coloration of old ivories. New bronzes can, when washed with nitrate of potassium (which in India, where we purified vegetables and fruit in potassium water, we called "pinky water"), achieve a patina. Anything can be distressed.

The moment one learns that the statue of David in the Piazza della Signoria is a fake, it is divested of all authority and charm (though it is a perfect reproduction); one feels one must immediately make a pilgrimage to see the original to make up for the hoax that has been perpetrated upon one.

According to Vasari, who may be too sour to be trusted, Michelangelo copied the work of "old masters"; and his works were indistinguishable from the originals, "for Michelangelo had tinged and given the former an appearance of age with smoke and other things, so that he had made them look old, and when they were compared with the original, no difference could be perceived." Michelangelo kept the originals in order to imbibe the spirit of the masters — which masters? one wonders — and today a Michelangelo copy of an "old master" would be a Michelangelo masterpiece.

The court favorite of the seventh-century empress Wu Hou convinced his lady that her paintings were in need of repair, and took them to a master counterfeiter. He sold the unblemished originals to a wealthy prince and returned copies to the empress. The prince was so burdened with guilt and so afraid of being found out that he burned them all, which was very naughty, as he should have burned himself.

We forgive Michelangelo anything.

> The cleverer I am at miniaturizing the world, the better I possess it. . . . Values become condensed and enriched in miniature. . . . One must go beyond logic in order to experience what is large in what is small.
>
> — Gaston Bachelard

The tiny and the immense are compatible.

Like Blake, who saw the world in a grain of sand, Cyrano saw the cosmos in an apple: "This apple is a little universe in itself, the seed of which, being hotter than the other parts, gives out the conserving heat of its love; and this germ, in my opinion, is the little sun of this little world that arms and feeds the vegetative salt of this little mass."

How small the schoolyard, the desk, the attic looks to us when we return to the stage of childhood dramas: miniaturizing, we are returned to the world of childhood.

One has heard of cherry stones hollowed out to contain ten dozen miniature tortoiseshell combs.

We are enchanted by things enfolded in other things, beguiled by things enfleshed by other flesh, things within things:

An expert employed by J. P. Morgan "once dropped a frame containing a valuable miniature. To his horror he saw it split as it struck the floor, but when he stooped to pick it up he realized that it was not broken. The impact of the fall had touched a secret spring in the upper half of the case which now turned out to be a double frame. Within the upper section, thus disclosed for the first time, lay a second miniature in a better state of preservation (because of its long protection from the light) than the first, already so highly prized." Better to find a magical hidden miniature world than to find a continent; the hidden miniature is the door to the secret garden, the proof of that which we know to exist, in common hours, only by a tried and attenuated faith.

When his escape was cut off from a burning building, a Japanese collector who owned a late-fifteenth-century painting by Sesshu slashed open his body with a sword; and when his half-consumed corpse was discovered, the priceless scroll was found contained in him.

On a nineteenth-century dig in Egypt, Dr. George A. Reisner found nothing but mummified crocodiles. A bored laborer kicked one and found, as the animal yielded to his blow and shattered into dust, what he identified as "old papyrus covered with strange pictures." The papyrus had been used as wrapping paper for the innards of the crocodiles; hidden in the beasts was what Dr. Reisner had been passionately looking for. . . . I hope this story is true. . . . It almost doesn't matter if it is true or not. . . . By the time he approached death, my paternal grandfather, whose friend Bruno Hauptmann was, had convinced himself he'd crossed the Atlantic with Lindbergh ("but nobody wants to know an Italian did it"); the metaphors contained in this delusion are, if not as interesting as truth, worth contemplating.

Saint Anselmo wrote this prayer to Saint John the Baptist:

> . . . You knew God before you knew the world;
> you showed your mother the mother bearing God
> before the mother who bore you within her showed you the day.

This is about the mystery of enfleshment, of the great held in the small, of hidden things contained, revealed, and understood. (Sometimes when I read this poem I grasp it immediately; and sometimes it hurts my mind and I strain for understanding; it is old and new, familiar and fresh.)

.   .   .

What shall I do when there is no more space for lovely things in these rooms that hold me high above the city of things? I can't imagine not looking (there will be grandchildren, after all): somewhere in a dusty attic there is a cameo bearing the likeness of the Queen of Sheba; in some forgotten garden there is a unicorn's horn.

5
MEN AND GOD(S)

Love is an ocean; its waves are troubled by the winds; it has no port or shore. The Lover perished in this ocean, and with him perished his torments, and the work of his fulfillment began.

— Beloved Ramon Llull, *Blanquerna*

PETER WIMSEY

And may her bridegroom bring her to a house
Where all's accustomed, ceremonious; . . .
How but in custom and in ceremony
Are innocence and beauty born?

> — William Butler Yeats, "A Prayer for My Daughter"

And what do all the great words come to in the end but that? — I love you — I am at rest with you — I have come home.

> — Lord Peter Wimsey

I DISCOVERED Peter Wimsey in a higgledy-piggledy bookstore scarcely bigger (and considerably more pungent in aroma) than a shoe-box, on Warden Road in Bombay. Actually he — which is to say, a used paperback copy of Dorothy L. Sayers's *Gaudy Night*, the romance in which Lord Peter is the hound-of-God detective hero — was in the shop's annex, a wheelbarrow that resided permanently outside the fruit-and-veg stall next door. It is the nature of Indian bookstores to be higgledy-piggledy and overflowing, alphabetization a form of order apparently incongruous to the Indian mind. I have never emerged from an Indian bookstall without a layer of ancient dust adhering to me, or without having had a book or books fall on my head. They are places one is best advised to enter without preconceived notions of what one wants; one invariably finds something that turns out to be necessary to one's happiness or gratification.

(Every time I tell myself I want never again to be in Bombay, I have only to think of Warden Road and the smells of spices and flesh and fish and mangoes and yellowing paperbacks and milky tea and attar of roses and boiling ghee and fresh-washed *khadi* cloth and the filth and brine of the creative sea that laps the greasy stones of the seawall . . . even the mold, which smells like the bloom of a venomous plant, and the heat, which is tangible, and which lodges in one's nostrils as well as in all the crevices of one's sensation-battered body . . . and I long even for the roil and the rot, the cow dung and the jasmine that combines its own fragrance with that of the dust that overwhelms it: life and decay; the ineffable silence at the heart of the brain-splitting noise; the silence so full of noise — the coincidence of opposites: the dance.)

Peter Wimsey came as a gift and a revelation to me in India (as Doris Lessing's *Golden Notebook* had when I lived with my husband in Tripoli).

Loneliness, and the overwhelming India-ness of India, sent me frequently to bed when I lived in Colaba, the dockside section of Bombay — a bed whose legs stood in tins of kerosene to lure and then to drown the bed bugs we'd inherited from the vacationing Dutch missionaries whose leased flat was our first residence in India. This ground-floor flat, its weedy garden home to a naked holy man with a permanent erection (and to rats), its kitchen home to the missionaries' thieving cook and man-of-all-work (and to rats), was in a courtyard complex of houses whose once hopeful butter-yellow paint was now stained with green slime, which flaked in the summer heat and oozed and blistered in the rains. The buildings were home also to a number of distinguished O.B.E.s, their honors ostentatiously displayed on their doorpulls; it was a wretched place, the missionaries having apparently taken Jesus' admonition to divest themselves of worldly goods as license to buy bulky furniture of extreme ugliness and darkness and dreariness and penitential uncomfortableness. It was an alien place, that flat — neither Indian nor Western, an inhospitable waiting room to an undisclosed, imponderable future.

I never entered the kitchen, having been told that the cook kept a sack of wheat in one corner for the delectation of the rats, who could then, he said (but I didn't believe him), be trusted not to rely upon the rest of us for sustenance.

I slept like a warden with my baby's crib wedged tight to my bed, seldom fully asleep, and seldom quite awake. At night I woke up to heat my baba's milk — *baba*, in India, being an affectionate term reserved for a baby boy; I passed the curtained windows that looked out on the garden, where the rats lived their disgusting secret lives, and crossed the dining room to the pantry, where I kept several hot plates upon which to cook my baby's food. (I felt the scrabbling presence of rats behind my back, in the raised kitchen above the scrubbed pantry. I told my husband I could smell the rats; he chose not to believe me; he attributed to me a talent for hyperbole. . . . But I can smell rats; and I can smell bat dung, too.)

I was again pregnant. I conceived my daughter six weeks after my son was born.

Over the dining room table, on opposite ends of a dark door, were two framed quotations derived from Scripture: "Lo! My Lord cometh quickly," said one. And: "Taste and see that the Lord is good," said the other. My husband refused to see the humor in this, he thought I had a nasty mind.

One night early on in our stay I entertained my husband's colleagues. I cooked veal cutlets parmigiana. An odd smile flickered across Mr. Harrison's face as his colleagues, Americans and Hindus, cut into their veal. Ah, Italian food! said the Hindus. *Veal?* an American inquired. Yes, I said, delighted, for I had gone to great lengths to secure the succulent meat. Later that night, after the hurried departure of the Indian guests, the babbled apologies, the baby's bottles, the crying (and the rats), it seemed to me that Mr. Harrison was right to have contempt for me —

what idiot wouldn't know that veal was baby cow and that the Hindus would be repelled by it, body and soul? Alas, I did not know. (There is no accounting for the lacunae in one's knowledge — even the fact that I was a city kid whose only acquaintance with farm animals derived from *Heidi* and the Prospect Park Zoo doesn't explain this curious lapse.) I thought veals were little animals that ran gladly up and down green hills, like lambs. I simply had no idea. But Mr. Harrison did; he could so easily have prevented the fiasco he allowed to be played out. (I never understood the mainspring of his pleasures and I seldom understood his ends.)

Now I think: How much he must have hated me.

Sometimes, expansively, he expressed his gratitude for my having married him; I learned to dread these effusions: acknowledged gratitude fueled and activated his hatred.

Great unhappiness is incompatible with the belief that it will ever end. In mysteries, everything is tidily resolved, there are no clouded motives; everything turns out all right in the end. (Let Right Be Done! is the clarion call of English common law; I count those among the most comforting and stirring words in the language.)

Lord Peter entered my life at precisely the right, contrapuntal moment (just as stories of wicked witches and of cruel stepmothers and handsome princes enter the lives of children when their fear and their longing would tear the fabric of their young worlds apart, if they did not find believable counterparts to their trembling, screeching nightmares in fiction). I fell in love with the silk-lined aristocrat, who patiently wooed the woman he loved for five years, subduing himself to his own ends because he perfectly understood that Harriet Vane's gratitude to him — his sleuthing saved her from the hangman's noose — was as likely as not to sour into resentment, human nature being, in this respect, intemperately ungenerous, people being so prickly about accepting gifts, so wary of disinterested kindness and detachment. Peter — whose manners are beautiful, whose tact and imperturbable, urbane courtesy would never allow him to engineer or to countenance such a scene as my Colaba dining room tragicomedy for the pleasure of seeing how it would all turn out; Peter — who lived in a settled world of ceremonies and rituals; Peter — passionate and principled; mischievous, jolly Peter — whose being born to privilege presents him with an everlasting occasion for guilt, and goes far to explain his "sudden withdrawals into the recesses of his own mind." . . . So wittily and self-deprecatingly self-effacing, not piteously self-effacing:

"You may say you won't interfere with another person's soul, but you do — merely by existing. The snag about it is the practical difficulty, so to speak, of not existing. I mean, here we are, you know, and what are we to do about it? . . . Our kind of show is dead and done for. What the hell good does it do anybody these days? . . . People will point me out, as I creep, bald and yellow and supported by discreet corsetry, into the night-clubs of my great grandchildren, and they'll say, 'Look, darling! that's the wicked Lord Peter, celebrated for never having spoken a reasonable word for the last ninety-six years. He was the only aristocrat who escaped the guillotine in the revolution of 1960. We keep him as a pet for the children.' . . . Only I have a cursed hankering after certain, musty old values, which I'm coward enough to deny, like my namesake of the Gospels."

The spilling of one's emotions like slop is in no way akin to profundity of emotion — and men whose affections are oleaginous can turn, in a greased moment, into snarling monsters of betrayal. What matters to them is the luxury of the emoting, not the fiber and durability of the emotion itself; their victory lies in painting the object of their emotions with the brush of their own humiliation and fear, which they try, by emoting, to exorcise. They wish to see another in the fear and degradation in which they by their lies and perversions are themselves condemned to live. They laugh at reflected pain . . . and then it starts all over again. They are grateful. . . .

Peter, never sloppy in his emotions, would never bully one. One would always know where one stood with him.

Never marry a man whose wet pity for himself masquerades as universal tenderness — he will be a tyrant. Never marry a libertine — he will withhold abundance from you.

"If anybody ever marries you, it will be for the pleasure of hearing you talk piffle," Harriet says during the course of the attenuated Wimsey-Vane courtship. Peter talks amusing twaddle; he never speaks lies. His masks hide no sordid secrets; his camouflage — he is apt "suddenly

[to] roll himself into an armadillo-like ball, presenting a smooth, defensive surface of ironical quotations" — protects a soft and restless heart. ("When I try to be serious, I make such a bloody fool of myself.")

On the morning after his triumphant wedding night (tender dynamite between the lavender-scented linen sheets — *license my roving hands to go, above, between, betwixt, below*), there is this delicious dialogue between the splendidly joined pair:

Harriet (drowsily): "My lord!"

Peter: "*What* was that you called me? *What* did you call me? . . . The last two words in the language I ever expected to get a kick out of. . . . Listen, heart's lady — before I've done I mean to be king and emperor."

He is, his wife says, the shadow of a great rock in a weary land. He regards his bride as his equal, encourages her to take the physical and mental risks her principles and proclivities oblige her to take, and protects her not by condescending to an imaginary exaggerated femininity but by the steadfastness of his dignified love and the just-mindedness that precludes his possessively regarding another as instrumental to his own needs and enables him to accept that his fellow creatures — even and especially his wife — are endowed with free will. (Or, if they aren't, they must be allowed to act as if they are, interference with this principle being the grossest form of impertinence.)

I had never in my marriage been so safe as to consciously feel safe; I was quite unable to imagine what form that state of grace would take. I wanted, in a land with no familiar guideposts (and a baby on the way), an ally — an equal — to live with in this strange, seductive world that challenged me and threatened me all day and all night long. I wanted — though you might have held my toes to the fire at that time and I wouldn't have admitted it, anticolonialist I — the fire-and-ice Englishness that in storybooks provides a refuge from the opacity and turbulence of India, a corner to hide in, safe from the exalting and bludgeoning wonder that one's mind uncontrollably and wearyingly comments upon, a respite from the puzzles and the conundrums that one works out in one's body and one's spirit, independent of volition, in India. Abetted by my not inconsiderable gift for acting and for mimicry — and needing to love and be loved and fearing more than all things abandonment — I tried to act as if I thought my husband was a corner I could hide in; and I vilified myself and mortified myself for practicing the vicious art of self-deception. I was so unhappy as to be permanently disoriented; I bent my will to act as if I were not. False to my nature and my needs, I bent myself — thinking it to be my duty — to another's will.

My blond baby raised and opened his arms to the blue enamel sky, to the butterflies and hawks that flew above us; turned his blue eyes upon me with uncontaminated trust; loved the world he found himself in . . . and only with him was my unhinging self-consciousness, the result of my scarily acknowledged duplicities, absent.

> *The worst sin — perhaps the only sin — passion can commit, is to be joyless. It must lie down with laughter or make its bed in hell — there is no middle way. . . . I will have no surrenders or crucifixions.*
>
> — Dorothy L. Sayers, *Gaudy Night*

Peter is civilized.

He never employs trickery to gain his ends; he never sacrifices truth to achieve his desire.

Harriet Vane, the daughter of a country doctor, a Bloomsbury bluestocking who writes clever, juiceless murder mysteries, neat but unfleshy abstract puzzles with stick-figure characters, is a prisoner at the bar when Lord Peter first lays eyes upon her. Peter, who has hitherto casually regarded beauty as a prerequisite in his women, sees the point of Harriet — her "devastating talent for keeping to the point and speaking the truth," her battered pride coupled to her steely courage, her irritable intelligence, and her untapped sexual generosity; he sees it right away.

And that really is all that one wants — to be seen; what one does not want is to be invented, however zealously, or to be put to the use of another's cloaked necessities and malignant appetites, however hungrily.

Peter is a paragon: younger brother to the richest (and contestably dimmest) peer of the realm, thus free to pursue crime as an avocation; collector of incunabula; connoisseur of Bach and wine but drunk, most often, on words, he is apt, at any moment, to quote *The Book of*

Common Prayer, Isaiah, *Religio Medici,* John Donne, Kai Lung, *Alice's Adventures in Wonderland,* Nietzsche, Machiavelli, Boccaccio, Apuleius, Conan Doyle, canon law, Shakespeare . . . or to raise his clear tenor in the service of Elizabethan love arias (or bawdy French ditties):

> True house of joy and bliss
> Where sweetest pleasure is
> I do adore thee;
> I see thee what thou art,
> I love thee in my heart
> And fall before thee.

He falls before her; whereas conventional judge and jury are appalled by Miss Vane, who stands accused of killing her lover, a long-haired poet "with advanced ideas — he for God only, she for God in him, and so on," in Peter's words; a conceited prig whose idea it was "that great artists deserved to be boarded and lodged at the expense of the ordinary man." (Cf. Dorothy Parker: "Authors and actors and artists and such / Never do nothing, and never know much. / Playwrights and poets and such horses' necks / Start off from anywhere, end up at sex. / People Who Do Things exceed my endurance; / God, for a man that solicits insurance.") Harriet saw to it that her lover's shoelaces were tied and his manuscripts typed (though her own work, being "commercial," meant nothing to him). The judge, with palpable amazement, tells the jury that Vane was angry with her lover "because, after persuading her against her will to adopt his principles of conduct [which is to say, to live with him], he then renounced those principles and so, as she says, 'made a fool of her.'" Harriet does not quarrel with this assessment: "He wanted devotion. I gave him that. But I couldn't stand being made a fool of. I couldn't stand being put on probation, like an office-boy, to see if I was good enough to be condescended to. I quite thought he was honest when he said he didn't believe in marriage — and then it turned out that it was a test, to see if my devotion was abject enough. Well, it wasn't."

The next five years — after Peter surprises and upbraids himself for impetuously proposing marriage to an imprisoned Harriet — are difficult for both of them. Peter is almost irritatingly undemanding after his first spontaneous outburst of need and desire; Harriet's severe sense of inferiority allows her to believe, for longer than any other sane and sensual woman would, that he thinks of her as his toy, a thing made attractive by notoriety, the symbol and emblem of his magnanimity; she regards his love as an artist's tenderness for his own creation. He has the grace to understand this.

I think of Peter in the current tense. I had a fight, once, with my friend Mary Peacock, over whom he'd love best, if he were to return to our midst, she or I. In the end I had to admit that it would probably be Mary — I don't think I could forever moderate my vulgarity to accommodate his manners and refined tastes . . . though I don't know: perhaps my vulgarity would be leaven to his wit; and to his self-consciousness. . . . No; Mary wins. (Mary's mother was in love with Peter too; he is at least as real as Hamlet.) He is, his entertaining line of chat notwithstanding, austere, obsoletely courteous and formally polite — overbred; my own feelings of inferiority, my own need to be told over and over and boringly over that I am loved, would come up hard against his austerity and be wounded by it. Harriet is a commoner; I am, by birth and upbringing, a peasant, unable and unwilling to disabuse myself of my working-class origins and sympathies.

But I cherished the fantasy: to be loved by a man like Peter — and to be told so, grandiloquently — would convince one that one was lovable. . . . Peter is my knight on a white horse. I know there is no one *yes* that can erase pain — even God cannot, or will not — but while I know there is not, I persist in having faith that there is. One man's validating *yes*.

You'd know where you stood with him.

Have I said he was funny?

He simultaneously cultivates and despises his "disastrous reputation for tom-foolery." He is so intuitive as to be almost female in his quick and sympathetic understanding. (Harriet "resented the way in which he walked in and out of her mind as if it was his own flat.") Male critics (and film producers) have mistakenly (perhaps jealously) taken his odd and compelling combination of sensitivity and garrulity, his upper-class drawl, his swift-moving, ruthless intelligence, to suggest effeminacy — they mistake him for a fop, an effete "chattering icicle in an eyeglass."

They have been at pains to interpret his guardedness — his talkiness combined with emotional inaccessibility — as fatuousness. In fact he is so virile as to be dangerous: Harriet knows full well she'd go up like straw if once she yielded to him — but sex is a weapon he does not exploit. She resists, as only a very frightened woman could, the promise implicit in his beautiful hands and in his gray eyes and his sidelong smile, his confident carriage and his unhurried stride: behind a rather foolish set of features dwells a man who loves women — "dynamite in a munitions factory, six centuries of possessiveness, fastened under the yoke of urbanity."

He has a terrible and endearing fear of appearing obvious. He is kind, almost morbidly analytical, undelusionally chivalrous ("a desire to have all the fun is nine-tenths of the law of chivalry"), decent, eligible, disarmingly sweet, effortlessly charming. His adorable mother, the Dowager Duchess, whom he has the good sense to love, believes that "if he were in [the] Inquisition he would exert social talents to entertain executioners."

And he pays Harriet the sublime compliment of revealing himself to her: "For some reason, obscure to herself and probably also to him, she had the power to force him outside his defences." What woman would not want to be the one chosen to pierce his defenses? Who wouldn't want to be married to the Scarlet Pimpernel, a man imperfectly disguised as a silly-ass-about-town, a marvel and a legend in bed, and a miracle of intellect, a strong heart united to a tough mind, a man who is a dreamy unity, perfect, of flesh and spirit. Who would not want to be the woman who unmasks him?

His playfulness is both real playfulness and a disguise for what embarrasses him about himself — given that he has all the riches of the earth, he is hard pressed to believe that he has the right to a soul, too (to say nothing of happiness): "In strict logic, of course, he would have had to admit that he had as much right to a soul as anybody else, but the mocking analogy of the camel and the needle's eye was enough to make that claim stick in his throat as a silly piece of presumption. Of such was not the kingdom of heaven. He had the kingdoms of the earth, and they should be enough for him: *though nowadays it was in better taste to pretend neither to desire nor deserve them.*" (I love that little tail to his

dissertation; Peter cannot take himself seriously for very long; and if
he is ever tempted to whine or to despair of his lot, he "makes a noise
like a hoop and rolls away.") He belts out Salvation Army hymns with
a friend who is a retired born-again burglar; he confers unpatronizingly
with the spinsters and widows he employs without condescension to
do his investigating — women his world considers supernumerary; he
has mutually soothing talks with the pope about old manuscripts on
the eve of war (at the behest of the Foreign Office, for whom, he says
modestly, he is a kind of plumber, plugging up leaks); he is capable of
engaging in a felicitous exchange of pleasantries with the female dons
at Harriet's college — in the course of which he proves himself to be
a distinguished scholar; with tact and persuasiveness he teases poor
Detective Sergeant Parker — who is painfully conscious of his place on
the ladder of class hierarchy — into proposing to his sister Mary, who
loves him. Peter has a way, baffling and heavenly and improbable, of
caring about tradition, but not about the nastier demands of class and
caste loyalty.

Harriet "understood . . . why it was that with all his masking attitudes, all his cosmopolitan self-adaptations, all his odd spiritual reticences and escapes, he yet carried about with him that permanent
atmosphere of security. He belonged to an ordered society, and this
was it. More than any of the friends in her own world, he spoke the
familiar language of her childhood. In London, anybody, at any moment, might do or become anything. But in a village — no matter what
village — they were all immutably themselves; parson, organist, sweep,
duke's son and doctor's daughter, moving like chessmen upon their
allotted squares. She was curiously excited. She thought, 'I have married England.'"

I might not have wished to marry England; but I wanted, when I
found Lord Peter in a wheelbarrow on Warden Road, to feel, if not
like a chessman upon an allotted square, like a person with perfect
freedom within set boundaries. (It occurs to me that my love affair with
Peter Wimsey is a love affair with the cloister . . . and why not? He
acts, after all, like an Anglican version of God, who sees the tears of
women.) What I did not want was perpetually to be primed for some
new emotional jolt and for psychological apparitions to materialize

around every corner. I didn't want to live my emotional or sexual life on the precipitous curves of the danger lane. I wanted to lie down in peace and wake up in such contentment as is allotted us. I wanted for there not to be so many departures from the norm that, in the end, there was no norm. I did not want to be married to volatility; I had a baby, I was expecting another: I wanted not to live on an emotional seesaw. And I wanted — it seemed a minimum requirement then, and it seems a minimum requirement now — to be liked.

This business of gratitude is troubling. Gratitude, Harriet says, "is simply damnable." What I don't understand is why it should be. Doesn't generosity consist as much in taking as in giving? One of the endearing things about God, we are given to understand, is that to Him no gift is unacceptable.

I have a friend who was cruelly afflicted with the inability to accept kindness — he interpreted it as a kind of demand to which he was unequal. The more he was loved, the more his fear grew and the more reprisals he exacted from those who had the temerity to love him. He entertained boorishly the love of his lover and flatmate for years, seeing in the detached unselfishness of his scorned partner a desire to steal his soul. It was not until he had a devastating illness that burned away the chaff in his soul that he was able to acknowledge that he was in debt to the man who loved him. . . . I loved him too; my love he hated intensely, choosing to regard the love of a heterosexual as a kind of virulent impertinence. But he never cast me off, though if he had really meant to, he could have sent me away with a word — indeed, he wooed me with words, for he too was drunk on words. . . . His illness, in which he now chronically and bravely dwells, has enabled him to accept the ministrations of those who love him, and to accept them with comprehending grace. Out of something sad and terrible, something good.

I never slept with him. One night, full of longing — his physical beauty was so overpowering as to be a character trait — I watched him climb the stairs to his bedroom, and the muscles of his brown calves (he is Indian) worked so beautifully as he climbed the stairs, his blue velvet robe hanging just to the soft of the back of his knees, that I felt I had, simply by watching, experienced an act of physical love. My genitals respond even now to that image of him, naked brown feet padding. (If one lives long enough, one comes to understand so much one would almost prefer not to: voyeurism, for example.)

I can't think what he would make of my love for Peter Wimsey. Until his sanguinary brush with mortality, I shouldn't have dreamed of telling him about it. Though I did once spend a heavenly day with him at Oxford, Wimsey on my mind. (It was Sayers who taught me to love Oxford, where, don't you know, bookish Peter and his brainy inamorata pledged their love. I never went to college; and I suppose that fact (no longer regretted) fed my imagination, too, and nourished my love for Peter, jewel in Oxford's crown.)

> True house of joy and bliss
> Where sweetest pleasure is
> I do adore thee;
> I see thee what thou art,
> I love thee in my heart
> And fall before thee.

All our loves are contained in all our other loves. (Like the pierced ivory spheres of the priceless chess set, balls within balls within balls, that Harriet consents to have Peter give her, abundantly mortifying her pride.) That song, which Peter sings to Harriet, I heard for the first time in the parlor of Arnold Horowitz, my first love, whom I love still. Curled on the window seat. The maple tree sending its winy fragrance into that room through which breezes swept. Kathleen Ferrier was singing it. Now, when I listen to Ferrier's thrilling voice, I am glad and sad: glad because Arnold, who died more than thirty years ago, is never so alive to me as he is in the music he loved (Ferrier, and Schubert's *Trout* Quintet); sad because on that night, we listened to Ferrier singing a love song about a woman with "soft brown down" on her arms, and I, warped by my desperation to secure love, to hear its words, took the playing of that song to mean that Arnold hated the down on my arms. Of course not. Of course he didn't. He was making love to me, my darling love. I was fifteen. He was my schoolteacher. Warped, I misinterpreted his love and took it for a reproach. I was fifteen and I had been taught by masters, taught to accept revilement as my due. . . .

How vulgarly melodramatic that sounds. Peter Wimsey would be incapable of such spoken violence of emotion (though he would immediately recognize its derivation). And yet what I say is true.

His hands, his eyes, his smile, the nape of his neck, the tender line where fair hair meets forehead; not these, but his very nearly self-defeating fair-mindedness wins Harriet over.

There is a poison pen at large in Harriet's college; her deeds maniacally escalate, until Oxford — which Harriet had conceived as the still point of a relentlessly turning world, a refuge from insistent personalities — is no longer haven. Harriet, called by the dons to help uncover the identity of the demented person, is quick to see the thing in terms of soured virginity, repressed appetites, deprivation, the witchy malice of a sterile celibacy. Peter puts it to her squarely:

"Your fears are distorting your judgement. . . . Having more or less made up your mind to a spot of celibacy you are eagerly peopling the cloister with bogies. If you want to do without personal relationships, then do without them. Don't stampede yourself into them by imagining that you've got to have them or qualify for a Freudian case book. . . . My dear, what are you afraid of? The two great dangers of the celibate life are a forced choice and a vacant mind. Energies bombinating in a vacuum breed chimaeras. But *you* are in no danger. If you want to set up your everlasting rest, you are far more likely to find it in the life of the mind than the life of the heart. . . . That is my opinion as an honest scholar, viewing the question academically and on its merits."

Wanting her heart and her hand, as he does — wanting her *informed* consent — this statement has the ring of a man "busily engaged in sawing off [his] own branch." He knows this: "When you have come to a conclusion about all this, will you remember that it was I who asked you to take a dispassionate view and *I* who told *you* that of all the devils in the world there was no devil like devoted love? . . . I don't mean passion. Passion's a good, stupid horse that will plough six days a week if you give him the run of his heels on Sundays. But love's a nervous awkward overmastering brute; if you can't rein him, it's best to have no truck with him."

I knew, even as I agreed to marry him, that I would never love my husband's body. This had nothing to do with his body *as* body. It was a warning signal to me — which I disastrously overlooked — that I did not love his soul; our bodies are the bodies of our souls. I had neither love nor passion for him; marrying him was like falling into a deep dark well (like an extended panic attack: like terror).

How could I not have loved Peter, whose disinterested piecing together of facts enabled him to see that the culprit was not a mean old spinster but a woman who wanted nothing more than to make other people — her children — her "job."

I had a child. And I was carrying another. But I was unable to see them as my job — as pieces of work, as manipulable clay.

I *had* no job. "Wife" is not a job; one is not the watchman or caretaker of another, it leads to hateful muddle and to the doling out of roles, strong/weak, that have essentially no meaning within a marriage of equals. And so to read of the union of this fictional man and this woman (so unlike my own marriage), who marry as equals, with love and with passion, and knowing exactly what they are doing, thrilled me.

Who knows what it is that gives one hope, that contributes to an unlikely optimism and an apparently deranged courage? I think the ghost of Lord Peter was standing at my side when I signed divorce papers in Mexico.

(When my children were three and four I was prone to give them speeches about how "good" their father was. I don't know why I did this. Nor do I know why my having done this is somehow connected in my mind with my infatuation with Peter Wimsey — who was good.

The children and I used to meet their father in the park, on his way home from work; in that happy place I could best pretend that I was doing what was ordained. They flew into his arms.)

The house where Sayers placed her married lovers (and their eight servants, not including Peter's "man," Bunter) is in Audley Square. The Georgian building that provided the inspiration for Lord and Lady Wimsey's townhouse is now the University Women's Club. When I am in London I stay there, in a little room with a sloping roof that must have belonged, in Sayers's novel, to an undermaid. I have tea curled up in a leather armchair in the library. I try not to prick myself with the knowledge that Peter plays better on the page than he would in real life — and that I'd probably, were I to serve him, drop the milk. Or in some way make a fool of myself . . . perhaps, like the ancient ladies sitting in the club's lounge, some of them old enough to have been Harriet's classmates at Oxford, I'd drop marmalade on my cashmere twin set and scrape it off with a butter knife.

His ghost has never visited me in Mayfair (it would not be like Peter to pay an illicit call to an undermaid's room; he did nothing in stealth). I have never even dreamed of him. But I love being in his house; and I am grateful to him — and to Warden Road.

Soon after I fell in love with Peter Wimsey, Warden Road gave me a gift more beautiful than lovely Peter. Anna Harrison was born in Breach Candy Hospital on Warden Road. When I go back to Bombay now I swim in the Breach Candy swimming pool; and I gaze at the windows of the hospital that adjoins the Breach Candy Club; I see the terrace of the room where I introduced my daughter to the Arabian Sea. I marvel at the unity and connectedness of things. Out of so much that was bad came so much good. My tears add salt to the sun-warmed water: "innocence and beauty, custom and ceremony." Here, where I was once so alien, amidst ghosts and memories and the bright colors of the living day, I am home. I float: safe from the perils of the past, I am so happy as to be conscious of being happy.

RED BARBER

And there used to be a ballpark,
Where the field was warm and green,
And the people played their crazy game
With a joy I've never seen.
Yes, there used to be a ballpark, right here.
And the people watched in wonder,
How they laughed and how they cheered.
Yes, there used to be a ballpark, right here.
Now the children try to find it
And they can't believe their eyes,

'Cause the old team isn't playing
And the new one hardly tries
And the sky has got so cloudy . . .
And the summer went so quickly, this year.
Yes, there used to be a ballpark, right here.

— "There Used to Be a Ballpark"

Someone once described Ebbets Field as the cathedral of the underdog. If that is true, Red Barber was the poet of the underdog . . . and he was summer's Sunday afternoons, the voice of sun and symmetry and yearning and resolution. I think of Ebbets Field — a small ballpark, a protected enclosed space of leisured ritual, in the world but not part of it — as a cloister; I think of a cloister as the architectural equivalent of a theological concept: perfect freedom and joyous spontaneity within established boundaries. And I think of the voice of Red Barber, who sings with the angels now, as the voice of goodness.

Whenever he spoke, he spoke only to me. That is what I thought. And that is what each of his listeners thought. He brought the gold of summer into an attic apartment in the bowels of Brooklyn; no kitchen has ever been so sunny as the kitchen into which the radio carried his charmed and charming voice.

No childhood is completely unhappy; of that I am quite sure. Held by the magic of that voice, one suspended disbelief in happiness — even now I can delude myself into believing that summers have never been so benevolent, so bright, so merrily green and happily rowdy as they were then. No one who heard him will ever think of Red Barber merely as a sportscaster, the play-by-play announcer for the Brooklyn Dodgers baseball team; he was a messenger of order and of joy.

Two or three years before he died I arranged to meet him; and it was only when I was airborne, halfway to Tallahassee, where he and his wife, Lylah, lived in retirement, that I had the sense to ask myself what I thought I was doing: if it's true that you can't go home again, it's surely true that you can't return to your childhood idol, the man who could do no wrong. What was I thinking of, interviewing a man whose perfection for years I'd assumed?

Jazzman — the first man I ever made love to and the last man I will ever make love to — often bewailed the determination of my emotions: "Can't you ever leave anything alone?" he said. I can't. I return to the scene of the crime. I return to the scene of bliss. I return to the past because I've never really left it. So here I was on a fool's errand, bringing my love, intact, to an old Southern man whose voice hadn't filled the airwaves in decades.

There are two ways of loving a public figure, neither of them unselfish: one is to inquire into his life in order to learn the minutiae of it, placing queasy claims on his privacy in order to foster an illusion of intimacy; another is to allow oneself, in one's quiet self-absorption, never to think of the icon's private life at all, which is tantamount to believing that he exists solely for one's own pleasure.

So what *was* I doing disturbing an old man's peace?

(When I told my brother I was going to interview Red Barber, he said, "Red Barber! That was summer afternoon in Bensonhurst! That was our life!" It wasn't our life. But it was part of our life that was as plain and good as bread. When I told my brother I was going to the White House, he said, "That's nice." The president lives there; he doesn't touch our past, he is — although he may determine whether we live or die — in some basic way peripheral to our lives, not woven in the fabric of them, not braided in memory. Whereas, Red Barber . . . he was summer afternoon; he was the good we salvaged from the dung heap, he was powerful magic, and real.)

I listened to tapes of his broadcasts before I flew to see him. I was carried back to a glorious day in 1947, two out in the last of the ninth inning; Cookie Lavagetto, a Dodger pinch hitter, chunky and obscure, steps to the plate and doubles off the right-field wall at Ebbets Field, bringing in two runners, robbing Yankee pitcher Bill Bevens of a World Series no-hitter and winning the game for the Dodgers, "Dem Bums" (there never was such a happy noise in Brooklyn, and there never will be again). I hear Red Barber's voice, soft and clear, cadenced and authoritative, and the shadows lengthen on the playing field as he takes us gently into dusk.

I remembered all the old feelings; and I understood that Barber's genius was to render a game so exactly that one was delighted both by virtue of its sameness and constraints and by virtue of its openness and unexpectedness: the rules never varied; the play marvelously did. For nine full innings the world was safe. And all of us listening to him formed a community.

When Cookie Lavagetto spoiled Bill Bevens's bid for a no-hitter, Red Barber, after calmly reporting the latter-day miracle, said, "Well I'll be a suck-egg mule." A red-clay Southerner whose vocal rhythms were derived from *The Book of Common Prayer* and who liked to talk about magnolias spoke to the hearts of the stoopball- and stickball-playing kids of immigrants who barely spoke English. And he beguiled us with expressions like the "catbird seat" (his, or that of anyone on the spot) and a "rhubarb" (a violent verbal exchange between an umpire and a player, and a frequent happening in Brooklyn); "He's runnin' like he's goin' home for Christmas," he'd say; or, "He is tearing up the pea patch"; "You could say he's hollerin' down the rain barrel," he'd say. You could see the perspiration on the players' faces when he spoke; you could hear the "piping shrill voices of the infielders as they encouraged the pitcher" and see the grin on his face, "wide as a slice of water-melon," when the pitcher struck a batter out; you could hear the crack of a bat, "as sudden as a pistol shot," when a player "put one in the icebox when it was really needed"; you could see the third baseman "like a restless cat in a new house" on a perfect summer day, "not a cloud in the sky, air is soft, see the leaves and the birds just poppin' out of the trees." You could smell the hot dogs and the sweet green grass.

He never said a careless word. You could see the game better when Red Barber was broadcasting it on radio than you can see it now on television, because, as Walter Lanier Barber says, "You see with your emotions." And (he was so skilled) all along his folksy way, Mr. Barber was delivering little homilies — chatty (and really rather sly) back-fence asides on character, time, and fate, urging us to charity and under-standing: "I don't want you to judge Pee Wee harshly," he'd say, in that persuasive drawl, when it appeared that Pee Wee Reese had lost a critical game for us; "only pop fly I've seen him miss in eleven years." Baseball, the unguent of his voice applied to it, was not a blood sport.

From the moment I saw him I knew that I had been right to love him; and I knew that nothing would go wrong, that love would be added to love, as indeed it was: the hours I spent with Red Barber and the woman he shared his life with for sixty loving years I count among the most blessed of my life.

He was eighty-two, slightly stooped and no longer sure-footed — he walked with a kind of proud delicacy; he wore horn-rimmed glasses; and such hair as he had was a faded ginger. (I'd have known him anywhere.) Curiosity and ardor breathed as steadily in him as they had years and years ago when he was my eyes, the lyricist of my childhood, a man who instructed me in the beauties of the body — he talked about the muscles and sinews and dance of a baseball player, and I saw the hand of God in His creation more vividly than I saw it at all the Bible studies my mother took me to; he talked about the glory of a summer day, and it was a form of praise more sanguine and sincere than the rote expressions of belief I heard at the Kingdom Hall. His play-by-play descriptions encapsulated a text on the necessity of law and the trans-forming power of grace. Red Barber remained to his dying day an orthodox believer; my mother, who relaxed her vigilance when I lis-tened to baseball, had no way of knowing that he undermined my assumed religious belief and strengthened my real faith — that he had the effect on me of a charismatic heretic, a divine provocateur.

He was necessary to my life. A gateway. A gateway out of a religion as bereft of life as it was of contradiction and into a world full of muddle and joy. And: no sweat. He made it sweet and easy.

For fifteen years, from 1939 to 1953, Red Barber ("the Old Redhead") broadcast games for the Brooklyn Dodgers, as fiesty, heartbreaking, eccentric, contentious, beautiful, and gritty a team as ever played the game of ball. There were no fans more loyal, ardent, knowledgeable, and vociferous — loudmouthed — than Brooklyn fans; true believers, we knew (in part because he told us so) that "if anything could happen, it could happen here."

Listening to baseball was a baptism into the melting pot for my generation of immigrants' children; it was our great good luck that Red Barber was courtly, impartial, and civil.

I loved Red Barber because he was lovable and decent, not so much avuncular as brotherly; the love I felt for him had nothing to do with sex. I was infatuated with the Brooklyn Dodgers, which was something else:

I had a crush on a pitcher called Ralph Branca, who gave up a homer to the Giants' Bobby Thompson, which robbed Brooklyn of a pennant (he later married into management); I used to hang out (loitering with intent) at the Oldsmobile dealership where he and Gil Hodges, Carl Furillo and Duke Snider bought their cars. This schoolgirl crush did not survive three summers; and it had everything to do with sex.

There was a Dodger called Pete Reiser who was forever knocking himself out and injuring himself on the right-field wall of Ebbets Field in a vain chase for fly balls. My Icarus, carried off on a stretcher. I wanted to protect Pete Reiser, to cradle his head in my arms. And that had everything to do with hormones. And with the magnetism of damage, the pull that damaged men had on my heart.

I saw a movie once — I can't remember its name — about an all-girl baseball team. It was a pleasant little movie, but I was unengaged — by which I understood that baseball for me has a whole lot to do with sex. I wonder if I had been born at another time and with a more sexually aggressive temperament whether I might not have become a baseball groupie. . . . I want to be safe, safe at home, in the arms of a man.

I did not tell Red Barber this, one couldn't. He was a moral absolutist and a Southern gentleman; and he never gave his wife "occasion to worry" when he was on the road. (Of how many men would you believe that? Believe it of him.) He once refused to review a baseball player's autobiography on the grounds that the player had behaved "unchivalrously" in discussing his marital breakup — he was, Red Barber said, "incredibly ungentlemanly." Red Barber refused to see *Bull Durham*, he told me, because "I read what it was about and I don't have to go. I know all about ball players. [He meant he knew all about their foolin' around.] I don't want to put things in my mind that I don't want there."

Bull Durham put something in my mind that I was pleased to have there — this manifesto, spoken by a burnt-out handsome and damaged catcher, Crash: "I believe in the soul, the cock, the pussy, the small of a woman's back, the hanging curve ball, high fiber, good Scotch, that the novels of Susan Sontag are self-indulgent, overrated crap. I believe Lee Harvey Oswald acted alone. I believe there ought to be a consti-

tutional amendment outlawing Astroturf and the designated hitter. I
believe in the sweet spot and soft-core porn. I believe that Christmas
presents ought to be opened Christmas morning rather than Christmas
Eve; and I believe in soft wet kisses that last three days." At the time
I saw that movie, I would have died for a man who made a speech like
that — never mind that real-life baseball players are tobacco-chewing,
spitting, crotch-scratching, womanizing swine (none of which I knew
when Red Barber sat behind his microphone). Their play is beautiful
to watch. Baseball's a church, *Bull Durham's* Baseball Annie says, a
religion full of music and cosmic truth. When she and Crash make love,
an organ plays. I am not averse to praying the prayer Blessed Julian of
Norwich prayed: *Mother God, Father God. . . .* But for me the living
gods are men.

One of the things Red Barber understood was the parochialism of
Brooklynites — a parochialism that could easily be mistaken for innocence. We were sophisticated about one thing: the Brooklyn Dodgers,
about whom our knowledge was encyclopedic. The psychological distance from Brooklyn to Manhattan was immense. When we went to
Manhattan we went, we used to say, to "the City." That city didn't
belong to us. We belonged to the tree-lined streets and the stoops and
the tenements of small shopkeepers and subway commuters.

I remember our first class trip into Manhattan: we went to the
Museum of Natural History to see the dinosaurs. Subsequently all class
trips took us to Manhattan. That was where everything *was.* We were
left with the indelible impression that Brooklyn was where everyone
lived and Manhattan was where everything happened. "OK, where's
the butcher? Where's the stoops?" my third-grade boyfriend yelled on
the steps of the great museum. He meant: If people live here, *how* do
they live? They were different from us. In our imaginations there were
no butchers — no shoemakers, no five-and-tens, no candy stores, no
Fifth Avenue, no back fences, no cellar doors. We were in exotic, alien
territory. The dreams of that city didn't belong to us. No one ever came
to Brooklyn to nourish a dream. No one but the Dodgers.

There was a kind of tension that was almost sexual between the fans
and the players. "When the Dodgers played the Giants it wasn't play,

it was blood on the moon," Barber said. "You had the small ballpark — the fans and the players were almost interchangeable. You'd see the perspiration on them and you could hear everything a player said. Manhattan had all those tall buildings, Wall Street, the theaters. The people of Brooklyn had only one thing. They had the ball club and they used that ball club as a weapon against Manhattan . . . especially when they played the Giants. There will never again be the natural genuine rivalry in baseball that there was when the Giants and the Dodgers were in New York. And most of that passion came out of Brooklyn. Brooklyn loved its players. Only the Brooklyn people called them Dem Bums. Nobody else could call them that. . . .

"It broke their hearts when O'Malley took the ball club to Los Angeles."

It did.

Every morning to the end of his life Red and Lylah Barber read the last verse of the nineteenth Psalm: "Let the words of my mouth, and the meditation of my heart, be acceptable in thy sight, O Lord, my strength, and my redeemer." He liked the Book of Psalms: "It's the only book in the Bible where man speaks back to God." (He wasn't a *sissy* kind of Southern gent.)

One of the things I found so lovely in Red Barber — and so encouraging — was that he was in love, deeply in love, with his wife. And she was — perhaps she would not put it in the past tense, for love endures and is stronger than the grave — in love with him. (I wonder how much of this I intuited when I was a child; I heard the love of living and the happiness in his voice — elements lacking in my parents' voices, my mother's either treacly-seductive or whining, my father's hard and fraught and occasionally (most frighteningly) wheedling — and perhaps I assumed he lived in domestic felicity; I assumed that he was an uncomplicated man. Ordinariness was precious to me then — the ordinariness of mastered emotions combined with candor and the bubble and flash of sanctioned spontaneity.) Sixty years is a long time to be in love.

I had never lived with people who were in love.

The feeling between them, Lylah said, "was very quick and it's been there ever since. At the time I met him, life was full and there for the picking." He was a janitor and a waiter at the University of Florida in Gainesville when they met. She was twenty-five, an independent young woman born into a matriarchal society of strong women, a nurse at Riverside Hospital in Jacksonville — one of the first five women in America to have been given a bachelor's degree in nursing, Red said proudly.

(He liked to be called Red.)

They were watchfully aware of each other's needs; once in a while something like flirting occurred between them, pretty to watch. She was sometimes tentative, sometimes astringent. He was laconic, always assured. Their personalities had not melded into one — confounding my image of marriage as a magnificent two-headed beast; they complemented each other and enjoyed the mutual comfort that is the product of profound trust.

"Not for one second have I doubted the love," Lylah said. I had to bend close to hear her whisper, "Not for one second of our lives."

The night Red died I thought of them, in their immaculate living room, which was singularly devoid of baseball memorabilia. Sometimes at night they listened to George Beverly Shea — "that magnificent light bass voice" — and to Ella Fitzgerald: "She did an LP of hymns, have you ever heard about that one? Singers singing the songs. That's our form of worship. Between your creator and yourself, everything you do is a form of prayer. Goodness, I look at these trees — what complicated beauty! How in the world is this tree created and what sustains it? Everywhere you look it's a spiritual experience."

He was almost too good to be true.

He was true. A man of brotherly courtesy and integrity, a steadfast man.

(Ah, what I wouldn't have given, growing up, for parents steadfast and serene; I love him because he was a safe harbor from cyclonic storms.)

He needed to be true: he had what he called "the hottest microphone in radio" — he was the man on the spot when Jackie Robinson broke the color barrier in baseball in 1947; his mettle was tested; it's unlikely that any other broadcaster could have handled that volatile situation with equivalent grace.

I am not talking about a man who escaped the limitations of circumstance; he was as the world and God made him — and he was made noble by the struggle to overcome the stumbling blocks of reflexive Southern racism (a struggle he viewed in pragmatic, not romantic, terms); this is what he told me:

"I was born in the Deep South, in Columbus, Mississippi. My mother was Mississippi, my father was North Carolina. When I was ten, my family moved to Sanford, Florida, which is very very redneck — Deep South, I mean redneck. As a boy I saw a black man walk the streets tarred and feathered. And I had never thought anything about the relationship between blacks and whites. There it was.

"Lylah and I, our first year in Cincinnati, went to the symphony. Sat way up there where the seats were twenty-five cents. And one afternoon a black couple came and sat down beside us . . . and we just quietly moved. Just as simple as that. Without thinking. That was the way we'd been raised.

"Mr. Branch Rickey [the Dodgers' owner and general manager] told me in complete confidence one afternoon in March of 'forty-five that he was going to bring in black players. He didn't leave any stone unturned, he meant to do it. This was before he even knew of Robinson.

"I came home and told Lylah I didn't think I could do it. The relationship between broadcaster and players was too close. And she said, Well, you don't have to quit tonight, let's have a martini.

"So I mulled."

Branch Rickey had told him this story: When he was coaching college baseball at Ohio Wesleyan University, a young black player was denied entrance to the team's hotel. Rickey found him crying, sitting on the edge of a chair, "pulling at his hands as though he would tear the very skin off. . . . 'It's my skin, Mr. Rickey. If I could just pull it off I'd be like everybody else. . . . It's my skin.'" That was one of the things Red Barber mulled over.

"In a few days I came to the point of economic determinism: I had the best job in the world; where would I get another one? . . . Then I began to think more deeply. I had no control over the parents I was born to, so why am I getting so high and mighty about somebody else whose skin is different because of the parents they were born to? I finally digested that. And then I heard a voice from the past, the World Series, Judge Landis, commissioner of baseball, 1935:

"'These ball players are the best in their business. You let them play — just report what they do. And the managers are the best in the business. Don't criticize their moves. You let them manage. You just report what they do. And the umpires are the best in the business. Don't be second-guessing any of their decisions. Just report. Report the reaction of the players, of course. Report the reaction of the crowds. But just report.

"'What I mean is, if a ball player gets a mouthful of chewin' tobacco and walks over to the box where you're sitting and spits it in your face, don't have any opinion. Report. Report his steps, the rapidity of his stride, report the accuracy of his ejaculation, if your eyes are that good. Report the reaction of the commissioner, if he has one. Leave your opinions in your hotel room. Just report.'

"And suddenly my dilemma was resolved. For goodness' sake. My job is simply to report. And that's what I did. I never once said that Robinson was black or a Negro. I didn't have to. Everybody knew it. All I did was, I just reported what he did — which was more than sufficient. Once he got on the bases and started dancing, we didn't need anymore. Physically he was the most exciting player — especially on base. And the most tremendous player spiritually.

"Robinson did more for me than I ever did for him. He made me a bettter man, a cleaner person. He got these scales off my eyes."

By the end of Red Barber's career, when he was broadcasting for the New York Yankees, I was living in India; baseball was far from my mind.

I didn't know this story: One day in 1966 the Yankees, a ruined team, played to an almost empty ballpark. Red, now doing television commentary, asked his director for a picture of the stands. His director wouldn't give him the shot he wanted; but he had the microphone, and he told the story — he just reported: "It is the smallest crowd in the history of Yankee Stadium . . . and this smallest crowd is the story." That week he was fired.

"One time a Brooklyn taxi driver volunteered to a friend of mine, 'Well, the trouble with that Barber is, he's too fair.' I like that. I'd put that on my tombstone — except I'm going to be cremated."

·   ·   ·

We chatted, that fine spring day in Tallahassee, about baseball as big business, about the designated-hitter rule, about why pitchers were the most selfish and self-centered of players. We talked about blood. Red Barber, trusted as few men ever are, was enlisted during World War II in the Red Cross drive for blood — *blood*, which had been a taboo word on the airwaves (the people of Brooklyn responded with a generous and steady supply).

Just before my mother became a Jehovah's Witness in 1944, Red Barber's radio spots almost persuaded her to give blood; but the Witnesses are, on patchy scriptural and quasi-scientific grounds, opposed to blood transfusions, and that ended that. Still; it's odd, isn't it, how many lives one modest man can reach. Giving her blood would have been the first communal act my mother had ever engaged in, a stupendous sacrifice of her myopic individualism, the proud isolation she confused with individuality and which she asserted (and simultaneously lost) in the bosom of her adopted family, her religion.

Red Barber knows he touched people; he doesn't take much credit for it: "I used at times to go to an institution called Rosary Hill out in Westchester — a home you qualified for if you had incurable cancer and were flat broke. The Sisters at Rosary Hill never had anybody there who was going to get well. I used to just drop by and talk with patients, you know; and I found out that their lives were so bleak, if a game was 20 to 0 it was still interesting to them because they didn't have anything else to look at. You know, when you have a game that's bang-bang-bang it carries you with it. But then you get those lopsided games, and that's physical work, you just want to get it done. But when I'd begin to get tired, I'd think of Rosary Hill and I'd say, Well, no. There's somebody out there that this is important to."

Red Barber, Presbyterian born, was for years a lay reader in the Episcopal church, entitled to read morning and evening prayer, the litany, and the penitential office, the offices of instruction, the order for the visitation of the sick, the burial offices. On road trips he was often invited to deliver a sermon; and he did — in Cincinnati, Pittsburgh, St. Louis, Chicago, Philadelphia, New Orleans. "Ball players are no different from anyone else. Every man is interested in religion, and there have been times when ball players have come to me to talk about God. I never pushed it, and I want to make that clear. Maybe that's why I never once have been kidded in a ballpark about being a lay reader. . . .

"In baseball, the good manager has made a careful study of each of his players. He knows their strength and their weakness. He only asks his players to do what he knows they can do best. And I don't believe the Good Manager is going to send one of us on an assignment that we can't do."

The "Good Manager . . . has created the universe, and the way his creation can continue is through human beings. . . . We have a job to do. . . .

"I sought perfection in my work," he told me; and it seemed to me I had been given a definition of a perfect world — everybody doing his job as he is supposed to on a summer afternoon.

"I don't feel sad about things and I don't look back. I'm like Satchel Paige: 'Don't never look back because somebody might be gaining on you.' I try and look forward and I try and appreciate the day: 'This is the day the Lord hath made. I will be glad and rejoice in it.'

"I was always appreciative of the work that I was given. I didn't choose it. It's a form of grace. I was given this work." He rested his arm lightly on Lylah's shoulders. "I was given this love."

And Lylah said, "I didn't have a chance. I loved him so much so right away."

I wasn't jealous of their happiness (one had always known — even a bad marriage could teach one this — how good a good marriage could be); I rejoiced in his presence, which allowed me to view my childhood through a mist of summer gold.

How do we live? We live in the vortex of our sorrows through the mercy of God, and we live by the example of God's-gifts-in-men. Red Barber was one of those gifts. I am indebted to him for providing me with the happy childhood I never had, and for giving me a person to love and a reason to praise in the desert of my days.

Love is the only game that is not called on account of darkness.

ARNOLD HOROWITZ

Let us go then, you and I,
When the evening is spread out against the sky
Like a patient etherised upon a table; . . .

And would it have been worth it, after all, . . .

It is impossible to say just what I mean! . . .

"That is not it at all,
That is not what I meant, at all."

— T. S. Eliot, "The Love Song of J. Alfred Prufrock"

Each day I salute the sun, the ocean and the land for your dear sake,
my love.

— Walt Whitman, *Leaves of Grass*

Sometimes, in the dark, at night, I hold out my hand to him, testing awful mysteries. I have narcotized myself with painkillers (so sweet, the lotus, the voluptuous inertness); and I want to see if he will take me, if — in one (finally) clear and unambiguous gesture — Arnold Horowitz will gather me to him; I will be his harvest, he will reap. Once I wanted unequivocal, transparent love from him, love like a church made of crystal, water, light. What I want from him now is to be the facilitator of my death. These are rehearsals. I stop short of actually willing the event, of calling on him with my entire heart and will, lacking courage, resolution — and (when it comes to it) lacking necessity; I do not press the point, though I would like him to vouchsafe some assurance that when I am ready, he will be there, there to take me to the broad and pleasant land. But there are no dress rehearsals for death. He can no more assure me now than he could when I was fifteen and — without reservation, qualm, caveat, with fierce intensity and longing — wholly in love with him. He gave me life; the least he can do is usher me into the country of death when I am ready for that Stygian journey. I have more questions for him than I have for God.

(I see a note of querulousness has entered my elegy — "the least he can do!"; I entertain the traitorous thought that simplicity would have served me better than the honey-sweet and perilous labyrinth he led me into when he gave birth to me by loving me. There never was anything of placidity in this love. In the labyrinth the shadows are dense and the sunlight signals elusively at every heart-stopping corner: I was captured.)

Everything in me was alive to him . . . and in him; nothing in him did not move me, astound me with wonder, fill me with joy (and its brooding stepsister, anguish: "Be not afraid with any amazement," Scripture says; I was afraid; and even my fear I loved because it sprang from my adoration of him).

He chose me. He marked me. Between the choosing and the claiming lay my anguish. He never (quite) claimed me; he never (quite) declared his love — not in the words I needed to hear.

It was famous, the attachment that bound us — my world whispered of it, and his world knew of it, and it was dangerous for me and it was dangerous for him; and I am attached to him still (though with what degree of danger I cannot say).

He has been dead for thirty years.

I once incorporated the only picture I have of Arnold Horowitz into a collage. When I moved, I left the collage behind. I have no need of it. I can summon up a picture of him at will; he is indelible. Look! He is here.

He read this poem by Archibald MacLeish once, in class, when I learned to understand that he loved me:

Not with my hands' strength nor with difficult labor
Springing the obstinate words to the bones of your breast
And the stubborn line to your young stride and the breath to your
        breathing
And the beat to your haste
Shall I prevail on the hearts of unborn men to remember
(What is a dead girl but a shadowy ghost
Or a dead man's voice but a distant or vain affirmation
        Like dream words most)
Therefore I will not speak of the undying glory of women
I will say you were young and straight and your skin fair

And you stood in the door and the sun was a shadow of leaves on
    your shoulder
And a leaf on your hair
I will not speak of the famous beauty of dead women
I will say the shape of a leaf lay once on your hair
Till the world ends and the eyes are out and the mouths broken
Look! It is there!

    I felt totally comprehended when he read this, and safe, and at home
in the magnetic field of his love. I felt valuable, and I felt good. I had
never attached value to myself before. It had not occurred to me that
I might be good.

Rumors swirled around him in New Utrecht High School. The poor
old crippled school librarian was in love with him, and came all over
girlish and giggly in his presence, and tried to convert him to Roman
Catholicism (and he was not incapable of making fun of her behind her
back; indeed, although he was in the ordinary way kind, he had a streak
of viciousness that accorded ill with the gentleness of his demeanor);
the "smart girls" all wanted to be in his classes and had crushes on him
and tried to decipher his mysteries. What were his mysteries? Why did
he appear, and not just to me, runic? They had little raw material to
work with; and they settled on his having had a generic "nervous
breakdown" the term before they entered school, which made him
more romantic than ever in their eyes. (But there was a teacher who
had gotten recurring malaria during the war; and sometimes he came
into class wearing a heavy overcoat when the rest of us were in summer
clothes, and he talked about his malaria — but he didn't succeed in
being romantic; and why this should be I don't know.) There were other
teachers who were younger and more conventionally handsome and
clever and good; but it was Arnold who attracted conjecture, and in his
presence fantasies multiplied; and for some reason — unclear perhaps
even to him — it was Arnold's approval the girls required . . . an approval so heightened as to be called love.
    I think it was his need that created their need. (I wonder if that might
be said of God.)
    Boys in Bensonhurst do not utter the word *love* lightly, if at all. Boys

did love him, though. The only punishment he meted out was exile from his classroom. The young hoodlums no one else could control sulked and skulked in the hallway like dumb wounded animals:
abandonment.

Why was he always and for so many the necessary person?

Some of these toughs became career criminals. He wrote to them in
jail and sent them paperbacks and packages of pepperoni. (He gave
away his old bow ties as rewards for good behavior and good work; and
sometimes tickets to Marx Brothers movies; and sometimes chocolate-
covered ants. He is a god to me; but he was a man complete with foolish
and provincial, capricious human gestures (which is not to say that God
is not capricious; how would one know?). . . . How I wish I had something physical of his now (though he lives in my blood and brain): a
bow tie. A silly, blessed bow tie. A fetish. A handkerchief he wore in
his pocket. A relic.)

The first time I saw him, he disappointed my expectations. I was
walking behind him on a school staircase, those caged-in iron staircases
that form an ecosystem all their own; and he seemed — his figure
slight, his fair hair slicked back, a bulging briefcase in one (beautiful,
blunt-fingered) hand — insubstantial. He was chatting amiably and
inconsequentially with some girls, upon whom his words worked as an
elixir. . . . It seems odd to me now that I should have expected to be
overwhelmed by a man I didn't know. Which in due course I was. And
for the rest of my life.

The English teacher I had before him, David Zeiger, was as decent
a man as I have ever known; and he was good to me, a good teacher,
tolerant, wise. He didn't make love to me; Arnold did.

Who did me the greater favor?

David was bewildered, as all my teachers were, that I was taking a
Commercial course, the course of study reserved for kids who didn't
expect to go to college. Shorthand and secretarial and nothing too
strenuous for the brain. ("Why is your last name Italian?" a teacher
asked me one day in the antiseptic-smelling hall, where, docilely, like
animals entering Noah's Ark, we walked in ordered lines, two by two
(gone are the days). "My name is Italian because I *am* Italian," I said.
"*Oh.*") Jewish girls expected to go to college and were "smart." Italian
girls expected to get married. (And everybody wore charm bracelets,

and corsages of sugar cubes when they were sweet sixteen (I did not).
It made David sad that I could not, by reason of my religion, which
forbade it, go to college (it filled Arnold with rage).)

David is still my friend (he is the first person who told me I would
be a writer); but this is a strange and perverse thing: I am not a good
(attentive) friend to him; and that is because he was Arnold's best friend
— and for years I thought he had the key to the "secret" of Arnold,
and I saw him primarily in this princely but utilitarian light, endowing
him with magical properties, for I believed he had a sorcerer's command
of the past — *my* past. He moved in the shadow of Arnold's mysteries;
and I am not a good friend to him because I have been unable to
transport him into the present where he lives and belongs; he is still
to me the keeper of the keys, an almost mythic figure because his life
and Arnold's touched. (And this looks to him like carelessness.) Lilah,
David's wife, knew Arnold too, and named her son after him. Impatient
with mysteries, she loved Arnold too, but not compulsively, and in her
peppery, confrontational way; and he is still alive in her. I envied
their ability to be (apparently) casual with him; I envied them because
their need was so much less feverish and obsessive than mine (though
far more obsessive — Arnold called obsessiveness into being — than I
knew).

On summer evenings, wet and sanctified with expectation, I would
walk from my house on Seventy-fifth Street to Arnold's house on
Eighty-fifth Street (where he lived with his mother and Orthodox
father in the narrow, monastic upstairs room of a wooden Victorian
house), hoping for a glimpse of him, exalted merely by the attempt. I
ran, accompanied by the scent of hedgerow blossoms and honeysuckle,
the homely streets of Bensonhurst my theater and my small town; and
sometimes I found Arnold and David together on Arnold's screened
porch (I could sense their presence and hear their voices a block away),
and it was all I wanted, what David had: to talk the dusk carelessly away
with Arnold, just as if Arnold were not oracle or savior but merely
mortal man. "Are you happy?" David asked. Such a good question, I
thought — the only question. (In those days we used to talk a lot about
whether it was right to believe in happiness or to repudiate it. We read
Fromm; we read Camus; we read Salinger. We talked about the impos-

sibility of reconciling the world's pain and one's personal greed for happiness — as if, dear God, happiness were there for the grasping (which Arnold knew very well it was not). Do people still talk like this now?)

These are some of the things Arnold instructed us, in his classroom — English 31J — to despise: racism, tail fins on cars, glass building bricks; musicals (in particular those starring Esther Williams under water), bigotry, religious fanaticism (which is to say God); bullfighting, unnecessary exercise (which "disturbed the balance of toxins in your system"), suburbs, school football heroes, dopey poems like "Trees," cruelty, celebrations of mediocrity and tolerance for the second rate; and small towns, which, stingy and claustrophobic and mean-spirited, shriveled souls. People gossiped in them about their appallingly small, wilted lives. People had otherwise nothing to do in them. How did anyone spend an evening in a small town? a vacant Sunday? We shuddered to think. We knew — because Arnold told us — that all kinds of terrible things went on behind the painted doors of small-town houses (we didn't know the exact nature of the terrible things, of course; we knew the word *hypocrisy* but not the word *incest*); the picket fences pierced our hearts. Everything important happened in cities, the larger the better. We read Edgar Lee Masters's *Spoon River Anthology* with Arnold's sensibility, and our hot blood was curdled by the small-town fates of Miniver Cheevy and Richard Corey . . . and some of their sorrow seemed to rub off on him, and the pity we felt for them was applied also to him, so that we felt for him a potent admixture of admiration and pity and sexual attraction and awe. He seemed so singularly alone. ("I have measured out my life in coffee spoons" — he read us "Prufrock.")

He battled with diabetes and with agoraphobia — he missed school for a whole term once, before I came, much of it, it was rumored, spent "crawling on his floor"; but I did not know that then. I am similarly afflicted; and I wonder sometimes if I have not inherited Arnold's diseases, or chosen to live out in my body the grandiloquently naive, imperially sad promise I made to my diary in those days: *I will make him mine by a kind of magic; I will become Arnold, buy the records he loves and read the books he reads. . . .* And sometimes too I wonder if my lust to collect things springs from my love of him. I have spent bittersweet days and driven days looking for a certain kind of fifties vase I associate with his house on Bay Thirty-first Street, the apartment he moved to after his mother died, the apartment with Picasso's Harlequin and a window seat and impeccable blond Danish-modern furniture . . . and a yellow vase. I have dreams of recreating the attic apartment of that old wooden house, his roof garden, too, which overlooked a garden a city block long.

It is terrible to me — one of fate's sinister and leering accidents — that an aunt of mine lives in that apartment now. She doesn't like me; I never go there; I want — sometimes — to live there with the fragrance of his ghost.

My love was fixed as ever can be; I raced ahead of myself in years, the emotion was mature (it did not fade); but I was, in that house, as socially awkward as any adolescent:

I had no idea how to pee in the bathroom of his apartment, which was next to the sunny kitchen in which he sat; what did one do about the noise?

We sat on his roof once with two of his old students and their three-year-old, who was naked and whose nakedness I called attention to by giving the child a pat on his pretty rump and calling it pretty, giving rise to a speech by the child's father about how they wished to maintain their child's innocence and how my (innocent) remark had stained it, the brat wasn't supposed to know he wasn't wearing clothes. . . . Isn't it remarkable that I should still smart from that insult? I was mortified, and my cheeks burn now when I think of it.

I was offered a drink at his sister's house once — gin, vodka, whiskey, Scotch — and my mouth could not form a choice. Gin. Vodka. Whiskey. Scotch. The world did not, after all, turn upon my choice; but to choose anything in his presence was suddenly impossible. I kept my eyes on the carpet and prayed for deliverance from choice. Perhaps he was irritated with me (who would not have been?), but he managed never to leave me open to reproach, he never suffered anyone to criticize me. Bursting with emotion, I was; and my most trivial gestures were (as a direct consequence) frozen: once I offered him a drink; but I forgot, in his presence, how to make a gin and tonic, I got it into my head that it required a cucumber.

Sometimes, in his apartment, I met his grown-up friends, and I was hostess, and I knew that he was pretending I was his wife. But I didn't stay with him at night. I was a quiet girl, well behaved; and I remember how, after one of those nights of play-acting, I walked home in a blur of tears and kicked over every garbage can along the way.

But that was later. The first time he invited me to his house — the house he lived in with his mother and his father — we sat on his screened-in porch, drinking black-and-white sodas, just like Jeanne Crain and Dick Haymes in one of those musicals he despised: *I'm as restless as a willow in a wind storm.*

Very great happiness is indistinguishable from very great unhappiness.

The first time he took me to dinner I had soft-shell crabs in a restaurant near Fort Hamilton where my uncle the cop, having been suspended from the force, was moonlighting as a dishwasher. I didn't know what to do with the fact that my uncle was, however invisibly to Arnold, on the premises; and I didn't begin to know how to eat the soft-shell crabs; I spread lettuce all over them and hoped he wouldn't notice.

Why did he love me?

He was agoraphobic; but he took long walks with me along the Brooklyn waterfront promenade, the world falling off into the sea, the bright day dissolved on the heart of the sea, the sea winds anointing our faces with brine; he held my hand. And did I make him feel safe? In those days I was incapable of doing harm, I was still a child in that way. And he was mother father lover god.

"Why does everyone look at you?" he said. That was later, too, after I'd left Brooklyn and moved to the East Village to make a life; I was twenty-two and still in love with Arnold Horowitz and I couldn't say: Because I am with you. "You are beautiful," he said. Because I was with him.

He had not the intention of perfecting his will to achieve happiness. Washes of panic. And melancholy. And wit. An irremediable malady.

.   .   .

"Did he love me, David?" "He loved no one else more," David says —
an answer worthy of Arnold himself. Lilah says, "He loved you — the
bastard."

I had not infrequently been the object of teachers' special attention. I
was smart and I was strange, and I was for all practical purposes an
orphan — my mother was supremely uninterested in anything that
happened to me at school, in anything that happened in my heart, so
long as my conduct conformed to the requirements of her religion;
my father was not fatherly (he was either not there or very much too
much there . . . but I have spoken of this and will speak more of
it later). Teachers know an *enfant sauvage* when they see one (perhaps
we smell feral; perhaps we smell of musk); and since third grade, when
Miss Silver came to the apartment we lived in under the el near Coney
Island, the apartment where my mother stalked naked at night (Miss
Silver with her clunky chunky silver jewelry, her dyed black hair and
bangs, her sibilance), one teacher or another had seen it as his mission
to make my brilliance known to me, to comfort the unhappiness I
imperfectly hid and to pierce and infiltrate my loneliness. (It is strange
that I do not remember them as well as I remember Miss Isaacs,
who did not seek to solace me. Miss Isaacs was afraid I'd try to convert impressionable young girls to my religion, girls like Shirley Gottlieb with crinkled dyed yellow hair, whose sister was a ballet dancer;
and Miss Isaacs warned parents against me. And that was hard because it meant I had no partner to stand in line with and no one to
eat lunch with. I used, before, to have lunch in the park of Seth
Low Junior High School with Shirley Gottlieb. When I was trying to
convert her. When I left junior high school, Miss Isaacs said to me,
"You are the most wonderful girl I have ever known"; and what was
I to make of this? She had been so cruel. I saw her years later in
the Botanic Gardens, walking down an avenue of cherry trees, and I
thought, I have triumphed. But I meant only that by that time I was
free of my religion, as free as Miss Isaacs to walk down an avenue of
blossoming cherry trees and with friends of my choosing. This triumph
felt unpleasantly like revenge. ("Loveliest of trees, the cherry now, / Is
hung with bloom along the bough." That was another of "Arnold's"
poems.)

I was used to special attention from teachers (and used to ostracism, too).

The quality of Arnold's attention was different. It bound me to him.

The first thing he asked us to write in class (after telling us that nobody in the world knew how to use semicolons, and therefore to abjure them, which I have not) was an exercise in self-indulgence — his and ours — called "Portrait in a Mirror." I lied. I lied about practically every single thing. I invented a self made of wishes and pretensions and paper lies.

I couldn't fool him. He saw through every one of my lies to a truth I had not been able myself to discover. I was never thereafter able to deceive him — one does not deceive one's creator. Of course I never again tried.

The beautiful girl with hair the color of sun-burnt wheat. . . . He wrote this on the blackboard and then he came to my desk and said, very quietly to me, *you.*

I think my mother understood before I did that I had opened my heart to a subversive love — just as, by primal instinct, she would have known if in the middle of an earthquake I had turned my key in the lock.

She sent my brother to the store for a loaf of bread. He came back with Arnold's Whole Wheat Bread. She threw it out the window.

Arnold hated my religion. I allowed myself to think that it was my religion that was keeping us apart. He would have broken the back of my faith if he could have; he would have torn the throat out of it with his fine white teeth, throttled the life out of it, twisting it in his strong hands like a mangy kitten and throwing it against a wall.

But when, inevitably, I did leave, years later, when I was twenty-two (and still in love with Arnold Horowitz, who, if this is important to you, was forty-seven), he cried. No one else did. I was scorned and cast out from the love of all my religious friends; and he cried: Now you will be like everybody else, he said. . . . To do him justice (I never ever *asked* him what he meant by anything he said), I think he meant: Without certainty, alone without God. And afraid. But it is true that he had told Miss Samuelson, another New Utrecht teacher who wished to adopt me, that the beautiful thing about me was my passion. And it is also true that the passion I felt for Jehovah God had long been subsumed by my passion for him. And true, too, that I had always been afraid — he knew this, he must have known.

What I will never know — what even David and Lilah do not know — is what his apparently chosen enigmatic glosses guarded or defended or kept at bay. What we know is that it is/was nothing so obvious you might guess at it; something was at work in him that was appallingly dark and devouring, he was locked in the jaws of the whale. He was cocooned in his despair.

He told Fatima Ouida, an engagingly madcap classmate of mine whom I did manage to convert (and who, as a result of my later defection, will not speak to me, which causes me vexation and pain, as she alone of anyone I know had knowledge both of my mother (her secrets) and of Arnold): Religion isn't the only thing that keeps a man and a woman apart. He told her this over the phone (the circumstances of this conversation, upon which my happiness hung like a thread, were not important enough for her to recall); and, Do you love her? Fatima asked; and he said what I would have known he would say: Yes.

I was pretty then. I had long, light brown, wavy hair; in my pictures — in the picture of me in which I wear a black silk faille skirt tightly cinched at the waist and a sheer white blouse with a red rose at the high neck — I look almost terrifyingly guileless.

(I say to that picture, O lovely girl, how I love you; I love you; I forgive you. . . . I have always envied and wanted to have and to be a twin — I have wanted to say to the other/not other: O lovely, lonely girl, I love you, I forgive you; rest, and be still. . . . He is standing at my shoulder now; he is asking me what it is that I have done that must be forgiven. . . . Darling Arnold, go away, and thank you, and come back, please, when I need you again and more.)

It would have been foolish of me to try to convert him; I thought my love could work hidden magic on his will. In my fantasies I perished with him at Armageddon with the wicked — if I had to die, I would die in his arms, floating on a sea of blood. *He* wasn't wicked, though; which presented an obstacle to this fantasy. (After I left high school, I was supposed — I was ordered by my religious elders and by my martyred mother — never to see him again. Of course I couldn't not see him.) Sometimes (because I still, in my divided soul, half believed, and acted almost entirely as if I did) I dreamed I'd live with him in the New World after the destruction of Armageddon. But he couldn't abide a god who destroyed "the wicked"; and there I was, without even a fantasy to grab on to. . . . How could God kill him?

At every school assembly he came and held my hand. Everyone else stood to salute the flag. He and I did not. Jehovah's Witnesses are not allowed to — and he, with great courage and risk to his own safety, while despising the reasons for my singularity and isolation, was determined not to have me feel like a freak. . . . It may be more accurate to say: If I were to be a freak, he wanted me to be *his* freak. (Arnold? Are you there? Are you listening?)

I was devastated when that term, English 31J — which has determined so much of the course of my life — was over. I had come to accept as casually as rain his presence every day, and to hoard the daily riddles I took home with me, riddles made by his softly spoken words.

It was thrilling, what came after that; how well he knew my clamoring heart.

And all this happened in Bensonhurst, a little town.

I could see the elevated train from the window of my homeroom, the train he took each morning to work; the trees obscured the long long staircase (seventy-six stairs) he descended, the staircase that ultimately brought him to me. I had no doubt that it was to me he was coming. He allowed me, from the start, to have no doubt: every day before he began his day, he stopped at the door of my homeroom and looked through the glass window and saluted me with his smile, a smile reserved only for me. My day did not begin — my sensate life did not begin — until I received the benediction of that smile. On days when he was absent, I was removed from myself, I wandered in a sterile wilderness; when I was parted from him I was parted from myself — really, the judgment of God was no more potent than Arnold's absence.

He knew this.

I don't know how he arranged it, but our free periods coincided; and on days when he left the door to his office open I let myself in; and I closed the door. Sometimes he had another guest — a woman, the crippled librarian, Miss Finelli, who flirted with him grotesquely; and her advances he met chivalrously. Once I cried. Love made my face all red and puffy; her love for him, and his kindness to her (love is a jealous god), made me cry. I moved as if to leave; but he eased Miss Finelli out of his presence; and then he kissed me on the forehead and said, "Why do you do this to yourself?" There were tears in his eyes.

I think Lilah believes him to have been a sadist. I do not. Lilah loves him nonetheless.

I have alluded to him — named him — from time to time in my writing. And every time I do, someone gets in touch with me, someone from New Utrecht, and tells me how he changed their lives, how good he was to them. (He loved no one more. I make it my first order of business to establish that he loved me more. I have satisfied myself that he loved no one more.) Sometimes these people want to organize reunions — the idea astounds and repels me — to discuss him. I would literally rather die. Sometimes, in their presence, I cry. Sometimes they bring gifts — like the picture of Arnold, a Xeroxed picture of him standing in front of a blackboard full of math equations, which I incorporated into a collage. (He taught math after I left the country, by which time I was twenty-six; he said math was less "embroiling" — or perhaps I said that.)

I saw *Room at the Top* with him in Greenwich Village, unable to look at him during the love scenes, our thighs touching. I saw a Sophia Loren and Marcello Mastroianni movie with him at the Loew's Oriental on Bay Parkway ("Her buttocks move up and down like pistons," he said, causing me to wonder how he could talk to me — me! — so casually about asses). We saw a lurid movie about Vincent van Gogh and we went to dinner at Ye Waverley Inne. We went with friends of his — other teachers — to hear high school choruses and orchestras. Most of the time we went to Mary's Venetian Restaurant on Bay Parkway; and then we walked and walked and for hours and hours we talked — and he murmured, once, resting his chin on my head, looking off into the ocean, where the sun was falling into the swelling sea: "I am safe." Then he took my face in his hands and gently shook his head.

I left school when I was seventeen. "You won't change your mind?" he said; "for me?" Even for him I couldn't change my mind and go to college. I used up all my courage loving Arnold; and this form of rebellion against my religion — against my mother — was beyond me. He'd asked me to take the entrance examination for the University of Chicago when I was fifteen, at the time the university, under the radical leadership of Robert Hutchins, was prepared to take students of any age who passed. We'd spent the evening listening to Beethoven's last quartets and reading poetry to each other, Shakespeare's sonnets (he chose well). I said yes to him as a gift; I passed the exam; I was offered a place at the university; I didn't go. He was exceedingly sad. He was not reproachful.

(The day after I knew what my immediate future might have been — I could have been a scholar! — I went to a Bible study where we discussed the "symbolic meaning" of Deborah's camels. Well, that's it, I thought; I must be nuts.)

He was not reproachful — it would have been easier if he had been — and I only once saw him angry. I'd been, with Witness friends, to see *Death of a Salesman;* they left after the first act ("obscene"). I had a talk about this with Frederick Franz, then the vice president of the Watch Tower Society: I suppose I should have gone to see *My Fair Lady*, I said. Franz said all worldly entertainment — that's what he called it — was equally bad, *My Fair Lady* as "distracting" as *Death of a Salesman* and therefore just as demonic. I reported this conversation to Arnold (substituting the word *obscene* for the word *demonic,* knowing there was a limit even to Arnold's patience); he said to tell Franz to get a copy of *Hamlet* and shove it up his ass, which, he said, was already accommodating his head; and when, he asked, was I going to use *my* head? He said a little brute force would do me good, but that unfortunately he wasn't the man to apply it.

Why wasn't he?

I don't know why I remember this just now: Arnold had studied at Columbia with Lionel Trilling, who told him that he, Arnold, was the wittiest man in America. (Arnold's favorite sentence was Ring Lardner's "'Shut up,' he explained.") Arnold's mother and father had come to his graduation; but he wasn't there. He thought they wouldn't notice his absence, and they didn't. He took a walk instead.

He was in analysis for nine years. "If fear of walking down steps is a death wish, what is fear of walking up steps?" he said. "Could it be that I have a life wish?" He was at the moment holding my hand.

I am afraid of steps.

When his mother died he sat on a lawn chair behind the old wooden house and said, when I called, as precisely as if he were a doctor prescribing for a terminally ill person: "Yes. Come. You will be good for me. No one else."

You see that I breathed him for many years.

For two years after I left New Utrecht, I was a full-time door-to-door preacher; to think of that time now fills me with a still sensate weariness, with self-disgust, and with amazement — and a kind of gratitude, for I learned much more than I taught (and I survived, working against all my natural inclinations). And I continued to see Arnold. As before.

I should have gone totally cuckoo without a form of ultimate commitment or of consummation: I was in need (I choose my words carefully) of drowning. So, clinging all the while to the hope that Arnold and I would be together, I applied to the Brooklyn headquarters of the Watch Tower Society, and was accepted, when I was nineteen, as a housekeeper.

And I continued to see Arnold. As before.

Nathan Homer Knorr, the president, then, of the Watch Tower Society, had commanded me, when I told him about Arnold, not to see him again.

Why did I tell Knorr? So stupid. (Knorr was stupid; and I was, to elicit his advice.) I wanted God's fires to burn me, to consume me, yes; but there was humbug in my offering my story to Knorr — it excited me. I knew, even as I heard his absurd and perfunctory advice, that I would never stop seeing Arnold. I could not.

It was prestigious, then, to be a woman at Watch Tower headquarters; and it was glamorous: men outnumbered women ten to one. And I had lots of flirtations and lots of kisses and I was danced with and courted and proposed to and I entertained fantastical infatuations. And sweet men fell in love with me. And I still loved Arnold. I still saw Arnold.

But the fissures in my soul were deepening. (Of this Arnold was unaware.) I wrote about this later:

> *One summer morning, as I left Watch Tower headquarters to go out preaching from door to door [having read Rilke's* Letters to a Young Poet *the night before], I saw two young men and two young women piling into a yellow convertible. They were laughing. They carried picnic hampers covered with red-and-white-checked cloths, very full. One of the young men turned on the car radio — a Mozart quintet. I wanted to be with them. I wanted to be them. I longed for their world of color and light and sound. My longing was so acute it was like a physical pain; and it was followed by an intolerable ennui: I didn't know what I was doing holding a satchel of* Watchtower *magazines, or why I was going to preach, or what I had to do with the Witnesses, or they with me. I wanted to run away. I didn't. But I knew at that moment that someday I would.*
>
> *The four young men and women had come out of a house on Pineapple Street, an old wooden house, white, with a forest-green door and forest-green shutters and dimity curtains and chandeliers that seemed to be lit even in the daytime. The garden of the house, with its cherry tree that had blossoms like crepe paper, was surrounded by a high white wooden fence, and set in the garden fence was a lime-green door with no doorknob on the outside. For days I imagined that if I knocked at that door, they would recognize me and let me in and we would sit in the garden under the cherry tree and I would never have to go back to the Watch Tower building again.*
>
> *Later that same week, on an impulse, I went alone to Birdland. Basie was playing, and Joe Williams was singing. I had two rye-and-gingers, and felt scared and exhilarated.*

The exhilaration did not last. The fear did. I wrote in my diary: *I am afraid afraid afraid.* I had been a Witness since I was nine years old.

I got a postcard from Arnold with a scribbled message: "Dear Babs [nobody else has ever called me Babs; and no one had better dare do]: Only that which everybody believes to be true is true."

I spent a lot of time walking in cemeteries, loving the dead, greeting them.

The first thing that went was my voice. Which probably got sick of itself: it had told so many lies; it was so many voices, all fighting for equal time. Toward the end, when I rang doorbells to preach, I opened my mouth and nothing came out. Nothing. As effective a paralysis as if God Himself had severed my vocal cords. . . . I stopped going from door to door. . . . Long, lazy Sunday mornings in bed: for the first time in almost fifteen years, Sunday mornings in bed. Doing nothing. Looking out at the harbor. Waiting. . . .

I was still going out in the evenings to Bible studies. Only I didn't talk to [my] would-be converts about the Bible anymore. I don't remember what we talked about (everything here gets blurred); I remember being fed a lot, plates of food and cups of tea, and holding children on my lap. How good people were! I wish I could remember who they were. . . . This is the part of the horror ride where the tunnel is dark. . . .

[Then] I couldn't walk down stairs. Every house had stairs; the stairs were always narrow. After the doors were shut and the voices and the warmth were over, I hugged the banisters and edged down sidewise like a crab. Sometimes it took me an hour to negotiate a flight of stairs. I stood paralyzed and nauseated at the top of the stairs — a void at the bottom of the stairs. . . .

During the day, nothing had changed. Except that I kept falling asleep. Every time I sat down, alone in my room, my eyes closed, and I slept, for what seemed to be five or ten minutes. Small blackouts. I didn't resist them. Delicious little secret deaths.

One night, late, I was on the subway. Tracks on either side of me that seemed to stretch into black infinity. Marooned. I remember the subway walls — blistery with ugly wet patches — and a dim, sick light. A train pulled in, and I couldn't walk to it. And then another, and another — and I couldn't make myself walk. . . . If I thought of anything at all, it was rats. In the damp, underground, there are rats. Waves and waves of nausea. I began to think I was hallucinating this. But the sweet-sour smell of vomit, mine, was real. (As was the unlovely fact that I had wet my pants.) At six a.m., as if a spell had been broken, I walked to a train. I had been standing there for seven hours.

I got to Bethel in time to shower. Doused myself with perfume (Lily of the Valley). I remember the morning text for that day: "What are these wounds in my hands. . . . Those with which I was wounded in the house of my friends."

I called my mother to come and get me.

I knew instinctively that I couldn't ask Arnold. I knew — though I loved him no less for understanding this — that his courage was not equal to my own.

After I left, I gathered up such courage as remained to me, and said, "I need — now, really for the first time — to talk."

"No," he said. "No. Please, I cannot help you, Barbara. I cannot help myself." I thought I heard him say "I love you."

At night my mother moaned and cried: "You are killing me!" she cried.

I continued to see Arnold. As before. Except now, when we parted, he kissed me — his lips were so cool — on the mouth.

I visited him one day at New Utrecht. We sat in the school auditorium, where we had sat so many times before. When we walked to the subway — on our way to Mary's Venetian Restaurant — he said, with more sadness than I had ever heard in his voice before, "You are so terrribly unpossessive." I have had forty years in which to consider those words. And, he said, "They thought — the kids — that you were my sister. Or my wife. I wish that you were either." I said nothing. Though the top of my head seemed to have gotten disconnected from my body and my feet could not touch the ground. I said nothing at all. And he said nothing more.

Two years later, after I had begun the affair with Jazzman that my body demanded, I said to Arnold, whom I still loved (whom I still love: are you listening, Arnold?), "It's too hot, being with Jazzman, all this hyped-up intensity of meeting and parting, jealousy and other women and violence and dope and stuff, his being married is not a good thing for my health." We were standing on the subway platform, waiting for the train that would take me back to my apartment — and to Jazzman, who might or might not show up on time but who would surely be there at night, because he was addicted to my body, and in love. "Isn't it possible," Arnold said, "couldn't you . . . isn't there someone else you could love, someone easier?"

"There are only two men in my life," I said. "There always ever have been, and you know it, and what shall I do, can't you help me?" The train had pulled up; by what means I do not know, I found myself inside. As the doors closed I heard him say, "Ah, this is terrible, terrible. This is what I have feared." He placed his hands on the glass door, like a condemned man in prison. I placed my hands on the other side of the impenetrable glass. He mouthed, "You are adored."

I continued to see Arnold.

My love affair with Jazzman lasted two years. (Thirty-five years later, it would resume.) And then I married Mr. Harrison, not knowing what else to do, wanting — so foolishly looking in the most unlikely place — peace, refuge.

When Arnold became blind, I was engaged to Mr. Harrison; what good, I ask myself now, would it have done if I had said: Arnold, my own dear heart, my love, my twin, my joy, let me take care of you, I love you, let me be with you all my life, I do not love Mr. Harrison, I love you, take care of me. I was afraid, I had always been afraid, of hearing him say: *"That is not it at all, / That is not what I meant, at all."*

I have never forgiven myself for leaving him.

He wrote to me when, soon thereafter, Mr. Harrison and I moved to Tripoli: "How I should love to be in that garden," he said — my garden of pomegranates and pansies and zinnias and date palms and sunflowers and violets and fat white roses. "There, silent, safe, I could dream away the days, never thinking of what I have lost. Perhaps," he wrote, "you wouldn't seem so impossibly far away from me if you were just across the Med in Italy. You seem impossibly far away. . . . How beautiful they seem now, like a dream, those nights so full of joy and love, the winy maple, the music, you. . . . Someone is playing the radio: the football season has begun. Somewhere someone is burning leaves."

I wrote back: "Come! Oh, come!" I could not imagine the consequences of his coming, nor did I care: I only wanted his beloved presence, his voice; I wanted Arnold more than I had ever wanted him before. I was a child again: believing. Believing in the possibility of perfect love. He never answered my letter. His sister did. "I see that it is I, once again, who must tell of Arnold's death. *Blah blah blah blah blah.* [I *hated* those commas — I comma once again comma — so full of herself. I didn't give a damn about the state of her heart, I was more greedy now than I had been when he was alive.] Thank you for the friendship which helped to make his life pleasant." *Pleasant?*

How Mr. Harrison — who presumed to comfort me — escaped with his life that night I do not know.

Grief does not end and love does not die and nothing fills its graven place. With grace, pain is transmuted into the gold of wisdom and compassion and the lesser coin of muted sadness and resignation; but something leaden of it remains, to become the kernel around which more pain accretes (a black pearl): one pain becomes every other pain . . . unless one strips away, one by one, the layers of pain to get to the heart of the pain — and this causes more pain, pain so intense as to feel like evisceration.

I hold him to my heart.

When I am dead, my dearest, / Sing no sad songs for me. Forget it, love. You knew there would be sad songs; *and world enough, and time.*

JAZZMAN

Men loved wholly beyond wisdom
Have the staff without the banner.
Like a fire in a dry thicket,
Rising within women's eyes
Is the love men must return.
What a marvel to be wise
To love never in this manner!
To be quiet in the fern
Like a thing gone dead and still,
Listening to the prisoned cricket
Make its terrible, dissembling
Music in the granite hill.

— Louise Bogan

So grant us again
the courage to begin,
to wish the morning well,
to kiss before we tell,
to trust enough to choose,
to take our days as news.

Here, in this trackless time,
where habit is our crime,
the amazing day begins,
forgiving us our sins,
and as we turn to bless,
the landscape answers Yes.

— Alastair Reid

"It was only the first night, but a number of centuries had already preceded it."

— Rafael Cansinos Assens

I read a little while ago that Robert De Niro was planning to reopen Minton's; by that time Jazzman had left me (or I him) for the last time (surely the second definitive exit must be the last?), and there was nobody else I wanted to tell. There was a picture of Minton's Playhouse in the *Times*, a decrepit shrine, on its façade the neon outline of a wacky champagne glass, the neon letters of the club's name leaning atumble this way and that, the windows and door sealed with cinderblocks. Teddy Hill used to stand at that door on 118th Street to greet his customers — or to glare at them if he had a mind to. For six months he treated me with exaggerated indifference, until one night for no reason that I could discern he hugged me, conferring upon me the benediction it was his pleasure generally to withhold — and to withhold especially from white girls, to whom one jazz musician was very much like any other jazz musician so long as he was black; and after that it would have been worth anybody's life to hit on me at Minton's, where I met Jazzman and fell in love with him at first sight.

I have a CD of Teddy Hill and His Orchestra (1935–1939): "Lookie, Lookie, Lookie, Here Comes Cookie," "Got Me Doin' Things," "When Love Knocks at Your Heart," "Uptown Rhapsody," "Would You Like to Buy a Dream?" "Where Is the Sun?" "Have You Forgotten the You and Me that Used to Be?" Dizzy Gillespie, Roy Eldridge, Chu Berry. . . . I can't play it. After the first time Jazzman left me (or I him), thirty-five years ago, I couldn't listen to jazz anymore because it hurt too much. Except for Billie Holiday — she hurt too much, too, and she made my hurt hurt more, but she made it hurt good. Once in a while Sinatra (who sings the autobiography of anybody who's ever been in love) did a riff that rocketed me right back into that smoky club . . . but he was bearable, was Francis, he made me cry, but he didn't scale my heart or scour it with acid (bye-bye Sonny, bye-bye Miles). Shit. When Jazzman came back into my life, we went back into the clubs and I felt like Lazarus: I could hear again. I was alive.

I don't listen to jazz anymore now.

I've torn up Jazzman's album covers (with my hands and nails and teeth). The vinyl records refuse to break. I could piece his face together again, if I wanted to, from the ragged bits I haven't been able to bring myself to throw away.

Teddy Hill used to say that Benny Goodman got all the credit for his — Teddy's — arrangements, which Goodman stole; he was permanently embittered, and wry, and dignified and austere.

I told Jazzman once that I couldn't breathe without him — I meant he was the air I breathed, he loosed all the restraints; but we broke up again; and now it has come (medically) true: I can't breathe. Vampire. Stole the breath of life. I know all about theft.

Twenty-two; and I was still seeing Arnold.

I was, after a series of part-time and temporary jobs (unable to secure one at the public library, where I thought to get drunk on library paste), working at Macmillan, when that publisher was housed on Fifth Avenue and Twelfth Street, in what is the Forbes Building now.

Every night, in her child's maple bed in the twin-bedded room we shared, my mother cried. I went with her to Bible study meetings, my body uncomfortable there, my soul shrieking out somewhere in the rain. I arranged to go to a class at the New School on Thursday evening — a meeting night. Slowly, by bits, I broke away (and nearly broke).

She watched from the window, twitching the curtains, when Arnold took me home and kissed me chastely on the lips. Leaving me at the door.

I walked through cemeteries a lot in those days — through Green-Wood Cemetery, a gorgeous city of the silent but so vivid dead, outside of which Rocco Quattracci and I used to park in his pink Edsel. There — separated by a wire fence from the marble Lady in the Bathtub, a memorial to a Victorian maiden who slipped and fell in the tub on her wedding night, cracking her young skull open — we necked.

I liked taking my heart to that soothing, sprawling place. The dead are sympathetic, unthreatening; they are like children, they do no harm. I liked their company. (I still do.) In that idiosyncratic and eclectic place, expressive both of individuality and communality, among simple markers and among mock castles, temples, pyramids, and marble gazebos, I was confirmed in the visceral knowledge that had entered me suddenly one day in a subway car, when for some reason all the evidence chose in my mind to accumulate and coalesce, and the conviction established itself marrow-deep that someday I would die; and I was comforted.

Coffee shops and loft parties and foreign films and (once) a meeting at the Young Socialist Club (Dan Wakefield speaking about Salinger) and dates. Volunteer work at settlement houses. Friends — a joy to me, such happiness after the apprehension caused by my having been weaned on Watch Tower propaganda about the carnality, corruption, triviality, treachery, and venality of the "worldly." But I was still living at home — and how she cried! *She is killing me!* my diary says. But I do not know who spoke those words, she or I.

My body was unoccupied. Rocco revolted me as much as he excited me. So did all the rest with whom I fiddled, giggled, played. Except Arnold, of course. Arnold I loved. I revolted myself.

One Sunday morning (I had stopped going from door to door) I saw a jazz trio — horn, bass, drums — on TV. They were playing at Minton's. I persuaded my friend Rosalie from Macmillan to go with me to Minton's.

When you walk inside (this is how it was), to the left there is a mirrored bar; and then there is the slightly raised platform where the musicians play; and across from them — directly across from them, which is where Rosalie and I sat — there are red leather booths and banquettes. I had a rye and ginger with four cherries. *Love comes in at the eye.* I had never seen concentration so hot and so intense. And also cool: detached/engaged. The communication, the communion — the signals wordlessly effortlessly joyously exchanged with other musicians, a form of sweet flirtation and of bonding and of testing the limits between self and others, the tension between isolation and solidarity, the competition and the complicity; and the integrity and delicate ego-balancing required to make it all work. (Perhaps making love would be like this?) But most of all the rapt communion Jazzman was enjoying with himself: he was the author of what he made; his soul (like that of a medieval mystic) extruded from him and expressed itself in explosions and in witty, driving, sexy phrases. He retreated, he advanced; he was silent and he stormed. He was a primal and a sophisticated force; his extraversion was the product of his introversion.

I loved his hands.

I thought his eyes were closed, the whole time, as if he were in church; but they couldn't have been; and he says they were not.

Oh Jazzman! The other night I called him in my sleep. I didn't know what I had done until I heard his voice. I loved his voice.

Well I knew I would go to bed with him. Which was as much a relief as it was an occasion for quickening: at last.

Maybe I saw this in a movie, otherwise I don't know how I learned that people behaved like this: I told the waiter I'd like to buy the horn player a drink. And when the set ended, Jazzman came over to me, almost in a mocking shuffle, rocking on the balls of his feet (but more like a tap dancer making his delicately swinging way on sand): "Did you mean for me to sit with you?" he asked. As if he didn't know. Purposefully emasculating his husky voice (his full-bodied, honey-ma-hogany voice). Causing me to babble: "Of course I did, why wouldn't I? Won't you?" Et cetera. And there followed his first little (very little) homily to me on the nature of oppression and segregation, which I listened to wide-eyed, and which of course was bullshit, he knew I was his, his *faux* humility was, thank God, an act.

But not entirely an act; and this is why, caught as I was, by Arnold before him, in the fascination of what's difficult, he secured me entirely — somewhere between his assumed humility and his aggressive virility was real fear, deep longing, a desire to win and a desire to hurt and a desire to love and be loved, and an overriding desire to have the bits of him put together — a desire, which terrified him, to be understood; and there were women who played with men, women who came to places like this precisely to play with men, to exercise the presumption of power they could find nowhere else; and could he be sure I was not one of them?

I hadn't come to play.

I would like to say I remember it all — the exchange of histories, the demonstration of his charm that made up that night — but I don't, perhaps because I was already in love with him from the moment he sat down. He knew whole worlds and ways of being that I knew nothing about — I understood that; and I grasped that he would share them generously. I remember the exchange of promises and telephone numbers on the rain-swept street outside of Minton's — my dreams don't allow me to forget. My nightmares always have the same codicil: I am standing on a street at a crossroads and the street is as terrifyingly strange as it is terrifyingly familiar and I am alone and don't know the way home; I don't know where home is, there is no one to tell me.

We had, in Chesterton's eccentric but accurate phrase, a "practical romance . . . the combination of something that is strange with some-thing that is secure." It perfectly met this criterion: "We need so to view the world as to combine an idea of wonder and an idea of welcome. We need to be happy in this wonderland without once being merely comfortable." The world in which we played out our fate was both an ogre's castle to be stormed and our own cottage to which to return at evening. It was practical, and it was desperate, and the two things were the same. Our love depended on an exact and perilous balance.

In all the days that followed, the trip back to Brooklyn from 118th Street was magic — tunneling through Central Park, the bent trees hung with snow (I was a princess in a fairy tale); or, on the subway, all alone, unafraid, mistress of myself — for the first time in my life — and of the city.

Once in a while he commandeered a car and rode home with me — he smelled of Choward's Violet and of Scotch and of Camel cigarettes (naked, his flesh is the sweetest I have ever smelled, it is like the fragrance of saints, it is the smell of an original innocence his life cannot belie).

My father waited for me, lurking underneath the stairwell of our four-story apartment house; he did not make himself known. Sometimes my father hid behind streetlamps in Harlem. He never said a word. He watched.

One night as we left Birdland, where Basie was playing, Frank Sinatra leaned out of the window of a passing cab and hailed us. Sinatra was drunk and with someone titled, and Jazzman and I climbed into the crowded cab, I with more alacrity than Jazzman considered fitting to his *amour propre*. I placed myself on Frank Sinatra's lap. Lovely bones, he had — all over. We went to an uptown after-hours club. Blind singer Al Hibbler made a circle around the room, touching faces, breasts, women's hair. Jazzman kept moving me away from Hibbler's outstretched searching hands; "I smell pussy!" Hibbler said; and I felt dangerous and safe, a combination of feelings that oddly enough had the effect of eradicating ambiguity: I belonged.

"Tell me," I asked Jazzman when he came back into my life, "is it true that Billie Holiday protected me at Minton's? Because I'm scared I make things up." "It's true," he said.

This is what I remember. Jazzman was playing. A black man placed himself across from me at the banquette where I was nursing a drink. "Who," he said without preamble, "are the Mau Mau?" "Black terrorists," I said; what did I know? Then he lashed out at me so viciously his face swam before mine, and then Billie Holiday — who had come in late, her boys, her poodle, her gardenias — said, "Don't mess with that girl — she's a nigger, she can be raped."

"So I didn't make that up?" I asked Jazzman. Thirty-five years ago, it was. "She loved you," Jazzman said. Aaaah. "And he hated you and lusted after you," Jazzman said. I said, "Who?" "Don't you remember? Don't you know who he was?" "I remember a cloud of fury," I said, "I can't make out the man's features." "Yeah," said Jazzman, "old Red used to come up to Minton's to score dope."

All this time I hadn't known we were talking about Malcolm X. . . . It was Malcolm, too, who told me about the woman who'd been murdered across the street at the Hotel Teresa, the woman whose body had been surgically and completely stripped of its flesh. I was emboldened to ask: "Why are you telling me this?" He never said.

He courted me, Jazzman did. I choose to be immensely touched when I think of this — when I think of him slowly taking his time, biding his time — for he was and is a calculating (he would say a *prudent*) man. He wanted — almost — to keep my innocence intact. . . . We are walking in the Village. "Dykes," he mutters as we pass two women lovers. "What are dykes?" I say, my mind serving up images of Holland. He loves this. . . . We are sitting in a bar on Fifty-second Street; he takes my hand in his and makes a little scratching movement on my palm accompanied by a quizzical look. I don't know what it means. It is a coarse gesture, it means, Will you fuck me? He loves that I don't know what it means.

I kiss him on Broadway. He told me later that he always carried a gun in his briefcase because of those gestures of mine, because they placed him in danger. This may or may not be true.

One night we are at the Metropole and Ben Webster is playing; and most of the crowd is white, and Ben Webster's funning himself by asking everybody, couple by couple, to kiss after a particularly splendid riff. When he gets to us, he says to Jazzman, "You got eyes?" (He means: Will you do it?) Jazzman, not so prudent, kisses me full on the lips.

We are driving in Chicago very slowly, because I have never been in that city before, and he wants me to see the sights; it has happened that

I have gotten separated from the girl singer, and in the car with me are only black musicians. Cops stop us for speeding; in fact we are going twenty miles an hour, if that. They haul everybody out and frisk all the men, taking a very long time; the trumpet player who is with us keeps edging his hand to his mouth, afraid they'll bust his lip . . . and that is the first time I have ever seen anyone — we are in the trumpet player's hotel, where he keeps his works — shoot up heroin (for which Jazzman had a fastidious disdain).

In Chicago in those days, when a crime was committed by a white man, the newspapers would say, "The perpetrator was not black."

It is not true that we are driving slowly so that I can see the sights. It is true; but it is also true that Jazzman's wife, from whom he is separated/not separated (who knows? does he know?), lives in Chicago; and he likes to tempt fate.

He is two men: prudent (calculating) and uncontrolled, uncontrollable, playing with the fates, coaxing from them the fire he believes his black skin calls down upon him.

One of the secretaries at Macmillan said, "But would you go out with him if he were a janitor?" She was going out with a (white) doctor; why wouldn't the question have applied equally to her? He was what he was and I loved what he was.

He lived at the Hotel Arthur, when I met him, across the street from Birdland; it was temporary home to many jazz musicians — and the only hotel in midtown where the cops regularly busted couples for "fornication," which was a law still on the books. The first time I went to his hotel I saw a framed picture of a pretty woman on his dresser. It was a photograph of his wife. I didn't know, then, that he had a wife — and by the time I did know, it was too late.

He has a mechanism like a Rolodex in his head. He flips to the card he needs and takes the script from it. (His eyes widen slightly while he searches for the appropriate file.) On the file, that night, was written that he and his wife had "a beautiful relationship." In which case, I said, what was I doing there? I no longer remember what answer he provided; what it amounted to — what all his lies and evasions amounted to — was that he loved me. And yet it wasn't a lie that he loved me.

He lived not so much in a world of counterfeit truth as in a world of contrapuntal truths. He was the most devious man I have ever known; and yet it was his painful candor that was lovable and mesmerizing, beautiful and valuable. And his deviousness engendered more tenderness than it did anger — he fought for survival even when (especially when) he had no need to.

The coverlet on his daybed was cerise. We talked about *Amos 'n' Andy*. He liked *Amos 'n' Andy*.

He made me say the word *nigger* that night. I couldn't. He made me do it. I said it, and I cried. He remembers that; he likes to tell that story.

> I'm wife; I've finished
> that,
> That other state;
> I'm Czar, I'm woman now:
> It's safer so. . . .
> — Emily Dickinson

In due course he moved to a rented apartment on Grace Avenue in the Bronx.

That is where we made love for the first time.

What I don't like to think about is that I wouldn't be able to find that place again. Or the mini-market where we shopped. Or the drugstore where I waited while he bought condoms. I panic when I think that Grace Avenue is lost (to me); it is a war zone now.

I told my mother — that day, so many many days and nights — *Wild nights! Wild nights! Rowing in Eden* (moored in him) — that I was at Rosalie's house.

My love for Arnold ran parallel to my love for Jazzman. But my body was occupied by Jazzman — and his body was the body of my soul.

> *Love is not blind; that is the last thing that it is. Love is bound; and the more it is bound the less it is blind. . . . The devotee is entirely free to criticise; the fanatic can safely be a sceptic.*
>
> — G. K. Chesterton

He never treated my body with less than exquisite empathy; he was incapable of a coarse gesture in bed (I don't mean his repertoire was limited, I don't mean that at all); but the week after we first made love — I was back at Grace Avenue — he handed me a mimeographed copy of a pornographic essay in which sex was described in terms of a horse race. (Cherry lost.) I cried. Did I expect John Donne? I had been raised by Arnold — Christopher Marlowe, Robert Herrick, Andrew Marvell, Robert Burns (*John Anderson my jo, John*). I cried. ("You are the bluesiest white woman I ever did see," his mother once said to me. She meant I bawled a lot.)

Did I trust him? One learns to love the world without trusting it, one has to. I trusted him.

One time when I came into his apartment he was on the phone with his young son (Jazzman was thirty-two and had two sons); and he was scolding the child, and he didn't want me to hear, so he brushed me away with the back of his hand. Every time I saw that dismissive gesture, perfunctory, brutal, and unnegotiable, I felt both the sharp pain of rejection and something other, coiled and dark — something I later identified as hatred. . . . There is another gesture he has; he hadn't it then, when I first loved him; it had accrued to him with age and suffering; and it is terrible. It is a gesture I had seen before only on the streets of India — beggars used it, a grubbing gesture, his hand cupped, his fingers slightly turned in, pawing. That is a nice necklace, he would say; and his hand would move in that awful way. Sometimes, unconsciously, he gestured that way toward the part of my body his sex wanted; I didn't hate him then, a starving man. I pitied him. But my need was always greater than my pity; and my need was to be needed by him.

There was a snowstorm the day he made love to me for the first time; I went back to Brooklyn by subway, cherishing my secret and my life-giving pain (and walking the last mile over hills of snow in an untenanted world). Oh how I had needed to be frankly fully used, hard and well used and lingeringly, liquescently, lovingly and in the daylight used by cock and hand and educated patient tongue. Chilled with snow and warmed by love I fell stunned into my maple bed, and dimly remembered, when I awoke, that I had seen my mother, sometime during the night, sitting on her own bed next to mine, rocking over me (*davening*). In the morning, happy and in the most wonderful physical pain, I was assaulted by her thin voice, issuing from a face turned away from me. "You said terrible things in your sleep," she said, "terrible terrible things."

The next week I rented an apartment in the East Village.

I loved that place. I had never lived alone before, I had never slept in a room alone.

SLEEP WELL YOUR NATIONAL GUARD IS WATCHING, said a billboard on my street, East Seventh Street (a street of tenements and laundromats and two funeral parlors and Ukrainian groceries); and I did.

"In solitude," Kundera writes, "it was possible for her to get the greatest enjoyment from the presence of the man she loved. If his presence had been continuous, it would have kept on disappearing. Only when alone was she able to hold on to it." Jazzman was on the road a lot; and I didn't mind, I lived with him wholly. ("He never separated her body from her soul and she could live with him *wholly*.") We were lovers whether he was in my bed, or in my city, or not in my bed and not in my city. I lived in an altered state of consciousness because I lived in the soft clutch of his love. In my ground-floor bedroom, its windows covered with plasterboard to keep the noise of the world away, the walls draped with green velvet, banks of candles lit when I listened to Casals, to Miles, I was happy.

And I always knew (but not because he told me) when he would be in town. I presented myself at the Blue Note or the Five Spot then . . . and he would be there. Waiting had not yet become a full-time occupation for me — the life I lived was, except for the fact of him, compatible with that of any Village girl in black leotards with brains and energy and curiosity; but I knew when to be at home for him. He would appear at my door looking sick with dread and nascent rage and longing and grab my arms, and, his mouth moving in my hair, would demand that I recount my infidelities; of course there were none. And then bed.

I don't remember ever having told him about Arnold. I didn't think he would have seen the point. (But I underestimate his intuitive intelligence; it is only when he is fashioning a story to protect himself that his own inventions blind him to others' truths.)

The first time I had knowledge of an event that was still in the future (I was living outside of time, waiting for Arnold to declare his love) I was sitting in a subway car on my way to Watch Tower headquarters. Across from me are two mousy men and a Puerto Rican woman, and I weave stories about them: She is an actress in B movies, a villain; the mice are her accomplices; and they are assassins. The next night, on my way back to Bethel from a Bible study, I pick up a copy of the *Daily News* in the lobby of the St. George Hotel and I see their faces staring out at me. (She was a minor movie actress.) They were the Puerto Rican nationalists who tried to kill Truman. I am neither surprised nor disturbed. I am living life on a tightrope (I was at that time readying my soul to leave Bethel); and I have skipped past logic and rationality to a foreign country where nothing but the ordinary is astonishing.

During the whole of the time I saw Jazzman, I knew when he would be in town — which was very inconvenient for him when he was tempted to have a fling, especially when he was trying it on with movie stars.

All the time Jazzman was my love and lover I knew things with casual assurance (there was nothing self-congratulatory about this knowledge, and nothing ravaging) that in the normal way I would not have known. I knew when my brother had been hurt in a gang war. I would go to Brooklyn and find him, nose bandaged, ribs taped — "Your brother fell down the stairs," my mother would say, a lie. I did not invite this knowledge. I neither liked nor disliked having foreknowledge; these psychic flurries seemed to go with the territory of love. One day I was riding in a cab and I understood (the thought was not a thunderclap, nor did it move me to an exorbitance of emotion or in fact to any emotion at all — I was unruffled; it existed simply as a given fact that owed nothing to temporal time or to volition): we will turn the corner and run the next light and we will hit a boy on a bicycle. We did. The boy was not badly hurt; but I asked, not knowing to whom my request was addressed, to be relieved of prescience; and I never moved lightly into the future again, it went away.

Except for one time more. I was sitting at my desk at Macmillan and I said (my friend Rosalie heard me say, I did not hear myself say this), "I will have to go to Jazzman now, he wants me." Then the phone rang, it was Jazzman's mother. That night I was on a flight to Gary, Indiana: Jazzman had tried to kill himself, she said.

He was, however, there to meet my plane. And randy. You wouldn't have thought this man — who upped the ante in every room he ever walked into, who brought with him the electrical charge of his charm — had ever entertained the idea of self-murder.

(Years later I formed the conviction that he was two people — there was a good Jazzman and a bad Jazzman; it was the bad Jazzman who would have tried to kill himself.)

His wife had had an affair with another man. (Who could blame her after all?) I don't think I knew this then; I don't think I was told what had given rise to this excess of suffering (or showmanship); his mother valued his suffering, which, I was given to understand, was of long standing — he was "different," his mother said. I don't remember. All I know is that he'd called for me and I was there. On the Hill in Boone Grove, living with Jazzman and his mother, Edie-May, and Aunt May-belle and Jazzman's little boy — six years old, he was — in a run-down wooden house on a dirt road. Going to Saturday night dances, offbeat dancing, and sleeping too late for Sunday morning church. Poker games. Lots of people, lots of talking, food.

I was the only thing white as far as the eye could see. Jazzman's kid held my hand and took me round to white storekeepers and when they looked at us uncertainly, "This is my mama," he said — ("They like to jump out of they skin, Daddy").

The first night I spent in that house I felt the covers being pulled off me in the double bed in which I slept naked with Jazzman: "Uh-huh," a woman who later proved to be Edie-May said, "B-plus." (She had been the madam of a whorehouse, presumably she knew.)

All the things I learned thirty-five years later — that he had been born with three testicles (very prettily, neatly surgically rearranged); that he was thought to be "slow" at school and obdurate and vain among the other boys his age; that he refused to work in the steel mills like everybody else; that he tap-danced for a living when he was eight years old; that he faked his age and joined the Merchant Marine when he was fifteen and worked as a cook in an officers' mess; that he took his mother with him on the road until he was well into his twenties; that one of his sisters had committed suicide; that he had a second sister who died of an abortion induced by her mother — I did not know then.

(I used to tell people, when he had retreated into mythology — after he had left me or I had left him — that my first lover had been a man without a bellybutton. I remembered him like this. Like a freak, or like a God; my *sacré monstre*. (Borges says that "'the man without a Navel yet lives in me' is the curious line written by Sir Thomas Browne to signify that he was conceived in sin because he was a descendant of Adam. In the first chapter of *Ulysses*, Joyce also evokes the immaculate and taut belly of the woman without a mother: 'Heva, naked Eve. She had no navel.'") There wasn't even the hint of a scar (I looked for it almost right away, thirty-five years later) where his bellybutton should have been, where (he said) a hernia had been, and something else had been rearranged. . . . He was unattached to his mother by an umbilical cord.)

Thirty-five years later, he plunged into his several versions of history (rifling through his mental Rolodex) and told me that he had planned to marry me but that Edie-May had said, She can't know what she's getting into, the child's too young. And he'd decided to give his son a home with his wife, Janine, and to make a family with Janine; and he didn't think — or Edie-May didn't think — I could cope with a child. "So then you did leave me?" I said. Because he had tenaciously held to the claim that I'd left him. "Well," he rumbled, "at least I didn't run away to India."

Who knew what to make of this? Scrambled motives, scrambled memories. And his cunning derails his intelligence. But I didn't care, thirty-five years later: I carried a mental picture of him sitting in the gutter crying, his head in his hands, outside the funeral parlor from which his sister was buried. The preacher had called the dead girl evil. The cops had the fetus in a bottle.

"And she did it all for just a thrill," he says to me, or perhaps to himself. We are in bed, this is the second time around, thirty-five years later. "Who? Who did what for a thrill?" I ask. "Janine." "But you were separated from her, you were with me." "Shhhh, quiet, girl," he says. He is too ready for love to root around for an encompassing motive for his acts, which are divided acts.

He told me lots of things. Some of them were true. What happened between us when we were alone was true.

"How I wish you could understand me!" he murmured thirty-five years later. Me too. I wished that too. But he sorted and picked his way among the facts, among the debris of the true and the near true and what he perceived to be the fatal lie. . . . Arnold used to quote Whitman to me: "Only that which everyone knows to be true is true." But Jazzman always had so much to lose and so much to gain on any spin of the wheel, truth seemed like an indulgence to him; he had more to gain, he thought, by dissembling.

Sometimes we took the car and sat on the hill and watched the molten steel of the mills shoot up in the sky, red volcanic rivers, orange-red, illuminating the velvet dark.

We drove to Michigan to see his cousins there. Such nice houses they had (and our congress was so easy). Only in the back yard, rats, hundreds of them, climbed in and out of garbage pails.

I loved the steel-mill town where he'd spent summers with his grandmother. ("Come here," he said, "I'll show you where the dykes live"). I was happy-go-lucky and protected, safe from the Saturday night knives and the dykes and the world that would have killed us if it could. There was no place in the world for a black man and a white girl.

One thing I was told then, but not by him. Sullie Jackson, who lived on Riverside Drive — where she moved after her husband came back from serving a sentence for armed robbery and hit the numbers — told me this: "When Jazzman sleeps in this apartment with his mother, only one of the twin beds gets messed," she said. It didn't seem strange to me. Very little he did seemed strange to me.

He hustled me out of Gary in the middle of the night. Someone had told Janine I was there. She wasn't having it. I got the first plane out. (I went docilely.) And after that nothing was the same. Before that there had been, for all the girl singers and French actresses in the world, no thought that we would ever separate. Now it was: Will I marry her? Won't I marry her? Will I leave her? Won't I leave her?

I was never sure again. One day I got a letter from him written in green ink, with circles — mandalas, actually — over the *i*'s, a squarish handwriting with glosses on the capitals. *I can't live without this woman*, he wrote. He meant Janine. Two weeks later he came to me unannounced and he was in my bed again. But I was tired by that time. Not tired of him. Just tired. I had spent my fortune. My fortune of hope and optimism and belief. I gave him bus fare to go back to Janine.

A year or so later, before I married (out of sentient weariness), I went to Chicago and had a taxi take me round to their house. I don't know what I expected. Blank supercilious windows — it was like any other house.

And I began a time in the desert.

1993. Thirty-two years ago, he left me. Or I left him. Or maybe it was thirty-four years ago. He went straightaway back to his wife. Or didn't. In any case he divorced; he remarried. I married; I divorced. He doesn't remember the apartment on East Seventh Street in which my memory has enshrined him; I don't remember how he got those terrible scars on the creamy flesh I love — he says I was there when he got them. I remember a letter I carried around like stigmata, a letter in which he said he was leaving me because of the love he had for another woman; he says he fled from me because of the love he bore for me — he left me, he says, in order to breathe, in order to come back to me . . . and I, he says, unable to wait out his fear, married precipitously, casting us both into a void of perpetual longing. (The letter he wrote was in green ink. He remembers the ink.)

What we both remember is the wrenching, the violence of unhappiness, and the passion, the wild tenderness, that preceded it.

He was my first lover. He will be my last.

I have had a rich and busy life since he left me (or I left him), a life that seems on the whole crafted, though every particular of it has felt spontaneous. I cannot say that I spent the better part of three decades mourning his loss or even thinking about him or being in any way true to his memory. Occasionally something would happen to remind me of him; I remembered him fondly, with no rancor, no animosity at all. I remembered the totality of my love for him.

It was a pretty artifact to consider: the first love of a girl for a man, the love of people who wished intensely not to do each other harm. I only got everything all at once — a love that was both physical and spiritual — the first time. That is what, before he appeared in my life again, I have told my daughter (who, had I not left him, or he me, would never, God forbid, have been born). I might have added that he was the best lover I ever had. I am not talking about technical virtuosity, although he was (I was to learn, as I went to bed with men who were clumsy or selfish or scared, men whose bodies did not love women) astonishing. I mean that his body loved my soul.

I wanted him from the moment I saw him; there goes my virginity, I determined (and that might well have been the first truly calculated decision of my entire life). I was twenty-two, innocent as dawn, and hurting; there was no question of morality or of consequences; what I knew (at first sight) was that he had it in his power to heal me.

I was very much in need of healing. I had just come out of a claustrophobic religious sect that had taught me to hate the world and the flesh; I needed a baptism of fire into the world I'd been taught to despise: he was a jazz musician; he brought me into that hot, hard, glittering world. (My unconscious must have enjoyed the irony: salvation of the spirit by means of the scorned flesh and the fleshpots of the world.) My love for him always had a religious fervor and intensity (and sometimes an edgy religious hysteria).

He brought me along beautifully. By the time we left each other, after three gorgeous and terrible and seldom pacific years, I was able — almost — to stand on my own feet.

Thirty-two (-four?) years later, feeling myself again in need of healing (a bruising business with a man, what else?), I called him.

I'd been bruised before, God knows, and sad before . . . why I chose this time to call him I can't for the life of me say. I don't even know how I came to have his telephone number. (He can't believe that I didn't use it earlier; he finds this strange, and not altogether easy to forgive.)

"I've been looking for you!" he said, his voice the warm mahogany bass rumble that had once been my entire delight. We told each other our lives. It felt comfy and cozy to talk to him — and that was a change; whatever we'd been before to each other, we hadn't been comfy and cozy; we had not been trusting friends. Those who knew us then remember us as almost mythic, certainly mercurial, lovers. And yet, somehow, the ease — the absence of Sturm und Drang that characterized our first conversations — didn't seem

at all like a diminution, a shift into lower gear; it was a spiral into greater intimacy, which fostered even greater desire. Before we'd had intensity; now we had intensity together with ease, excitement combined with an unhoped-for, delicious familiarity . . . and this added up to a feeling of safety that was almost palpable. "We can never harm each other," I said, "we've done all that already." "We never did harm each other," he said — all he can remember is the good.

Days after our first talk, in a bitter snowstorm, he came to me. "I want to hug you for about twelve hours," I said. He had something else in mind (and so, to tell the truth, did I).

After the first five minutes of mutual terror, we read each other's altered bodies like Braille. What followed (if this were a nineteenth-century novel, I'd say, Dear Reader, close the book and read no more) was thrilling. It didn't matter — except to technique on a most superficial level, and one could accommodate one's technique to the altered, instinctively understood demands of altered flesh — that our bodies were older. We saw our bodies through the sympathetic eyes of love (and the relevant parts worked very well indeed). And sex didn't have, and didn't need, any element of the forbidden to make it thrilling: we had belonged to each other for a long long time, we were taking up where we'd so stupidly left off. (I don't know that either of us knew this before we made love; we took it profoundly for granted after we made love.)

Maybe what had prompted me to call him was the unconscious urgency of intimations of mortality; I'm fifty-eight — I don't have a lot of time to fool around. He takes a more mystical view of things: he thinks it was ordained; he says, when he's in a forgiving mode, "We weren't ready for this page of the book before."

I'm fifty-eight, he's sixty-four. I was slim and beautiful when we were lovers the last time. I'm not now. He was dazzling. (I once found a note in his pocket from Ava Gardner — a scribbled invitation and her phone number — after he'd played a date at a jazz club; mad jealous scenes followed.) He's not, I suppose, objectively dazzling now. He's an old man with a gut who snores. So what? (My kids think he's handsome, however; they say I prepared them for a little old man and presented them with a provocative charmer instead.)

He doesn't come wrapped in a glamorous world anymore. When I first knew him, I entered his frame of reference entirely. I entered his world, having not yet constructed mine. His friends, his life, his family, his milieu. Now I have a world and a life; if the euphoria we both feel now subsides, if there is a leakage of innocence (surely the conviction that one will always be loved is the most sublime form of innocence), it will be because we are negotiating a meeting of worlds. The meeting of minds and bodies has been beautifully accomplished.

Thirty-odd years ago he was guarded, wary, cool. Cool, hip, determinedly inarticulate. He could not have said then: I miss you. He seldom said then: I love you. It wouldn't have been cool, just as it wouldn't have been cool for him to consider my wishes — to say, for example, as he does now: Did you mind when I left you to talk to the musicians? Thirty years ago I wasn't supposed to understand that he cared if I minded anything at all.

As a result, I thought then that he held all the cards, had all the power. "Didn't you know I worshiped you?" he says. I did not know. It's dangerous to be the object of worship. No one deserves it. And the worshiper eventually spends an awful lot of time trying to destroy the image he's made to worship. That's what happened the last time. (I think that's what happened. He takes a simpler view: "My mother said you were too young to know what you were getting into," he says.)

I don't feel worshiped anymore. I feel — and this is far better — completely comprehended. He knows me; he loves me; and this is the highest compliment I've ever been paid.

There are ways in which life has worn him down. Me too. I wish he hadn't been battered (I wish I hadn't been battered); but suffering opens up parts of the heart you didn't even know you had. And now his love is articulated, and mine is marginally more patient. His is not jealous anymore, and mine knows limits to its possessiveness.

Do I wish he weren't complicated and difficult? I can't really say I do. James Baldwin once said we don't choose our loves, we accept them; and he is the man I accept . . . I have no choice (I certainly am not going to make the same stupid mistake the second time around). Does he wish I were less complicated and difficult? Perhaps. In the end does it matter? I think not; the poor man doesn't have a choice.

I could be wrong.

I didn't know how much a disastrous marriage had wounded me in my womanhood. He has healed me in my womanhood. No matter what else changes, this will never change. I have been held in someone's heart for a lifetime, cherished for all the years of my adult life. This makes me feel old and young, new and ancient, all at the same time. It has brought both closure and renewal.

"I don't remember that you made me laugh so much before," he says. We laugh a lot now. I cried a lot before. "The bluesiest woman I ever met," his mother, who loved me, called me. Now it's possible for us to tease each other — as we couldn't when he played god to my goddess — and even to see in each other elements of the ridiculous and the absurd (and to be absurdly touched by them).

Some things haven't changed: the smell of him, his eyes, his hands. Some things have changed: he never could accept the idea of pain or defeat before; he thought he could outmaneuver and outrun it. Real life has caught up with him and chastened him. If this makes him less godlike, it makes him more human. It makes me more human, too; I used to regard only my pain — thinking him capable of resolving his by an act of will; now his pain is more terrible to me than my own; his unhappiness squeezes every drop of anguish from my heart (which I rejoice to know has grown so few calluses).

I think we've saved the best for last.

What if we had married then? My mind recoils from this question. There's just so much deconstructing one can do. I guess I take a mystical view of it too: we needed to grow apart so as to grow together. (We do regret not having had children in common, though; and, though we fantasize, there is nothing we can do about this very real sorrow.)

If we were to meet for the first time tomorrow, would I be drawn to him? I don't think so. History — the simultaneity of continuity and rebirth, familiarity and revelation — works in our favor. In a way this scares me. It scares me to think that because I disapprove of his politics — I think they're nuts — I might not, if he were brand-new to me, see the point of him. He counters that his politics, and his somewhat paranoid view of the world, come from his experience; and he is right. His opinionated bellicosity is belied by the softness of his heart. He's been afraid of exposing that softness; I think it is only because we knew each other in that other, young life that he can offer it to me. We've paid our dues. His strength and his sadness he shows me; he's not carving out a persona anymore. On his part there's less need to posture, there are no "acts." What would be the point? When we were young we made up in attitude what we didn't have in wisdom. Now that we're no longer young, we're not trying it out for style anymore; we've dropped the pretenses.

That's not to say we can't fool ourselves and each other; life isn't so forgiving that you can fashion yourself entirely anew and be born perfectly again in love. Unconscious guilts and patterns exist to sabotage us. I don't know, for example, if my undermining need for reassurance — which hasn't been strongly tested — has been entirely tamed. I am aware of dangers.

We have said, not as a vow but as an irrevocable fact, that we will never leave each other's lives again. I believe this in some profound way to be true. While I am scared by the thought that our superficial differences might, had we met tomorrow, never have given us the chance to know that we were ordained to love, I count it as an immeasurable gift to know that something — some essence, which you may or may not wish to call "soul" — remains intact over the years; what he loved in me then, he loves in me now. I love him for loving it.

Our ease extends to sex. I would have said we had perfect sex before. (As a consequence of which, I'd often rued, it was all downhill after that — thirty years of downhill racing.) Can I say it was perfect then if I can also say it is more perfect now? I am conscious now, in the new freedom we enjoy, of the little reticences, the withdrawals, that marked our lives in and out of bed then; I'm conscious of them because now, having nothing to lose and everything to lose and consequently nothing to protect, I'm aware of how large and silly and dangerous a part trivial embarrassment plays in young love. Silly, also sweet; but we don't have time for it now. We may sometimes behave adolescently; but we are always aware that time is a gift. We love, and we will die; this knowledge governs us.

He sees me as I was and he sees me as I am. He has entered me and healed me again. I am so lucky. To explore all that is new and all that is old with the first object of one's desire seems like a miracle to me . . . he thinks God has brought this about . . . and he has healed me so much I believe this too.

We've learned to preserve ourselves from the shoddiest demands of our imperfect natures.

You don't get to be our age, however, without being encumbered; and on occasion even the great joy I feel doesn't altogether chill out the fear I entertain that the encumbrances of years will do us in (history, which works so much for us, can also work against us). If he were to leave me tomorrow (that demon need, the insecurity he thinks I have risen above, asserts its ugly head), everything I have said would still be true. Life and love are hard. Life and love are wonderful; I've been twice blessed, and my gratitude is forever.

What is truth? I wrote that — I *fashioned* it — after the first time we met again, after a three-decade absence (and an immediate return to bed). Imposing order upon chaos necessarily involves a degree of invention — if nothing else, connective tissue needs to be supplied, and brevity demands an editing; and if even one bit of connecting tissue is faked or flawed (or dross), and one essential truth is edited out, can the body of truth not be crucified? (But — Blake — "Everything it is possible to believe is true.") I believe that if each of us was stripped of layers of civilization, personal history, culture, enervating sadness and exhausting lies, dogma, certainty, and disbelief, we would find each other. Howling. And connect. I believe that when we are soul to soul, on some unknown ground where fundamental soul-matter meets, without the accretions of harm, the damage and the shit, where characters and personalities were what they were meant to be before the world disfigured us, that at this basic (anima?) level we will meet (we *do* meet) and recognize each other. Alas, we live in the world as the world is, and with our histories as our histories are.

> *When sense from spirit flies away,*
> *And subterfuge is done;*
> *When that which is and that which was*
> *Apart, intrinsic, stand,*
> *And this brief tragedy of flesh*
> *Is shifted like a sand;*
> *When figures show their royal front*
> *And mists are carved away, —*
> *Behold the atom I preferred*
> *To all the lists of clay!*
>
> — Emily Dickinson

I had called him once (from the desert). I'd seen his name outside Fat Tuesdays, where he was playing, and I had not gone in: vanity (I was old! I had been young) and a swift thrust of fear and an overwhelming sense of displacement and disorientation made the panic rise in my throat. And when I gathered my courage to go back, he was no longer playing there. So I called him on the telephone. We cannot agree on when this was. Five years ago, or ten. . . .

All the time I was with him and for all the years I was away from him — those years when I did not allow myself to know that I missed him — I had a recurring nightmare: I would wake, drenched with sweat and crying, and trying to put together the digits of a phone number, getting them wrong, losing him. . . .

He had stabbed a man; and he wanted to come right over. He had stabbed a man because he believed his (current) wife — he is always married — was having an affair with the man. ("And the funny thing is, I was wrong about that bitch!") He wanted to come over — right now! — and start all over again. No, I said; and retired the active thought of him — that knife! (I took a plane to Italy.) And whatever the value he attached to his property — his wife, his sons, his house (he lived in a pretty little suburb on a street with a Norman Rockwell name which had turned into crack alley) — he was determined to hold on to his fiefdom (he was the only black father left on his block; and his nature is to form intimacies not with people but with circumstances, as a cat is said to do, only in a cat's case this is not true; he lives not from enjoyment to enjoyment but from want to want — he can never be satisfied).

It is true, though, that a thing must be loved before it is lovable, and (Chesterton) "when you do love a thing, its gladness is a reason for loving it, and its sadness a reason for loving it more." His bluster and his greed hid sadness.

Five — or ten — years later, I called him again. (He had tried angrily and clumsily to reach me; he couldn't find me.)

The look on his face when he makes love is the look on his face when he makes music.

He came to me that wintery spring of snowstorms; and this is what I wrote — fashioned — while I waited for him to come, our intimacy already having been established on the phone (he was more closely tethered now to house and home, the stabbing had seen to that; it had done the opposite of liberating him).

I have just come from my swimming pool, I feel all loose and easy in my limbs and in my soul (from the cool waters of the pool to the hot waters of the gushing Jacuzzi and back again into the forgiving cool); my flesh feels caressed, feels like silk, feels lovable, feels relaxed and expectant all at once; and now I am in bed, smelling of chlorine (which smell I love) and of tuberose perfume; my damp hair rests on velvet pillows, candles burn, and their scent (syringa — the white flower of the mock orange bush) mingles with that of the blowsy yellow roses I send myself each week. (For a long time somebody sent me roses, I never knew who; they arrived mysteriously wrapped in virgin white; and then they stopped coming; and I, having become used to roses, made myself a present of them thereafter.) I am listening to Ben Webster and Oscar Peterson; I feel the phrasing of their music in my pulse . . . in my genitals . . . deep in my vagina, to be precise; an unaroused clitoris has never been the locus of my juicy desire, which is indistinguishable from sweet, aching, penetrating pain. . . . This is nice. New York is shrouded in fog. I can just see, fizzing through the clouds, the fantastic deco doodles of the Chrysler Building and the flashing red lights of the Empire State Building ("in the dark the just exchange their messages"); planes fly low, fog curls around my roses.

Waiting is a kind of silken foreplay. All the answers are in the flesh, in touch. He is the body of the evidence.

I love best the moment when he first enters me; the first introduction of otherness into my body literally takes my breath away, pierces my soul as well as my body. Sometimes, after hours and hours of sex, I find myself (while still in the act of love) adrift beside still waters, floating on ocean waves, in fragrant gardens, in the happy childhood I never had, in a trance illuminated by catherine wheels and flashing pictures, kaleidoscopic lights.

Nothing I do with him could make me feel guilty, could make me feel anything but new: "O my America! my new-found land." I am at home in the exotic world of love, safe in known arms, rowing toward milk and honey, a securable distant shore. This is the perfect willed dance, the joined intention enfleshed.

"There's one thing I have to tell you," he said, "knowing how you hate religion and all. I'm a Baptist now." "It's OK," I said, "I'm a Catholic now." "The Man knew we weren't ready for this page before," Jazzman said.

You know how it ends.

It ended.

Never leave me again never leave me again never leave me again, he said. Oh there will be trouble this time if you leave my life again, he said (by trouble he meant: someone will die, and by my hand). But he said — he had a way of talking to himself, as if just to the right of him someone else was in the room, someone to whom he was confiding his secrets: She won't make this hard (he meant me), she is more secure now (he meant I would make few demands). Alas, love makes demands. He demanded to be understood — when he was out of work, he lived like a homeless man under his own roof, he said. I understood what I needed to understand: that I was central to his life. He played again. We made plans; he was going to form another group; they would rehearse at my house. . . . At the Vanguard, a drummer said to me, He says you've healed him, baby, you've made him whole again. Jazzman said, That emptiness I feel, that vise around my head, it's gone; you made me well, you healed me, baby.

He said to Anna, You should have been *my* daughter!

He took his wife to Bermuda — a trip sponsored by her church, he said (and I believed him); she took him, he said; he went along to keep the peace. I see lace nightgowns and a reconciliation, I say. I don't, he says.

He had never in thirty years of marriage been unfaithful to her, he said. His idea of fidelity was to come back home before dawn, no matter whom you were fucking, or where.

He slept with me till dawn. He slept with me till noon. After sex his body, for all its availability to me, might have gone under a turtle shell — it made his nerves jangle to be touched after fucking, he said (and I remembered this from the past; I knew the terrain of his back very well). He wasn't good at cuddling unless he was dressed. But he never stayed dressed very long.

After he woke up he'd say, I could move right in! And he walked on my rooftop garden, a drink in his hand, surveying the city of the perishable dream.

He said he prayed for his family. But when I quoted to him words from Saint Paul that I love, he made that back-of-the-hand dismissive gesture that turns me cold. He goes to church for the reason he does so much else, to cover his ass.

Every once in a while a *we* would creep into his conversation — he meant her and him. It was the absence of that *we* that had allowed me to believe I was not committing a mortal sin.

Jazzman didn't know why he was still there — in his crack suburb — he said. Maybe it was because he was waiting to regain his children's affection. Maybe this maybe that. But he was with me. And after sex he cried out, throaty, like a woman. He had only to see me to be aroused and erect. Once a week, twice a week, three times a week, phone calls every day. For a year, for more than a year. And old friends back in our lives again.

So why did I think I was shining him up like an apple, polishing him up so that he would be all shiny and new for her? (They hadn't fucked for years.)

It ended by erosion. (You are far from perfect, he said to me on the phone — as if love requires perfection, as if his love did. It is comfort that requires an approximation of perfection. And misery requires conditions so perfect that misery looks like comfort until it feels like death. Love does not require perfection.) And during this time we required and experienced fiercer delights and experienced a fiercer discontent.

We went to Suzanne's wedding. I had a fever after the ceremony; that night I tossed restlessly in bed and dreamed the lost-telephone-number dream. I knew it had frightened him — a house and a garden full of people black and white and golden children and race not an issue at all and Suzanne my (black) sister-in-love; it meant it was possible, to live an open life like this, a good life, and one not predicated on anticipated harm. It brought him into the realm of the ordinary, the real. He started getting scared after the wedding, and more scared after we went to Zimmy's house. Zimmy is an old man, a trumpet player, and he has an old and conventional white wife; and their life is not glamour and froth, it is real. Jazzman did a line of coke at Zimmy's house (I had never seen him do coke before); and on the way home he stopped a cop's car and asked for directions to my house — he was calling down the fates again; but the fates turned their heads away. Intoxicated, he experiences the ecstatic equilibrium of danger.

When we return from the wedding, he steps into another version of his life as soon as he steps off the plane; he talks street talk, his verbs and his pronouns are at war (as he is, with himself).

He tap-danced in my kitchen. Poured salt on the parquet floor and did a sand dance. Drove my daughter wild with his jive talk: "Is a pig's pussy pork?" was his way of saying yes. With her — with his wife — he was proper.

With whom was he the impostor? I don't think he knew.

Whenever we went to a club, the old musicians, whom he hadn't seen for years and years ("must have closed Long Island down and rolled up the streets"), greeted him like a little brother, and like royalty. Hugs and kisses and tears and drinks all around. Once, at the Vanguard, Japanese tourists took his picture, they thought he must be an American god. He was irresistible. (He upped the ante in any room he entered.)

He was still a hipster, and jive was his talk. He believed he was conversing, but, aside from the usually indecipherable comments addressed to the Man Who Wasn't There, he just rapped — and waited to be capped. Tell me why, I'd say; and his amazement was real: I've told you! There was a torrent of words in his head; sometimes I just got the tag line of his conversation with himself — and he took for granted that I had command of the entire conversation he'd had silently (roaring) in his head.

And yet he thought — and it was not untrue — that he was telling me his life. Nobody else is interested, he said. And I think it is true that he told me more about his past than he had told anyone else. It came out with such difficulty, with such difficult breath to his lips.

He said his wife didn't know about his sisters who died. I believed him. For one thing, she aspired to propriety, and marrying a man whose sisters had died in circumstances she would have identified as squalid would not have pleased her to hear about; he would have known to censor his speech. (He didn't censor his speech when, before his "homelessness," he gave his boys lessons on how to pleasure a woman orally; he drew a diagram. His wife fainted into the dishwater.) While he was courting her, he was simultaneously courting an elegant call girl. I found this out from my friend Decima, his cousin, whose being, in my friend Anne Tabachnick's words, "a *kachladel*," a spoon that likes to stir the gossip pot and watch it boil over, doesn't prevent me from believing it. A man about whom it is said that he slept with his mother needs more than one woman in his life.

I went to a private detective (I lied to Jazzman and told him the guy owed me a favor) and had him track down Jazzman's twin nephews. I presented him with lists of possible phone numbers to reach the children at. He had stood in my kitchen and cried for his lost sister.

He never called the numbers.

("Don't you ever leave anything alone? Why do you have to charge at things?" he said.)

He wore red suspenders.

I will never slow dance with him again.

He played bridge! "My little old Negro man," I called him. Just imagine: bridge, and church (deceptively sedate).

He was short. I had remembered him tall. It was the only physical trick my memory had played on me.

Three of his children had been aborted. I would never have aborted a child of his; he knew this.

He hated that his wife made more money than he did. "The white world doesn't give the black man a chance," he said.

"What if I were poor?" I said. "We'd be cryin' on each other's shoulders," he said; we were eating lobster at the time — *he* was eating lobster; I couldn't eat in his presence. We'd made a pact when we were young, he said (we had done, I remembered), and it didn't matter which of us would make it first because we held all things in common.

Musicians told him white women gave black men money without even asking what they needed it for, he said, talking to the Man Who Wasn't There. This was the bad Jazzman talking, the one who lied and grasped and was disturbed in his mind.

"Don't make her wait so long before you get to her house," Tabachnick said, "it makes her so unhappy." "I'll train her," Jazzman said. What a pimp would say.

The good Jazzman never mocked me, never humiliated me (and how we laughed), and taught me gentleness, and never tried to scare me. The good Jazzman had no tricks.

Parties at my house. Weekends at Gurneys Hotel, near his house. Playing with fire. Book parties where flashbulbs popped.

I asked him for my birthday present to take me to the East Village; I wanted to look at those windows on East Seventh Street with him (and I love to be driven by the man I love). He did a quick spin around the block, said to The Man Who Wasn't There, "My daughter comes down here on weekends." He looked scared as hell, and said — to me, "We didn't spend as much time here as you think." We stopped at Decima's house. "I'm going to Chicago," he said. Decima nodded in my direction with an inquiring glance. "No-ooo," he said with that dismissive brush of the hand, "my grandchildren will be there." Could he mean this? That he wouldn't take me there because his grandchildren would be there? The children of the little boy whose hand I had held in that mill town? What did that make me? Decima's son came in, and declined his mother's offer of a meal: "Gotta eat at home," he said. "Yeah," said Jazzman, "we know how it is, gotta go through the moves, gotta eat one place and then eat another." "I don't know how it is," said Decima's son, who likes me (and who loves his wife). Jazzman took his time at Decima's house — and later, when he was already two hours late for a ballgame (he was a part-time agent, that was another of his gigs), he said to me, "See? That's why I hate coming to see you." Decima had to be restrained from slapping his face, and her son walked out in disgust. In front of Decima's house I jumped out of the car — "I did nothing to deserve this," I said, banging my head smartly on the door. He pulled me back in. And wheedled: "Don't be mad, I hate it when you're mad. I can't live when you're mad at me."

Middle of the night calls: "I can't stand it when I'm not with you." Whispered calls: "Turn on Channel Thirteen, there's a program you gotta see." So many calls from work that a man who bore him a grudge tried to seal the receiver down with Elmer's glue.

When he called me and I wasn't in, all the old interrogations began: "Where were you?" Basso profundo.

When my children were young, I would grieve over their boo-boos for days — days and days after they had forgotten an unkind word, a fall, I'd be hurting for them still. It was like that with him. Weeks and weeks of fretting, and laying the putative blame at the white man's door, that he wouldn't be put on the full-time work roster — he worked at a tennis club — and then he wasn't, and I couldn't bear his having to endure this insult. But he could. He shrugged it off.

When your wife slept with your best friend . . . "Oh, that?" he said. "Nah, that never happened. That was just something my head made up to keep me mad at her." Oh.

If his wife had done such a bad thing, why was he there? Because he had me. If she hadn't, why hadn't he troubled to tell me that history had been revised? Because it is the current version of history — his revisionism — that he totally accepts; and this is what allows him to forget the past — which makes it something of a miracle that he had held me in his heart and not forgotten me for decades of changed times and reasons.

> *You are not alone, when you are still alone,*
> *Oh God, from you that I could private be! . . .*
> *When I am from him I am dead till I be with him.*

After that day at Decima's house, waiting became a full-time occupation.

Friday night at Gurneys, and a call late Saturday morning: "Can't come. Have to pay the mortgage. She found these papers, said the mortgage wasn't paid." "What do you mean, you have to pay the mortgage? On a Saturday?" "You don't understand how black people live, baby, trust me." I almost did.

I wrote this letter, and tore it up — it lacerated me then, and it lacerates me to read it now:

all thats happening is that im leaving you before you leave me. Honeybunch im outta here. youre wrong to think nobody'd get hurt; eventually there'd have been blood on the walls — mine . . . like last time: its not me you cant live without. im just leaving you before you leave me. the end of your healing would have been that you wouldnt have needed me any more to make life w her — your real life —

bearable. let me go; stay well; god bless. you were joy to me, and all of love.

"This is Sultan . . . this is Sydney . . . this is Whisper McCool's brother, remember him?" Incorporating me in his life wherever he went, wherever he was.

Cupping my face in his hands *never leave me never leave me never leave.*

> *Poetry is sane because it floats easily in an infinite sea; reason seeks to cross the infinite sea, and so make it finite. The result is mental exhaustion. . . . To accept everything is an exercise, to understand everything a strain. The poet [the lover] desires exaltation and expansion, a world to stretch himself in. The poet only asks to get his head in the heavens.*
>
> — G. K. Chesterton

Your husband left these things, which I am sending back, at my house; he claimed to be in love with me — and I suppose for awhile he was. We made love, effortlessly and beautifully, and often. I loved him; I still do. But his conniving, his cowardice, his lies, his weasling and wheedling have made me ill; he lives like a man picking his way through mine fields, waiting for the world to blow up in his face — I care about this and hate this on his account as well as on my own. I have to live in the truth or not live at all. I am bound to believe that my motives in sending you this are mixed; but I do believe the truth sets one free — so I'm telling you this, not to inflict more pain but so that we can all live truthfully, and heal. (He once told me he would feel like a rich man if he had $5000; so I wrote him a check for $5000. . . . I would have given him my life. . . . I would have taken him from you if I could; he has never wanted to leave you.)

I wrote this letter to his wife but never mailed it, and not just because it was maudlin (and because I have never been sure how much my giving was a perverted form of taking). I didn't mail it because he had done something again — I don't know what, it might have been simply cupping my face in his hands — that made me so happy again. Perhaps it was because he remembered how, thirty-five years ago, he'd tried to get my whole breast in his mouth, and, interrupting himself with his own laughter, tried and tried and tried again to do it now. Perhaps it was because he told me how to cook the steak or because he told the supermarket checkout girl not to send up chocolate ice cream when I ordered it. Perhaps because my friend Jan's eyes filled with tears when she saw us together — "as if sex is never stale, you two," she said. The sex was never stale. Perhaps it was because he claimed me so publicly at the Village Vanguard. Perhaps because he moved the bedroom furniture around to suit his pleasure.

I mailed this letter:

u told me you had a lot of confusions and fears — I know that you do — i know that you're scared to death of making big changes in your life at yr age, and you think im pushing for change. i ask you to tell me what yr confusions and fears are, and to trust that i will not take advantage of them or use them against you. i think (tho how can i be sure) that i can live w what u are able to give and not torture you for more. u sd a lot was going on w you; i know you have another life — i ask you to tell me whats going on inside you, to the extent that you can. i know this isnt easy for you to do. i need to feel this is good. i want to work w you to make something good and beautiful — i dont know if we can, and i dont think you know if we can but if we are honest maybe we can love ea other without causing ea other or anybody else pain. i think we have a chance if we're frank w each other. i want us to be beautiful again. dont be scared by me. its scary for me too. i say stupid things. so do you. it doesnt matter to me. you dont have to be perfect. . . . dont be scared. *dont be scared.* talk to me. let me be a good friend and lover to you — when you want me. you saved my life thirty-five years ago; i owe you my life — do you think i can ever forget that? if we can be together, when we can, and help each other in the ways that we can, i will be happy (I am happy). sweetheart, whatever life has done to you and whatever you have or havent done and whatever you will do, i am here and rejoice in you and love you. . . . . forgive me when i am stupid. forgive me for all the things i dont understand.

Are there no other stories in the world except yours; and are all men busy with your business? . . . Perhaps when the man in the street did

*not seem to see you it was only his cunning; perhaps when the
policeman asked you your name it was only because he knew it
already. But how much happier you would be if you only knew that
these people cared nothing about you! How much larger your life
would be if your self could become smaller in it; if you could really
look at other men with common curiosity and pleasure; if you could
see them walking as they are in their sunny selfishness and their virile
indifference! You would begin to be interested in them, because they
were not interested in you. You would break out of this tiny and
tawdry theatre in which your own little plot is always being played
and you would find yourself under a freer sky, in a street full of
splendid strangers.*

— G. K. Chesterton

He says, "Why do I sometimes feel like an impostor?"

It can't be denied: he saw few things through to the end. Before we
were reunited he'd stopped playing ("tired of waiting for the phone to
ring"); he'd lost a job as manager of a jazz club ("Mafia boss"); the city
councilman whose assistant he was got evicted or impeached or whatever it is they do to corrupt officials — crack, and embezzling. "So did
you do crack? Did you embezzle?" I asked. He said, "I *never* did crack.
Hand in the till." He was a housing inspector, and that job fell through,
too. He had a plausible reason for everything. Every mistake he made
(I believed) sprang from his failure to remain true to his calling; he was
an artist who did not make art. I said nothing so highfalutin to him;
there was no point telling him what he must have already known. But
when he was with me he started to play the horn again. How I loved
him for that. And I couldn't think less of him for having failed in other
jobs — of course, as his wife might have said, he wasn't the provider
for my children. He didn't perceive himself to be loved by her, either,
that's what he said. "This relationship is going nowhere," he said — a
relationship of thirty years, his marriage, he meant. I do think love
would have made him lovable. And employed. He was already lovable
to me. He still is.

Life is hard for a black man, I don't have to be told that.

He didn't know who his father was.

But he turns emotions into political homilies. How does he really know what he feels — how does he truly feel — when he blusters on about white society being good to black women and bad to black men, "and that bitch makes more money than I do." His rhetoric deadens his intelligence, of course, but worse, his emotions, too.

"How come you get so many mail-order catalogues? Black folks don't." He has found a way — a way demeaning to his intelligence — to interpret the world. I hate it.

He struts on the small stage of his created world, and everybody else — his wife, Decima, the man in the elevator, the supermarket clerk, me — is a supporting player. Yet underlying all the polished maneuvers, the postures, the ready attribution of blame, is a palpable sense of duty and honor and loyalty — a desire to be better than he is, a hunger for virtue. Sometimes I think he despises me because I know he is better than he is. He is two people, one of them capable of saying, no hint of bravado in his voice, "Sometimes I blame the white man for everything, I'm so full of shit." His self-absorption serves his pride — and defeats it. He lives like a hostage, pleasing his captors, identifying his enemies. "Oh how I wish you could understand me!" he says.

It hurts him to try to make sense of life.

He doesn't read books anymore. In fact he doesn't read anymore.

Who is he, really?

Thirty-five years ago he said, "If it hadn't been for you, I wouldn't play anymore."

The last time I asked him to tell me once again why we broke up thirty-five years ago he said, "You got between me and my art."

Does he ever know what he believes?

Is he crazy?

My head feels like it is slamming into the wall of his madness. I watch him drawing, constructing, a new picture of himself to accommodate present crises and exigencies; then I see him crumple the picture and start again; and when he comes back into himself and sees me, he understands that I am in possession of the earlier image of him, which he has chosen to discard — so I become strange to him.

Both of his sisters tragically dead.

I want to eat his pain, to *be* his pain. I want his pain to be my pain and not his pain. I am greedier than he.

He is like a man who makes his own death mask and conforms to it convulsively, a man who projects his illusion onto a screen and steps into it.

He used to paint by numbers, he had those paint-by-number kits.

It is Good Friday, and I haven't seen him for days. I dread Good Friday (I won't fly on Good Friday), I hate it and I fear it too, there is no one minding the candy store, God is dead and His absence fills the world and now Jazzman is gone from me too. ("You are having the real Good Friday experience," my daughter says, wistfully. Yes, always. But I never have the commensurate joy of the Resurrection. So what does one make of that?)

He sends me a dime-store greeting card: *Your love brings me the greatest joy.* I am absurdly happy.

Palm Sunday, Passion Sunday. All through the sound of lamentation, the chanting of Saint Matthew's Passion, wound round and round with grace, I felt Jazzman's presence, refreshing my belief in the Incarnation (without which I could not believe in God). *Were you there when they crucified our Lord? Oo-oh sometimes it makes me tremble, tremble, tremble.* I was happy.

That Easter, the Easter of my love, my hibernating orchids bloomed; and my friend Jan sent me lilies; and I woke up with the cats astride my chest, biting each other's dear faces. I exulted. I had awakened into the thought of him, music for organ and brass: *The appalling strangeness of the mercy of God.*

I was in my mind married to him; I was the center of his life as he was of mine — "I don't regard this as adultery," a Jesuit friend had said; and then I saw I was not married to him, nor he to me.

It ended explosively.

That morning I read Nancy Mitford's letters — a letter to her lover of decades, decades of devotion, Gaston Palewski:

Dear Colonel
I don't understand your policy. I saw your marriage in the DAILY AMERICAN & my whole life seemed to collapse — now I have reconciled myself to it, so reasonable, such a solution to all your problems. But you always said you would tell me — I quite understand NOT telling because almost too difficult & I know when I once left

somebody who minded I did it in that way, anything else seemed impossible. (The question is, too, what have I ever been in your life . . . about like Gaby or Marella or something different — I've never understood.)

That night we were going to B. Smith's. Before he came to me for dinner, he called to say, "Look, we don't have to be kissing and hugging all the time, we know what we are to each other. My daughter goes to that club."

"Oh. So who am I supposed to be?"

"My friend," he says, "a business acquaintance."

The question is, What have I ever been in your life?

I make his dinner mechanically.

"Are you dressed for the club?" he asks.

"No, I'm not going to the club. Eat your dinner. It's no big deal."

"It's World War IV," he says.

We sit on my bed. Clothed, while the dinner congeals. He is addressing his words to the Person Who Isn't There. It is all gibberish, it is a language I do not understand, full of ellipses and grunts and jerks and aborted laughs — it is a foreign tongue.

I am frozen into silence.

And he goes away.

I wake up to a day empty of him. I wake up every day knowing that every other day stretching forever and forever to a gray horizon will be like this day, without him. And my body is the moon — vast, dead, unpopulated, white.

The first night we made love (the second time around), when I said "I love you," he said "Still?" with all the wonder of the world in his voice. That shining word is a jewel I hold in the palm of my hand.

Did he think I could understand him without there being consequences to my understanding him?

Always trying to cover his ass. And never knowing how to save himself.

> *If souls are separate love is possible. If souls are united love is obviously impossible. . . . Love desires personality. Therefore love desires division.*
>
> — G. K. Chesterton

*I **Am** Heathcliff.*

— Charlotte Brontë

Tell me which is true.

He said I healed him. It is strange; I have had panic attacks for as long as I can remember; I have lived with terror. When he came back I was as happy as I have ever been in my life; I was at home with him. I belonged with his flesh — riding in his car, at dinner, everywhere, he was never alien to me; but the old phobias came back. A measure of the panic that had been chemically ameliorated and that had of recent years abated came back; and I understood that when I am estranged from my rooted sadness and grief — the sadness and grief that reach back into my childhood — I feel terror. . . . Mind over matter, he said; it might have maddened me, but it only made me sad that he said that.

He didn't stay away. He played hide and seek. Testing me. Playing with my need, which, overwhelming, overwhelmed him. He wanted everything now, everything I had been prepared to give him; but he wanted — as he had years before — to put space between us first. I ran away. And defeated the purpose of running away by telling him I was doing it. I was going to see Suzanne. "When you come back from your little vacation in St. Croix . . ." he said. Little vacation? I was running for my life; so:

"You know, Jazzman, I think I'll tell your wife."

"That won't make my life easier."

"Bye-bye."

I called her. "Hello, Mrs. Jazzman," I said, "did your husband tell you I was going to call?" "Who's this?" "I'm about to tell you," and I did. "Why are you calling me at work? [Strange question?] I have no reason to believe my husband has ever been disloyal to me. . . . Can I ask you something?" she said. "Are you black or white? I won't tell my husband you called," she said. "He'd hurt you."

She told him, of course. She told her children first.

For six months after that, I called him almost every day (I did not identify myself). I called to read the runes — to hear his voice. Which was now thin or querulous. I recognized this compulsion as a species of madness. Once, soon after I had told his wife, I called him and identified myself and said, "Do you want to talk to me?" "No," he said, his voice clotted with loathing.

Sometimes in the middle of the night he calls. "I love you," he says; and he hangs up. "I have nothing bad in my heart for you," he says. I say *sometimes;* I mean twice. Once to say I love you and once to say I have nothing bad in my heart for you.

And now all that I know, I know from Decima; and I have made Decima promise not to talk about him to me anymore; and I do not talk to Decima about him anymore.

I know that he spent Christmas in bed. Alone.

I know that every time he calls Decima he says, "How are they?" Meaning me. Not even daring to use the pronoun. Suzanne predicted that he would "just wind down," and I suppose he has. It is amazing what men can do — men can do this: "They do best who, if they cannot but admit love, yet make it keep quarter, and sever it wholly from their serious affairs and actions of life; for if it check once with business it troubleth men's fortunes, and maketh men that they can no ways be true to their own ends." How are they? he says; how are they?

Why did I tell his wife. Nothing so simple as a need to hurt him (when I hurt him, I hurt myself, it goes without saying; and if that had been my motive, it would have had the virtue of simplicity and a kind of purity). To get the monkey off my back? To throw the ball into his court? (All the metaphors are crude and inexact.) Because I couldn't bear the weariness of holding on to secrets? Because I couldn't stand to be in the crucible alone, with nothing known by her and everything engineered by him while I was told only what he permitted me to know and granted only enough to satisfy his needs? How petty that sounds. . . . Wild; I was wild, living in the vortex of my love and grief. . . . And the act seemed to me to be not petty but large —

consequential, and I had been denied consequentiality. I was contingent. (He cut his finger washing his hands in the dishwater "at home," he says; and I cry because real things happen there, there is a bathroom with Band-Aids, and I don't know the color of the bathroom; and I am contingent.) Did I imagine it would give me remission to tell? terminal (terminating) satisfaction? Did I think of it as one conclusive act, the world rolled up in a tidy ball? Did I do it to see if I would fall off the face of the earth?

And what if, I am now obliged to suppose, I had told my mother, fifty-five years ago? What if my telling had taken the form of an indictment: Because you are not giving Daddy what he wants, he takes it from me. To insist upon framing things in terms of pattern is to perpetuate the pattern. This interpretation smells of the sickroom (and of the talk show); it is so contemporary, so glib, it makes me ill.

His wife, a year later, called Decima: "Decima," she said, "did you know my husband had an affair with a white woman? Did you know he ate her tootie?"

Decima told me. Decima said that his wife was laughing, and Jazzman was in the family room with her. *The family room.*

I called Jazzman. I told him that if he ever laughed at me again I would kill him.

Decima said, "I told him, 'Aren't you afraid? Her brother's Mafia'" (which he is not). "I gave that thought," said Jazzman — an unutterably despicable (and untrue) theatrical response; which prompted me to call him again. (Was I being used — Tabachnick told me this — as a teasy sex toy between them, to ignite their fraudulent passion?) "If you are using me to keep that shitty marriage of yours going, I feel sorry for you." That's what I said, not eloquently. His response was elegant — a single sound that lay somewhere between a sob and a groan: "No," he said. "Don't you know I worship you?" He had said that . . . thirty-five years before. I made it up that he said that again. I made up what I wanted to be true. What he really said was: "I feel sorry for you if you think I'm laughing at you. I have you in my heart." Words with which I'll have to make do.

·　·　·

The circle has closed; the world is not flat; and I'm not going to fall off.

I give you a miracle: I am not afraid to die. He did that for me, he saved me from the fear of death, a fear that had been my familiar. I don't know how. I don't know why. Never in my life could I have said this before: I am not afraid to die. Because of him. He gave me this gift.

But I am greedy; that gift, inestimable, was not enough to satisfy me. I wanted present gold. I wanted back what I had had before — I wanted to open my eyes to the thought and being and breath and love of him as I did when we loved. I wanted in his absence to dwell with him. I had lived and breathed and had my being in him. Do you think this is idolatry? Perhaps it is. But — *The appalling strangeness of the mercy of God* — I got what I wanted, what I had longed for and begged for, though not in the way I had conceived. If in the early hours of the morning I emptied myself, stilled myself; if I eschewed analyses of cause-and-effect and slammed the gates on blame and vindication and meditated only on love and not on the reasons for loving, this miracle is possible (it is possible to create a vacuum that God will enter): I walk through a door, I pass over a threshold. On the other side is that bath of bliss, that untrammeled garden of joy that was mine when I walked within his brilliance. I am simultaneously narcotized with peace and energized with joy — sheathed in light. This intensity of happiness is no longer attached to or dependent upon my love for Jazzman (which still however exists); there is a way in which this bliss, this love, exists independently of him. I can cross through that door at will. I compose myself; I let it be known that I want it; and I step over the threshold into radiant and perfect love. I abjure choice; I am chosen.

There have been others. Don't think not. I offer no excuses — and no explanations — for not writing about them.

Just today Salim asked me to marry him, imagine.

Why does one love the men one loves? Perhaps, as Iris Murdoch says, there is no such thing as a question without an answer; but this is such a bald question as to be both boring and risible. Is it scent? history? mother? father? fate? accident? caprice? fashion? vanity?

All our knowledge brings us nearer to our ignorance. . . .
There is, it seems to us,
At best, only a limited value
In the knowledge derived from experience.
The knowledge imposes a pattern, and falsifies,
For the pattern is new in every moment
And every moment is a new and shocking
Valuation of all we have been. . . .

> — T. S. Eliot

So:

For God sake hold your tongue,
And let me love.

> —John Donne, "The Canonization"

Filled with . . . love, may I be rather grown
Mad with much heart, than idiot with none.

> —John Donne, "The Dream"

FREDERICO SECUNDO

Henceforth, from the mind,
For your whole joy, must spring
Such joy as you may find
In any earthly thing.

> — Louise Bogan

So now I'll climb trees in the Hesperides and tell you why I love Frederico Secundo, Emperor (*Stupor Mundi*, Wonder of the World, 1194–1250), regarded by many as the progenitor of modern scientific collecting and of falconry (that most aristocratic and romantic of sports), hailed by Bernard Berenson as "one of the most dazzling figures in history," and accorded this encomium by an historian (before the revisionists set to work on his full-blooded and enchanting person and

achievements): "Was there ever so glorious a history of youth's achieve-
ment as that of Frederick from his 17th year to his 25th year?" (David
G. Einstein, *Emperor Frederic II*)

Real life will never give me an opportunity to love such a man as
Frederico Secundo, a man of sorrows, acquainted with grief — and
acquainted with Moslems and Jews, whom he treated with a respect
and lack of condescension that made him unique in his time; a man
who loved women and served the poor and the cause of law and order
and justice and loved luxury — and tempted Saint Francis of Assisi with
naked nubile dancing girls; a man who lived lavishly but in the knowledge of treachery and deceit, and one who lived his private life without
fear of papal reproach, troubling to conceal nothing. The world will
never produce such another.

He was as hideously flawed as he was magnificent; but by the time
I knew the gorgeous poetry of his life (which I first encountered in
H. V. Morton's *Traveler in Southern Italy*), nothing so flimsy as fact
could dissuade me from loving him. (It is a related truth that by the
time one knows enough about a man to have contempt for him, one
knows too much to have contempt for him.)

One loves someone not least for the questions he asks, and I loved
his questions: "Tell us whether one soul in the next world knows
another and whether one can return to this life to speak and show
oneself. How is it that the soul of a living man which has passed away
to another life than ours cannot be induced to return by first love or
even by hate, just as if it had been nothing, nor does it seem to care at
all for what it has left behind, whether it be saved or lost?"

He wanted to know about oceans and volcanoes and geysers. Where
is paradise? he wanted to know. Where is purgatory? Where is hell?
"In which heaven is God in the person of His Divine Majesty and how
does He sit on His throne, and how is He accompanied by angels and
saints," he asked, "and what do they continually do before Him?"

His intellectual curiosity was limitless. He once asked the Scotsman
Michael Scot, court astrologer, mathematician, and scholar, to measure
the distance from the top of a church tower to heaven. Scot contrived
to do so. Without telling Scot, Frederico lowered the top of the tower.
Then he asked Scot to measure again. He did, and reported, "Either

heaven has receded a little or the tower has shrunk," delighting Frederico. (Scot, who was also patronized by the pope, translated Aristotle into Latin for Frederico, and made medicinal sugared violets for his emperor.)

It is said of Frederico (but I am obliged to consider this calumny) that he put a condemned man in a barrel for the express purpose of seeing, in the event of his suffocation, if the poor man's soul could be seen to leave the barrel. Frederico — who had a digestive disorder, ate little, and exercised much — is also reputed (but I refuse to believe it) to have experimented on human digestive organs to determine whether exercise or rest was more beneficial: "He fed two men sumptuously; after eating he commanded one to rest and the other to labor and then suffered both to be put to death in order that their digestive organs might be examined, and his craving for knowledge satisfied" (Einstein).

According to one of his biographers, a contemporary friar wrote that "he sought to learn the origin of language: particularly which of the languages, Greek, Latin, Arabic, or Italian, the children would speak first, if left unaffected by the presence of others. To make proof of his experiments he forbade nurses for the babies, who soon, for the want of their nurses' care, perished, and with them, apparently the origin of language, which still remains a secret of nature." (I choose to believe that the friar was inspired by enmity or envy.)

He was sentimental, ruthless, affable, bold, friendly, dignified, mystical, pragmatic, rational, skeptical, irascible, messianic, tolerant, stubborn, pacific, prodigal, profligate, virile, cunning, happy, gracious to people of all stations and class, vivacious: glorious.

Legends accumulate around those we love, and some are flattering and some are damning; never mind. I have formed my picture of him; and now historical judgment of him is irrelevant to me. The historical pendulum will swing this way and then that; what does it matter to me? As for his politics and his social policies, some of which drew me to him and enamored me, they are in some respects now being called into question; and so what? I care no more than Cinderella cared about the politics of her prince. When one falls in love at first sight, the aggregation of evidence (whether it be positive or negative) serves only to enlarge the image of the person loved, and to engage one's imagination fully in the service of love.

The great love of his life, Bianca of Piedmont, was not of royal birth; he took her as he found her, and he found her "worthy of the love of Jove."

She was tall. He was short.

Whatever cruelty resided in his nature she expunged. With her, he was the best he could be . . . fulfilling woman's fantasy: *I soften your nature and I enlarge you.*

I love his gift for invective. He once addressed Pope Gregory IX as "Your Fornication," instead of "Your Brother" (*fornicacioni vestre*, instead of *fraternitati vestre*).

He was wounded as well as flawed; and his life is a succession of fairy tales.

He was king of Sicily, where hot surprises are found in dark places and murderous secrets ripen in the sun. He was plentifully endowed with the imperturbable Sicilian courtesy that coexists with the brutishness and brutality of the Mafia. He was elegant.

Far more Norman than German in temperament and sympathy, far more Sicilian and Oriental than Western European in outlook and style, Frederico was the grandson of Frederick Barbarossa and the great-grandson of the Norman Robert Guiscard, who delivered Sicily from the Saracens who had defeated the native Italians and Greeks.

("You love a *German?*" a friend of mine asks me, illustrating how ignorance feeds the flames of bigotry. Then: "Would you save me if the Germans came to get me?" she asked. "I hope so," I said (declarations of one's own putative goodness and courage and charity smacking not a little of hubris); but this wasn't enough for her; and I am impatient with this. . . . During one of our last fights, Mr. Harrison said to me, addressing his words to an audience that acted as a third-person catalyst and emboldened him, "The kind of person you are, you would save the Jews next door before you saved your own children." God knows what he meant. But why should one be tested in this way — asked to measure and to give an account of one's love and one's future? I call it vile.)

Frederico Secundo was born in a tent in the market square of Jesi in Apulia, to Constance, the Sicilian wife of Henry VI, who had only the day before in Palermo — Christmas Day — been crowned king of Sicily and Southern Italy, heir to *imperium regnum monarchatum:* empire-kingdom-monarchy. Nineteen cardinals and bishops were in attendance at his birth, the more precious because it ended nine years of marital barrenness.

Of all places on earth, Frederico was ever to love Sicily best; it is one of the ironies of his life that neither was he born there nor did he die there. (When he saw Jerusalem, the desire of Christendom's heart, he said, "Had God seen his Sicily, He would not have chosen Jerusalem for special commendation.")

Apulia is a witchy place (Horace called it a dry and thirsty place). Nowhere but on its long Murge plateau are to be found *trulli*, strange round buildings with cone-shaped roofs, made, without mortar, of large gray flat limestones arranged in overhanging, concentric circles. The cones are topped with diverse and eccentric finials — balls and pyramids, stars, quarter-moons. (They seem to be more than merely decorative; they seem to symbolize something, but one doesn't know what — they repel intimate knowledge.) Some of these houses — to which one might attribute simplicity of construction but never, in a million years, simplicity of intent — are whitewashed. It is said that they can be dismantled overnight, if need be. They are mystical and dreamlike. They are bizarre and cavelike-cozy, fantastic and earthy and otherworldly (otherplanetary?). D'Annunzio saw their charm: "I would like to lie down in a *trullo* with a vault of gold and there dream."

Passionately maternal and passionately Catholic, and widowed soon after the birth of her son, Constance, before her death, committed the four-year-old to the guardianship of Pope Innocent III, who became regent of Sicily during the years of Frederico's minority.

The poor little boy had a loveless childhood surrounded by protectors and court enemies, who were more often than not indistinguishable one from the other, flattering and sycophantic, deceitful, fraudulent, and venal.

The boy king (delicious, isn't it, how much sympathy the words *boy king* evoke?) was sturdy and intelligent beyond his years; and he lived as kings live in fairy tales (or in Errol Flynn movies) — horseback riding, fencing, distinguishing himself with sword and arrow.

But it is most pleasant to imagine the boy king wandering through the magical labyrinthine souks of what was called "semi-African" Palermo; and most disturbing, too, for he sometimes walked hungry through the market, La Vucciria, which, even now — with its dark green awnings and its perpetually burning naked light bulbs abolishing distinction between day and night and creating a scented sinister wonderland of filtered light and deep shadow — is at least as Oriental as it is Italian. Sicily had been, from the ninth century, a gathering place of Jews and Arabs and Christians; the child wandered among synagogues and mosques and churches as if they were all related, imbibing wordless homilies on ecumenism. He was ravenous — for more than food — in the sunny center of world trade, his precocious sensuality nourished by honey and jewels and rugs and tapestries, pepper and spices and sweet violets and violent beauty.

Innocent saw the unfathered Frederico only once in his lifetime; but the Vicar of Christ on earth — who held to the belief that the primary duty of Frederico was necessarily to preserve the authority of the Church in both the temporal and spiritual realms — addressed his young charge with authoritarian solemnity: "God has not spared the rod. He has taken away your father and your mother; yet He has given you a worthier father, His Vicar, and a better mother, the Church." Perhaps these words were meant to be magnanimous; it is unlikely that the child perceived them as loving.

He issued his first spirited challenge to the pope when he was only fifteen, making it quite clear that in his estimable view the crown did not owe its existence to the pope and that the king was not the vassal of the pontiff.

Indeed the stage had been set very early for the central drama and the terminal struggle of Frederico's life; Innocent III wrote, when the child was four, that God "instituted two great dignities, a greater one to preside over souls as if over day, and a lesser one to preside over bodies as if over night. These are the pontifical authority and the royal power. Now just as the moon derives its light from the sun and is indeed lower than it in quantity and quality, in position and power, so too the royal authority derives the splendour of its dignity from pontifical authority."

For his entire adult life Frederico — who loved God — contested the ironclad determination of the Roman Church that it was endowed by God with total temporal power as well as spiritual power. He was for all his life a respectful child of the Church — he had no quarrel with liturgy or dogma; but he disputed the divine right of the Church to rule the state. Frederico believed *he* ruled by divine right, and that there was not and need not be an intermediary between God and the king: "I hold my crown of God alone; neither the pope, the council, nor the devil shall rend it from me! What! Shall the pride of man of low birth degrade the Emperor?"

(When Innocent's successor, Honorius III, reproved him for his independence, declaring that his acts subverted his mother's will, Frederico replied that the agreement with Rome, having been made by a woman, was not binding on him.)

He did battle with a succession of popes. Their admonitory correspondence is wonderful: "Take heed," Pope Gregory wrote, "that you do not place your intellect, which you have in common with angels, below your senses, which you have in common with brutes and plants. Your intellect is weakened if you are a slave of your senses. If these two lights, knowledge and love, be quenched, if those eagles be brought low and turned to earthly lusts you will not be able to point the way to salvation to your followers."

(Another of the Church's devoted children, Teilhard de Chardin, Jesuit geologist and paleontologist, 1881–1955, took as a matter of fact the yearning of plants, which incline to the light, but was prompted to ask if even rocks did not yearn, in some way that we are as yet unaware of. Teilhard came very close to being excommunicated for asking uncomfortable questions and loving the world and believing in the sanctity of human activity. Frederico *was* excommunicated, *four times.* So many of the most lovable people do suffer at the hands of the Church they love, one must only regard it as odd — and love them the more.)

Frederico was a man of vast sexual and sensual appetites. From the time he was thirteen he chafed, believing himself to be a man treated like a child. Innocent — who had never laid eyes on the woman —

arranged Frederico's marriage to Constance of Aragon, from whom
Frederico was to spend most of his life geographically separated, when
he was fourteen. Constance, upon whom Frederico had never laid eyes,
was widowed, a mother, and ten years his senior. She was also sage and
faithful, admiring and affectionate; she considered herself well wed; he
returned her affection. Upon their marriage her young husband assumed rulership of the Kingdom of Sicily, which for all practical purposes meant Messina and Palermo. In 1212, when Frederico was eighteen and Constance was twenty-eight, their son Henry was born and
blessed in the Cathedral of Palermo, where, ten years later, good
Constance was entombed. Frederico had been a generous and grateful
husband (though his ambition and the imperatives of popes — especially that of Innocent, whom he venerated as the benefactor of his
childhood — took him away from her to Germany and Naples and
beyond): she had not wanted him to fight for the German crown;
Constance wanted him in Sicily, which was after all large and beautiful
enough (as was she). But her love had increased his ambition. During
the course of her brief lifetime, loyal Constance had seen her husband
become the single most powerful temporal ruler in the world. When
he was crowned emperor of the Holy Roman Empire he requested the
pope to crown her as his queen.

Frederico was loved both in Germany and in Rome. Who else was
loved both in Germany and in Rome? No one. He didn't, having
secured the crown, spend much time in Germany; perhaps he would
have agreed with Edith Wharton, who opined, whilst in Italian Lake
Country, that while Germany had no choice other than to be German,
Italy was foolhardy to look as if it might be; Germany can be forgiven
for being German, as it is Germany, she said, but Italy cannot (and I
agree).

Sicily soon became famous — as later Apulia would be — for the
brilliance of its court life. Frederico, a man of broad scholarship and
broader tolerance — a man of the most uncensuring cast of mind —
spoke six languages and held itinerant court at palaces and hunting
lodges. (I would like to be married to a man who was uncensuring!)
Like Kublai Khan, he held court amidst travelers and wandering min-
strels and poets and philosophers and jugglers and ribald troubadours

and dancing girls who gyrated on revolving glass globes. Sometimes he sang. (I would like to be married to a man who sings! . . . in fact I will not marry again.)

. . . Go to any Catholic church for mass and you will likely ask yourself, Why is Catholic music so bad, so listless and so pale? It is perhaps because during the Counter Reformation a pope took it into his head to ban all music on the ground that ribald ditties had been sung to sacred music, rendering the music itself obscene. Frederico sang very naughty ditties indeed. . . .

He had a traveling menagerie. He sponsored democratic carnivals on the emerald plains of Apulia.

When Saint Francis of Assisi came from the Holy Land to Bari, Frederico was holding court there. The king-emperor tempted the saint with dancing girls he had imported from Egypt. Saint Francis remained oblivious to their charms — he held them at arm's length with hot coals from a brazier. This the emperor saw from a peephole he had drilled into the bedroom wall of the saint, from whom Frederico then begged forgiveness. (Well, it isn't quite like drilling a hole into a Howard Johnson's motel room — Frederico, being only human, wanted to test the goodness of a man too good to be true, as who would not?)

He received gifts from the sultans of Egypt — a jeweled instrument that was both a clock and a map of the heavens, an Albino bear.

He had friendly leopards, trained by him to behave like domestic cats; three of them he sent to the English Henry III, who consigned them to the Tower of London, where they were later joined by a polar bear and an elephant; these animals became the nucleus of the Royal Menagerie (their descendants may be seen at Regent's Park, in the London Zoo). His menagerie in Apulia, kept by black custodians, included lions, hunting leopards, elephants, cheetahs, hawks and hounds and camels, and dromedaries upon whose backs were carried royal treasures. The imperial elephant carried the standard of his Hohenstaufen father, German Emperor Henry VI. His animals escorted him through Palermo to the wild Calabrian mountains wedged between two seas, and from that land of exuberant loneliness and hills honeycombed with caves and dark unexploited forests to witchy Apulia.

He wasn't that mean and repugnant thing, a secretive collector: he rejoiced in revealing his treasures.

Admit: Andersen and Grimm between them could not have invented him.

It is odd that in Apulian folktales the falcon always represents evil.

Frederico shared the esoteric pleasures of hawking with the women of his court, who rode on horses with ornamented saddles and hangings, female peregrine hawks perched on their protected arms. He so loved the sport that "when the great khan of the Mongols wrote one of his tiresome letters telling Frederico to submit to his might or forfeit his crown, Frederico remarked that he might gladly resign his throne if he were allowed to become the khan's falconer." He had more than fifty royal falconers; and his representatives in southeastern Italy were instructed to catch the live cranes he used in training sessions. "From Greenland to the Dar al-Islam Frederico sought his falcons and information about them."

He instructed falconers to sing to his birds at feeding time, and always the same song, and to love them, and wash their hands and pet them.

(So wouldn't you love him? adore him? Can't you see why Constance did?)

Inspired by Aristotle's *De Animalibus*, he researched the habits of birds, approaching his subject observantly and with deductive reasoning. He felt no compunction about contradicting Aristotle if the evidence of his eyes led in a contrary direction; he wished, as he so nicely said, "to show those things that are, as they are." He made records of the nesting habits of birds, and especially of cuckoos.

When he wanted to know how vultures spot their prey (a question I often asked myself when I saw the necessary loathsome birds gather in India), he sealed the eyes of captive vultures, and his experiment proved that it was by sight, not by smell, that the carrion birds zoomed in on unresisting flesh. He worked on *The Art of Hunting with Birds (De arte venandi cum avibus)* — the first scientific book on ornithology written during the Middle Ages — for more than thirty years.

And when did he find time for all of this? In between wars, one supposes, and in between quelling civil disturbances in Apulia and Calabria, and in between establishing prototypical universities and in between pleasuring himself in his harems and in between confrontations with popes. And in between Crusades.

One shares the grief of H. V. Morton that Frederico's original two-volume copy of *De arte venandi cum avibus,* "beautifully illustrated with pictures of birds, some said to have been drawn by Frederico himself, and enriched with silver and gold," is lost. "It was heard of last in 1265 but has since vanished without trace." (Copies of the book appeared at least up until the late 1950s — a mark of Frederico's scientific acumen.)

The king-emperor cared, Morton (who is so simpatico) says, not for the kill, "but only for the thread of understanding between man and bird: the skill which enabled a man to extend his will into the sky and to draw back his emissary from the clouds."

My paternal grandmother was born in the ruins of one of Frederico's hunting lodges in Calabria, in a little village called Oriole. (It was a whitened sepulcher when I saw it — a cave; it had been a cave at the time of her birth; and it had probably been a dungeon in the Middle Ages. . . . And in the nearby church where she and my grandfather married, excavations were going on, and bones of the dead mingled with the broken mosaics of the church, protruding through the earth, dispersed as casually as wildflowers. . . . My grandfather's name was Frederico.) My daughter danced in a ruined castle in the seaside town of Rocca Imperiale in Calabria; naked colored bulbs provided light and loudspeakers provided disco music — this was said to be a castle belonging to Frederico; does it not challenge one's idea of progress? Would you not rather have been there then, when the world was called Dark, than now? (But my daughter was happy there. And these events are suggestive to me of the thrilling and comforting work of synchronicity in the world.)

Castel del Monte, the Apulian castle–hunting lodge that is generally regarded as Frederico's masterpiece, is composed of eight massive towers of pink-gold stone, eight rooms on every floor. (And all around it are those strange, mystical *trulli,* holding their own against this magnificence.) It has been suggested by Louis Inturrisi that the castle's perfect mathematical proportions are due to "a ground plan carefully worked out around the mystical number eight, . . . the use of the divine proportion 1618 in its measurements, and its positioning . . . determined by the movements of the sun so that shadows struck its walls when the sun entered different signs of the zodiac." The divine proportion, by which a part multiplied by the number 1618 equals the whole, is based on a belief in the human body as the measure of all things. ("As soon as I got home," Inturrisi writes, "I . . . measured the distance between my navel and the soles of my feet, then multiplied that by 1.618. Within a centimeter it equaled my height.")

All his castles had plumbing. He cultivated roses and grapes. You can still drink wine named for Castel del Monte (where Chinese celadon ware was found).

I have yet to measure the distance between my navel and the soles of my feet. I hold the pleasure of 1618 in reserve.

There is the matter of the Crusades. Frederico was a most reluctant crusader: he equivocated, negotiated, postponed. He hadn't the belly for it; he couldn't quite bring himself to see the necessity or the justification for this war of wars; he wanted to recover the Holy Land by peaceful means.

In 1220, when he was not yet thirty years old, Frederico, king of Sicily and of Germany, was crowned Holy Roman Emperor to the soberly stirring sincere strains of Gregorian chants. Before a dazzling congregation he kissed the feet of the Holy Father, Honorius; and he was presented with the sword, the globe, the scepter of justice, the ring of faith, the mantle, the holy lance, the Golden Apple of Mercy, and the crown. And the people of Rome assigned their fate to him, loving him, believing him capable of miracles. (They were poor.)

Reiterating a former vow, he vouchsafed his willingness to go on Crusade.

When, a year later — Frederico having found many reasons to keep himself at home — news that Egypt was lost reached Europe, Honorius heaped the blame upon Frederico, to whom he wrote: "For five years men have been expecting your Crusade. . . . We shall spare you no longer, if you still neglect your duty: we shall excommunicate you in the face of the Christian world. Take heed like a wise man and a Catholic Prince."

Frederico saw Yolanda, his second wife, heiress of the Kingdom of Jerusalem, as the means to the peaceful end he envisioned (meaningless though her title essentially was). This marriage was an affair not of the heart but of state, arranged by that conniver Honorius. Frederico was twenty-nine (twenty-nine-year-olds are such babies today, aren't they?); Yolanda was not yet fifteen, and had, poor thing, lived a cloistered life, her solitude nourishing her sad grandiose fantasies that glamorous Frederico would cleave to her and adore her; he did not. (According to accounts I prefer not to believe, he slept not with her but with her cousin on their wedding night, and he virtually entombed her, poor girl, in his Saracenic harem, there to enjoy as best she could the company of eunuchs.) Poor Yolanda died before she was eighteen years old, ten days after giving birth to a son, Conrad.

Frederico's promises to go on Crusade did not, meanwhile, materialize. It must have seemed stupid to him — the Saracens were not his enemies; and they had shown themselves capable of compromise. A patron of the arts, Frederico was enthralled by the languor and luxury and elegance of Arab and Saracenic life; he discussed astrology, astronomy, and religion in his court with Arab, Saracen, and Jew, and learned from them what they had to teach; they were his friends. Why should he kill them?

His reluctance inspired Honorius once again to take up his poison pen: "Why do you boast yourself in wickedness? Take care that God does not root you out of the land of the living: we must excommunicate you if you persist in your wickedness. . . . You used to thank the Church, after God, for your safety and your life. . . . What have you done for her? What can she hope from you? We are angered: . . . It was others who sowed, that you might reap; . . . but here is the Apostolic Chair, ready to check you."

Honorius died, and like Innocent before him, did not see Frederico embark on a Crusade.

I am not quite sure, having never had the experience, how it is possible passionately to love a man who is unchallenged and unencumbered with enemies or antagonists. You want a man — I think — whom many see the point of (and many adore), but one who arouses also intense feelings of disapproval, hostility, opprobrium, or hatred. One wants oneself to be the only one who *entirely* sees the point of one's beloved and, reciprocally, the only one unreservedly adored. You sharpen your love on the ire and disapproval of his enemies; having to defend a king is a noble and pleasurable and exciting thing, an opportunity to luxuriate in the exercise of loyalty (and perhaps to congratulate oneself on one's superior sensibilities), and a chance to suffer for the gift of love.

You don't agree?

Perhaps you are right.

Frederico was loved in equal measure as he was hated.

Gregory IX, on the day of his accession to the papacy, called upon Frederico to fulfill his vow. And on this occasion the king-emperor did. He set sail for the Holy Land — accompanied by an ill wind. His ranks had been depleted on shore by an epidemic; and in heavy seas he too fell violently ill; and so he returned to Italy.

Given Frederico's past record, perhaps old Gregory (the pope was eighty) came honestly to his belief that Frederico had tricked him, and that his illness had been, as it were, prearranged; in any case he excommunicated the thirty-three-year-old emperor.

Gregory sent a humdinger of a communication to the Apulian bishops, inveighing against the armies of the infidels, the rage of tyrants, the folly of heretics; "false brethren and wicked sons [who] by their perversity, disturb the bowels and tear open the sides of their mother. . . .

"To combat these matters, . . . the Holy Apostolic See reckoned . . . in a nursling whom she had taken up . . . as it were, from his mother's womb, fed him at her breasts, borne him on her shoulders; . . . and to crown all his blessings, bestowed on him the title of Emperor, hoping to find him a protecting support, a staff for her old age. . . .

"But he, breaking all his promises, bursting every bond, trampling under foot the fear of God, despising all reverence for Christ Jesus, scorning the censures of the Church, deserting the Christian army, abandoning the Holy Land to the unbelievers, to his own disgrace and that of all Christendom, withdrew to the luxuries and wonted delights of his Kingdom, seeking to palliate his offense by frivolous excuses of simulated sickness.

"That we may not be esteemed as dumb dogs who do not bark, or fear to take vengeance upon him, the Emperor Frederick who has caused ruin to the people of God, we proclaim the said Emperor excommunicated; we command you to publish this our excommunication throughout the realm; and to declare that in the case of his continuancy, we shall proceed to still more awful censures."

What, one wonders, might they have been?

In the Cathedral of Anagni, in the company of the Princes of the Church, Gregory excommunicated Frederico, consigning him to eternal darkness. He cursed the king-emperor; and, chanting dirges of despair, cardinals and clergy extinguished their torches and plunged the church into darkness, in token of the darkness that had entered the king-emperor's soul. (It was believed, in the Middle Ages, that sin makes us opaque, and that if we were without sin, we should be transparent, beacons of light.)

Frederico, unchastened, proceeded to take the water cure near Naples . . . and to make preparations for a new Crusade.

Gregory had confirmed the formal excommunication in 1227 at St. Peter's; after Frederico took the cure and returned to Apulia — where clergy and nobles pledged their allegiance to him — Gregory excommunicated him for a third time, during Holy Week.

He condemned him as a heretic and sent him to hell: "In the name of the Father, Son, and Holy Ghost, and of the blessed apostles, Peter and Paul and ourselves, we excommunicate and anathemize Frederico the so-called emperor." The bells of Christendom with many tongues proclaimed his damnation.

Frederico, however, had friends in Rome, having provided bread for the starving; the imperial Frangipani family in particular was indebted to him. So, with the consent of the Senate and the people, a member of the Frangipani family, a professor of jurisprudence from the University of Bologna, publicly read a vindication of Frederico. When next Gregory elevated the Host at mass, the entire assembly hissed and shouted their defiance of their pontiff. The city rose in a fury of passion and shouted allegiance to their king-emperor; and Gregory, poor beleaguered old man, was obliged to leave the Eternal City.

Now that Frederico had prepared his soul to go to Jerusalem, which he hoped to secure by peaceful negotiations, obdurate Gregory sought to keep him back. Frederico sailed on this Crusade without his blessing.

No one could accuse Frederico of modesty. So many lives had been lost in the battle for the Holy Land; and he banked on his own understanding of the East, and on the power of his personality.

In the event, he was right to do so. His journey resulted in the Treaty of Jaffa, under the terms of which Jerusalem, Bethlehem, Nazareth, and the Church of the Holy Sepulcher fell to him; the Temple Mount remained in Moslem hands. He guaranteed the religious rights of all Christians and Moslems — prompting Gregory to call his remarkable treaty, so much in advance of its time, an alliance between Christ and Belial.

All this that he did, he did without a single death. It was an astonishing moral and diplomatic success, which fell short only in one particular: the Church would not crown him king of Jerusalem. He himself placed the golden crown on his head. There was no mass, no consecration of the crown, no celebration for the man who had won the Holy Land for Christianity. It must have been a quintessentially lonely moment — alone in his victory; and bitter? He never returned to Jerusalem.

A Moslem official said of him that he was "red and bald; he had weak eyes: had he been a slave he would not have fetched 20 drachmas." Leaving that (and the fact that by the time he was forty he was fairly fat) aside, so what? It is what the official said next that is interesting: "Whenever he spoke he railed at the Christian religion." Of course he railed against the pope, and against the hierarchy that took Gregory's part; but (I don't know why this should be so hard for non-Catholics, then as now, to grasp) this did not reflect upon or negate his love for the faith, "the story" of the faith — for the doctrine and liturgy of the Church and, therefore, for the terrible Church itself.

Magnanimous in victory, Frederico agreed not to tax the churches and not to interfere with the election of bishops. He was then belatedly recognized by Gregory as king of Jerusalem; and the Church recognized (again) his rule in Italy and in Sicily. More importantly (on September 1, 1230), he was received into the Church formally again, the joy of the sacraments erasing "the darkness of sorrow. . . . We went to the Pope, who, receiving us with fatherly love and with the kiss of peace, . . . calmed our passions and reversed our rancour, so that we were unwilling to speak of the past. We have forgiven our foes, one and all for their offenses against us."

Perhaps you think this is all politics tarted up as spirituality. I do not. God speaks to us through our individual temperaments and in the idiom of our time, that is what I think. (I also think that there is seldom one motive for any one act — and perhaps, as we are made in His image, that may also be true of Him.)

In any case (the Montagues belonged to the emperor, the Capulets to the Church), every love story has political implications. . . . I think of mine.

Perhaps I have distorted the facts to support my love for him; I hope that I have not; but I recognize this to be — always — a danger. (I hope that I may have a fine regard for facts — but facts are not entirely sensitive measuring instruments; *fact* does not equal *truth*.)

These are some of the accomplishments for which the ages have honored him: He formed a code of laws to deliver the weak from the strong. The constitution of the Kingdom of Sicily effectively abolished serfdom.

He gave to the peasant the right to inherit land.

He protected pilgrims and travelers from bandits, and merchants from usurious tax collectors.

He crushed the accusation that Jews ritually crucified Christian children to mock the Crucifixion; false accusations were condemned and the libel against the Jews was outlawed.

Establishing governmental complaint courts, he deprived princes and clergy of their power to adjudicate and administer justice — with one exception: clerical courts had jurisdiction over adultery. His representatives administered the law impartially, giving no preference to nobility above peasantry, assuring equal justice for rich and poor.

Crimes against women were vigorously punished.

He granted female succession to the land of princes, making redundant the absolute need for a male heir and its attendant cruelties.

He encouraged the participation of the poor in public events, narrowing the separation between rich and poor.

The state reserved the right to legitimize children of the clergy; in effect, he said that there were no illegitimate children. He himself had fifteen children out of wedlock, all of whom he recognized and supported.

Saracens and Jews were guaranteed complete freedom of worship.

He established model farms (he was also a horse breeder and a lover of Arabian steeds, most of which he allowed to run wild, the remainder of which were sent to stud in Calabria).

He restored the University of Salerno to its former splendor and decreed that only those physicians who served the poor without remuneration might keep their licenses.

He founded the secular University of Naples ("the foundation of knowledge and the seed plot of learning") in the belief that all people — regardless of class or financial status — were educable, and that it was the duty of the state to provide them with a free education. The university — where Arab, Greek, and Saracenic teachers taught philosophy and the natural sciences — was based on the principle of discussion and debate, not conformity.

To the professors of the University of Bologna he said: "We have always loved knowledge from our youth; whatever time we can steal from state affairs we cheerfully dedicate to reading the many volumes stored in our library. We have stripped the works written by the Greek and Arabic philosophers of their garb; we have had them translated by chosen men, maintaining faithfully the virginity of the words. We do not wish to keep them all to ourselves; you are the first to whom we send, since you are the nurslings of philosophy who shall draw water out of old cisterns. Do you make them public for the use of your students, to the glory of your Caesar. We do not wish to keep them all for ourselves."

It is said by his admirers that he civilized Sicily, and bequeathed to the Sicilians his elegant manners.

His was the only harem in Europe. He was indeed licentious (and had a lyrically happy sex life). Some historians — attributing to him silken manners and a dark suave majesty — manage to make him sound unctuously Eastern, Basil Rathbone in a turban. For some reason I am glad he was short.

There is a legend that the Mafia originated in Moslem guerrilla resistance against the Kingdom of Sicily — an intriguing idea. Like the bandit Giuliano who roamed the mountains of Sicily in the 1940s, disobliging Moslems during Frederico's time roamed all over the western hills, unresponsive to the demands of the king's centralized government. Frederico gathered twenty thousand rebellious Saracens and transported them to the mainland of Italy — to Apulia — placing them at a greater distance from their African brothers. He built for them a great city in which the muezzins called the faithful to prayer from the minarets of mosques that Frederico built.

Eventually some of these transported Saracen Moslems were converted to Christianity, though no interdiction was ever placed on the practice of Moslem religion or law. Frederico, a kind of guerrilla warrior himself, respected them for having fought so hard in the mountains.

(He was a guerrilla warrior, three popes his enemies; a contemporary historian, David Abulafia, writes, however, that "far from being an implacable foe of the papacy, as he is usually represented, he was sincere in his attempts at compromise, even appeasement." In other words, he didn't have a death wish; and he did love his terrible Church.)

He did exercise his kingly prerogative to move people around. When he conquered Djerba — the isle of the lotus eaters off the coast of Tunisia — he invited its North African Jews, craftsmen and agriculturalists, to settle in Sicily.

One of the crafts they brought with them was the making of exquisite tiles. In the interior city of Caltagirone, in Sicily, there are staircases of magnificent tiles, no two alike. (I have some Sicilian tiles; I bought original eighteenth-century tiles for less than I could have bought reproductions because, according to the junk dealer from whom I secured them, "Signora, the men who make the tiles today are poor, they need to feed their families. The men who made the old ones, they are dead." It is not often that lunatic logic works so well to one's advantage.) . . . And when I lived in Tripoli, I often went to visit a lonely old Italian man in his beautiful courtyard, a man whose people had come from Sicily, but, before that, from Djerba. He made tiles. He was the last man left who made decorative tiles in Tripoli; soon all the Italians were gone from Tripoli; and he is dead.

It is likely — although revisionists call it into question — that Frederico regarded the Saracens as brothers. But he was king. And he was cruel. When the leader of a Saracen revolt, Ibn Abbad, having wisely surrendered after an eight-week siege, prostrated himself before Frederico, the king-emperor would not pardon him; he could not abide even the hint of treason. It is told that he dug his spur into the body of Ibn Abbad and tore it open. The wretched man refused to die; a week later he was hanged in Palermo.

Does it seem to you that I am writing a blueprint for the hero of a romance novel?

I have said he was flawed (love is not about justification; it is about acceptance):

From the time his son Henry was nine to the time he was twenty, Frederico did not see his firstborn. The son of Constance and Frederico ruled Germany arrogantly and without regard for his father, from whom he had the temerity to wish for political independence. (Imagine being the son of the Wonder of the World! It can't have been easy.) In this Henry had the sympathy of the Lombard League — pesky descendants of whom wish still, today, to separate themselves from their southern brethren; Lombardians promised him support if he rebelled against Frederico. In 1234 hapless Henry was so ill advised as to do so, raising the standard of open revolt near Coblenz. (The boy must have been an idiot. Either that or he belongs in a Freudian casebook.)

Frederico, with the blessing of the pope (who had this time excommunicated Henry), entered Germany to the acclamation of the masses. . . . History moves so fast (faster then than now? Mustn't our ancestors also have suffered from future shock?): Frederico was received as conqueror of the Holy Land, and he, once condemned as a heretic, was now proclaimed the protector of the Holy Roman Church.

Poor Henry was imprisoned, first in Germany and then, after a witless escape attempt, in Apulia. Frederico then married the English Isabella, whose hand he had denied Henry. It is hard to imagine a more complete rout.

What a difficult balance all these players in this grand drama were obliged to maintain. In contravention of the pope's will, Frederico moved against Lombardy, which threatened the unity of Italy then as it does now. The rancor between king-emperor and Gregory, coiled, waiting for its opportunity to explode, was revived.

Frederico to Gregory: "You charge us with the faults of our officials in Sicily, just as if we could see clearly from Germany into Sicily with the eyes of a Lynx and the voice of thunder. . . . We think that we do you no wrong . . . Italy is my heritage and all the world knows it."

Gregory to Frederico: "Kings and Princes were humbly to repose themselves on the lap of priests; Christian Emperors were bound to submit themselves not only to the supreme Pontiff, but even to other bishops. The Apostolic See was the judge of the whole world; God had reserved to himself the sole judgment of the manifest and hidden acts of the Pope. . . . Let the Emperor dread the fate of Uzzah, who had laid his profane hands on the ark of God."

At this time, Gregory was one hundred.

In what was to be a final burst of rebellion, Frederico affirmed his right to tax the Church and to determine the election of bishops. He also — insatiable orphan that he was — laid claim to the island kingdom of Sardegna: he married his golden-haired, sweet-voiced fifteen-year-old son Enzio (born out of wedlock) to the ugly widowed queen of Sardegna (who turned against luckless Enzio with hatred when she felt herself to be used as a brood mare).

Gregory excommunicated Frederico again (the king-emperor was a man of incontestable splendor; but the drama of which he was protagonist has an undeniable element of farce). "May the Lord God of vengeance award [Gregory] his just retribution," Frederico bellowed. "Cast your eyes around! Lift up your ears, O sons of men, that ye may hear! . . . We hold Pope Gregory to be an unworthy Vicar of Christ . . . who sits in his court weighing out dispensations for gold, himself signing, writing the bulls, perhaps counting the money. He has but one real cause of enmity against me, that I refused to marry his niece to my natural son Enzio, now king of Sardegna. . . . But ye O Kings and Princes of the Earth, mourn not only for us, but for the whole Church; for her head is sick, her prince is like a raving lion; in the midst of her sits a frantic prophet, a man of falsehood, a polluted priest. . . . This father of fathers, who is called the servant of servants, shutting out all justice, is become a deaf adder; refuses to hear the vindication of the King of the Romans, hurls malediction into the world as a stave is hurled from a sling; and sternly, and heedless of all consequences, exclaims, 'What I have written, I have written.'"

Drawing from the mad and beautiful visionary Book of Revelation, the old pope declaimed: "Out of the sea a beast is arisen whose name is all over written, 'Blasphemy'; he has the feet of a bear, the jaws of a ravenous lion, the mottled limbs of a panther. . . . He openly sets up the battering engines of the Ishmaelites; builds schools for the perdition of souls, lifts himself up against Christ the Redeemer of man, endeavoring to efface the tablets of his testament with the pen of heretical wickedness. . . . He has risen to extirpate from the earth the name of the Lord. Rather . . . we exorcise the head, the body, the extremities of this beast, who is no other than the Emperor Frederick. . . . In truth this pestilential king maintains, to use his own words [which it is almost certain Frederico had never uttered], the world has been deceived by three impostors, Jesus Christ, Moses and Mohammed: that two of these died in honor, the third was hanged on a tree; even now he has asserted distinctly and loudly that those are fools who aver that God, the omnipotent Creator of the World, was born of a Virgin." Gregory furthermore accused Frederico of having Saracen concubines — which he did.

But Frederico applied the words of Revelation to the frothing old pope: "From the time of his accession, this father, not of mercy, but of discord, not of consolation, but of desolation, has plunged the whole world into bitterness. . . . He is the anti-Christ of whom he declares us the forerunner."

Frederico made a clear distinction between the office of the pope and the person of the pope; then (as now) the people were not prepared to make this distinction between the person and the office, the pope and the Church, the prelates and the body of Christ. The fickle masses turned against their once beloved king-emperor, seeing in him the would-be destroyer of Mother Church. Gregory commissioned the Franciscans and the Dominicans to crusade in all of Europe against the king-emperor; Frederico promptly turned both orders out of Sicily and Apulia. Gregory — tit-for-tatting, the boys' game — publicly promised remission of sins to those who would defect from Frederico, and to their mothers and fathers as well.

The separation of church and state was proving an impossible dream.

When Gregory at last consented to give up the ghost, in 1241, in the August heat of Rome, Frederico addressed the crowned heads of Europe: "Pope Gregory is taken away from this world, and has escaped the vengeance of the Emperor of whom he was the implacable enemy. He is dead, through whom peace was banished from the earth, and discord prospered. For his death, though so deeply injured and so implacably persecuted, we feel compassion; . . . God we trust will raise up a pope of more pacific temper; whom we are prepared to defend as a devout son, if he follow not the fatal course and animosity of his predecessors."

In the matter of Henry: Called to his father's presence, in the apparent belief that the king-emperor had it in mind to kill him, Henry, riding in Calabria, urged his horse over a precipice and plunged to his death. We have varied accounts of the king-emperor's response to the death of his firstborn son (all of them heart-melting):

"The feelings of a father overpower those of a judge, and we are forced to bewail the death of our eldest son. Cruel fathers may perhaps wonder that Caesar, unconquered by public foes, should be mastered by a domestic sorrow; . . . We confess though we could not be bent by our son when alive, we mourn him when dead. We are not the first or the last who have wept for an undutiful son."

Abulafia: "A flood of tears wells up from the depth of my heart, even though heretofore held in check by the memory of the wrongs I suffered, and of the exercise of stern justice.

"We mourn the doom of our first-born. Nature bids flow a flood of tears, but they are checked by the pain of injury and the inflexibility of Justice."

. . . History is a fairy tale. And I have told the parts of the fable that touch my heart. If I had attempted to tell the whole, "objective" truth, it would be no more and no less true than what I have told. All love affairs are fables. . . .

Henry was buried in a shroud of gold-and-silver tissue into which eagles' feathers had been woven.

European internecine quarrels delayed the election of Gregory's successor; Frederico was prompted to issue another broadside to the Princes of the Church: "Sons of Belial! Animals without heads! Sons of Ephraim who basely turn back on the day of battle! Not Jesus Christ the author of peace but Satan, Prince of the North, sits in the midst of their conclave, inflaming their discords, their mutual jealousies. The smallest creatures might read them a salutary lesson: birds fly not without a leader; bees live not without a king. [God, I love his words, I love his love of words; they are practically edible, his words.] They leave the bark of the Church to the waves, without a pilot."

Innocent IV, visiting the alleged sins of the fathers upon the sons, excommunicated Frederico's grandchildren. Terrible, really, because Frederico had regarded him as an ally, Innocent's fortune having derived from Frederico's grandfather Barbarossa. Trouble comes from directions we least expect. The nature of accidents is that we are unprepared for them, that's why they are called accidents.

Innocent offered Frederico peace and reconciliation on humiliating terms. (The drama appealed immensely to Italians of course.) Frederico was fifty. And doomed. The Church, terrible and immortal, renews itself. Frederico, mortal, and aware of encroaching death, could not. As his life wound down, and his attempts at peace weakened and failed, a council was convened to try him; and his representatives, eating an extraordinary amount of humble pie, speaking for their king-emperor, averred that Frederico would ally himself with the pope against all of Innocent's enemies, restore church property, and again (this must have cost him a lot) go on Crusade. Innocent dismissed these "fine words and specious promises. . . . The axe is at the root of the tree and he would avert it. If we were weak enough to believe this deceiver, who would guarantee his truth?" At the mass that concluded the council, Innocent said, "See ye, who pass this way, was ever sorrow like unto my sorrow?" He rehearsed Frederico's heresy and superstition, and offered the women and the Moslems with whom he consorted as proof of his infamy: "Nothing remains but ignominiously to depose a man laden with such manifold sins," he said.

Frederico, wearied and defeated: "We submit ourselves to the spiritual penances, not only to the Pope, but to the humblest priest; but alas! how unlike the clergy of our day to those of the primitive church, who led apostolic lives, imitating the humility of the Lord! Then they were visited of angels, then shone around by angels, then did they heal the sick and raise the dead, and subdue princes by their holiness, not by arms! Now they are abandoned to this world and to drunkenness; their religion is choked by their riches."

Innocent: "The Emperor doubts and denies that all things and all men are subject to the See of Rome as if we who are to judge angels are not to give sentence on all earthly things."

Crusaders turned their attention from the Holy Land and united against Frederico; Innocent had command of the treasuries of France and Spain and England; pilgrims joined the papal armies; the pope's tentacles — priests and friars — extended into every part of the empire. The tide had for the last time turned. Frederico Secundo, *Stupor Mundi*, Wonder of the World, Holy Roman Emperor, was deposed: "His sentence is absolutely irrevocable! . . . He is condemned and forever. His viper progeny are included under this unmitigable proscription."

Frederico, mortifying his pride, submitted himself to a test of orthodoxy; he demonstrated his belief in the Creed, on which he was examined. Innocent was unmoved.

Frederico grew ill. On the morning of February 18, 1248, he went hawking; when he returned to the palace he had built near Parma, he found his army slaughtered, his possessions dispersed, his crowns stolen.

He believed that he would be murdered in his bed. On one occasion he changed places with a servant — who was stabbed, subsequently, in the royal bed.

Nothing about his amazing life should occasion surprise.

No less a man than Dante regarded him as the father of Italian poetry.

Frederico had shared many intellectual pleasures with Pietro della Vigna, jurist and statesman and court poet. One day, searching for his friend, the emperor wandered by chance into his bedchamber and discovered Peter's beautiful young wife asleep and uncovered. In the process of covering her, he dropped his glove. When Pietro della Vigna found it, he reviled his wife for her unfaithfulness: "On a vineyard another plant trespassing came, / And ruined the vineyard, / O, villainous shame!"

True or not, Pietro soon found himself in prison, charged with having conspired with the pope's physician to poison his king. Suspicious, Frederico had asked Pietro to drink from a cup of medicine offered to him; the physician overturned the cup. The residue was given to a prisoner, who died in great agony. And Frederico, betrayed, said: "This Peter, whom I thought a rock, who was the other half of myself, has plotted my murder! Whom can I now trust, betrayed by my own familiar friend? Never can I know security, never can I know joy more." The physician was hanged. Pietro was blinded and paraded through the streets of Apulia. Imprisoned in Frederico's Apulian dungeon, he dashed himself against the pillar to which he was chained, and his brains fell out of his head.

Frederico's last definitive act, a lovely one, was to marry Bianca, so as to legitimize Constance and Manfred, his children by her, in the eyes of the world. He died in Manfred's arms, the archbishop of Palermo in attendance. He was fifty-six; the year was 1250, whose digits add up to eight, his favorite, chosen number.

Merlin, assorted mystics, and myriad quacks refused to believe that their Emperor, *Stupor Mundi*, the Wonder of the World, was mortal. . . . And of course they were right.

A litter hung with crimson velvet bore his body to its resting place; he was surrounded by hundreds of weeping Saracens — his honored bodyguards — and by nobles and prelates; and barons, black cloaks over their armor, followed on horseback. The body of the king-emperor — draped in embroidered cloth of silk, his feet spurred and shod in boots of silk — was brought over the seas from Bari to Messina — to Sicily at last. He wore his crown; his right hand was placed on the hilt of his sword; he wore a large emerald set in a gold ring.

And a crusader's cross was sewn on the red silk mantle over his heart.

His earthly remains are in the great red porphyry urn resting upon marble lions in the Cathedral of Palermo — that wondrous Spanish baroque church that looks like the fires of the Inquisition translated into stone. He has many lovers: red roses are brought to him every day.

The Te Deum that followed the announcement of the death of the Wonder of the World was led by Innocent IV: "Let us rejoice and be glad." The congregational responsory to Innocent's readings from the Psalms was "Down to hell he went."

Heaven is the hell where Frederico is.

6

NOTES
FROM ABROAD

This is the aim of my explorations: examining the traces of happiness still to be glimpsed, I gauge its short supply. If you want to know how much darkness there is around you, you must sharpen your eyes, peering at the faint lights in the distance.

— Italo Calvino, *Invisible Cities*

Everything beyond a certain distance is dark, and yet everything is full of being around us.

— Teilhard de Chardin, *The Divine Milieu*

MY GOOD AUNT MARY says that when I was a small child I would climb the steps to the bedroom floor swinging my bottle of bedtime milk and chanting, "Now I'm going to Germany, now I'm going to France. Now I'm going to London, now I'm going to Rome." "How did you even know about those places?" she asks. I don't know. I don't remember that little girl at all, though if I try very hard I can see a pair of sturdy little legs, feet shod in slippery rayon socks trimmed with shiny lace, moving away from the laughter of the grown-ups into warm, vast, intimate, comforting space. That child longs to take the journey across the threshold that will separate her from the cacophonous noises of strangers — people who claim to know her better than she knows herself; she travels to foreign places to play hide and seek.

When I was nine years old I made a friend in Buffalo at a religious convention (that year — 1944 — there was a plague of caterpillars, and they fell from the trees into the light cast by streetlamps and formed a slimy carpet of yellow-green stuff and guts, and dropped sticky and squirmy into one's hair; one was afraid that they would veil one's eyes, insinuate themselves into one's mouth); my new friend lived in Niagara Falls. One day when I was ten, I told my mother — who was studying the *Watchtower* magazine at the kitchen table at the time — that I was going to see my friend in Niagara Falls. My mother nodded without removing her eyes from her apocalyptic reading matter; and I went, by way of Greyhound bus, to Niagara Falls, where — at midnight — I rang my friend's doorbell. No one answered. I walked back to the bus station, and arrived home the next morning. My mother was still sitting at the kitchen table, consulting Strong's *Bible Concordance*. Her blue eyes took a while to focus on me. "Hello, dear," she said, and returned to Strong's.

> *Elsewhere is a negative mirror. . . . Your footsteps follow not what is outside the eyes, but what is within, buried, erased.*
>
> — Italo Calvino

It terrifies and saddens me how much I used to lie.

It is not that way anymore. I do not fear the approach of old age because, when I concentrate and reflect, I find myself always and again in a garden of white flowers; or a bazaar where all of human behavior is ritualized, solemnized in accordance with ancient civil rules; a haunted forest. . . . I am picnicking again on the ramparts of Golconda; I watch a volcano pitch its thundering fire into the yielding sky; in the deep well at the bottom of the garden, a serpent turns iridescent colors before it is shot; I am watching lean dark boys lounging in the port shadows of Anzio; yellow hummingbirds sip nectar from a purple jacaranda tree; an old lady under an avocado tree talks about her mother (dead), Plague Inspector for the port of Bombay a century ago. As long as consciousness exists, memory and its nuances exist (happiness exists); I cross over the threshold.

But there was a time for a long time when my curiosity was deadened, battered, and diseased. And I feared death; and I lied.

TRIPOLI, LIBYA, 1961

I am sitting in a little square with Mr. Harrison, in an outdoor restaurant run by the soon to be dispersed children of Italian colonists . . . a green painted fence — green is the color sacred to Mohammed — a picket fence; and more exotic to me than Libya is the recognition that I and my husband have nothing to say to each other although it is only our second week abroad in a new place and a new life. I am reading a paperback mystery. Absently I remove an olive from his plate and he mumbles in disgust. He really doesn't like me very much.

> *Often I have wondered how a Roman wore his toga. Here rich and poor wear it, be it dazzling white or dirty greyish, new or in rags, and stride along utterly unaware of how Antique they look to us. Old men recline on stone benches waiting for the hour of the evening prayer, as distinguished and impressive as the figures in Bellini's Naples "Transfiguration."*
>
> — Bernard Berenson, *The Passionate Sightseer*

I do not have a guidebook. In all the years I lived abroad with him — in Libya and in India and in Guatemala — I never once thought to read a guidebook; and this is inexplicable to me, my self at that time is a self foreign to the avid self I am now. Where — what — were my appetites?

I can't see. I am expending all my energy on pretending that my marriage is a good one, a happy one. My lies blind me. I understand from this, now, that it is not introspection but numbness that promotes narcissism, solipsism, and alienation; I was numb.

We lived in Tripoli fourteen months. I told myself many lies. Even my dreams were censored; invisible policemen, when I dreamed the unthinkable, appeared at the foot of my bed to direct the traffic of images.

(I asked Mr. H. if he ever masturbated; and he reacted in appalled — simulated? — shock.)

The dream police will not let me have sexual fantasies.

Among the lies dwelt facts: Four cats were born in Tripoli under the jasmine tree — black-gray-orange cats. One, fat and greedy, and given to biting its mother's tit, was called Orange Sinner; and one was called Lemons, which was later emended, because of its resemblance to a pop-eyed friend of mine, to Jimmy Lemons.

It is 109 degrees. The kittens, who rest near our bed, have fleas. I buy flea powder, made in West Germany, in one of the two main arcaded streets of Tripoli, streets lined with cafés in which, because I am a woman, it is improper for me to sit; and the flea powder poisons the kittens. I feed them with an eyedropper, three times a day and three times a night; but two kittens die anyway, writhing, convulsing.

. . . Before I married Mr. H. I had a cat called Squiggles, whom I loved. Squiggles slept in my double bed on East Seventh Street, and I was late to work every morning because his warm snuggling and his wet little kitty kisses were deliciously impossible to leave. So when Mr. H. moved into 69 East Seventh Street, he exiled Squiggles from the bed. Squiggles climbed into the courtyard — which from time to time he had visited. Blinded, I didn't realize until it was too late that he was not eating the water beetles and the mice he had previously gone to hunt; my bold predator was starving. So the vet said, "What has happened to change your life? This cat is committing suicide, he is starving himself." Thereafter, whenever I had reason to hate Mr. H. I thought, Murderer! Though it was my negligence that killed Squiggles (how badly a bad marriage distorts). . . .

Jimmy Lemons played in the garage and in the back garden (about which Mr. Harrison had very Zen-like, minimalist ideas) and in the front garden (which was mine to plant along more riotous lines: florid gardens I like); and for all I know, Jimmy Lemons played in the caves the Italians who had built our seaside villa dug into the ground for protection from air raids during World War II. (I never went there, past the arcade in the back garden that led to the steps at the bottom of which, according to my husband, were rooms clearly distinguishable as kitchen, living room, and bedroom. I never went there because the roofs of the caves (he told me) were thick and black with bats . . . and my curiosity was at that time tightly reined; once I started asking questions, where would I stop?)

At night, when all the other cats — by this time we had five (I wanted millions) — were immaculately asleep, Jimmy Lemons went out to prowl. At three or four in the morning he would return, managing to enter a window and announcing his imperious presence with thick sounds from the back of his throat, or else he scratched the glass door of the bedroom (which led to the Japanese back garden and the caves and the bats) to wake us up and let him in. Mr. Harrison resented this intrusion upon his sleep. So he gave Jimmy Lemons away — with, I am so sorry to say, the dim consent I called by the name of wifely support in those blind days. He gave Jimmy Lemons to Mohammed, our houseboy, who put the pop-eyed explorer in a box and put the box in a suitcase with air holes and put his cargo on the back of his motor scooter and drove Jimmy Lemons to his farm. To do this, Mohammed had to negotiate the labyrinthine streets of the old souk and then to take the coastal road to his village oasis, fifty kilometers away. I missed Jimmy Lemons, I missed his eyes peering out at me from the apricot tree. Three weeks later there was a weak mewing at the bedroom window, a kind of shadow wail; and it was Jimmy Lemons, fevered, one leg broken; he had come home. After that, one couldn't send him away again, of course.

The cats had to be taken to the air force base to be vaccinated against rabies. Wheelus Air Force Base was the largest American overseas base in the world. It had a hospital where King Idris, Qaddafi's royal predecessor, indulged his many illnesses; and it was closed to nongovernmental civilians (but not to us, because Mr. H. was employed by a quasi-governmental aid organization); it was closed to all Americans except for rabies vaccinations, God knows why. If the families of oil workers — or workers themselves — were injured or became ill, they had to fly to Italy. The pimply boys with bayonets who stood outside the base to guard it were told to "engage militarily" any nonaccredited Americans who tried to get into the hospital. And one woman, feeling herself about to give birth prematurely, allowed the pimply toy soldiers to keep her away; and her twin babies died. (Surely they wouldn't have killed or even detained her. The soldiers were children. Surely she could have marched right past?) An oil worker whose leg was squashed by a rig in the desert died on the plane to Italy; if he had gone to Wheelus, he might have lived.

Some of the Air Force wives never left the pampered grounds of Wheelus. They waited at the commissary for the arrival of wilted brown American lettuces and moldy tomatoes and lived from the produce of cans . . . and all around them, outside the base, were the bright products of the Mediterranean soil — melons and figs and dates and tomatoes. Sometimes the ocean, where tomatoes were dumped in bumper years, tasted of tomatoes, divers said.

(The Libyans import food now; the desert has been allowed to encroach upon the fruitful coastal strip — old aerial photographs tell a very different story; this is called progress, and is the result of oil.)

"Accuracy takes too many pages," I wrote in a letter to a friend. I meant — even my letters were coded — that my life was a garment I wore, like an enveloping barracan, to hide my soul. My letters had a jolly, manic tone, or a treacly sentimental one.

Numbness and hysteria are two sides of the same coin.

"[Mr. H.] is a perfect angel," I wrote. "Remember all that beautiful leisure time I was going to be so creative in? Now I have it," I wrote. "All I want to do is eat chocolates." I was all the time bored, and reproachful of myself for being bored, and bewildered.

The witch down the road knew I was pregnant before I did. She knew everything. I used to crouch on the floor of our Land Rover to give her the evil eye when we passed her hut (a preemptive strike), sure that she was preparing bad magic for me.

The Arab ladies in black barracans stood at my tall green gate, their babies in their arms, their kohl-lined eyes ringed with flies they never bothered to brush away, regarding my belly. Kindly. Flies skated on their babies' eyeballs.

One lady beckoned me to follow her to her dun-colored hut. In a dark corner was a naked baby covered with flies and weak as a kitten. He needs medicine, she said to me, in a combination of sign language and Italian; and it was patently clear that he needed more than that; but she wouldn't let us drive the infant to the hospital or to a clinic until her husband came home from the oil fields and gave her permission, and she wouldn't go unaccompanied by a man of her family; her husband would be home in six months, by which time the baby would surely have died. (In fact the baby was, at the time I saw him, almost a year old, but so malnourished as to look like a newborn.)

There was a midwife in the old town. The woman with the sick infant would not entertain her in her hut — the midwife's morals were suspect, she was suspiciously progressive. One night a man went to the house of the midwife and said that his wife, for whom the midwife was caring, was about to give birth before her time. The young woman protested that she could not go alone with him; but he pleaded: She is in pain, she will die, my baby will die. The midwife could not refuse his plaint, which was a ruse. He kidnapped the midwife, who for ten days was raped by seven men. When she was released she returned to the house of her father in the old town; but he would not take her in, nor would the man to whom she was affianced speak to her. She found refuge in the Egyptian embassy; and foreigners took up a collection for her, and she went to spend the rest of her days, her honor ravaged, in Cairo. She knew the identity of the men; but they were never punished for their deed. "She was asking for it."

I crawled under tables and beds to escape the sound and blast of Wheelus's jets; the Cuban missile crisis was on, and I knew we would be the Soviets' first target. I hated Kennedy, whom before I had loved, and I hated Mr. H. because he had urged me to vote for Kennedy. I walked down the sand road lined with cactus and orange prickly pears to the sea and, loving my harbored baby and hating my life, asked myself: Is this all I will ever have? I had read this sentence in a book: "What he was now he would always be; what he had now was all he ever would have; he had come to a place, and life would hold nothing more or less for him than it did at this moment." I was thirty years old.

"The thing is, I'm pregnant," I wrote. "I've just missed my second period. The symptoms are, I wear a bra to bed, I take three-hour naps, and [Mr. H.] drinks a quart of milk a day. I don't really believe it, though, because I'm not in New York with everybody to talk to me about it. I probably won't even believe it when the baby is born — February — because no one in New York will see it. Please tell everybody in NY I'm pregnant, and tell me you've told them, so it will begin to have some reality. The other symptoms are, I read a lot of poetry and I feel invulnerable. I'm not so much afraid of the jets that break the sound barrier over my head any more. Or of bats. Or of rabies. I'm not worried that it won't be beautiful, normal, healthy or that I won't know what to tell it about God, or that it will hurt. I swim better. I love [Mr. H.]. Can it really be happening."

Mr. H. was learning Arabic and calligraphy. Two morose Russians from the embassy, friends of his, frequently came to our house in the evenings and got drunk and listened to *Boris Godunov* and *Carmina Burana* and cried; and Mr. H. got drunk.

What was true was that I knew my baby would be beautiful, normal, and healthy. I never doubted it.

Dancers, Martha Graham alumni, came to the villa and did the twist and sat on the floors of our house crushing cigarettes out on the tiles and getting drunk.

From their various embassies came Africans and Koreans and Americans and I cooked elaborate meals and I missed Birdland and the possibility of seeing Jazzman; a Nigerian mother held her baby to one side at the dining room table so the infant could pee on the tile floor.

The cats peed in the fireplace, where eucalyptus logs were burned.

The skylight of the living room roof leaked. There were scorpions.

Old Italian workmen came to fix the plumbing. First they dug up the septic tank and then when they found nothing wrong they went fishing in the toilet bowl with a clothes hanger and brought the dripping junk to me, triumphantly, in the living room. They asked for olive oil (I thought for their lunch); they swallowed it from the bottle and spit it at the rusty door handles they had been asked to fix.

I read Philip Roth, *Letting Go;* and Iris Murdoch, *An Unofficial Rose;* and Jimmy Baldwin, *Another Country.* And Dr. Spock.

I wrote to my family that I was swimming and floating in the sea. In fact I didn't swim and I didn't float. There were ancient Roman villas in those beautiful seas — those seas that tasted of ripe tomatoes — but I didn't swim under water through their porticos, I never swam at all. In shallow pools formed by black shale rocks I waded. I could not learn from the man to whom I was married to swim or to drive a car. If sex had been good I could have learned.

There were rules I couldn't learn, or learned only after I had made my first, bad impression: I didn't know one was supposed to serve one's seated husband first at a buffet dinner and only then oneself (it seemed impertinent to me to anticipate what someone else would desire to eat

— impertinent and theatrical and smug). I didn't know one was supposed to bring one's new neighbors casseroles when they moved in. We lived four kilometers outside town in a sparsely populated village called Gargaresh. (Our villa had been in its time the home of a Libyan patriot, and before that the home of the Italian consul, during Mussolini's rule, after which it had suffered degradation as an ammunition dump. We had one eighth of an acre of land, on which, when we took residence, were poinsettia trees and citrus trees, date palms, carnations, corn, hot-pepper plants, watermelon, squash, eggplants, and string beans.) I knew the rules of New York life, not this transported Welcome Wagon life. I was numb to the sensitivity of others, though not calculatedly unkind. I felt more at ease in wordless communication with the Arab ladies in their huts than with oil wives from Texas. I didn't know how to behave.

I got an official letter from the aid agency Mr. Harrison worked for: "We must all be pretty Americans. Remember you are not just a person, you are an image."

I got a letter from a friend: "Don't you think superficiality is okay anymore?"

"One of our cats, all black, is afflicted," I wrote; "he opens his mouth to cry and nothing comes out. He closes his mouth and a faint squeak hangs in the air.

"Lovely crisp autumn days are here, our house is beautiful, last weekend we drove out to a waterfall and picnicked on a blanket of spring wild flowers, and we're hunting for Roman artifacts. We have found coins; melted glass, pale blue and iridescent; fish hooks; ceramic tiles; pottery shards; and one complete vase: we dig in three mounds five minutes away from home."

Was this true? If it was true, where are these things? Where have they gone? (It is true that American neighbors had found a marble pediment and a cistern several kilometers away from Gargaresh.) I don't think what I wrote in that letter was true; I think I appropriated someone else's experience in order to feel real.

I wrote that I was so happy that hanging clothes on the clothesline was heaven. In fact it was Mohammed who put the clothes on the clothesline.

We took a long drive from Tripoli to Benghazi (which John Gunther

called the most miserable city in the world); all along the coastal road
were wild flowers, and I covered the jeep with them so that our vehicle
distantly resembled a hearse; almost immediately they died. Bodies of
crushed and rusted cars and smashed trucks lined the road.

He was pedantic in his expressions of affection, and wildly unruly —
anarchic — in his sex life (but not with me). Once when he was drunk
he kissed me wetly while I was having a shit on the toilet; I felt mortified
and revulsed and murderous.

We drove to Tunis. There is a huge colosseum that rises in the desert
somewhere across the Libyan-Tunisian border; I wonder that it occa-
sioned no wonder in me. I had a peach melba in a town the name of
which I do not remember, outside the city walls. In Tunis, with Sadiq,
our driver, we went to a café where brothel girls entertained their customers; and, drunk, my husband danced with me flamboyantly — such
great swoops and such unfocused intensity — while Sadiq looked on
and smirked (the tango, it was); I felt mortified and revulsed and murderous. The brothel girls were amused, but sad for me, too, I thought.

In the *jebel*, the rocky plateau that separates the coastal strip from
sub-Saharan Africa, there are rusty cages. Human beings were held
here during the time of the slave trade by African dealers; Sadiq calls
black Africans "Kiwis" — the name of black shoe polish.

You would think I would exquisitely remember sleeping in the desert
— the Fezzan; I can't. In the desert foxes dig holes under your head,
Sadiq said; they like to see your head flop back, it makes the little foxes
laugh. I remember that; and I remember stories of men on horseback
or in jeeps racing gazelles until the gazelles dropped dead of exhaustion;
and I remember stopping at the king's guest house — a filthy one-room
cement house — and being served, by the caretaker, rancid camel meat
for dinner and a carafe of water with a tadpole in it. The bed bugs were
as big as my thumbnail.

I was not an active participant in my own life.

The person who wrote letters home was a person living in a movie

— a not very good movie of someone else's life; I wrote the script; I made myself up.

Do you understand that this is why I hate masks?

In the icy morning, at dawn, we drank coffee made on a Primus stove and eggs and hot fish soup — this sounds wonderful; I don't remember it.

We drove, in the desert, a distance equal to the distance between New York and Chicago; and we saw not a soul.

In the pre-Islamic oasis of Gadames I drank fifteen cups of tea in one day — very sweet green tea, strong red tea, mint tea, tea with peanuts. Each time tea was brewed there was a cup for each guest, a cup for the host, and a cup for "the house."

The dwellings of Gadames were built shortly after the birth of Mohammed. (Oh how I wish I could be there now — now, when I am able to see, and not perfunctorily, when I am so much more happily astonished by the world than consumed by ignorance of my place in it.) The *mudir* — the mayor — took us on a walking tour of the two-leveled city. The visible, aboveground level was the abode of men; the underground level was the abode of women; interior steps connected the separate worlds of separate sexes (and the women came out, from time to time — two hours a day — to draw water from the well). There were separate mosques for men and women, separate baths, and separate schools. The underground streets of packed sweet-smelling mud were cool and clean; the designs painted on the gleaming underground white archways and walls were fifteen hundred years old. Massive tall carved wooden doors, useful in times past (when they were locked at night) for separating warring tribes, connected clusters of whitewashed houses by way of vaulted tunnel-like communal chambers with latticed skylights. Life in caves: massive low ancient wooden doors for entry into family quarters. All the household goods belonged to the women — who slept apart from their husbands, and wore the household keys around their necks.

The women gave me dates, and sugar, and woven flags. (I showed them how to mix powdered milk.) They giggled; and they stripped. They wanted me to see their flesh. (What kind of needed confirmation was this?) They wanted to see my pregnant body: I stripped. Sadiq, who went to the Tripoli cinema on women's day wrapped in a barracan so he could see the faces of women, said he had lived with his brother's wife for five years and never seen her uncovered — "and they are with you fifteen minutes and you see all."

(Young girls marched in Tripoli to support the independence fighters of Algeria; heady, intoxicated with freedom, they removed their barracans and marched in their school uniforms. They were stoned. Attention shifted from the French in Algiers to the "unwomanly women" of Libya.)

> *I . . . love to muse and dream and visualize ruins as a scene, as romance, as a transporting evocation. Leptis is, all considered, one of the most impressive fields of ruins on the shores of the Mediterranean. . . . The great sculptured pillars are so delicately undercut that the effect is almost of lace work, reminding one of the best Indian sculpture, . . . or of Carolingian ivories. There is still much to be excavated. . . . Will the Libyans want to carry on and preserve what may seem to them an intrusion from a hostile world?*
>
> — Bernard Berenson, *The Passionate Sightseer*

We meet the Italian ambassador at Leptis and proceed to crawl over — and under — sand dunes at Leptis Magna; under the direction of the Italian superintendent of public works, laborers are engaged in the ongoing work of excavating the circus and the amphitheater on the sea. "We were on hands and knees for what seemed like hours through a partially excavated tunnel, clawing shifting sands for footholds. When we finally emerged gasping into daylight we found ourselves at the edge of a deep abyss, and there were workers like toy-men hundreds of feet below. I couldn't tell, in that dark, whether I had climbed up or down," I wrote. Below us was the sea.

The gentle old merchant in the souk loves to bargain, as do I — it is a finely choreographed art; the tiny cups of tea (like dollhouse cups) grow sweeter as the price between us narrows. Mr. Harrison likes to have it done with, depriving the merchant of his pleasure. Mr. Harrison believes in money.

This old man (whom I remember in my prayers) presented me with shawls of fine Egyptian wool, and Berber cloth, for birthdays . . . a special one for the birth day of my son.

In an alley in the old city were the remains of a slave market, seven hundred years old.

"My Sasha cat died and all her kittens were blind from enteritis. I cried very much, and if all my cats die, what will I do with babies?"

From the letter I sent to my family announcing my pregnancy (a letter I found after my father, who kept all my letters, died), my signature is torn off. What does this mean? Why do I persist in believing it betokened something fetishistic? (It makes my skin crawl.) (What did it mean that he said, just before he died, "Never trust that Barbara, never trust that girl"?) Was this the work of the witch? Which witch?

"Every time you write Dad a letter," my brother wrote, "he reads it to about half the people in Brooklyn. And when he fights with Mom he tells her he's moving to Tripoli."

"Do you ever buy huckleberry pies at Ebinger's? They have delicious crumb buns, too," my mother wrote; Ebinger's was on Eighteenth Avenue in Brooklyn, she was mad.

Nicely and Namby were born under a jasmine bush and moved thereafter to the morning glories on the terrace that belonged to the nursery that was being prepared for my baby. Nicely was orange and fawn, and Namby was a tiger cat, and they roamed among the marigolds and zinnias and the poisonous yellow jasmine, the larkspur, the stock, irises, the daisies, the white moonflowers (which, closed by day, opened at night to release a strenuously sweet and soporific fragrance — a moonflower under your pillow and you sleep a dreamless sleep; eat a moonflower and you die).

"We have a cactus called a century plant — it lives 1000 years, it produces, at the end of its life, a magnificent white mammoth flower, its first and last, and then it dies, all its life energy having gone into making this one beautiful thing."

"The doctor says I have the most luxury-loving baby he's ever seen — he's sprawled all over the place, not curled up in a fetal ball." Lovely to be so occupied.

Mr. Harrison asserted that children would be easier than cats to care for, as children would "listen to instructions."

There was trouble over our contract with the Libyan government, and we didn't know — I was five weeks away from my due date — whether we would have to move, and if we did move, whether we would go to Rome or to Sicily or to Afghanistan or to the Gaza Strip.

At Christmas we had houseguests for ten days, a cocktail party for fifty, and a brunch for twelve (and I passed off chocolate pudding from a package as chocolate mousse, and Mohammed cut his finger and dribbled blood all over the pudding. The day after Christmas Mr. H. and the houseguests went to Djerba; and while he was gone I sprained my hip washing dishes and when he came back he made fun of me, walking behind me saying *quack quack* and flipping a towel at my ass the way jocks do in locker rooms. I was less than a month away from childbirth.

A colleague of Mr. H.'s came to the villa to tell me he'd gotten a cable saying that his father had died. "How tiresome," he said; I had never heard anyone talk that way before outside of books.

I had a terrible cough and cold. The doctor at Wheelus — with whom I fought when he told me he wanted to induce labor so that the baby would be born "at an opportune time" (for him) — did nothing for the racking cough I was to bring with me into labor, but diagnosed "acute anxiety" and gave me pills and said in an offhand way, "These are for borderline schizophrenics." I said I didn't think I was a border-line schizophrenic. He said, "Probably not. Manic depressive, more likely." He was a very small man, and after my baby was born he stitched me up too tight (asking me to admire his work).

"[Mr. H.] was with me all the time, providing love and comfort and moral support and back rubs and sips of water." This was not true. This was life as I wanted life to be. I was in labor for twenty-one hours — alone, for most of that time, in a narrow room with a caged light bulb dangling over my narrow bed, alone in the shower when my water broke. Mr. Harrison was in a little cubby down the hall with an air force sergeant, discussing the mechanics of birth (and crying).

"I think the hour I spent in the delivery room was the happiest of my life." I'd had no drugs for twenty-one hours; when I began to bear down — and at last felt as if I were actively engaged in this event, not just the plaything of pain — I laughed with relief and anticipation: "Tie her down," the doctor said. He wanted to knock me out with drugs. I screamed, *"No no no!"* I wanted to claim this part for my own; my baby — whom Mr. Harrison always called "our baby" but I never did — cooperated; and, while I was not allowed to hold him (my hands being pronounced unsterile), I was awake to see his beautiful/ugly red, squashed, precious face — the face in which all his future was written, my darling darling ever darling boy.

"I gave my husband a son," I said.

"I feel like I'm the luckiest girl in the world."

Did we all lie? Did all of us, adrift in the new world of motherhood (wearing regulation jammies, sitting on regulation rubber tires to ease our regulation episiotomies, eight of us to a room, our babies, crying, down the hall away from us), lie to one another about our happiness?

I was lonely, I wanted my baby. And I wanted to read *Little Women*.

I never wrote to anyone that my breasts were dry, these great stupid things I had carried with me forever.

When I took him home from Wheelus I walked each day to the local market with him. I shook hands and said in Arabic, "Good morning, how are you?" and bought two eggs so that the villagers could get used to my baby and to show the witch I was not afraid of her bad magic.

My closest and nicest neighbor was forbidden by her husband to talk to me because while I was in the hospital Mr. H. had had a drunken fight with him.

A young Italian woman from the old town came to visit and shook my baby up and down and said, "This baby has not enough milk"; which was true.

Sometimes Mr. H. endeared himself to me. I brought him hot beef broth and lime Jell-O for a stomach upset and he wanted to know in what order to eat them.

"I read an article about 'perfecting one's love for one's mate.' But I don't really know what that means or how you'd go about it. It sounds like polishing silver."

I felt a spiritual affinity to the Arab women in veils.

There was nothing in my letters about my loneliness, or about Mr. Harrison's wrathful melancholy, his drinking.

My baby was nineteen days old when we were ordered to go to Bombay. "I'm a little chilled by the practical considerations of a move at this time, but happy to be going."

I was terrified.

Mr. Harrison said the cats would be quite happy in the garden, "don't worry about them." Packing with one hand, my baby in the other arm, I allowed myself to believe him — a sin — and left my cats behind. A sin.

"Our soft life continues."

I wanted to stand again in the courtyard of Patchin Place and yell up at E. E. Cummings's window, as we had done in days past:

> Buffalo Bill's
> defunct
>   who used to
>   ride a watersmooth-silver stallion
> and break onetwothreefourfive pigeons justlikethat Jesus
>
> he was a handsome man
>   and what i want to know is
> how do you like your blueeyed boy
> Mister Death

My letters meant: Love me. Hear me. Know me. Read through my lies. Tell me who I am.

I began to have nightmares again about forgetting Jazzman's telephone number.

Sometimes at sunset Mr. H. and I took a thermos of martinis and drank them overlooking the sea, breakers twenty feet high.

I knew that I would miss my garden ruefully.

The TV Mr. H. had rented for me broke; and I wrote: He "is not guilty enough to capitulate to my one-more-possession-will-make-me-happy plaint and rent me a piano."

There were burlap curtains made of natural linen in the baby's room. An orange tree crushed against the glass. There were Bedouin blankets on the beds and sheepskin rugs on the floor.

I began to read ads in old copies of the *New York Times* for apartments in the Village.

On Malta, dancing underneath bright lights, we saw two young men, gay twins with matched pink hair and matched pink poodles and matched pink dungarees.

During the whole of my engagement I had worn black.

NORTH AFRICA REVISITED, 1993

In the exotic and terrifyingly familiar landscape of dreams — in which the impossible is the inevitable and the alien is one's brother; in which the dreamer is simultaneously visible and invisible, caressed and as-saulted in her dreaming flesh which is disembodied matter — rivers run through deserts, flowers bloom along paths where seductive dangers lurk in gardens of paradise that are fed by streams of excrement, houses are caves through which the dreamer's tunneled unconscious searches and stumbles. In this territory, where the known and the unknown are identical twins and what happens in the heart resounds in the receptive universe, objects and events telescope and melt into a unity that is more perilous than chaos; stasis and flow, monotony and variety — repetition — are indistinguishable, as is the prince from the toad . . . and from this country no one returns undisturbed.

In my dream I make my way through dun-colored honeycombed rooms so low I have to crawl from one to the other. Sometimes a green door punctuates my journey, which has no end. The tunneled rooms are brilliantly lit and full of wondrous things — hands made of gold and milk-white cats with emerald eyes and carpets of edible colors and warriors in silken robes. Will somebody be cruel to me? Why is nobody cruel to me? When I wake from this dream I am sad.

Before I went to Morocco I thought this dream was about Libya, where I once lived, although its features only dimly resembled the streets and shops of the souk — not dun-colored but white and blue; not darkly tunneled but latticed, light, and airy — where I bought copper hands of Fatima to keep away the evil eye and camel bags with lozenges of colors (like jujubes) and where once, in impenetrable alleys, my favorite cat got lost (and later found); and cruelty came from unforeseen directions. After I went to Morocco, I was inclined to believe that the dream was prescient and prefigured it. And now it doesn't matter anymore whether the dream belonged to the past or to the future, prefigured Morocco or harked back to Libya. It closed a circle. In Morocco I found a great deal not to like; nevertheless I am beholden to it — it helped me to reclaim Libya, which my memory had chosen to misplace and thereby to malign; without Morocco I would not have grasped the measure of love I entertained for that time and place . . . after a while, time and place become one entity, one cannot be considered apart from the other. . . . "We shall not cease from exploration / And the end of all our exploring / Will be to arrive where we started / And know the place for the first time. . . ."

Four men in long white cotton gowns sit, with biblical simplicity and intensity, under a date palm, turbans wound around their heads. No one could ask anything of them but to keep their unselfconscious pose. A young girl carrying reeds and sweet grasses emerges from the shadow of a glade, papyrus rustling; a glance at us and she is gone with the grace of a gazelle, leaving us to wonder if she was ever there. . . .

A profusion of red poppies, vivid and frail, among the green wheat, the amber wheat with silvered plumes; an olive tree bearing both flower and nascent fruit, like a metaphor for bounty; carpets of wild flowers, gentian, violet, purple, pale buttercup yellow, acid-lemon yellow, alternate with aggressively tidy fields of grasshopper green lined with neat rows of olive trees. A riot of poppies sways among onions whose long slender stalks culminate in many-headed white blossoms emerging from vellum jackets. The astringent smell of onions is added to the mint-scented air, and yeasty-smelling milk is sold in plastic orange buckets under eucalyptus trees in the heat of day. . . .

A Sufi poet says, "The world is a mirror. . . . In every atom are a hundred blazing suns. . . . If you examine closely each grain of sand, a thousand Adams may be seen in it. . . . A world dwells in the heart of a millet seed." . . .

What lies behind that clutch and huddle of whitewashed houses on tangled sandy lanes? (The smell of woodfires and of musk and of the distant sea and orange blossoms makes me wild with an indefinable longing, and at the same time comforts me.) That little village is not a secret to me; I lived in it once; but that was in Libya. . . . "Let me bring your baby to the doctor," I said to the Arab woman down the road, the witch who knew when I was pregnant before I did but whose sorcery could not heal her own child. "No," she said. "Your baby is dying," I said. "It is Allah's will," she said; and then, relenting, "When my husband comes home from the oil fields we will go," she said. "When?" "He will be back in six months." In two weeks the baby was dead. I thought thereafter that she wanted my baby; and I made the sign to take away the evil eye. . . .

A ruined city on a windswept plain above a sea of grain through which the wind soughs mournfully. . . . What is left of Roman law and sensibility and vivacity here? All gone; the colonnaded women's bath populated now only with geraniums; the once luxurious rooms of the bordello a home for nettles and scorpions; an olive press left like the skeleton of a dinosaur to rot; the merest trickle of rusty water in the troughs where white and purple togas once were washed. The rocks are worn where clothes were beaten centuries ago — it is lovely in the sun to touch the smooth rocks; touch nourishes fantasy. Even lovelier are the faded mosaics — a relief from the Moslem interdiction against portraying animals, birds, humans, and flowers in art. Here are dolphins sporting; a man riding a horse backwards; a jolly squid; a witty prawn.

On a stone block there is a representation of an enormous phallus (three feet long).

Under an aborted triumphal arch a young woman faints from the heat. . . .

I used to walk for hours alone in Libya's Leptis Magna, magnificent, coherent ruins by the sea. I gathered loose chunks of mosaics and amethyst and lapus lazuli as if they were wild flowers, and sat with them in a Roman house that still echoed with life and looked as if it might have been deserted only yesterday, imagining what my life would have been like then, in that house . . . which exercise was scarcely more difficult than imagining why I had chosen the life I lived. The past yielded its meaning more readily than the present. . . . It hurts my mind to think of Qaddafi and those ruins; perhaps the sand has covered them all. . . .

Twilight is the magic hour. We pass through white horseshoe gates with green enameled tiles and we are in a market square and in another and very old world, a world of incantatory charm and voluptuousness. Hallucinatory confusions have been preparation for this moment; weariness and irritable exhaustion have been wayposts on the journey toward delicious languor and untroubled acceptance. Now no question demands to be asked, no conflict resolved. We are in the south, the Sahara. Erfoud. Where every thing and every body is self-possessed and necessary, and every object has unquestionable integrity. The bruised and excited uncertainties of the daylight hours have led to this resolving moment at dusk; time is timeless here, endless and circular, as it is in arabesques. There is nothing one could possibly quarrel with, each thing being indisputably what it is and whole-unto-itself. White-turbaned men sit along palm-lined walls, their faces turned to the storyteller in the center of their rapt group. Lanterns light the way for cartloads of black-robed women heavily veiled — and even this seems right, even the kohl-lined eye (only one eye peers out from the devouring garment) seems poetically right: "All the mystery that awaits us looks out through the eye-slits in the grave-clothes muffling her. Where have they come from, where are they going, all these slow wayfarers of the unknown? . . . Interminable distances unroll behind them, they breathe of Timbuctoo and the farthest desert. . . . These wanderers have looked on at the building of cities that were dust when the Romans pushed their outposts across the Atlas" (Rebecca West). Blue men, tall handsome men wearing indigo turbans and blue robes that stain their skin, ride on white camels, their faces veiled (black eyes flashing) to keep the sand from their severely beautiful dark faces. . . .

In the morning the square has lost its magic, it is just a provincial square, tawdry, sober, penitential. . . .

Dust to dust. The Kasbah of Rissani — three centuries old, built by Sultan Moulay Ali Sharif, first king of the ruling dynasty of Morocco — is of the earth, earthy, a cave. We walk through cool underground streets, tunnels . . . tunnels in a womb. Pools of light from high windows illuminate great doors, great hinges. Women in black glide through distant arches, lovely in this prenatal light. Four beauties lean negligently against a low doorway. This is like our first home; and what we can imagine of our last. No wonder these men think women are dangerous — they are wombs within wombs, the beginning and the end. Outside in the square — it hurts our eyes to see the sun — four little girls in pink play with a sardine can, a ribbon is attached to it, and they pull it as if it were a cart. Already they smell of musk. . . .

I saw blue mountains in the light of a sinking orange sun; I was in the Djemma el Fna, the great dusty square of Morocco, a perpetual carnival from which the souks radiate — Vanity Fair, Bedlam. My first impression, as I walked through circles of human onlookers surrounding circles of acrobats and witch doctors, snake charmers, and letter writers, was that hell was better organized than this. Birds of carrion flew overhead. Dentists sat at wooden trestles with heaps of loose teeth and ready-to-wear dentures, pliers. Lice pickers sat next to hair cutters. A Punch and Judy show incarnate: a little boy is beaten with a bamboo stick (this is a charade) to force him to perform; I watch for ten minutes, he is still being beaten, the crowd is still laughing (with a marked lack of merriment); the foreplay goes on too long and I leave without knowing what acrobatic wonders the little boy performs. A man does a lewd approximation of a belly dance. Another wears rubber flip-flops on his ears, the better to mimic a donkey. A three-piece band — flute, drums, a kind of guitar — punctuates the storytelling of a Berber. A snake is draped around the shoulders of a protesting tourist. Cobras and monkeys compete for the attention of men who take onanistic pleasure in fishing with red plastic doughnut-shaped hooks for liter bottles of Coca-Cola. Crowds collect at numbered food stalls: fish in cauldrons of fat, yellow cumin-stained grease rising to the surface; eggs in vats; chicken tripe with chickpeas; lamb sausage; pots of harira, rough-hewn wooden serving spoons; fried offal; foul-smelling gray meat, grasped and pulled apart by hands, from a deep pot of boiling liquid. Electric light bulbs compete with the fires of the braziers, burning pale against a pale sky.

I leave the hurly-burly for the terrace of the Café France, above the mandala of circles, the crowds. . . . And suddenly, while I'm not looking, the pale hour turns into night, the night lights no longer compete with day, and it becomes possible to believe anything . . . that people feast in the anticipation and consciousness of satiety, that the stories they hear are true, even that they are happy. I am. Everything rises and converges: incense, smoke, voices, flutes; and the enduring, punctual call of the muezzin threads its way through this tapestry of sound which amounts to a kind of silence that encompasses singing, drums, wailing, ululating. Voices curl in the smoke, all part of the intricate pattern, a sensory flash frozen, stasis and movement: a unity. Long ago in Libya a friend told me to see North Africa from the corner of my eyes; I didn't understand him. Perhaps he meant that everything happens when you are not looking.

BOMBAY, INDIA, 1963

It was hallucinatory, that time in Bombay.

I know the road. When I am on Warden Road, coming back from Breach Candy swimming pool, I see it, a little wooden pointer: Nepean Sea Road. But for some reason I have never been able to ask the taxi driver, any taxi driver, to make the sharp left that would take me onto the winding road to Malabar Hills where I lived with my son, my husband, and the new baby I conceived six weeks after the birth of my son. I don't know the address of the flat on Nepean Sea Road; and this gives rise to panic. I have been back to Bombay; but I have never seen that building overlooking the Arabian Sea again . . . the building where the fruit-eating bats with the pterodactyl wings flew over my baby girl's crib, lusting for the banana she dribbled from her perfect mouth . . . the building where the rat tried to climb into her crib . . . the building where I fainted in the fifth month of my troubled pregnancy one starry night at a rooftop party amongst jeweled and disapproving Indian women (advising myself, as I blacked out, to cut it out, feeling, even as

I fainted, like an impostor) . . . the building where Jehovah's Witnesses came to tell me the world was ending.

I am sometimes tempted to believe it is not really there at all.

"We've been having rather a difficult time, and when I think of it, I'm amazed at our hardiness and resilience — our cheerfulness must be visceral or glandular — it certainly owes nothing to the facts: I very nearly had a seven-month baby — went into labor during a routine visit to the doctor, who popped me full of medicines to avert a spontaneous abortion and sent me home in an ambulance and now I am flat on my back, where I will remain until the baby is born. Josh, meanwhile, with whom I used to play all day, no longer cries; he looks bewildered because I won't — can't — pick him up, an adaptation that, though necessary and good, I'm sure, distresses the hell out of me. . . . I run the house from between the sheets, and entertain guests in my bedroom between seven and nine. . . . India is going on just outside my bedroom windows, but I never believe it except at night, when the pavement dwellers play their flutes and sing."

Mr. Harrison's office windows on Arthur Bundy Road were level with the tops of flame trees, and monkeys swung from branch to branch, and cuckoos sang, and larks.

Mr. Harrison exercised his prerogative to read my mail. He saw my lies.

From our terrace we saw the vultures circling over the Towers of Silence, vultures fat from the flesh of the exposed Parsee dead.

My son waves at the children who crouch on the steel beams of the building in progress across the road, the beams where tribal workers cook, eat, sleep, make love. I go to bed at night wondering why they don't come to kill us in the dark.

Crows pick the food from my baby's plate. My pampered sweet baby who sits at the front door with an airplane bag slung over his arm saying "Bye-bye plane," and sobs "Da-da da-da" when his father goes on field trips. "He knows the sound of [his father's] car, and when I take him to the terrace to see his father arrive he practically throws himself off in transports of joy." He was such a sweet child, the little boy who tried to smile with his eyes flooding and his fist in his mouth to ease the pain of teething. Where is the little boy who when he stood up alone for the first time waved his arms and sang to himself in pleasure, the boy who fingerpainted with his shit, the little boy whose first and favorite word was *good* (and he called himself good). . . .

> *All growth is a branching out. A woman loses a child even in having a child. All creation is separation. Birth is as solemn a parting as death.*
>
> — G. K. Chesterton

We went out on our friend Gayle's fishing boat off the coast of Bombay, an hour across the marshes and then another hour on a bullock cart to his holiday shack — dung floors, kerosene lamps on the sand, village weddings and dances along the beach, and the Queen's Necklace shining across the crescent bay. And bumping on the bullock cart my son ate the whole of the chocolate cake I'd baked, and drank coconut water straight from coconut trees that shaded the shack, and played all day under the coconut trees and on the pressed cow-dung floors of the shack . . . and the new baby in my womb bounced along the rutted trail with me.

Dinner at the Tatas' house — pictures of J.R.D. Tata with Princess Margaret and with Lindbergh (and when he went to the American South, the great Parsee industrialist and philanthropist drank, on principle, from the fountains that said FOR COLORED ONLY). Such an unprepossessing little man. And he flew alone, in a plane he engineered, from Calcutta to London, while Lindbergh was making his more acclaimed but no more amazing flight. Not bitter, though. Family money from the legal opium trade. J.R.D.'s grandfather built the Taj Mahal Hotel (that Victorian splendor, like a fort on the outside, facing the stone-arched Gateway to India; all lacy carving and marble and delicacy of florid decoration within); he built it because he was not permitted, in South Africa, to stay in the hotel where his shipboard mates stayed: NO DOGS, INDIANS, OR BLACKS ALLOWED. So he built the hotel for the peculiar purpose of having a sign made that said NO WHITE SOUTH AFRICANS ALLOWED. If you know where to look for the sign, you can find it still.

I like the story Alice Turner tells about the Tatas: When her family was in the diplomatic corps and she was a schoolgirl in Indian hill country, she spent a holiday with Thelly Tata, and in the heat of noon all the women, wrapped in saris and scent, climbed into the great lacquered charpoy, with all the little children, so much eggshell-colored and brown flesh, shielded with mosquito netting and in the shade of a great peepul tree, and slept, their bodies, Alice says, like little puppies' bodies, everyone this way and that, limbs soft and warm and overlapping and loose. . . . There are times when all of India seems to gentle you and a great maternal sound rolls off from the sea and down from the high mountains and across the great plains to embrace you in its echo.

HYDERABAD, 1963

Great elaborate dusty chandeliers and slow churning fans in huge high-ceilinged rooms lined with heavy dark furniture and masses of un-polished silver, and verandahs, and enfiladed never-used public rooms, gardens with chairs and tables still arranged for the teas that nobody ever takes in them anymore. This is Percy's Hotel in downtown Hy-derabad. It is gone now.

We stay here two days and then we move to the Rock Castle Hotel in Banjara Hills, among the lakes and boulders and hillside burial tombs of Moslem wives of renowned beauty, the royalty of Golconda.

Josh found a puppy in Golconda Fort, a little brown thing with great black eyes whining among the cannonballs. He took his first step unaided toward the puppy. We took it home.

In the night someone killed the puppy. Josh sees tigers in the bath-room. *Is a fish going to bite my pee-pee off? Is a goat going to bite my pee-pee off? Is the telephone man going to bite my pee-pee off?*

He cries — he is angry — when we shoot the krait; he cries. In one day we kill a cobra, a python, and a krait; they are in the garden where the children play. The venom of the krait attacks the central nervous system. Its bite kills in seconds.

In a house close to Golconda, the garden is infested with snakes. A magic man comes and throws magic powder over the garden (colored chalk) and not for a year — to the day — is a snake seen in the garden again.

Dancing bears and snake charmers outside our door.

A man comes to our house looking for a job. He dies in the court-yard before I can reach him, before Panji, our ayah, can bring him rice water.

Josh has malaria. Well one moment and raging with fever the next.

There is a high-voltage power line on our property. A workman is curing cement on the flat roof. Water from his copper vessel hits the wires and returns to the pot, where it fries; I call an ambulance; the shocked man lives. The year before, we are told, a woman climbed a mango tree to pick a ripe fruit, and the wind blew her hair onto the wires, and she was electrocuted.

I live in sorrow and in fear. Mr. Harrison has the local authorities move the power lines down the hill, where no one lives, thank God.

I fire the cook, who beat his wife in the courtyard.

I cook with Anna in the crook of my arm and Panji hovering. Joshi-baba peels all the onions in the bin; we are happy, Panji and Anna and Joshi and me.

Letters from New York:

> Brace yourself, Bob. I've just come home after seeing your mother. She is doing as well as can be expected. I had a long talk with her doctor and he told me that he took out her ovaries where the cancer was but he said that the damn thing will spread. Mother doesn't know that the matter is malignant (bad) and we've decided not to tell her. You, your Aunt Angie, your brother and I and my family knows and we've pledged that no one else will know. Tonite she was telling me to bring some raisins that will build her blood. She thinks that because she lost a lot of blood and no transfusion was given is the reason she felt so weak. Barbara dear when you write do not mention the truth. Goodnight.

My mother lived for twenty years more; she never did allow herself to know the truth.

> In the seven years that we have lived here I have not had a mail key. Dad brings the mail up on his way from work. It's been alright, only

lately we've been more than usually anxious to hear from you. And I've wished I've had my own key to pick the mail up in the morning.

Dilemma. I sent dad to the store with a shopping list and prices carefully marked out. I showed him the sale folder and told him not to pay a penny more for the pastrami, rice, cheese, toilet paper and other things. As he checked out he noticed everything was a few pennies more. He made a fuss with the checker and then found the manager and made a fracas with him. He refused to pay for the goods after they were checked, the manager almost threw him out and did tell him to get out. There were about 80 people in the store, Saturday morning. He came home to get the sales folder — he wanted the manager to eat it, and found that I had sent him to Dilberts instead of to Packers. . . . He went down to apologize. It seems to have started a lifelong friendship. The manager knows dad has two married children, etc., etc. . . . So every day I'm still hiding my identity.

From my father:

A good daughter always makes a good mother. I was watching tv and was drinking a glass of wine and I realized that the liquid was dripping from my mouth. I went to the mirror and noticed that my face and mouth was out of kilter. My mouth pretty near touched my ears. I went to the doctors and was told it was Bells Palsy. I'm taking electric shock treatments and the doctor says that in a few more weeks I will be ok. The nomad in me makes me envy you.

Mr. Jung, an advocate from the court of the Nizam, before that miserly rich ruler's retinue was reduced by India's central government to three thousand people, takes me to the old city, through mazes of doors into ratty old houses, into courtyards where dealer-hoarders have stacks upon stacks, shelves upon shelves, crates upon crates of precious, dirty, dusty, exciting things. Women sit in the courtyards picking lice from one another's hair and nursing babies. Mr. Jung says that as recently as sixty years ago — in 1900 — Chinese tradesmen and their families crossed the Himalayas to southern India; and some of their wares are still here, where we sit. Jade bottles of perfume, unopened, nest in scarlet China silk. Mr. Jung gives me a string of unpolished, carved Mogul emeralds for my birthday, and six Renaissance glasses, crystal green and gold. We picnic on a lake, punka-wallahs cooling us with the tail feathers of peacocks; gold dishes; jackals' voices bouncing off the naked hills; armed Gurkha guards; and ancient rugs under a white silk tent. Now Mr. Jung lives in exile at the Rock Castle Hotel; and he is sad.

"Go way, Mommy, I love you, Mommy," Joshi-baba says. Were his sunny days tinged with melancholy? Sometimes he retreated into a silence and a stillness complete, impenetrable; radiating sunshine one minute and the next minute far, far away. . . . In the harmless dusk he struts down the village streets clowning: he jumps, hops, waves his arms in the air, suddenly drops to a crawl, shouts, sings, and every few minutes turns around to be sure he is getting attention from the older village children. He takes his toy drum and marches with the musicians of an Indian wedding party on our road. He pulls plants out of the garden and waters his baby sister with the gardener's hose and says: "I *mali*." His superego flourishes in the Indian sun; he yells to himself when he's doing something "bad": "Joshi, don't!" Then he hides under a table. On an airplane: "Plane fall down now? No, this nice plane. . . . No, Mommy, can't stop here, dangerous." Anna says, "Where is God?"

> *A very old Kikuyu came up and talked to us: "You were up very high to-day," he said, "we could not see you, only hear the airplane sing like a bee. . . . Did you see God? . . . Aha, then you were not up high enough; . . . but now tell me: do you think that you will be able to get up high enough to see him? . . . What do you think? Will you get up high enough in your aeroplane to see God?" . . . "Really I do not know," said Denys. "Then," said Ndwetti, "I do not know at all why you two go on flying."*
>
> — Isak Dinesen, *Out of Africa*

In the daytime, the children sometimes splash in the river that runs past our house, the river where the water buffalo wallow and the Indian village women wash their saris on black rocks; and after the sun has gone down they wade in their red plastic pool, the trees flaming gold and red and purple and green, the garden alive with the scent of white jasmine.

There is a wall of windows in their nursery playroom; in the heat of day it is covered with *tatis* — reed blinds that the *mali* throws water upon so that their fragrance fills the sun-speckled false dark.

The children come out to watch the cows that are milked for us in the servants' courtyard. They clap their hands and watch the foraging goats eating all of the *mali*'s plants, scampering sliding skipping on smooth black stones, sending up a shower of gravel.

Panji is dead now. She lived in the civil lines where the British lived when Hyderabad was extraterritorial. When my children sailed to New York from Bombay: "Oh Panji, Panji, why have you left me?" they cried. She was very beautiful — regal, when we first met her, in her white rags. The letter we got in New York from her husband said she died "of stomach ache and grief."

I went to bed one night with an Englishman who lived in a house down the road. I didn't like him, that wasn't the point. I went to bed with him the night before I boarded the train that was to take me to Bombay, where a boat would carry us to New York. His son claimed also to be in love with me. I did like his son, but he was eighteen (I was thirty). I was in love with a third man, who lived in the big house with the man and the son who loved me and another brother and two daughters and the mother of these children. They were wildly anti-British English-men and -women and broke every possible rule, their only regret being that there were so few social rules, in our little society, to break. Sometimes, late at night, early in the morning, after hours of political and meaning-of-life talk, I would climb into the bed of the third man, ever hopeful, and he would look at me and say, "What? You again?" and roll over and feign sleep. All of this ceased to matter the moment the ship that was taking me and Anna and Josh back to New York sailed out of Bombay harbor.

Anna wants to be a can opener when she grows up — that is what she says.

HYDERABAD REVISITED, 1993

It is the steamy time after monsoon; my lungs are sponges saturated to bursting point with almost palpably sticky air. In the moldy air-conditioned chill of my Bombay hotel I vainly telex a hotel in Hyderabad; no answer is forthcoming — all communications have dropped into a hot wet void.

I decide nevertheless to go to Hyderabad, where twenty years ago, for three tumultuous years, I lived.

The small family-run hotel that ignored my imploring telexes is high in the rocky hills that surround the congested, once princely city. It is a short walk from untouristed Moslem tombs of superlative beauty, and a ricksha drive away from Golconda, the fort whose name is synonymous with fabulous wealth, the place where the Hope diamond was found, the fort on whose crenelated ramparts in the still and fragrant night I picnicked, laughed, sang ribald songs and sad songs and made love, in my youth, a quarter of a century ago.

The Rock Castle Hotel (a jumble of bungalows of diminished splendor and undiminished charm built at the time of the Raj) overlooks the house — now occupied by a razzmatazz Indian film star — where I lived. That wonderful house with its fountain and gardens and infinite varieties of green (its snakes, its scorpions); its sausage trees, its yellow cassia and gold mohur trees and flaming tulip trees and mango trees (fruit warm and ripe in the morning for eating); its frangipani and purple jacaranda and fern trees and night jasmine, its poison oleander.

I take a ricksha to the Rock Castle Hotel from the deplorable modern hotel in which I am obliged to stay. I have it in mind to glare at the proprietors.

There is a very old man in a very old rusty black suit at the switchboard: "Mrs. Harrison, memsahib! How we are knowing it is you that is telexing? Are many Mrs. Harrisons! How is sahib? How is Joshibaba? How is Missy Anna-banana?" Muftar, the old man, who is in a frenzy of welcome, has not seen or heard from me or my children for a quarter of a century. I am in floods; my sobbing engenders his, and he says through a veil of tears: "Now you are having breakfast here. Are staying in your old rooms two missionaries, we are not liking those people. In two hours I am having your rooms ready and you are staying with us again, I am sending now the boy for your bags."

In two hours I am in the old rooms; happy, the excesses and voluptuousness of India rendering me careless and profligate, I caress my skin with all the perfumes I bought in the bazaar in Bombay, everything all at once, patchouli and honeysuckle and roses and musk and heliotrope, and the oil of *khus-khus* extracted from the root of a sweet grass. At the windows are *chiks* — shades woven from *khus-khus*; a servant is hunkered down outside sprinkling the *chiks* with water . . . and the stone bungalow is dark and cool and fragrant in the beating sun. The bungalow sleeps; I sleep, as if in the belly of an accommodating beast.

In the evening everyone I have ever known in Hyderabad is on the terrace to greet me.

How could one not love India? And, loving India, how could one not love? The real reason women fall in love abroad is not that they are free of domestic inhibitions but that they translate their love of stone and place into love of flesh. . . . Is this true?

In the days to come I apply myself diligently to the gnarled pattern of my past, carrying past sorrows and gladness to the old tombs, miniature Taj Mahals where I sit dreamily in the shade of mango trees.

I manage to have a love affair with a fellow hotel guest, losing myself in his hungry embrace . . . and losing any grasp I might have had on the truth of the past. (He is a German who in exculpatory, halting English declares, "I am not a war man." He is, however, a married man.) And my liaison bruises the sensibilities of my conservative Indian friends; it bruises my own sensibilities as well, and this I regard as a definition of sin: hurting oneself in the act of pleasuring oneself.

I never have casual affairs in my own city. The air of my own city does not caress my flesh so wantonly, silkily, in the scented dusk. Today is the feast day of Ganesh, the elephant god, the god of great good luck. It was a foregone conclusion that I would go to bed with the German, from the moment I agreed to have a drink with him on the flower-draped terrace . . . and the fizzy lights of the city shimmered below us and the sounds of the Ganesh festival floated up, flute and timpani, their distant music seduction disguised as blessing . . . and the creamy white moonflowers opened to receive the night air and to release their heady fragrance.

How extravagant India is!

In the gardens of my old Hyderabadi house there is a tree, the asoka, which blooms with effusive orange and scarlet flowers, but only if it is kicked by a beautiful woman.

I have sometimes thought that I fell in love in India all those years ago for lack of anything better to do, arranging flowers in vases and being charming to one's guests not being a full-time occupation. It occurred to me in Hyderabad that falling in love was a way of cauterizing my senses; there was too much to love in India, and altogether too much — heat and poverty, beggars, leprosy, filth, ignorance, vipers, dust and difference — to hate, or to fear. When I lived in India I learned nothing in a systematic way about Indian religion, tradition, and history; I learned by osmosis, using the demands of my two small children as a defense against my moral and mental sluggishness. I guarded my soul against India; perhaps that is what those love affairs were all about.

My old friend Nandita, who has chosen not so much to forgive as to ignore my present liaison, suggests that my narrow unremitting attention to my Indian past is a form of vanity. I see her point: imagine regarding India as the background for one's own tedious affairs of the heart, solipsistic indeed. I tell her, in my defense, that I look for patterns. This strikes her as a peculiarly Western form of lunacy and/or arrogance; "utilitarian and reductionist," she calls the (Western) impulse to (psycho)analyze love. "What could be more utilitarian than an arranged marriage, Nandita?" I ask. But her husband, Potla, and her son and three of her grandchildren are walking up the steps to greet us, and their tender ease and unburdened love for one another removes my words of any sting; their happiness is a reproach to me.

Nandita's eyelashes lower, and from her huge black eyes issues forth one of those shuttered, oblique looks, so Indian, that sometimes serve to convince me that East and West are in fact the twain that will never meet. "Let the problem solve itself," Nandita says, vexing me. "Oh, you sound like a television guru, Nandita," I say. She waves a jeweled hand at me and leaves in a cloud of silk and chattering grandchildren.

The next morning Nandita brings me Indian holy books, with a stern admonition to read them — "It's time"; and she brings me Lady Lawrence's memoirs of the days of the Raj, *Indian Embers*. Lady Lawrence's family owed their lives and their prestige to the service of

Empire in India, and she loved the subcontinent with an undivided heart: "She, unlike me, was happily married, which of course made all the difference," I say to Nandita, who slithers her fish-eyed look at me again. "Remember the banyan tree," she says, the tree whose branches drop shoots to the ground, which take root and support the parent branches. When a banyan is very old and very large it is difficult if not impossible for the eye to discern the progenitor from the offspring; past and present coalesce and are united. It is a bloody waste to spend one's time looking for the pattern when one could be playing among the branches: "Remember the banyan tree."

The German goes away. Ranting. He is serving the Indian military in a way I cannot fathom and do not choose to fathom. He is now convinced I am a spy. I think this is funny. Nandita says I am making progress.

I stroll each morning and evening in the village in the hills where my children once played. "It's one of those Indian places," says my daughter, whose joy it is to return to it, "where absolutely nothing happens and everything happens." A few little stores selling desiccated veggies and overripe bananas; a tailor; a *bidi* shop; a café with cauldrons perpetually on the boil with hot peppery oily stuff, and tea that coats the tongue with sugar and burns it with heat; rickshas carrying skinny uniformed children to school; women, their hair wet and sleek from morning ablutions, balancing copper pots on their heads; goats and sheep and swineherds, and sometimes a dancing bear and sometimes a snake charmer; and in front of every house, till dust and bare feet sweep them away, the beautiful, intricate patterns drawn in colored chalk by village women each morning to greet the day and the gods. "A cosmos within an atom," the holy books say; "an atom within a cosmos."

I love this place. I am full of excitement inspired by the holiness of the ordinary; coincidentally I am calm.

On the Lloyd Triestino Line, sailing from Bombay to New York, an attendant brought me Josh in the middle of the night — three-year-old Josh, dressed in his plaid bathrobe from Rinascente: he was on deck leaning over the rail; he wanted to see the moonlight on the water.

A special purser was assigned to guard the children's wading pool:

Anna didn't see the point of swimming clothes, my Indian baby (who chose to believe that her father was a maharajah and that her brown eyes were green, *"They are green!"*).

On the New York pier my mother said, "They don't wear that shade of lipstick anymore, dear." Her first words to me.

GUATEMALA

In Guatemala City, Anna ran away from nursery school because: "I don't want to be little-lord-jejus-no-crying-he-makes. *(Oh come. Yeah. Faithful and tri-ang-le.)* The little-lord-jejus-no-crying-he-makes has no words, Mommy, he sits in a basket, so no."

They played with the children in the shantytown around the corner. Anna piled her baby-doll carriage high with cans and clothes because in one shack a baby was sitting propped up in a basket, her neck raw from her unnatural position, and five children in the marital bed. "Why those children have no shoes?" The houses of the poor exist no more; the children they played with exist no more. An earthquake killed them.

In the house next door to us rich people lived. They had six Doberman pinschers and a ramp on the façade of their house on which the Dobermans prowled. One day I heard Josh making odd little curdled noises in his throat as he stood by the cinderblock wall that divided us from the rich people. Our dog, Blue Dooley, was hanging, bloodless and lifeless, from the jaws of a Doberman, his neck broken. The maid of the rich people brought him over wrapped in a towel. "The signora says please wash the towel and give it back," she said, "the signora needs it." Josh burned with fever and did not speak for days.

I can never go back to Guatemala; things have only gotten worse for the poor.

"Chi-chi-casta-*nan*-go. Chi-chi-casta-*nan*-go." For hours Anna chanted on her way to the mountain village. She never stopped except to sleep briefly, and as soon as she opened her eyes: "Chi-chi-casta-*nan*-go."

Josh trails his hand in a mangrove swamp and it is sliced by the tailfin of a baby shark. Our hosts on the Pacific are a doctor and his wife, Roberto and Cathy Rendon. Roberto medicates Josh's hand. He accepts gifts of sweet baby shrimp (which we boil in sea water and eat, unshelled) from the villagers he treats with antibiotics. I sit on the bank of a river that flows into the sea and count: "One two three four five six seven eight nine ten." I am counting heads. The Rendons have eight children. All of them, boys and girls, have some form of *Maria* in their names. The sands burn during the day. At night we sleep in hammocks. Anna, who has burned her feet in the burning sands, sleeps, tucked and fetal, behind my knees, curled like a kitten.

A circular arrives from the embassy: "A pestilence of sorts, variously diagnosed as mononucleosis, a virus, glandular flu, and, by the husbands of those afflicted — it seems to have hit only women — as laziness."

John Bosco, founder of the Salesians: "It is enough for you to be young for me to love you."

Afterward, after the divorce, they went back to visit their father at his several posts; they spent one school year in Bombay and another in Lima. In their New York school they had been taught how to be happy but not how to spell (a mistake I would not repeat); Jesuits in Bombay and American schoolteachers in Lima took a markedly different approach to pedagogy.

They wrote. Josh, from Bhubaneswar (where they biked to the erotic temple sculptures and received an education in stone), in 1971: "Mommy, we have seen five monkeys, Mommy. Mommy, when they jumped off the trees it looked like they were diving on their stomachs. Mommy, I've seen two elephants, Mommy. A crow shat on me two times."

Anna: "Mommy we've gone to the zoo here, and the Indian man there touched the bear's nose, and the bear had a white stomach and the rest of it was black. There is a road in Bhubaneswar by a lake, and in the middle of it there is a white temple. Mommy to me it is one of the prettiest roads in Bhubaneswar. I miss you very much guess what daddy and [his wife] are going to have a baby today we went to the beach I have three new friends. A crow shat on me three times. Here is a book of love for Barbara — a shooting star falls down from the sky and brings love to you."

Josh, from Bombay, to his grandfather, whom he addressed as Junior

(1975): "Already I've missed two days of school because first, I felt sick and then I had something wrong with my eye — bronchitis and then conjunctivitis everybody but the cook and dad had conjunctivitis. School is okay except for that I don't have any friends and it's much harder than the schools in New York I also have to wear a uniform to school and a neck tie. Junior, sometimes I carry that old knife you gave me for good luck. Do you have a photograph that you could send me? It's been raining a lot here. We haven't gone swimming lately because everybody had conjunctivitis and Anna and I have been going to school. Every Tuesday in school I have to run two miles so that's one more thing I don't like about the school and after running the two miles we are not allowed to have any water. I miss you very much."

Josh, to me: "Mom, don't worry about the teacher hitting me in school if the other boys can take it I can. p.s. I was never hit by a teacher."

Their letters are animate.

Anna, at fourteen, from Bombay: "Oh it's incredible for me to imagine my stupidity last year . . . one thing I still have is laziness. Oh I've realized how rich people are here! Why don't you like Somerset Maugham? I do. I'm playing tennis!!! I LOVE YOU I LOVE YOU I LOVE YOU."

Josh, Christmas, 1975: "Christmas is going to be very strange without you, mom. Could you please buy ¼ lb of ham for the cats for Xmas. Send me the bill and I'll pay you back. Lately I've been feeling sick because next Monday are our midterm tests and I hardly know anything I'm supposed to know for the test.

"The other day I got my school exams report. I did much worse than last time. I failed three subjects history, literature and mathematics. Dad says I'm going to have to take math tuition over the holidays. My finger is fractured. So far I haven't met any friends and I don't like my class mates. . . . Signed: Sweets Kineval."

From Anna: "All my friends are leaving Bombay for hols and what makes it worse, they all live in Europe and I may never see them again. *NEVER.*"

From Josh: "I sort of have a friend now his name is John. I don't like him too much because he is always cheating in games and he always tells you what to do and stuff like that. I didn't really get hit I just got my neck all sore like when you do those pressure points behind my neck but they really mean to hurt you. Signed: Funky Fantom."

Josh: "What do you do about being an architect because that's all I want to be when I grow up."

Josh: "There is just one problem with being an architect, I stink in math."

From their father to me (from India): "Josh continues to be happy but I do hope he works harder this next year. He works in my office half days or whole days — coffee, mail, errands. I pay him a pittance — Rs 5 a day — but explain to him that Rs 5 a day is about Rs 2 more than a laborer in the countryside makes working hard for 7 hrs. . . . It is very important that the children write thoughtful thank-you letters to [relatives and friends] in Santo Domingo, Barcelona, and Bombay. It is expected of them. In Bombay even withholding their allowances was sometimes insufficient motivation for them to write to you."

Anna, from Lima, 1978: "I am so worried about school transcripts. What am I to do? What if they ask me exactly how many classes I've failed? Altho I don't know exactly. I couldn't lie to cover up the extent of classes which I did fail — what would happen if I lied? wouldn't I be in serious trouble? I am afraid my friends' feelings for me will change."

I wonder what meaning the word *exotic* has for them.

Anna studies and writes about medieval women mystics; she volunteers in shelters for the homeless.

Josh paints; he feels at home in the Amazon.

> *What he sought was always something lying ahead, and even if it was a matter of the past, it was a past that changed gradually as he advanced on his journey, because the traveler's past changes according to the route he has followed: not the immediate past, that is, to which each day that goes by adds a day, but the more remote past. Arriving at each new city, the traveler finds again a past of his that he did not know he had: the foreignness of what you no longer are or no longer possess lies in wait for you in foreign, unpossessed places. . . . The*

traveler recognizes the little that is his, discovering the much he has not had and will never have.

— Italo Calvino, *Invisible Cities*

A JUNGLE STORY, 1993

So much of life in India consists of waiting. Waiting and rejoicing. Rejoicing and waiting. Endless cycles. Waiting for the rain, rejoicing when it comes. Waiting for the rain to end. Rejoicing when it ends.

The air is white with rain. It stops as suddenly as it begins, and the skies are scrubbed and pure; the intoxicating light coaxes an unbelievably opulent fragrance from green grass and even the mud smells clean.

Maharajahs entertained the Prince of Wales and Russian grand dukes in the hunting lodge where we sit on deep verandahs in plantation chairs. I could sit here forever watching the shadows lengthen on the green lawn while the honey-rust voice of our host, kind Colonel Wakefield, a seventy-year-old Anglo-Indian once of the Army Engineers, waxes nostalgic, with a soldier's affection, for "the pukka days" of the India-Pakistan war when, as the Pakistani side had the breweries and the Indian side the good distilleries, officers of both sides drank together . . . until the morning and the regimental command to kill.

Monkeys, kept from us by a ring of fire, eye the mutton curry and saffron rice pudding that we eat in the thatched hut on the river. The husband of a honeymooning couple from Bandra, a rich new suburb of Bombay, says, "It is too quiet here, there is nothing to do." The air is alive with kingfishers and flying owls and spotted blue doves and eagles. "Read a book," I say. He is as much surprised as if I had suggested a novel sexual perversity. We have just returned from a brown backwater of the Cauvery River; our saucerlike coracle slips through mists; the world looks like an illustration in an old Bible of the first day of creation. Our boat is made of willow and pitch and cowhide; and it would not come as a surprise to me — time, as waters slide over waters like the liquid notes of a Mozart quintet, being an illusion — if we were to find Moses in just such a boat among the bamboo and the reeds that whisper to the water. The young husband is the owner of a Taco Bell restaurant in Bombay.

The headlights on Colonel Wakefield's jeep pick out pocked orange toadstools on felled trees. We are in an envelope of preternatural calm; in the jungle the breath of the world is suspended. Everything is simultaneously still and full of movement. The calm is broken but the silence is not when ugly boar and two-thousand-pound bison, phlegmatic and atavistic, cut across our path. Spotted deer, the descendants of those to whom Buddha preached, are caught in our lights. "Do not be afraid of any amazement," says the colonel to the deer, quoting from *The Book of Common Prayer*, endearing himself to me forever. (He talks to the animals; he murmurs, he croons.) In this wet season there is little reason for elephants and cats to take advantage of man-made salt licks and artificial lakes; but they have left their spoor — we see the prints of tiger paws, we smell tiger dung. Almost more exciting than actually seeing the tigers, I tell myself, scanning the dense jungle growth for golden eyes; and I almost believe it. Packs of wild dogs with malevolent pale yellow eyes and upright bottle-brush tails race before the headlights, grinning, leaping like gazelles; even tigers and lions are afraid of them, the colonel says (I wonder if he is carrying a gun). These dogs were the trained companions of Paleolithic man; they look like Original Sin.

I take leave of my surroundings and find myself back in my childhood. I feel a strong and sudden yearning for a Brooklyn neighborhood, a frame house. . . . Of course! It is the smell of elephants. The smell of elephants is the smell of the Prospect Park Zoo. I see myself quite clearly, a little girl in a pink pinafore holding her father's hand, standing in front of the elephant cages. And it is in that moment that a herd of elephants appears in our headlights (I think drowning must be like this). Peacocks and jungle fowl agitate the tall grass.

"Goldie Hawn saw a tiger on the road," says Colonel Wakefield. Goodness. We are back on the macadam road in our little Ambassador car; and a rogue elephant moves toward us. Huge, measured, blasé, terrifying, and oddly delicate. And unstoppable. Like damn fate, inexorable. "Look at the sun on the tusks," says my companion, Mrs. God, barely moving her lips. "Shut up," I explain. Our driver backs up, one kilometer and then two, trying to move without moving an inciting muscle. I don't remember what happened next — a motor scooter, a bus, a truck, rock-throwing idiots — I think the elephant was hemmed in, front and back; and after trumpeting the fear of God into us decided to amble away. He disappeared in any case, crashing into the illogical branches of banyan trees. I wake up now to the thought of him (nemesis), his foot crushing me, his soft and pulpy tongue big as a city.

> *Foolishly no doubt I am at times assailed by the thought that the vividness of those days, now quieted forever, may not be entirely subjective. Perhaps they exist outside Time, and still continue their measured way in the scheme of things.*
>
> — Lady Lawrence, *Indian Embers*

⁊
ROOMS:
SIGNS AND
SYMBOLS

> *The houses that were lost forever continue to live on in us; . . . they insist in us in order to live again. . . . How much better we should live in the old house today! . . . Not only our memories, but the things we have forgotten are "housed." Our soul is an abode. And by remembering "houses" and "rooms," we learn to "abide" within ourselves. . . . Come what may, the house helps us to say: I will be an inhabitant of the world, in spite of the world.*
>
> — Gaston Bachelard, *The Poetics of Space*

I HAVE OFTEN fantasized that if I were to become rich, I would buy all the houses I ever lived in; and these houses will conform to my dreams of houses: objects will take the place of people, they will be like characters in a story (and they will have integrity; and they will never change). I want rooms where rituals have taken place and memories have accreted and left ineradicable impressions.

> *The places in which we have experienced daydreaming reconstitute themselves in a new daydream, and it is because our memories of former dwelling-places are relived as daydreams that these dwelling-places of the past remain in us for all time.*
>
> — *The Poetics of Space*

First I will buy Grandma's house on West Fifth Street. I will sit very sweetly on the roof terrace Grandpa built, where I am forever smiling, sweet, and blond; I will sit under grapevines and cross my ankles and fold my hands in my lap and direct my imperturbable gaze to an invisible camera (a Brownie); I will contemplate the future that is now my past, an Augustinian exercise. I will not mourn lost innocence; I will own it. And if I tire of that — and tire of trying to see, over the maple treetops, the parachute ride in Coney Island — I will go through the double doors into the bedroom where Aunt Lulu died. But this will be before her death, and the object of my desire will be the vanity table of kidney-shaped glass, its legs hidden and swathed in white bridal net. I will rummage through the jewelry box (a licensed pleasure) and I will find the magical amethyst that is set, floating, in old gold stamped with fleur-de-lis and tree-of-heaven leaves. I will adorn myself with a brooch of red cherries and a Bakelite sailor boy and a rhinestone Christmas tree. Years later I will meet them in a flea market and recognize them and claim them.

In Grandma's room silverfish darted in and out of high-buttoned shoes in a musty closet. I have never again seen silverfish — *Lepisma saccharina*; they are like dinosaurs, gone. I was frightened of them, so clever and quick, secretive and shiny. They lived on wallpaper starch; behind the falling roses of that papered room they led their busy, hateful lives.

The day Aunt Lou died she was to have taken me to the circus. This was in the days when circuses had three tents and oom-pah-pah calliope music and we watched the tightrope walker as if our lives depended on him.

We were sitting in the sun parlor, alone in the big house, when she fell ill and asked me for the spirits of ammonia which for some inexplicable reason I was able to find. Her illness came on suddenly and daintily. After that day — a day that had been lying in wait since she'd had rheumatic fever as a tenement child — she never left her bed; she was twenty-two. She was twenty-three when she died and tiny, hair crimped and eyebrows rebelliously shaved (shaved when my father, the Modesty Monitor, said: "Don't tweeze"). She was adorable. She was laid out in the parlor in a yellow ruche dress she made, a greeny yellow (the color of melancholy). Aunt Lou made my mother's wedding dress, too, a sheath for dreamy virginal beauty, and she made a dress I covet still — her own bridesmaid's gown of crimson velvet that flared provocatively to crimson satin slippers from white breasts deliciously cupped in a shirred Empire bodice.

(The circus is an unhappy place. My friend Tessa says: "This is how I felt before I left David, before I left the kids — I felt like the lady in the circus who twirls from the top of the tent with a bit in her mouth; I wanted to scream for help but I knew if I did I would fall and die." Tessa, glittery and beautiful, intensely sweet and dying in her chains, ran away from her ordered life to the wild beaches of a Caribbean island; now she spends most of her life under water, dreaming, as she dives and plummets to play with dolphins among enchanted coral reefs, euphoric dreams of the diaphanous house she will someday build under healing waters.

(A known writer made Tessa the occasion of a column when she ran away; the columnist — whose goodwill and easy friendship Tessa had always assumed — wrote the kind of harangue that I might once have written about the generic phenomenon of women who run away from their children: What is the price of fulfillment? I might have fulminated. What needs can justify abandonment? What does such a woman *want?* But when I understood the lineaments of Tessa's grief, I was robbed of my hectoring voice; the valves of my heart opened to embrace her peculiar pain. In the particular may reside the universal; it does not follow that what is generally true contains individual and universal truth. This is what I learned in my consciousness-raising group; it was not the lesson I was supposed to have learned.

(. . . My lover, who is black, said to me, "The trouble with black women is that white people have told them they are better than black men; and black men can't get anywhere." My daughter said, "Well, isn't there a way in which they are better? Don't you admire black women more than you admire black men?" "Yes," I said, "I suppose . . . perhaps, generally speaking" . . . but I am obliged to see through the scrim of my lover's pain, which is not abstract; my loyalty to him precludes argument on this point, because this is the locus of his pain. . . . The world has worn him down, beyond the claims of ideology. There is a way in which one's beloved *is* the truth, and his truth cannot be gain-said. . . .

(Tessa's Cambridge kitchen was yellow, lacquered lemon-yellow, and the boys sat at the table, and over their bowed and lovely heads David prayed. And I went home to Brooklyn and painted my kitchen yellow, because I thought it would make me as happy as Tessa was. And all the time Tessa was dying in her chains.)

> *The importance of memory as a part of our existence in the environment has frequently been denied in this century and by some is even now rather embarrassedly characterized as "nostalgia" and dismissed again.*
>
> — Kent C. Bloomer and Charles W. Moore, *Body, Memory, and Architecture*
>
> *Imagination is nothing but extended or compounded memory.*
>
> — Giambattista Vico

Aunt Lou's flowery double bed was a playing field: among fuchsia chintz flowers we made paper dolls and dressed them; and it was the theater for my first sexual reproach as well: "What are you doing?" Aunt Lee said. "Sitting with my heel in my pee-pee, it feels good to sit like this," I said. "No no no no no no no," said Aunt Betty and Aunt Lee; and it was the bed in which Aunt Lou died. Sex and play and death among fuchsia flowers. The bed where I lay when Grandma put hot mustard plasters on my chest and back when pneumonia struck and leeches failed.

(A haunted ragwoman masquerading as a collector, when I go to the flea market I look for those fuchsia flowers — hybrids on which, later, drops of blood would bloom; of course I never find the right stuff.)

Aunt Lou designed her clothes on a dressmaker's dummy in the first-floor garden room, a glassed-in porch, a sun parlor — sun dappling cubist linoleum, old rugs and streaky-marble tables, radio-shrine, and highchair and ferny plants, pots of tuberous begonias, rickety wicker furniture and chintz-covered overstuffed furniture and old suitcases overflowing with stuff — that Grandpa added behind the sunny kitchen proper (he was always accreting, adding: every time he came back from a mercenary martial expedition, another domestic space, and another child to Grandma's womb). That was a house of many hearts — that room, where Lou patiently sewed and Grandpa listened to the radio news in a language he couldn't understand, was one heart, one side altar. I wandered from heart to heart, side altar to side altar, insinuating myself into the core of things, learning about grown-ups by reading their rooms, storing memories in those rooms.

"Do the stairs go up or down?" I asked this question once, idly, when someone told me he was renovating a house — on the face of it a foolish question. But: "There are the stairways: one to three or four of them, all different. We always *go down* the one that leads to the cellar, and it is this going down that we remember" (Gaston Bachelard). That house was like a Hindu temple — many hearts, many side altars, and one "germ cell," or "womb." In my Church, the metaphor is light — light unto light, a journey into the light and love of God. In Hindu temples, proceeding from blinding light to darkness and to black darkness greater still, one feels as if the truth has been turned upside down, inside out. The Indian mystic enters realms "far beyond the comparatively tawdry heavens where the great gods dwell in light and splendor. Going 'from darkness to darkness deeper yet' he solve[s] the mystery beyond all mysteries . . . he reache[s] a realm of truth and bliss, beyond birth and death, joy and sorrow, good and evil." (In the heart and womb of darkness, Krishna plays his flute. He calls women to leave their marriage beds and dance with him in the moonlight. In the heart of the stillness is the dance.)

The great pulsing heart of that house on West Fifth Street was the basement kitchen, an echo-image of my grandparents' hut-cave-subterranean dwellings in the Old Country, a place proximate to earth in which to dream Old Country dreams and reenact Old Country rituals in surroundings that partook of the New. In this subterranean place everything happened — meals, words, intimations, precise gestures that defined the world. In the basement — the room with the lion-clawed round oak table painted chippable ivory and the old Sears hard wooden chairs with horsehair seats that were painted to match, the room where Grandma cooked, and where we ate, and where we played the Victrola ("Don't Sit under the Apple Tree with Anyone Else but Me"), and where the dog (always, in every incarnation, "Teddy") rested in the heat thrown by the great black oven — there was a veneer of Americanism: aspidistras, mission lamps in whose pools of pink light white arms and pink fingertips were collected. Guests were received here, if they were intimately and greatly liked; the parlor was reserved for funerals and Christmas drinks and formal encounters with the insurance man and tolerated relatives. The kitchen proper was for "American" family meals — Campbell's soup lunches (tomato, with a pat of butter; chicken noodle, made with only half a can of water, for richness; and white toast) and Cream of Wheat breakfasts; the garden room was sacrosanct family space, dedicated to work and news. Nobody ever ate or was received in the dining room. The front sun parlor was where one read the papers and peered at the life of the street — it was from that sun parlor, an anteroom, friendly defensive/protective space dividing Us from Them, that I was called at dusk. (I see a shadow standing in the doorway: hide and seek.) The bedroom floor was never visited by any stranger (except for Santa Claus); and on the honey-suckle-wreathed and vine-dappled roof terrace, the Brownie pointed only and always at me.

One learns about hierarchy from houses.

(My teeth hurt when I think of the grapes those vines bore, thick-skinned, the essence of green, and obscenely pulpy (a little *pop* against my palate and I felt obscurely guilty, as guilty as I felt when, after tracing them round and round with my finger, I pierced paint blister after paint blister while I thought about boys).

Three steps down from the basement was a kind of ultra-cellar with whitewashed walls and packed whitewashed earth. White "Thursday cheese," made each week and stored in green-smelling reed baskets. Yellowed magazines, a universe of books. Old sewing patterns. A barred window, small, that looks up to the narrow front garden. . . . I am a princess in a barred room, a dungeon; outside is a mulberry tree with ripe white crushable fruit, its slender limbs sweep the ground, I want to lie coiled in its cool embrace; I want equally to stand here at the window, looking up at the object of my desire, my tree, from which, in centralized solitude, I draw nourishment. I want to be inside and outside simultaneously, inside the fantasy and outside the fact, inside the fact and outside the fantasy; I want fact and fantasy to be the twins whose hands I hold, separate and together. I want every room I ever live in to be white.

I want, I want, I want.

Upstairs, crouched in the linen closet, knees jammed under my chin, I found the consolations of the cave — rosemary-scented sheets and sugar-cube boxes hidden in silk embroidered pillowcases. Satin coverlets edged with Grandma's lace.

Years later, I stained one of those pink coverlets with my menstrual blood, which crusted and then corroded the lovely stuff, the work of days.

It was from Lulu's room that we peered, in the dark, through binoculars to watch the girls next door undress. The "girls" next door were elderly spinsters, sisters nicely matched. I never saw the naked flesh of my Aunts Betty, Lou, or Lee; they wriggled out of underclothes and into nightgowns while wearing overclothes, a cunning trick. The girls next door were Jewish. Years later, we had a house in the country in whose precincts I delivered messages at the top of my voice to my brother, whom I believed to be an imbecile; and my aunts (their shadows framing yet another door) said, "Don't let the Jews down the road know what we're having for dinner"; and I bludgeoned the planted thought that nakedness and Jews partook indivisibly of darkness and illicitness. (The woman who wore a silk dress and no brassiere on the West End train — her breasts were firm and pert — was Jewish; this I took to be a fact.)

In Aunt Lou's bedroom my father told me I couldn't have my 25 cents allowance because . . . I don't remember because. Because I wasn't "nice." Because I "answered back." Because because. I thought promises were unnegotiable; I thought contracts were unbreakable — holy; I thought I was supposed to get my quarter no matter what. I was ready (always) to receive punishment; I wanted some punishment to be invented that satisfied the sin; I sobbed and bawled, my hot, teary bewilderment could not be stanched. (What was the sin?) That encounter of crossed moral purposes, which I perceived in my body as betrayal (so small an incident, a drop in the sea of years), darkens the house on

West Fifth Street for me. My father's shadow is huge (he was five two). . . .

So I leave that room. I walk into Grandma's garden — little rambling roses like babies' fists, sweet William, mint, sweet peas, stock — and I crush basil between my fingers, releasing the fragrance of goodness (basil grew at the base of the Cross).

> *The American single-family house maintains a curious power over us. . . . Its power, surely, comes from its being the one piece of the world around us which still speaks directly of our bodies as the center and the measure of that world.*
>
> — Bloomer and Moore, *Body, Memory, and Architecture*

> *Here is the ancient floor*
> *Footworn and hollowed and thin,*
> *Here was the former door*
> *Where the dead feet walked in.*
>
> — Thomas Hardy

No one has ever died in the house I live in now. When Aunt Lou died, her body was laid out in the parlor and candles were lit and wailing relatives brought flower offerings. I was relegated to an upstairs bedroom and forbidden to come down; but it was much more scary upstairs — where I could hear the wails and smell the flowers and the incense and imagine that the shadows on the wall would eat me up. So of course (how could they not have known I would do this?) I came trembling down the stairs one night — a single candle left burning near the black coffin lit my way; and when I saw my aunt (who was no longer my aunt, who was no longer; in the coffin lay a ghastly effigy, an emptiness dressed in a yellow dress), I was violently sick over the patterned rug. I love that house. That fact is obdurate. But Grandma and Grandpa and Aunt Betty and Aunt Lee could not stand to live in it after Lulu died; there was a time — vanity, narcissism, guilt, and shame and remorse being indistinguishable in the heart of a child — I believed it was my sick that was to blame for this chosen exile; they mourned their double loss thereafter: house, and Lou.

In memory recaptured through daydreams, it is hard to say through what syncretism the attic is at once small and large, warm and cool, always comforting.

— Bachelard

Try as I may, I cannot get exactly right the smell of the attic room on Seventy-fifth Street, although it was the dry pungent smell — rosin/raisins/sap/yeast/ammonia/musk — that contained me as much as the raw-wood space itself. We called it the attic room; in fact the whole apartment was an attic apartment in the eaves of a wooden house at the level of treetops, a cozy space, steadfast and tidy, containing so incongruously the passions of four unhappy people — my mother, my father, my brother, and I.

Adolescent sorrow is suffused with the dry-fruity perfume of maple trees, a sweet breeze threads its way through currents of sadness, ruffling the mind, oxygenating pain.

An attic closet — a crawl space — in an attic room: smallness contained in smallness. ("And there is almost no space here; and you feel almost calm at the thought that it is impossible for anything but the large to hold in this narrowness." — Rilke) No light illuminates the corner where the wall slopes precipitously down to meet the floor; such a small space — but in my mind it goes on forever and ever, a tunnel into regions of benevolent and thrilling darkness, into "the mystery beyond all mysteries . . . beyond birth and death." My mind, in this womb space, in this ancient natal fragrance, goes on forever and ever, to a vanishing point in which "birth and death, joy and sorrow, good and evil" converge in a "realm of truth and bliss."

In this space my mother kept the snapshots and the keepsakes of her courtship; my brother's baby pictures and mine; a poem she wrote to my father . . . which I endlessly perused, which I ate with my mind. She had loved him once! This poem told me so. And in this room, as a consequence, my mind was an enormous, ravening beast; I never for a moment vanished from my own awareness: "everything comes alive when contradictions accumulate." My brother kept dirty pictures in the attic; I kept nothing — I rummaged and, ravenous, read. I read other people's lives. One day they all disappeared — the dirty pictures, the snapshots, the poem. And there in the back yard, near the garage where I play handball, is my mother, greasy with sweat, in a flowered house-dress and felt slippers; she — fatally beautiful — is making a bonfire of it all, the pictures, the poem. She turns to me, and when her eyes focus, she smiles a greasy smile; and then she drops a rosary on the burning heap, while I go up in flames.

> *One does not love a place the less for having suffered in it unless it has all been suffering, nothing but suffering.*
>
> — Jane Austen, *Persuasion*

> *Only in a house where one has learnt to be lonely does one have this solicitude for* things. *One's relation to them, the daily seeing or touching, begins to become love, and to lay one open to pain.*
>
> — Elizabeth Bowen, *The Death of the Heart*

My brother slept in the old mahogany bed with my father; my mother slept in my room, in one of the maple twin beds. Sometimes, in the languorous sunny afternoons, she rested, blue eyes closed, on her back, her dress rucked up, her legs apart in an exaggerated *V.* My own flesh felt invaded then; I did not dare to think of what was between her legs (a predatory animal, asleep but eminently rousable, was be-tween her legs). Sometimes, during the night, she laughed; more often she cried: my flesh screamed.

Her eyes were of a blueness so blue, the blueness southern Italian country people call "white."

"Tell your father," she said, "that I can't sleep with him. Tell him I have a cold." I was ten years old. I have forgotten to say how seductive she was. And how icy and how sorrowing. I told him. He beat me. She never — till death seventy years later did them part — slept with him again, or knew his flesh.

Of these strange and terrible things no word was spoken among us.

When I was eighteen and my brother was thirteen, "You may have noticed that I don't sleep with your father," she said to him. They were sitting on the vast sofa, covered in some slippery wine-colored stuff, in the living room. "That is because" — my mind curls like fog among the neighboring chimney tops — "I had to help him in order for you to be conceived," she says. My brother cried. My heart bled into my brain.

Is there a time tunnel from that moment to the moment when I said to my lover (this morning, in my own house, in space that I love, space in which I live alone), "I need you I miss you I want I want come be my love my own"? ("Stay sweet," he said.) Mother. Father. House. My knowledge of them is stored there, in that house. . . . I am acquisitive, I want I want — things and houses and love and the knowledge that is buried in the listening walls. "The houses that were lost forever continue to live on in us; . . . they insist in us in order to live again."

I have never known a kitchen so sunny as the one on Seventy-fifth Street. It was grand, and everything fitted so nicely — the intelligent ironing board in its cupboard that opened with the merest touch of a finger pressed against its springs, altogether hidden and altogether there. . . . If only memory would yield its secrets like this, with the pressure of a whisper, a wish. So orderly and nice — reserved, but available without protest when required; how one wishes one's life could be like that — reserved, available for service, tidy. ("We should want life always to be well oiled.") But the shelf lining and the decals and the clever ironing cupboard were witnesses to the chaos of animate and inanimate things: roaches flew from the oven; and one night all the cupboard doors flew open — in protest against the killers in our midst, in sympathy with the tremors of our hearts — and a poltergeist flung all the cups and saucers to the floor (dumb objects only appear to bear silent witness to our shenanigans and pain). That was the night my father tried to kill me; and the next day, the next sunny morning, he sat by the window and hummed and crooned and made love to himself, groaning. My mother was not home.

How many killers were in our midst?

I have lived in houses with introverted porches and houses with extraverted stoops; that house had a porch. . . . Although I have lived in houses that had both a porch and a stoop — that house on Seventy-fifth Street was one of them — in memory houses have one or the other, not both. There are houses made for stoopball and late night girls' secrets ("I choose auburn hair and green eyes"; "for me blond hair with gray eyes" . . . we talked the dusk away, longing for transformations); and there are houses — those with porches — made for unaffected solitary inquiry behind a veil of parched flowers and juicy vines. . . . The house on Seventy-fifth Street had two sets of stairs, front and back. We used the back; the tradesmen, the insurance man, and guests the front. On Saturday nights, my hair in curlers wrapped in a kerchief to demonstrate, to anyone who cared, that I had a date (I was not a datable girl), my mother assigned me the task of scrubbing the back stairs. I scrubbed; she ate an Ebinger's huckleberry pie ("Barbara has a water-retention problem"). Also she laughed. It would be hard not to hate a mother like this, hard to see the pain she bore in the pain she rejoiced to inflict; but she is dead, and one cannot hate the dead . . . though one can love the dead, this being one of God's peculiar tricks.

"I want a house with a porch," I said to my future mother-in-law, an architect. "Nonsense," she said, "nobody ever uses porches, people only think they want porches, a romantic delusion." As a consequence of which sentence I knew I shouldn't warm to her. I love porches, defended/undefensive space, innocent space: protected intimacy, porches are the architectural equivalent of rose-colored glasses, they speak of leisure and grace, they permit one to be alone while not alone. To be all the time in the world but not of it, daydreaming, seeking inner space from within gauzily shielded outer space, that's what porches are about; and drawled unguarded lazy conversations. Every week my mother-in-law cooked, and she and her husband ate, on alternate nights, a roast beef and a ham, sometimes dressed up with canned mushroom soup and sometimes with pineapples, a detestable frugality.

The old landlady (who was perhaps the age I am now) weeded the front garden as I watched from the safety of the porch. Landladies all wore flowered housedresses in those days, and white nylon socks and landlady shoes — fabric wedgies with crepe soles securely strapped to fat ankles; and this one wore no underwear. She weeded and I watched, bemused, a great black wiry bush protruding from her flowery dress; I didn't allow myself to know what it was. A man passed, and he saw her bush and looked at me and grinned in complicity, and I grinned back, but I was frightened, sickened, his smile was oily.

Another time a dog took up rowdy residence in that weedy garden near the porch, he was foaming at the mouth and scrabbling at the ground and snarling, a demented thing. My mother watched from the attic window. I left the safety of the porch and navigated around him, and went to the corner bakery — my assigned task — to buy Italian whole-wheat bread. When I came back my mother was still at the window, the mangy dog was gone.

Porches are America's lost rooms.

> *The master's farm business, the mistress's selections of goods and produce, the home craftsman's sales, and sundry emotional negotiations of the cooler sort (with the hired man, the foreman, the slave or house servant, the distressed or disgruntled neighbor, even with the unpredictable stranger from the muddy road) could all be conducted in the civil atmosphere offered by the shade of a prominent porch, apart from the sleeping and feeding quarters and without serious risk to the family's physical and psychic core.*
>
> — Reynolds Price, *Out on the Porch*

In Hyderabad, the enclosed courtyard formed by the walls that framed our house and united it with the servants' quarters was this kind of civil space: the Muslim butcher entered from one door, the Hindu butcher from another, each with separate weights and scales; they maintained a mutually satisfactory distance from each other; and we bought pork and beef.

On the terrace of that house — that wonderful house with its fountain and gardens and infinite varieties of green, that house on a boulder-strewn river where goats gamboled and buffalo bathed and beautiful Indian women washed their beautiful saris (and my naked children nimbly, triumphantly ignorant of danger, jumped from rock to rock), endless nights: *nimboo-pani* (gin and lime), buckets of ice; endless conversation (Nandita, Potla, Jim, Jake, Babe, Simon, Bobby, Usha, Prodipto, Joyce); and I fell in love. With a man who had no known sexual proclivities, no gift or appetite for gossip, reminiscence, intimacy. He loved — if love is a word that can be applied to a neutrality as total as Switzerland's — facts. My husband was as mercurial, as volatile, as India itself; unlike India, he was exhausting without being nourishing. I chose an unrequitable love that flourished in my mind and left my frightened body to maintain its fragile peace. Lovely terrace, with its intimations that life held more than it held now, lovely moonlight vibrating in the still trees. Hot.

Behind the wooden verandah jalousies of the old houses of Bombay the punkas churn the viscous heat; a woman opens a wooden shutter and holds her baby out to the street, his bottom bare; his pee splashes onto the crowded ground below.

In southern India, in Kerala, on the islands off Cochin, gracious old wooden houses — *tarawads* — have lived for centuries; they look, with their pagodalike ventilation eaves, almost as Chinese as Indian. Their pillared verandahs are deep, and cool as caves; symmetrical wings of these deep porches encircle courtyards ringed with pots of flowers. We sit in the shade of a nutmeg tree. The white satiny shell that contains the rich brown nutmeg is pickled for curry; the nutmeg itself has satiny brown "hair," attached to which is a scarlet bean — mace. All this in one neat package; geography does inform belief — no wonder Indians believe an atom contains a universe.

Here is a wonderful porch: it is furnished like a comfortable living room; but the fourth wall is the striated sea, colored fishes swim amidst coral reefs (and the world has no boundaries . . . this is in Jamaica).

Of all chairs, rocking chairs are the most haunted; they have the most *presence*. Their natural habitat is the porch; evening.

Porches are egalitarian, homely and democratic, formal and domestic — wicker chairs amidst Ionic columns.

The peace and the excitement of rainy days spent behind the screens of porches with wide, sheltering eaves: to be out of the rain and part of the rain. The smell, brown and green, wet and sweet, of rain falling on fallen leaves. What could possibly go wrong?

When I look at pictures of Gainesville, Florida, and see turreted houses with chimney stacks and shutters and glassed-in conservatories and back porches and bedroom porches and front porches, I find it hard to believe that a serial killer was at work in this town. That is because when I was a very little child I believed all bad and crazy people lived in one great dark house and a demon let them out at night. I formed this belief the night my father and I went for a walk and he told me there was no heaven — at that moment all the hypnotic lights of all the tranquil, self-possessed houses on that Brooklyn street, which had before seemed so palpably expressive of happy lives different from my own, seemed slightly to lose their warming brilliance, and slightly to retreat from me, and I was aware of a bleak emptiness where the sky was. And I progressed from this thought, this conviction, this eviscerating feeling, to a new, more alienating one: the apparently empty skies were stacked with row houses, stack upon stack, invisible to me, self-same but alien; the world was endless and unknowable, and I was untethered to it, unanchored in space. This infinity imposed a rigorous solitude upon me, a dislocation, a rupture, a bewilderment tantamount to cleaving pain. I could not conceive of empty space. Perhaps that summer night predisposed me to find likable the Indian temples I saw a lifetime later, temples — their shapes determined by ancient treatises and metaphysics — that reflected the Hindu view that "the world is a structure pulsing with inner life, an organism swelling with productive juices. . . . Everything — space itself as well as the matter and beings within it — is alive" (Zimmer, *The Art of Ancient India*). An atom contains a cosmos; empty space does not exist. (All southern Indian temples, crude and exquisite, have in common vitality and *horror vacui*, exuberance and elaboration upon elaboration.) But in the crowded emptiness of that long-ago summer night my father (whose voice — casual, unapologetic — hung in the parched air) said, "There is no God." My hand resided in his like a wounded animal. He peered too closely at me (he always did), to see the effect he had produced. He loomed, he always did, no boundaries between us: no shade of my expression was lost on him, no sigh, no smile, no change. I don't know what he saw in my face; he laughed.

(I hate masks.)

I sat on the wraparound porch of the first man I loved, Arnold Horowitz — oh lovely summers, sad and sweet, full of thrilling painful hints of love — and we had strawberry malteds and talked about God and happiness. A block away the el rumbled its way to Manhattan, an ironic subtext to our pastoral emotional obliquities. I never saw his room in this, his mother's *faux*-Victorian-shingled house, but it is as vivid to me as if I had — a single bed, a Danish-modern desk, a Picasso print: a cell. When I journey to Brooklyn to visit that house — these pilgrimages are like the first summers of love, sad and sweet — I see a plaster Madonna on the grass outside the now glassed-in porch; he would have been appalled. He would have laughed. Now, dead, perhaps he is more tolerant than he was then.

I am as confused as I ever was about heaven. It is difficult for me to believe in a God who does not suffer. But if we die and go to Him and are united with Him, do we then not suffer too? *More* suffering? ("The whole world's longing and pain mingle about you." — Saint Gregory of Nazianzus, theologian, Father of the Church) Is that what makes God God? That He can contain happiness within His suffering and suffering within His happiness? It would be too awful if Arnold were suffering still. ("What minds' affinities with heaven can pierce the veils above the clouds?" — Saint Gregory of Nazianzus)

Ideal houses have swimming pools and piano rooms and window seats.

My maternal grandfather: his mean brown house — which smelled of the loo and of the wine he made in the basement and of the cheap incense Grandma burned, and of moldy sheets and Drake's cake and dusty, greeny black clothes and aging diabetic flesh and the mold that was covered over by stamped-tin ceilings — had a player-piano room; Grandpa smashed and splintered the piano one day with an ax. I do not want to think about this, about the ax, about the hand that slammed the faces of his children (my mother, so beautiful).

I call the man I love, on whose account for an entire year I have been distracted: "I'm stuck," I say, "I can't write." "What are you writing?" he asks (he never asks to see what I've written about him, which lack of curiosity is flummoxing, and on certain days frightening, to me). "About rooms," I say, "and what happened in them." "Fear," he says. Fear? "Write about fear," he says, "that comes first." That comes first? Before love? "Love comes later," he says, "fear first. If you grow up in the ghetto," he says, "you don't want to read about nice rooms, nice people." (I don't think he ever reads what I write.) In any case he has given me a key to his psyche (and to his absences): fear comes first; and a shadow falls over my heart. His mother alternately abandoned and indulged him; when she was obliged to be away from him, he slept in his grandmother's wooden house in the country. His bedroom was four hundred feet from a blast furnace fifteen stories high; and outside his bedroom window the freight trains of the Erie-Lackawanna Railroad ran. (Noise causes heart attacks in certain mammals; he is defended, armored, scared.) There were rickety stairs leading up to an attic crawl space in that room; he thought devils lived there; and he never, caught between the blistering light and the peopled dark, told his fears. He seldom *tells*; he is a hipster and his sentences are epigrams, aphorisms, clever, waiting to be topped. (We are after all cannibals, a Mexican-Indian writer, Catholic, gay, said to me; my ancestors ate people, he said. . . . And we eat the Host; and I want to eat my lover's pain, I am greedy for his pain, it is sustenance.)

Yaddo has two pianos in its piano room. One day, as I was writing a love letter in that artists' retreat in Saratoga Springs, three deer came to my window, silent in the silent snow; I tore up the love letter. I sleep and work in the servants' quarters of West House, a mini-mansion; I love it here — a brass bed, oak floors, two generous rooms and bath divided from the other bedrooms of West House by green baize curtains. One night I heard a rustling near the curtains, then shuffling footsteps down the hall; the aromatic smell of pipe tobacco. Who? I cried. In the morning, at breakfast: I heard footsteps last night, I said; did anyone come to see me while I was asleep? Shuffling footsteps? Susan asked. Yes. Pipe tobacco? Yes. A cough? Come to think of it, yes; why? My father, Susan said, paid you a visit. Why me? Because you're reading my manuscript, Susan said, and he doesn't like it, and those were the rooms he always slept and worked in. Well, I said, I don't like these nocturnal visits. Ask him kindly but firmly to leave, she said. But the ghost of John Cheever never visited me again.

"O sluggish, servile, and most dejected mind, which includeth itself within the narrow bounds of his own house," a Jacobean traveler wrote; so wrong: a house contains a universe. ("In my father's house there are many mansions.") I am unclothed without the skin of all the houses I have ever lived in, my skin's skin.

ROOMS THAT TELL STORIES, ROOMS THAT SPEAK

CHARLES RENNIE MACKINTOSH: KIND HEART AND WHITE ROOMS

> *On the second floor of a modest building in the great industrial smoky town of Glasgow there is a drawing room amazingly white.*
>
> — B. E. Kalas, *Charles Rennie Mackintosh*, 1905

When my children were babies, they sat in highchairs provided for them by the dining room staff of the Imperial Hotel in Tokyo; one was pink, the other blue, and both were decorated with painted bunnies. I don't think I have ever seen anything so incongruous; in the vast, damp, and empty space of Frank Lloyd Wright's colossal room, my juicy babies looked like God's mistakes, drowned by Wright's immense ego. (He was a very little man.)

Wright's buildings invite you to admire his cleverness. Charles Rennie Mackintosh's buildings are an invitation to defy unhappiness. They make the soul buoyant and set the body and the mind at ease; they are joy.

Mackintosh — Glasgow architect, theorist, and designer — died in virtual obscurity in London, of tongue cancer, in 1928. Categorizing him stylistically is a teasing game: one sees Japanese influences in his work, elements which are formal, chaste, rectilinear, and dramatic; in the vigor of his early, massive furniture one sees English Arts and Crafts influence — though he disdained the worship of craftsmanship or materials for their own sake, and concerned himself instead with spectacular visual impact; and, particularly in his stained glass and sinuous decorative details, one feels the influence of art nouveau. He despised art nouveau; he called it "melted margarine." (He compared Parisian Metro lights to "slightly deliquescent lard.") In fact Mackintosh is *sui generis* and his furniture is so fresh in concept and in execution one might think he invented not only furniture but the idea of furniture itself. His rooms induced in visitors "an almost mystical sense of peace, . . . an impact of monumentality, broken only occasionally by a small, superimposed ornament [the effect of which] is of a jewel" (Kalas).

He played with light and dark, the circle and the square, the geometric and the organic; he "fashioned" light and made it do his bidding.

His own sitting room had plain white walls, a white carpet, a white-washed fireplace, white furniture, and floods of light.

A bed hung with textiles of his design was a world entire, as beguiling as a Renaissance canopied world/bed. It is simultaneously romantic and austere, severe and sensual — a cocoon of joyful inevitability. Walls, furniture, and ceilings were white in the many white bedrooms he designed; and the whiteness of these dream machines was punctuated and emphasized by his elegant ladderback chairs of unrelieved black. Insets of colored glass made wardrobes enchanted enclosures (one expects to find in them sugar cubes and the bracing smell of lavender, order and secrets; they are like Alice's looking-glass — one feels that to enter them would be to find a world that both reassuringly conforms to one's expectations of paradise and thrillingly surprises one); traces of rosy pink in fabrics subtly softened his geometry, his squares and oblongs, perpendicular and horizontal lines.

Every embodied metaphor that makes a house magical is contained in these rooms: niches and window seats, fireplaces and hearths, open space and secret space, intimate space (light and dark). Steps that pull us upward into fantasy and familiarity.

The white lacquered cupboards he and his wife, Margaret, made for these rooms — and the improbable, gravity-defying T-shaped black-lacquered cupboards — are worlds unto themselves. They are miracles of fresh simplicity, new and unexpected, that speak to us as if we had been longing to live with them all our lives (stained-glass inserts and hammered metal doors). I have never encountered enclosures I loved so much, complex, extravagant enclosures with nothing to hide.

He had a clubfoot, a profoundly loving and abiding marriage to a wife he regarded as his equal and faithfully adored (Margaret, his "silver light"), and (he was a depressive, and, after fifteen fruitfully creative years followed by ten of rejection, poor) a life that is generally reckoned to have been sad ("antagonism and undeserved ridicule bring on feelings of despondency and despair," he wrote). He painted watercolors of flowers. He loved fat Scottish roses, which show up frequently — highly stylized and often invested with symbolic meaning — in the wall stencils of Mackintosh murals.

"Architecture," he wrote, "is the world of art and as it is everything visible and invisible that makes the world, so it is all the arts and crafts and industries that make architecture. . . . Architecture is the synthesis of the fine arts, the commune of all the crafts."

He understood the importance, the mystery, of doors; his doors were appropriate portals to bewitching space; the clean lines of his white doors were interrupted (checkered) by cutout cubes and colored-glass lozenges, like candies, or jewels. Beyond the doors were rooms that in their intelligence and simplicity were "spellbinding. In the studio–drawing room I genuinely felt that I was standing in a complete and perfect work of art," Alistair Moffat writes. "Not looking at it like a painting on a gallery wall, but standing in it, inside it. . . . With great architecture or great art, . . . I've had to work at it in order to enjoy it. But in Mackintosh's house none of that effort was needed. I got it right away." One does.

His niece, Margaret Rennie Dingwall (who ate meringues for the first time in "Uncle Tosh's" drawing room), talked to Moffat about the charming game Mackintosh made for all his nephews and nieces at Christmas: "You went into the white studio drawing room, with that beautiful pale carpet and the lovely chairs, and you saw that he had made a maze there out of coloured wool. Around these chairs and cupboards that are so famous now, he'd got six or seven different colours (one for each child) wound so that the room looked like a spider's web, criss-crossed with bright colours. You had to follow your own colour until you found a Christmas present. . . . I liked his house."

He was as ruthless as he was tenderly alive to beauty: "If anyone else touched his work, he'd have literally torn them apart." On the other hand, when a house of his catches fire, what comes first to his mind is that "if any of the children's dresses had gone on fire it might have been terrible."

He sometimes collaborated with his friend Herbert MacNair; and he and MacNair — this is like a fairy tale — married two artist sisters, Margaret and Frances Macdonald. "The Four" thereafter collaborated on elements of design. According to the latest scholarship, Margaret was his coequal in all elements of design. This may account for the yin and yang of feminine and masculine elements critics see in Mackintosh architecture (the organic curve and the lock of the grid; the circle and the square); it is the work of a man and woman in spiritual and intellectual harmony, and in love. Mackintosh and Margaret's house, a friend remembers, "was always so pretty and fresh. A bright red glowing fire, the right sort of cake, a nice tea, and kind hearts — and a lot of fun."

When a stubborn mark got on the white furniture Margaret cleaned it with warm olive oil.

Everything he did was practical — he abhorred froufrou; and everything he did was magical: he "covered the walls of his dining room with coarse grey-brown wrapping paper and stencilled them with a rose and lattice motif enlivened by silver-painted dots" (Moffat). The "dots" were cascades of silvery circles, in color and form not unlike the transparent petal of the Scottish plant called honesty. It was his lovely assumption that the world was composed of a unity of the visible and the invisible that accounts for the lyrical work of his heart and mind and hand, the lasting magic of his white worlds.

The Glasgow School of Art is generally regarded as his masterpiece. (I stood at the doors of the school for uncalculated time, smiling, and wondering how anything so utilitarian — glass, white wood, and brass — could be so guilelessly charming.) The library of the school is its *sanctum sanctorum*, calm, warm, magnificent, congenial — a glassed-in soaring cathedral of learning, and brilliantly functional, vital, and romantic, a happy and an awesome place. Its exterior — which borrows from Scottish baronial architecture — is as unfussy as a fortress and as whimsical as a fable: the exterior metalwork, decorative and practical, is fantastical — his *rosa mystica* appears on curving wrought-iron window supports; the stylized flowers, birds, seeds, plants, and berries of his iron fences invite you into his private mystical world and tell stories in iron, stories that lend themselves to magical interpretations and are reckoned to be beautiful even by those who have an unimaginative cast of mind; they provide sufficient evidence to give the lie to the libel that the Scottish are dour.

"The Mackintoshes were perfectionists and they couldn't have an ordinary key. The door had a special plate and to open that interesting door of the new School of Art [in Glasgow — 1899] there had to be a proper key and that key had to be laid on a cushion, and they couldn't have just bought a Victorian cushion for a Mackintosh key." ("When a conflict between lock and key appears in a night dream, for psycho-analysis this is a clear sign, so clear, in fact, that it cuts the story short," Bachelard says.) So Margaret made a cushion for the formal opening of the school — "a small, oblong, pale, pearly silk cushion with a silver fringe around. . . . I remember the key quite clearly now, shining pale in this grey afternoon when it was raining slightly, a drizzle, a real Glasgow afternoon. I was six" (Mary Newbury Sturrock, talking to Alistair Moffat, 1985).

He — they — were *sui generis*. Mackintosh buildings and artifacts ap-pear to have no progenitors and no direct descendants (although it has been said that he acted as a "purifier," preparing and cleansing the way for moderns). He subdued his ego to the organic and mystical elements he and Margaret incorporated in their work — the stars, moon, the sun, the sphere of the world. His work renews our love for the natural world (it owes as much to a fat Scottish rose as to mathematics), and renders it, paradoxically, more mysterious. The Mackintosh world is an alchemical mirror.

One of life's strange coincidences bemuses me: next to the terraced Victorian house on Blytheswood Square where Margaret and Charles Rennie Mackintosh lived (having reconstructed its interior) is the house of Scotland's most notorious Victorian, Madeleine Smith. She is said, at the age of twenty-two, to have poisoned her worthless lover, whom she used for sex, with arsenic. (A jury returned a verdict of Unproven.) She did this in her basement bedroom next to Margaret and Charles Mackintosh's white rooms. She later married William Morris's man-ager. Had she been born a few years later, she would have been drawn, I like to think, into the artistic circle of women from which Margaret and her sister came, the group self-christened "the Immortals," for whom sex was not forbidden territory. But a few years made all the difference. Madeleine Smith moved to the Bronx and was buried in Westchester.

HENRY JAMES: HIS FEATHER DUSTER

> *I went to the French exhibition at the Metropolitan. . . . I really went up to see the winter sunlight on the floor of the long room downstairs in the American Wing. I often do this, during the winter; the room is so gracious and beautiful, and the sunlight pours in, broken up into squares, onto the floor, and the whole thing gives me bunches inside, I can tell you. . . . There's something about the fact that the room is on ground level that gets me; H. James could do a story about that, something about genteel atavism, and wanting to live in the 18th cent. Yes; there's something in my blood that wants to look down into a long ground floor room with the sunlight in it. You can figure that out, if you can.*
>
> — *What the Woman Lived: Selected Letters of Louise Bogan,*
> Ruth Limner, ed.

Given the cramped brown ordinariness of her house in Albany, the romantic heroine of James's *Portrait of a Lady* was almost doomed to fall in love with that civilized swine Gilbert Osmond, "the old cabinets, pictures, tapestries, surfaces of faded silk" that lived so perfectly in the soft spangled light of his perfect Tuscan villa. (Poor Isabel Archer, poor lamb. Like most romantics, she believed herself to be rational, whereas people who go around saying they are "incurable romantics" are, one has had occasion to notice, quite often shrewdly calculating, cynical and ruthless, and have too many ideas about themselves.)

One can see her doom reaching out to embrace Isabel on a hilltop in Tuscany, as she and her companion, Madame Merle, wind "between high-walled lanes into which the wealth of blossoming orchards over-drooped and flung a fragrance, until they reached the small suburban piazza, of crooked shape, where the long brown wall of the villa occupied . . . by Mr. Osmond formed a principal, or at least a very imposing, object. Isabel went with her friend through a wide, high court, where a clear shadow rested below and a pair of light-arched galleries, facing each other above, caught the upper sunshine upon their slim columns and the flowering plants in which they were dressed. There was something grave and strong in the place; it looked somehow as if, once you were in, you would need an act of energy to get out. For Isabel, however, there was of course as yet no thought of getting out, but only of advancing."

But Osmond — who looks like "a prince who has abdicated in a fit of fastidiousness and has been in a state of disgust ever since" — isn't grave and strong, he has only "a great dread of vulgarity." (He thinks Rome is vulgar, an extraordinarily vulgar thing to think.)

"Your rooms at least are perfect. I'm struck with that afresh whenever I come back," Madame Merle, his rottenly complicitous lover, says. "I know none better anywhere. You understand this sort of thing as nobody anywhere does. You've such adorable taste." Isabel, whose generous nature is moved by the fact that Osmond's income is not ostentatiously large, cannot see beyond the beauty of his rooms — his "adorable taste" — to the evil of his character; it is like women to confuse the characters of men with the character of their work; and his rooms are Osmond's work, the work of thirty years of guile.

In these rooms he has no magnificent bold masterpieces. ("Old curtains and crucifixes," his sister, Countess Gemini, says dismissively.) It is precisely this that stirs Isabel, who has an inherited fortune to burn and a heart full of untapped love to confer; and who better to confer it upon than a man who seems to her gentle, sad, exquisitely modulated and refined, a man who lives diffidently in "the atmosphere of summer twilight that pervade[s]" his villa. She has it in her power, she grasps immediately, to make someone happy — to give. (Of course her giving is a form of taking, giving always is; just as taking is a form of giving when the heart is pure; Osmond's heart is not and never has been pure.) What Osmond has is small and perfect, and what he has made of what he has is full of artifice. ("Even the little girl from the convent, who, in her prim white dress, with her small submissive face and her hands locked before her, stood there as if she were about to partake of her first communion, even Mr. Osmond's diminutive daughter had a kind of finish that was not entirely artless.") It is not that Isabel does not recognize the artifice as artifice; it is that her soft heart is ineffably affected by it: "I don't see any horrors anywhere," she says; "everything seems to me beautiful and precious." "A few good things; indeed I've nothing very bad. But I've not what I should have liked," he says, with the diffidence that so recommends him to her (a feigned diffidence); "He seemed to hint that nothing but the right 'values' was of any consequence." "You'd have liked a few things from the Uffizi and the Pitti — that's what you'd have liked," says Madame Merle, who knows her man. Isabel, led to the precipice by her goodness, led to the slaughter by her readiness to love, sees in his things and in his arrangements "the kind of personal issue that touched her most nearly; . . . a lonely, studious life in a lovely land; . . . an old sorrow that sometimes ached today; a feeling of pride that was perhaps exaggerated, but that had an element of nobleness; . . . a care for beauty and perfection so natural and so cultivated together." She is betrayed by the ancient civilized Tuscan landscape, as gorgeous as an illuminated manuscript: "the vistas, the ranges of steps and terraces and fountains of a formal Italian garden — allowing only for arid places freshened by the natural dews of quaint, half-anxious, half-helpless fatherhood" — serve as an anteroom to the villa with which she has fallen in love, an anteroom to the citadel of her heart.

Poor, good Isabel has read and translated Osmond's rooms with tragic incorrectness. When they marry, Osmond moves Isabel around the way he moves his furniture around (she is as decorative, and as obedient to his wishes).

(And poor James loved the Tuscan landscape so much, so almost frenziedly, he couldn't allow himself to trust it. He had to transform it into the locus of Machiavellian evil so as to quiet the delirium it inspired in his womanish heart. . . . Did you know that James owned to killing a cat one night in his English garden because it was caterwauling?)

It is an interesting exercise to reflect upon the words of James's friend Edith Wharton (in *The Decoration of Houses*) when one is contemplating Osmond's capacity to create beauty out of his own ugliness: "Architecture addresses itself not to the moral sense, but to the eye. . . . Architectural sincerity is simply obedience to certain visual requirements."

When one thinks of the books and movies in which rooms and houses are the catalysts for actions benevolent or malign (Howards End; Lizzie Borden's house . . . houses that have character and are characters in our imagination), it's hard, rather, to see this as clearly as Wharton did.

The room that Merton Densher enters and is obliged to cool his heels in, in James's *Wings of the Dove*, a room so unamiable as to be mercilessly alien, causes one to doubt Wharton's dictum: Densher has only to see the vast drawing room of Kate Croy's Aunt Maud Lowder to know that his cause is lost; the cruel room sounds the death knell to his hopes; he will never be permitted to marry Kate.

"As he walked to and fro, . . . taking in the message of her massive florid furniture, the immense expression of her signs and symbols, he . . . found himself even facing the thought that he had nothing to fall back on, and that that was as great an humiliation in a good cause as a proud man could desire. It hadn't yet been so distinct to him that he made no show — literally not the smallest; so complete a show seemed made there all about him; so almost abnormally affirmative, so aggressively erect, were the huge heavy objects that syllabled his hostess's story." In this room, where Maud Lowder is so present in her absence, and her *things* — "so fringed and scalloped, so buttoned and corded, drawn everywhere so tight and curled everywhere so thick" — speak of her and for her, her colossal vulgarity takes on for him a kind of "freshness, almost, . . . beauty, since there was beauty, to a degree, in the play of so big and bold a temperament. She was in fine quite the largest quantity to deal with; and he was in the cage of the lioness without his whip — the whip, in a word, of a supply of proper retorts. He had no retort but that he loved the girl — which in such a house as that was painfully cheap. Kate had mentioned to him more than once that her aunt was Passionate, . . . uttering it as with a capital P, marking it as something that he might, that he in fact ought to, turn about in some way to their advantage. He wondered at this hour to what advantage he could turn it; but the case grew less simple the longer he waited. Decidedly there was something he had not enough of.

"His slow march to and fro seemed to give him the very measure; as he paced and paced the distance it became the desert of his poverty; at the sight of which expanse moreover he could pretend to himself as little as before that the desert looked redeemable. . . . He read more vividly, more critically, . . . the appearances about him. . . . It was the language of the house itself that spoke to him, writing out for him with surpassing breadth and freedom the associations and conceptions, the ideals and possibilities of the mistress. Never, he felt sure, had he seen so many things so unanimously ugly — operatively, ominously so cruel." In this Victorian room, fiercely British, imperial (*Em*pire-al), among the heavy horrors, "the solid forms, the wasted finish, the misguided cost, the general attestation of morality and money, a good conscience and a big balance," among things that "finally represented for him a portentous negation of his own world of thought," he quailed, as if before the throne of a false god; and his fate was sealed.

Rupert Brooke said of his house in Cambridgeshire: "This is a lonely, dank, ruined, overgrown, gloomy, lovely house: with a garden to match, . . . it is all five hundred years old and fusty with the ghosts of generations of mouldy clergymen. It is a fit place to write my kind of poetry in." How lovable it was; he went "through the dew-soaked grass of the meadow over the mill-wall leading to the pool, to bathe naked in the unseen water, smelling of wild peppermint and mud" (*Writers and Their Houses*, Kate Marsh, ed.). The house and the meadows speak in this, his kind of poem:

> If I should die, think only this of me:
>   That there's some corner of a foreign field
> That is for ever England. There shall be
>   In that rich earth a richer dust concealed;
> A dust whom England bore, shaped, made aware;
>   Gave, once, her flowers to love, her ways to roam,
> A body of England's breathing English air.

He died when he was twenty-eight.

Darwin wrote *The Origin of Species* in a former parsonage.

Like olive trees, mulberry trees live for hundreds and sometimes thousands of years (the mulberry trees belonging to Saint Thomas More's house still bear fruit). I had an invitation once to visit the house of a man who said, "We have little to offer you, but you can sit under the mulberry tree Milton's tutor planted." I think it was the most romantic invitation I have ever received.

MURDER

Ugly, foul, gaunt, mean, stupidly cluttered, the Borden house in Fall River, Massachusetts, smelled of spoiled mutton soup (bubbles of putrefaction rising to its slimy surface), of urine and excrement and soaked menstrual rags, chamberpots and slop pails, warmed-over fish and vomit and sweat, kerosene and the unwashed flesh of the crevices of Lizzie Borden's stepmother's lardy body — of parsimony and unspoken hatreds. In the sitting room of that house, with its drab-colored walls and dark brown trim and its junky florid carpet — a house in which privacy was a blessing impossible to secure — Death, if it were fastidious, would be an unlikely guest. What happened there was what had to happen there: Murder. An ax. Forty whacks.

. . . "What does it matter now? The old man's dead," I said to my doctor. "And you're afraid to cross avenue streets," he said, which is true: unseen dangers rush at me, I feel their wings; the earth does not feel firm beneath my feet. "In any case," I said, "he never penetrated me." (At night: "What do you do with your hands under the covers?" my father said. "That's not nice," my mother said; she was naked. . . . Whose hot breath? . . .) "He never penetrated me. He did try to kill me, you'd never know it to look at me now, would you?" My doctor says, "I'm not laughing, Barbara."

He is right, it isn't a joke. And it isn't an anecdote either, though I've done my best to turn it into one, sanitizing it, ordering and neutralizing it, skimming over it lightly in flat, uninflected sentences, denying the present pain, the leaching fear. (Did you ever doubt there was a censoring wily writerly presence behind the words you read?)

When he was dying: "Who are those other guys in the room, kid?" he said. "Are they good guys, Daddy?" "Yeah, they're OK. OK. Don't trust that Barbara!" He has bolted upright in bed (his cotton-polyester sheets, his rubber sheets), and his voice, a whisper for weeks, is a bellow: "Don't trust that Barbara!" he shouts to the shadows crowding his room. "But I'm Barbara, I'm here, it's me, Daddy. Daddy." "Good guys," he whispers. "But there's that other one," he moans, turning his face to the wall. "What other one?" "The one that did all the bad things, the one that followed me around doing bad things. All my life." "You were never bad, Daddy," I say, believing it. But I can't kiss his loose flesh. And when I think of it now, his slack flesh, I feel an abhorrence that induces vertigo.

I don't know how to tell myself this story honestly. The event itself, though logically I see it as part and continuum of the shameful life we led on Seventy-fifth Street, I see also, simultaneously, as an island stranded in time. It happened to me; it seems almost to have happened to somebody else. (Poor little girl at the other end of a telescope . . . but it is I who can't cross streets.)

Well; with no confidence that I can tell this without doing something wrong (wrong . . . warped . . . wicked . . . bad), I will tell it. (Did you think for a moment one wrote only for other people?)

It is Christmas Eve. My mother has announced her intention of going from door to door to preach the Jehovah's Witness gospel of bloody universal doom with her brother, my Uncle Tony. When my Uncle Tony comes to dinner, my father, who detests him, says: "Did you stuff dolls today, Toe? How many dolls did you stuff? Did you have fun? Did they like it? Did you stuff them good? Hee-hee-hee." Uncle Tony works in a doll factory; he is a Purple Heart veteran of the war, Burma-cuckoo (and too present in his flesh: his flesh outweighs his intelligence). My mother — who has been successful in converting Uncle Tony, her least-favorite brother, to her religion, dismal and bloody religion — sits stony-faced at the kitchen table. Uncle Tony turns bright red but doesn't protest. I play with my food. (One pork chop per person, never a second, bounty will bury you, don't you know.) I don't know what they're talking about, how could I? Well of course I do, how could they behave like this, what is wrong with them? . . . My father goes nuts, ranting impotently, forbidding my mother to go out preaching, causing my mother to laugh her peculiar half-trilling, half-belching laugh. She likes this part, the wrath, the courage it takes for her to go, the anticipation of baroque troubles when she returns. I am left home to wash the dinner dishes. (But why? Usually I pray and beseech and feign stomachaches in order to be left behind; she laughs and takes me with her. So why am I left behind? Is this part of a larger scheme? What does she know? Damn her.) Now I am washing dishes and my father is singing "Soliloquy" from *Carousel* ("When I have a daughter . . . she'll be sweet and as pink as can be . . . a neat little petite little tintype of her mother is she") and punctuating the lyrics with indecipherable words and wails, and he is crying and drinking wine. Now the cupboard doors swing open and pots and pans and saucers come flying out. Now, in his undershirt and shorts, he is twisting a towel in his hands, and the towel, wet and smelly, is around my neck. He pulls and twists and I fall backward against a body I am even now loath to say I hate . . . in every particular . . . his Linotype operator's ink-stained hands, his horny toenails, his stale breath, his mouth so like my own. . . . And now there are blanks. He is on the front stairs, making his way to the apartment below ours, and I am with him (tied to him by what?). "Is this a nice way," he asks our neighbors, Bea and Bill, "to spend Christmas Eve?" But he is calm now; maudlin and calm. "Shhhh, go to bed," they say, "you're drunk." Well; that's all. One doesn't wish to make more of it than it was. Or less. Presumably my mother came back that night, accompanied, as always, by the odor of sanctimony and martyrdom and perhaps by horrible Uncle Toe (who, when I see him now at family funerals, tells me, "Be good").

Where was my brother? What did the cat, Princess, do? Who restored order to that kitchen, which on Christmas morning was again sunny and serene, smelling only of the silence of snow? He tried to kill me. When I say those words I feel only weariness. Well; not always. The other day an acupressurist came to my house to give me a massage, nice Chinese man, soft-spoken, modest. He put his hands around my neck, his thumbs working to exorcise my body's pain. I made myself lie there quietly so as not to embarrass him or myself. That night all the muscles in my body pulsed and twitched, and my nerves contended with them, a demon dance; my skin was a useless cloak that could not contain my body. . . . I have questions. (But the old man is dead.) Why are we, my father and I, at the doctor's office across the avenue from our house? Why is he talking in a voice so loud it fills the world? Why am I pleading with him to speak softly, please, please; and why does he smile, his voice saluting and staining the air. A minor mystery. He tried to kill me, you'd never know it to look at me now.

Sometimes I can't breathe.

WHAT THE EYE DEMANDS

From my bedroom windows, my living room windows, and from the windows of my mirrored office (mirrored for the light I am voracious for) I see a huge poster painting, seven stories high, of a young boy of indeterminate race holding a gun. The gun is pointed at me, it invades my bedroom, my living room, and my mirrored office. Affixed to the windowless side of a blameless turn-of-the-century cast-iron building, the poster painting is red, white, blue, and black: STOP THE VIO-LENCE, SAVE THE CHILDREN, it reads. Who is responsible for this atrocity? I see it from my roof garden, too. When it first went up the obscene thing occupied all of my visual horizon; my eye was drawn only to it, and the Chrysler Building and the Empire State Building (which I can also see from my bedroom, my office, my living room) might not have existed; its brazenness obliterated the urban landscape. (Some people claim to see, in the black irises of the child's eyes, white skeletal faces; I see fetuses.) When the poster first appeared it contaminated the city view and my mind. Now I hardly see it anymore. I have censored it, the way the eye selects what the mind will remember, for example, about the roofline of Florence — memory doesn't summon up and the recollecting eye does not see the TV antennas and satellite dishes that litter the romantic view. . . . So if it can be censored, what good is it, what purpose does it serve? What purpose did it serve when it evoked our rage? For months it riddled the conversation of my fellow residents with rage: *Who the fuck did this? What can we do about it? I want to throw a grenade at the goddamn thing.* Nobody did anything about the violent artifact; now we hardly see it anymore. Of course writing about it revivifies it, just as the exclamations of guests do; and I want to throw a grenade at the damn thing.

Proportion is the good breeding of architecture. It is that something, indefinable to the unprofessional eye, which gives repose and distinc-

tion to a room; in its origin a matter of nice mathematical calculation, of scientific adjustment of voids and masses, but in its effects as intangible as that all-pervading essence which the ancients called the soul. . . . The line . . . is what the eye demands.

— Edith Wharton and Ogden Codman, Jr.,
The Decoration of Houses

The immense stoniness of the Metropolitan Life Building's curvilinear façade — the first thing I see when I enter my apartment — hurts my teeth like the sound of chalk on a blackboard; so I have hung in my living room white crinkled-silk translucent curtains that can in an instant be swept aside from the windows of my twenty-fifth-floor apartment. "The better the house, the less need there [is] for curtains," Wharton says; alas. When I lived in the smaller apartment next door to this one, a quintessential skyline view was framed by my windows (the failed neoclassicism of the Metropolitan Life Building obtruded only slightly on my view; Park Avenue was my highway and my tunnel to the magic city). Now that view is only a bit off center, several feet off center; and it makes all the difference. I had no curtains in the haremish bedroom of my old apartment, which served as a living room as well (nobody, though, ever sat on the carpeted steps that surrounded my multipillowed bed); and while women invariably loved this space — my friend Emily says my bed looked like an altar — my sixty-four-year-old lover, who surprises me by being conventional at the most unexpected times, used to sing, and sometimes to grumble, "I Am Climbing Jacob's Ladder" every time he navigated those steps (he wants a bedroom to look like a hotel room, with a king-size bed). In that one-person-sized apartment I fitted as sweetly as a nut in its shell; now I see that apartment, with its fireplace that served and cheered both bedroom/living room and dining room/office, as the house of my indulgence — everything served my own needs, including, I understand now, the needs of my unconscious. I see the apartment I live in now as a house that in some way conforms to social obligation and to custom; in this larger space I feel more connected to the world. But it's odd: in spite of the cream-colored sofa and the (functioning, but essentially iconographic) fireplace, most of my guests still sit at the round dining table to talk. I have not succeeded in quelling the vague unease

I feel in my living room. I liked it better when I felt unconnected, in my aerie, to the world. Perhaps it's the curtains — I'm afraid they are finicky: "Lingerie effects do not combine well with architecture." But without the curtains I feel an obscure restlessness, almost as if I were sitting in a bus station.

I look to Edith Wharton for help: "It must never be forgotten that every one is unconsciously tyrannized over by the wants of others, — the wants of dead and gone predecessors, who have an inconvenient way of thrusting their different habits and tastes across the current of later existences. The unsatisfactory relations of some people with their rooms are often explained in this way," she says. "The beauty of a room depending chiefly on its openings, to conceal these under draperies is to hide the key of the whole," she says; but: "The concealed door is a useful expedient," she also says; and "in a narrow room, no one cares to sit in a line with the doorway."

I am having an argument with myself about how much I want the world to intrude upon private space. I am having an argument with myself over the relative merits of introversion and extraversion. I want a house that thoroughly protects my solitude at the same time as it invites others to enter. I love the ancient Tuscan town of Lucignano, built of five concentric circles on a hill: from the front windows of houses one sees the world — the town, the cobblestone streets, the markets, the cafés; from the back windows one sees gardens and the silent hills beyond. Introversion/extraversion; and one feels girdled, sheltered, embraced, befriended; one experiences solitude but is not alone. . . . I have contrived to put curtains (nubby Indian silk) between my front door and the living room proper. I literally cannot bear to sit on my cream-colored couch with the door and its three locks in view. Without curtains I should feel that I were living in public space; that there was no demarcation between public and private, no transition between safety and chance, inside and out. The door mourns departure (in the case of my lover, a series of departures in one long endless departure) more declaratively, more terminally, than it celebrates arrival; rooms should be entered in stages and left in stages — I wonder if anything less than a series of enfiladed rooms would silence fears of abandonment.

. . . In Rome one makes the transition from Bernini's Piazza Navona to the small, intimate piazza of the Church of Santa Maria del Pace by means of a pedestrian tunnel behind the Church of Sant'Agnese, a tunnel formed by the Church of Santa Maria del Pace, which straddles two narrow cobblestone streets; one feels the weather in as well as on one's body — sunlight to dark, dark to light, a passage full of delight, an exit that is at the same time an entry, a fulfillment. The transition from life to death should be like this. . . .

"There are but two ways of dealing with a room that is fundamentally ugly; one is to accept it, and the other is courageously to correct its ugliness," Wharton says — romantic advice; there are but two ways of dealing with a lover who is fundamentally flawed: one is to accept him and the other is courageously — magically? arrogantly? futilely? — to correct his ugliness.

"Symmetry," Wharton says, "is the sanity of decoration." The bones of my apartment are bad. The odd protruding angles of walls, sense-lessly interrupted space, conform to no logic but the zoner's and the contractor's — this building was made from the outside in, to present an interesting and pleasant face to the world; and perhaps as a result of projections and regressions in interior space that make no aesthetic sense, I am always looking for a way to soften and conceal rude lines with *things*, decoration to mask deficiencies. I want comfort, airiness, and a sheltering intimacy. I want the elements of a bazaar (not a museum). I want order — the internalization of outdoor civic spaces; I want rooms simultaneously to be clean and cluttered — like a bazaar, coherent and organic in their clutter. Like Keats, I want "luxuries bright, milky, soft and rosy" — but nothing superfluous.

From my living room I see the Flatiron Building, and Broadway cutting diagonally though the Cartesian grid of Manhattan — a symbol of larkiness and caprice, nice surprise.

I forgive the bad bones of my apartment — all those clouds and the persuasive light incline me toward happiness; but I cannot deny that the only perfect rooms I have ever lived in were the rooms of my childhood; they had/have the perfection of the immutable, they have entered eternity, whereas everywhere I live now and until I die will be in the sphere of time. They were/are perfect because they *were*. They are wired into the labyrinth of memory. They exist outside time.

When we lived in Jamaica, Long Island (I was five years old), we had a house that was covered, sheathed, separated from the world with ivy. Choked with ivy, my mother said. I felt abidingly safe behind that densely woven curtain of green. One morning I awoke to find it had all been chopped away. Witch chopped it all away.

One would like to be in a place like the Farnesina Palace, of which Vasari said it was not built, but really born — *non murato ma veramente nato*. One feels this of the homes of one's childhood.

Still (happy chance), in my bedroom I am content, at ease, at rest.

In his introduction to Wharton and Codman's *Decoration of Houses*, John Barrington Bayley — the snob — says, disdainfully, "the social pyramid — once so glossy and steep — has disappeared and we have instead a cluster of ethnic towers à la San Gimignano." Fiddle-de-dee. In fairy tales, the princess, gentle and virginal, resides in the tower: the patron of San Gimignano is Santa Fina, a slender and blameless girl who once accepted an orange from a young man at a well, died penitentially on an oak plank, and in paintings embraces the walled city in her tender arms. The fortress towers of San Gimignano — stalwart, friendly, formidable, delightful; reserved, hospitable; compact, patrician, and, on the one hand, as George Duby says, "the unreal space of courtly myth, the vertical flight of mystic ascension . . . and, on the other, a . . . compact universe, profound and solid" from which one could lean out and exchange recipes, or throw arrows or collapsible wooden bridges — reconciled me to a life of insertion in canyons, in a building many of its residents call The Fortress. As I fall asleep in the crook of the neoclassical Met Life and the Empire State buildings, which form an angle, I think of the friendly towers of San Gimignano, from the crannies of which butter-yellow violets grow; and I feel safe. I drift to sleep in a world of birds and clouds and light, airplanes, freed balloons, unmoored kites ("I should like my house to be similar to that of the ocean wind, all quivering with gulls." — René Cazelles). The nearly mystical Chrysler Building — as much a paean to self-similar forms as are the temples of India with their repetitive motifs, like rows of prickly asparagus stalks and bunches of cauliflower florettes — shines purely and discreetly. The Empire State Building inspires lovers' fantasies: I feel like I have the Empire State Building in my mouth, I say to my lover, who growls with pleasure.

Skyscrapers are not by nature affable. It is easy to regard them as antisocial. Mine — the one I live in and the ones I see from the one I live in — are, by reason of association, both awesome and affable. Grand.

Their soaring bulk and their lights are reflected in the mirrored walls.

Sometimes I allow myself the pleasure of two painkilling tablets before I climb under the white covers; and then, voluptuously inert, I drift, neither awake nor asleep, into waking dreams; I listen to the welcome silence of my body, which I dreamily interpret to mean all is at rest and well (the noises of the world softly funnel into my room); I channel surf — blessedly losing all discrimination; I play Bach's B Minor Mass; the Gloria and the Magnificat wash over me. . . . Tonight the sky is a pure, intense, cool blue; the northwest vibrates with a greenish pink glow. The scattered lights in buildings black against the sky blink out indecipherable messages. The cupola of the Metropolitan Life Building's tower culminates in a halo of golden lights; it is washed cream with light, and then the cream cascades into white, which turns, then, into pale aqua. The Empire State Building is a cerulean blue; its red tower-lights flash like the Just in Auden's poem, exchanging messages.

The queen-size bed in my white bedroom is rococo iron, painted white with brass trim, c. 1860 (Toronto). A white quilted bedspread, pattern: Tree of Life; white linen sheets and four bed pillows of white linen; two cream-colored velvet pillows; two fringed chenille pillows colored white, green, blue, cream, yellow; one white chenille pillow. Two round bedside tables, one twenty inches round, swathed in thrift-shop embroidered white cotton covered by an antique shawl of cream silk chiffon and geometrically patterned bittersweet-orange silk velvet fringed in bright orange; it is topped with glass, and on it are a halogen lamp, Museum of Modern Art; a blue Depression-glass bowl from a Salvation Army thrift shop in Brooklyn, with the business card of the estate-jewelry boutique at Barney's resting in it; a lacquered vermilion Chinese covered reed basket (from a department store on Canal Street in Chinatown), and in it small bottles of perfume oils — musk, from Kiehl's 1890 pharmacy; honeysuckle, from Kiehl's; two bottles of *khus-khus* oil from the bazaar in New Delhi, and one of lotus; attar of roses (New Delhi bazaar); atomizers of Calyx and Rain. Also on the table:

three Post-it pads, yellow, pink, green. A large spray bottle of Anique Goutal's Eau de Camille; two 1920s small silver-and-ebony capped glass bottles, one round and one rectangular, one holding attar of roses and the other the residue of *khus-khus;* one Lalique dragonfly perfume flask, empty; one Lalique perfume flask in the form of a woman with butterfly wings, filled with musk oil the color of grass. Two old Hyderabadi perfume bottles, amber glass and Persian-blue glass with attached brass caps, each two inches tall. A large ugly bottle of Yves Saint Laurent's Champagne. A frosted pink 1930s perfume bottle, from Gargoyle Theatrical Properties, in the shape of a fan. Books: Colin Dexter, *The Silent World of Nicholas Quinn;* Steve Runciman, *Sicilian Vespers; The T-Factor: Fat Gram Counter; The Shopper's Guide to Fat in Your Food; No Pictures on My Grave: A Spiritual Journey in Sicily; The Complete Poems of Emily Dickinson; The Collected Works of W. B. Yeats,* Vol. I, The Poems; *Commonweal,* May 8, 1994; *The London Book of Afternoon Tea;* Edith Sitwell, *Book of the Winter;* Dennis McFarland, *School for the Blind; Diamonds Are a Girl's Best Friend: Women Writers on Baseball; Martha Stewart Entertains,* open to "Weddings"; *French Textiles from the Middle Ages Through the Second Empire.* A bookmark–café menu from Barnes and Noble. A remote control for the Denon sound system across the room and one for a Toshiba TV.

During the Renaissance, Wharton reminds us, and until the late eighteenth century, "it was customary for the lady of the house to lie in bed while receiving company. In many old prints representing suppers, card-parties, or afternoon visits, the hostess is thus seen, with elaborately dressed head and stiff brocade gown, while her friends are grouped about the bedside in equally rich attire." Only the very poor and the eccentric rich — pity the hygienically minded middle classes, for whom mobility means wanton change — now die in the same beds in which they were born. . . . I love the Davanzati house in Florence: in this fourteenth-century merchant's house, generations mated, birthed, and died in a great four-poster bed; generations of babies opened their eyes to a magical frescoed world of knights and ladies dallying in tame forests, men on horseback and men playing chess, and men and women diaphanously clad, exchanging lazy embraces in that same four-poster bed. These frescoes were a world. . . . "Your command post," my children used to call my bed, half in amusement, half in exasperation, so loath was I, at one time of my life, to leave it. . . . Until he was five or six, my son played rolling pin on my body, giving my body a massage with his body, rolling his way from the back of my neck to the small of my back — I paid him 25 cents.

At the foot of my bed is a cream-colored silk shawl embroidered with cream-colored vines and flowers (from a thrift shop in Saratoga Springs).

Above the bedside table is an old Mexican painting on tin (from the Sunday flea market, Twenty-sixth and Sixth) of a young Madonna dressed in blue (Mary's color) and gilt and gauzy orange. In a circle of red roses and white roses she rides on clouds, holding a fat baby Jesus whose fat dimpled hand rests on her ample breast; Jesus is clothed in gossamer clouds and in a loincloth of pearly peach. I have surrounded her with ex-votos of silver and stamped tin — representations of body parts offered to God in supplication or thanksgiving: a pair of pendulous breasts, two lungs, and a baby in embossed stylized bunting — these three from Spacca-Napoli; from Lipari in the Aeolian Islands a female head, hair dressed in a bun; a man in a tightly buttoned business suit; and — from a market in Venice — a torso exposing intestines (an assemblage of ropes and beads), a jumble of organs, and a heart shaped like a conch shell; from Greece two eyes; a heart. From France pewter medallions the size of a half-dollar: the Sacred Heart of Jesus; Saint Teresa clasping roses and a crucifix; Saint Joseph holding a sheaf of wheat in one hand and a draped toddler Jesus to his heart in the other; a beautiful Pre-Raphaelite Mary, Queen of Heaven, around whom angels fly.

On the other side of the bed — I am making a circle of my room — a round table, sixteen inches across, covered in old picked and embroidered linens and a Mackintosh table runner, burlap-colored and embroidered in a rose and green and blue floral and geometric pattern (from the market in Camden Passage, London); three candles, partly burned, in pink Weller art-pottery candlestick holders; a two-liter bottle of diet ginger ale; a malachite perfume flask, circa 1930, holding a 1940s Gruen watch and the lead pencils — gray, black, silver-and-gold, made in Taiwan — that my daughter gives me every Christmas; a yellow Post-it pad; two water tumblers, one empty, one half full; Xanax; Mylanta, cherry creme flavor; Percocet; a pair of distance glasses, broken, held together with dried-up Scotch tape; a cable-box remote control; a black telephone.

Above the table and above an early-American rocking chair (St. George Thrift Shop, Park Avenue South) is a Tabachnick, an acrylic painting of a Madonna and Child who know everything and are beautiful; it is called *The Second Child.*

On the oak windowsill there is an art book, *Clarice Cliff: The Bizarre Affair;* a Bible, King James Version; and a manuscript called *A Splendor of Saints: Readings from the Lives and Words of Saints,* by Anna Harrison, in a loose-leaf notebook decorated with a decoupage of saints, a gift from my daughter last Christmas (a book that forms the basis of my devotional life). It is open to May 13, yesterday's date, and to the biography and the words of the solitary Beloved Julian of Norwich (1342–1423): "Among the greatest of the medieval theologians, Bd. Julian produced some of the most extraordinary writings on God as Mother," my daughter writes.

"On May 13, 1373, when she was thirty and a half years old, she was privy to sixteen visions of her Savior. She was very ill at the time, in great pain, and she believed she was on the verge of her own death. She received last rites, and while meditating on a crucifix placed before her she soared into ecstasy: she plunged deeply into the pain of the cross and experienced the extraordinary joy of the Trinity. . . . Like a Mother, Bd. Julian wrote, Christ encloses the soul in himself: 'Our Savior is our true mother, in whom we are endlessly born and out of whom we shall never come.' Christ suffers like a woman in labor when he gives birth on the cross, and, like a mother, he continually sustains us, feeding us with his own body: 'We know that all our mothers bear us for pain and for death. O, what is that? But our true Mother Jesus, he alone bears us for joy and for endless life, blessed may he be. . . . He carries us within him in love and travail. . . .

"'The mother can give her child to suck of her milk, but our precious Mother Jesus can feed us with himself, and does, most courteously and most tenderly, with the blessed sacrament, which is the precious food of true life. . . .

"'This fair lovely word 'mother' is so sweet and so kind in itself that it cannot truly be said of anyone or to anyone except of him and to him who is the true Mother of life and of all things. To the property of motherhood belong nature, love, wisdom and knowledge, and this is God."

On the wall facing my bed is a long low bookcase. Atop the bookcase are a 19-inch TV and a cable box; a frosted-glass fruit compote dish, with blue bowl and pink stem from Tolouse, and a blue cylindrical glass vessel, four inches high, with a diagonal slash of pink paint applied by an artist's steady hand; a pot of white dendrobium orchids — five still in their tender green pods, seventeen in bloom (twelve on one stalk, five on the other), the white flowers tinged with the palest, freshest green, droplets of water collecting on rubbery green leaves — in a terra-cotta pot; a porcelain chocolate set with a pitcher, creamer, and sugar container, gilt-encrusted as if with a pastry tube with diamonds and medallions and flowers of blue and pink and gold, handles of gold (marked "Made in Germany," a wedding gift to my mother, which she hated and which I appropriated . . . begged . . . borrowed . . . stole from my aunt's dining room breakfront); three unmatched deco bronze candlesticks, the candles partly burned; one Indian tribal ankle bracelet, bronze; a brass Indian perfume holder on four unsteady legs; a dancing Shiva; Hanuman, the monkey god, brass (God saves souls as the monkey carries her babies to safety: they have to work to hold on — that is one version of salvation; the other is that God saves souls as a cat carries kittens — no work is required of the kitten at all); a carved brass Indian nutcracker in the shape of a flying horse; a temple dancer's pelvic ornament, brass, in the shape of an outspread peacock tail; and a memory jar (shard art, jars used as grave markers: flea market) in which, embedded in a kind of epoxy, are these tangible memories of a life long gone (I read this jar, it tells me stories, it keeps its secrets):

A chartreuse glass wrist bangle, in the center of which is a plastic sea
    shell marked faintly with the words *Los Angeles*
        Shards of green glass with white frosting
A mother-of-pearl button with a center of glass
Strings of glass beads (probably fake pearls that have lost their coat-
    ing), many missing, leaving pea-sized holes
Peppermint-striped glass
Two black ebony buttons
A square piece of ivory, indecipherable

Clasped mother-of-pearl hands
The shards of porcelain dishes, gold and green, rose (roses) and gold;
       blue and white
Shards of carnival glass
One dangling earring, black glass
Oxidized object with hook, one-inch wide, five inches long (fan
       holder?)
Three plain white shirt buttons
Pieces of peachy white shells
Three miniature belt buckles
Political-campaign-style button, two men, bow ties, slicked-down hair
Fan-shaped gilt brooch or button
Four-inch-diameter starburst, silver and glass
One-inch glass slipper
Two $\frac{1}{2}$-inch American Indian clay dolls
Two $2\frac{1}{2}$-inch terra-cotta cigarette-sized and -shaped cylinders
Barrette of blue glass
Silver button, floral design
Blackened ring (Cracker Jack box?) with two glass stones
One aggie
Clay cocker spaniel
Barrette, yellow stones
One-inch clay baby doll
Fake pearl dangling earring
Small oblong gold brooch, $\frac{1}{2}$ inch, initials indecipherable
Pieces of shiny rock
Marble-sized balls, brown and green and blue
Coinlike object (button?), Greek woman's head, dated 1901
Three-inch white porcelain doll's arm
Miniature dutch clog
Red glass (button? brooch? toy-bicycle lamp?)
Button, shield-shaped
Barrette of red glass
Cloudy white marble
Beetle-shaped button or brooch
Dulled brass souvenir, 2 × 1: AKRON 1825–1925 Centennial

Amidst the books (religion, poetry, travel) are a brass toy, made during the time of the Raj by an Indian artisan — a boy/man ten inches high, rifle at the ready, to tweak the nose of the Raj; two Jaipur bronze caskets; one Minton tile (Camden Passage antiques), Persian blue, two lovebirds perched on twigs that bear bunchy roses; a brass Indian elephant Juggernaut; seven brass bowls of different sizes and designs; a brass *pan* container; five television remotes in an iron basket, none of which works.

On the wall above the bookcase is a mounted photograph of a pink-washed house and grape terrace on the island of Panarea (a pink and purple curtain stirs in the ocean breeze) and another of a jetty in Lipari, where children sliding down mountains of pumice like the smoothest talc make the blue Mediterranean waters milky (a red dinghy; I am a fleck in the milky blue water).

COMPACT DISCS:

Mahalia Jackson, *Gospels, Spirituals and Hymns*
Wynona, *Tell Me Why*
Faire, Sweet and Cruel
Schubert, *Trout Quintet*
Trumpet: Boncini, Telemann, Purcell . . .
George Strait, *Ten Strait Hits*
Handel's *Messiah*, Neville Marriner
Kathleen Ferrier, Vol. 2: J. S. Bach, *Saint Matthew's Passion*, arias and
    choruses
Beethoven, *Late String Quartets*
Bach, *Mass in B Minor*
Cecilia Bartoli, *If You Love Me, Se tu m'ami; Eighteenth Century Italian
    Songs*
Bob Dylan, *Hard Rain*
Randy Travis, *Greatest Hits, Vol. 2*
Bach, *Toccata and Fugue*
Teddy Hill and His Orchestra, 1935–1937 (Dizzie Gillespie, Roy
    Eldridge, Bill Coleman, Dicky Wells, Frank Newton, Sam
    Allen, Chu Berry, Bill Benson . . .)
Bob Dylan's Greatest Hits
Billie Holiday at Storyville
Frank Sinatra, *Only the Lonely*
Branford Marsalis Trio
Mozart, Symphonies 40, 32, and 38 (Concertgebouwe Orchestra)

Kathleen Ferrier, *Song Recital*
An English Ladymass — Medieval Chant and Polyphony
Mozart, *Great Mass in C Minor*
Andre and Bilgran, *Trumpet and Organ* (Handel, Bach, Albinoni,
　　　　Loeillet, Marcello, Telemann)
Mozart, Symphonies 39 and 31
Bach/Vivaldi, *Gloria/Magnificat*
Carole King, *Tapestry*
Kathleen Ferrier, *Blow Thou Wind Southerly*

TAPES:

Bach, *Brandenburg Concertos*
Beethoven, *Ninth Symphony*
Ben Webster/Oscar Peterson
Vivaldi, *The Four Seasons*
The Band
Sinatra, *Nice & Easy*
Les Canteuse de Saint-Eustache
Rossini, *Stabat Mater*
Nazi band playing and singing swing music with lyrics adapted to
　　　　Nazi propaganda
Sinatra, *This Love of Mine*
Sinatra, The Reprise Collection 1, 4, 3, 2
Sinatra at the Sands with Count Basie
Verdi, *Requiem* (Leontyne Price, Jussi Bjorling, Giorgio Tozzi)
Haydn, *Mass in Time of War*
Bach, *Magnificat and Praise God*
Simon and Garfunkel, *Greatest Hits*
Ben Webster/Coleman Hawkins
Larry Gatlin and the Gatlin Bros., *Cooking Up a Storm*
St. Thomas Choir, *Silent Night*
Coltrane/Hartman, *My One and Only Love*
Oscar Peterson Plays Cole Porter
Bach, *Cantatas*

In a green and white Balducci's shopping bag: Fabric swatch book
(bought at auction for $400), glued fabrics removed, marked Pape-
terie des Jeuneurs, 30 Rue des Jeuneurs, Paris; Mon. Henri Durand;

A. Royer and F. Roux-Mollard, Fabrique de Registres, Perfectionnes. Typographie Lithographie, Gravure, #99346; Articles pour Maisons de Tissus. Black interfacing fabric; white interfacing fabric. Scissors, straight pins; in fifteen Ziploc storage bags, 388 samples/swatches of women's dress silks, France, 1860–1900, color coded (purples, lavenders, pinks, grays, reds, greens, blues, yellows, blacks, whites; figured, textured, flower embroidered, polkadotted, ikat woven, gold and silver threaded). Six rolls of 1940s silk moire ribbon, orange, peach, scarlet, gray-and-green, purple, gray; and two rolls of multicolored (browns and blues and oranges) ribbons.

These things reassure me. I know I will not die until I have made a tapestry of them.

In a Ziploc sandwich bag in the Balducci's bag: black Bakelite cross, superimposed on which is red Bakelite cross; gold cross with emerald; Mexican *milagros:* arm, kneeling man, young girl, man's head; black Bakelite with purple and lavender cubes, marked Lea Stein, Paris.

(From the moment my lover entered my door, however — after an absence of thirty-five years — I ceased to be afraid of death.)

On my bed are two cats, mother and daughter; they lie akimbo and entwined, Maggie and Dinah are their names. They are calico cats. They were both orphaned, mother and daughter, when I got them. The nails of their front paws had been removed by the owner who abandoned them. You'd never know to look at them that they are maimed.

When I open my eyes to the morning northern light, the orchids, their leaves and stems, casts a latticed pattern of light and shadow over the picture of the pink Lipari house, overlaying the latticed pattern of the reed canopy of that magical house: light upon light; and I am instantly happy.

8

SCARS AND DISTINGUISHING MARKS

ON MY LEFT WRIST where bone meets gristle there is a tidy thread-like white scar, three quarters of an inch long, separated by two inches of unblemished flesh from a liver spot the size of a tear.

(Why are they called liver spots? Are they called *fegato* spots in Italian? . . . When I was seventeen it came to me with absolute and damascene finality, standing in a rush-hour crowd on the Culver Line train, that I would someday die. (The apprehension of inevitability was not without its peculiar exhilaration — in a shifting treacherous world, this fact was adamant and lapidary; it did not, however, occur to me on the Culver Line that I would get old, the loosening flesh on my hands settling into patterns resembling tiny rivulets on a silty riverbed. Hands never lie.)

This is how I achieved the scar. My mother and father went to the house across the alley — this was when we lived in South Jamaica and I was not yet five — to play cards with the neighbors (poker, it would have been, or gin rummy). I was comfy in bed, the lights in the house next door casting reassuring slanting light on my coverlet; I had the radio for company. I listened to Ginny Sims, a singer who wore a ribbon on top of her head, drawing her crinkly hair away from her broad, flat, almost Mongoloid face. I listened afterward to *The Dinah Shore Hour,* vowing my allegiance to Dinah (a Southerner rumored to be part Negro), withdrawing my favor from Ginny Sims (this was an act of substantial significance — to Ginny Sims, Dinah Shore, and to me, that is what I thought). I listened to *Inner Sanctum*. It was Saturday night. Every episode of *Inner Sanctum* began with a door creaking open, increasingly loud and increasingly scary, and the portentous voice of an announcer inviting us into the mysteries of the dark. On this night — oh what can they have been thinking of! — children danced on gravestones with careless impropriety; and, as the world of *Inner Sanctum* never permitted crime, however guilelessly committed, not to result in catastrophic punishment, the affronted dead rose from their graves, at first creakily and then with racing purpose, and their clicking bones, draped with tattered flesh, invaded the suburban lawns of the sleeping children — children peacefully asleep in beds just like mine — and the children were drawn to those whose homes they had defiled and were crushed in their hard and mangy embrace.

I yelled out the window facing the promising lights across the alley, *Mommy Daddy Mommy Daddy Mommy Daddy come home come home!* I waited, scrunched in starchy sheets, for Mommy Daddy; and then — I heard faint sounds of laughter from the house across the alley — I waited with terror for the dancing bones. I waited and then I vomited, projectile vomit gushing forth like the bones who flew like linked arrows from the ground. Then Mommy Daddy came home. If I rise above myself, above the body that remembers this, I see a white-faced girl, pale gold curls wetly clinging to her head, her teeth chattering Mommy Mommy Mommy, trying vainly to smile; and my mother, viewing the scene, smelling of cigarette smoke and Heaven Scent, gave vent to mutters and yelps of rage: *My clean sheets damn you work work work all I do is work.* Daddy has left the unclean scene, he removes himself from my mother's grating wrath and I am not surprised, he is a master of disappearing acts. Mommy directs me, still in her fashionable tipped and feathered hat, to scrape off the vomit, and then she watches me tie up the sheets in bundles; then she makes the bed (hospital corners), *All I do is work*, her voice rising in crescendo.

I am clean (my breath stinks) between new sheets. I take my teddy bear, make inquiries of it to which there are no responses, and, to punish myself and teddy and the dark and the voices and the unforgiving night, I tear one of his sweet blind brown eyes out of its socket. I

am appalled at what I have done. And then — having established who
the criminal is — I gouge my wrist with the prongs of my teddy bear's
eye, so as to wear the stigmata of my unnameable unknowable crime.

The clean new sheets were patterned with clowns. She chose them.
This evidence confuses me, alarms me, thrills me. Clowns and roses:
love? Do they mean love? How can I add the story up, how can I
balance, how can I add?

If I look at the palm of my right hand I fancy I see, on the meaty part
below the index finger, a spot where a wart once grew. (One did not
speak of physical deformities to my mother, whose nostrils narrowed
in the presence of ugliness.) I came rather to like it, it engaged my
interest and dispelled loneliness even as it disgusted me: I sat at a
religious convention with my beautiful mother dressed in a coat with
ocelot trim, her chestnut hair in a black snood, and I played with the
wart, its knoblike stems — tubercles — like the paths of a microscopic
labyrinth; I peopled it — the stems were castles in which lives with
infinitesimal but stupendous happenings were lived. I traced the paths,
causing the wart to bleed, with the cardboard program for the day:
GOD'S KINGDOM THE END OF THE WORLD AT HAND. Even
now I remember it with a kind of affection. And revulsion. I felt it to
be responsive to me, to my will, to my raking fingernails. It offered me
proof that I was alive. Cupped in my palm, it exists now as a shadow
of that long-ago loneliness.

On my left buttock there is a crosshatched strawberry stain, rose
and purple, an inch square. Jazzman lover once played ticktacktoe in
the spaces of this blotch. No he didn't. I made that up. If I had a lover
with a stain like this, I would play ticktacktoe on his ass. Then I would
kiss it.

On my white stomach there are six faded jagged scars, pale rose,
narrowing, like an inverted triangle, from bellybutton to pubic hair,
and this is how I got them: I was mad at Paul Kelly, with whom for a
year I lived, and I put a pillow over his head (his hair was red; his eyes
were blue; he had a Guardsman mustache and he drank; he sang
Gregorian chants and Irish sea chanties; he was the first person to teach
me the Hail Mary — which he did over beer and whiskey shots at the

Lion's Head Bar — the rhythms of which I love; he wrote a prose poem, in parallel columns, for six years; he researched a book I wrote on Jehovah's Witnesses, and all the librarians at the Brooklyn Public Library, male and female, fell in love with him; he was an accomplished lover who showered every time he took a crap; he was a fiend on the subject of my hygiene, which he regarded as slack — he always knew when I was pretending to take a shower and just letting the water run, I don't see the point of water baptism before and after every fuck; he was witty and tall and depressed and gorgeously anecdotal and forgetful and he made Yorkshire pudding and a sixteen-layer cake and he was cherished by my children and he died of alcoholism when he was forty-five); I meant only, with the pillow, to show my displeasure, hurting him was not in my mind. I got caught up in my love-rage and applied too much pressure as I leaned over him naked, my breasts sweeping the golden hair of his chest, and, strong as an ox, he reared and devilishly scratched. Sometime later, after Paul had died, I made up a story about a man I knew who'd driven me through Prospect Park and tried to rape me, scratching me through my leotards. I kept this story in reserve for future lovers who might ask about the scars; I never used it, though. The reason I was mad was that he'd beaten me at Ping-Pong playing with his left hand; and then he laughed at his deception. Cecil Beaton took portraits of his mother; and when he was a child — a rich Roman Catholic child in England — he played with Antonia Fraser. That is what he said and I had no reason not to believe him. I sent his pious mother a letter of condolence when he died; I said that oddly enough it was Paul — who professed loudly and in original epithets to hate his Church — who had, in a roundabout way, brought me to the Church. I thought that would make her happy. She wrote back that she could never approve of Paul's "arrangements," missing the point about God.

These scars do not trouble me — they did when I was young and heedless and lovers came and went, always a new one for the taking.

I hated Paul for a very long time, with a hatred bitter and corrosive, because his drunkenness had made our lives dreary and quarrelsome and dulled his wit, and after he'd had a vasectomy his poor member, without its nimbus of orange-gold hair, revolted him and he came home

less and less and fell into gutters more and more and finally I kicked
him out (the children, after all); and when I could no longer live with
this hatred I prayed to God, in whom I did not believe, to relieve me
of it because it was eating at my soul like acid. And He did. The next
morning I woke up without hatred; I woke up with love — love was,
that first morning of my new world, the air I breathed. I prayed the
Hail Mary, taught to me by Paul, who is now, in my life, a faded story,
more sweet than not, poor Paul, God's unwitting missionary. Or pawn.

(I have a theory that He — God — gives you the whole candy store
once, as He did when He cleansed my life of hate; and this brings you
to your knees and to Him, and after that He is less generous, you never
get the whole candy store again. His hook is inescapable . . . and then
He gives you slack.)

On my right thigh, dimpled, now, with fat, there are the marks — dead
white — of six teeth. They form a circle the size of a half-dollar.

I am standing in the back yard of my house in Jamaica talking to the
dog who lives in the yard that backs up to ours. I am wearing lime-colored leggings with velvet spats attached, a lime-colored coat of pilled
wool with a lime-colored velvet collar, and a lime-colored cap that ties
under my chin with a velvet ribbon; mittens are tied to my sleeves; I
am four. Something about the dog — with whom I talk every day —
seems strange to me. . . . And after that I forget.

I know — I bear the signs — that he bit me through the lime-colored
leggings. I know I felt betrayed (I also know that betrayal was not a
novel sensation to me); there was a fight between the families; the dog
was shot. I would like to say I felt sorry for him — I think I did — but
this may be a perverse form of vanity. Twelve rabies shots in the
stomach I had, twelve. On twelve successive days. (Isn't it odd: I just
looked out at the Empire State Building and felt a wave of nausea: the
needle.)

My mother didn't see the need to come with me to the doctor's office,
so I made my way alone. I remember nothing about his office. I
remember walking home, past modest pleasant houses, vacant lots; I
remember the world tipping over, tilting; ah what spinning days, the
ground failing to rise to meet my feet. I remember — this thought was

simultaneously inchoate and as clear to me as the waxed blue sky —
that the world would never rest for me, that my purchase on the earth
was tentative and dearly bought.

What could she have been thinking of?

She called my moles — I have two pale brown pretty ones on my right
shoulder, just where my lovely daughter's are — "beauty marks"; and
wasn't that kind of her? Sometimes she was kind.

I went to school wearing adult castoffs. In Seth Low Junior High
School, Mrs. Scalice took me one day to the bronze honor plaque in
the main corridor and said, "Look, not one Italian name on that — I
want your name on that." All the time she was speaking I was trying
surreptitiously to pull my socks up from beneath my heels, where they
had slid into the secondhand sandals I wore; I also wore, that day, a
cerise ruffled blouse of slippery synthetic satin and a fuchsia skirt.

I longed for bobby sox and saddle shoes. But one day *she* — on an
impulse that confounded me (as, perhaps, it did her) — bought me a
pink angora sweater in a shop under the West End elevated line. I loved
it so much I kissed the image of my face over and over in the bathroom
mirror (one didn't kiss *her*). One day she took me out preaching with
her; as usual I didn't want to go. On the way, some boys, horsing around
in front of a produce store, heaved a rotten eggplant in our direction
(perhaps my mother's beauty excited them) and it landed, squooshed,
in my hair. She didn't let me go back home to wash it out. She said she
needed me to be with her, she needed me (I had no doubt that she
needed me). Its stench and its slime adhered to me. At times like this,
when I was as far away from active defiance as the North Pole and as
close to tears as my next breath, my mother would laugh. Giggle. Her
amazing blue eyes, their intensity exaggerated by the nearsightedness
she refused to ameliorate with glasses, would shrink and retreat, and a
kind of greasy veneer would cover them, like an oil slick, the oil of
lunacy.

She watched *A Doll's House* on television and she moaned and shook
her head uncomprehendingly: "How could anyone abandon her children?" she said. "Oh Mommy," I said, wanting her so much; and she
stared straight ahead.

One Sunday morning I gathered the courage to avoid going from door to door with her by lying doggo and pretending to be sick (this involved a great deal of groaning and writhing on my part). The door to my bedroom — the room I shared with her — was left open, and after she'd gone and I returned to myself, I heard funny panting noises and gasps coming from the sunny kitchen I could see from my bed; and it was my father and he was looking out the window and masturbating and I saw him. Did he know that I was home? (I was ten.) This left — it surprises me to understand — no mark on my body, no scar. . . . Although it is true, of course, that I cannot breathe, and that I have wreathed and shrouded my body in fat.

Even during the Depression, Uncle Joe got three eggs for breakfast; my mother adored her ugly intensely charming blue-eyed bullying sentimental brother. . . . When one danced with him at family weddings, one forgot his history; his charm felt like goodness, a goodness his ugliness served only to underscore. Suspended from the force on allegations of rape, suspended for soliciting a bribe from a building contractor who — Joe's luck — happened to be the son of a judge. . . . It must have been crowded with family that weekend in the house in South Jamaica; when I awoke he was in my twin bed. I saw an immense morning erection, and peered at it with childish curiosity mixed with a sense of danger, and revulsion; whereupon he slapped me hard, my cheek burned. I cried. "Now go downstairs," he said, "and tell your mother you said bad things so I had to hit you." So I did.

Just now I brushed my cheek to see if it was burning.

In his later years Uncle Joe returned again and again to the land of his mother's birth, restlessly searching . . . for the field of grass she danced in, he said, the long white, sweet grass.

These three things have seemed to me either blind or all-seeing: the eyes of the great white whale; the eyes of teddy bear; the eyes of God. They devour.

The car accident that broke three of my ribs massively bruised my left breast, against which Alice, who was driving the car, had hurtled. My breast looked like a huge purple eggplant deformed and splotched with green. When my son, called by the police, came to the hospital emergency room (his measured saunter at odds with the grimness of his face, the tightness of withheld tears — "internal injuries," they had warned), he was obliged by the attending physician to remove my hospital gown; and I said, anticipating his delicacy of feeling escalating into panic, "Just regard it as flesh." By which I meant neutral, anonymous matter (meat), not the breasts at which he had suckled. And he did, with grace; all the worry was in my mind. . . . And when he was little and he and his sister fought, it seemed to me, unceasingly, I spanked their bottoms once when I was fresh from the bath and my top was bare, I hit them with my breasts exposed. So for a long time I wondered if at that moment some ghastly complex had been formed, if they would associate women's breasts with punishment and pain — God knows what I thought, to what frivolous pain my imagination urged me. All the worry was in my mind.

9

SWIMMING
LESSONS

I MET Johnny Weissmuller at the 1939 World's Fair, at Billy Rose's Aquacade in Flushing Meadows. Deeply embedded in my memory is a picture of me standing on the high diving board shaking the Olympian's hand, my eyes fixed firmly on the furrows of his magnificently muscled torso. Of course this cannot be the literal truth of the matter; it is, though, an accurate photographic emotional memory: there I am, poised to fly in the air so as to sink into the water and rise again. It is an image of perfect surrender.

To surrender one's vulnerable body to water has always seemed to me a limpid act of will that has no counterpart or equal, unless it is sex.

(Shelley, who drowned gracefully off Viareggio, never learned to swim. "Why," he had once asked Trelawny, "can't I swim? It seems so very easy." Trelawny, all practical good sense, said, "Because you think you can't," whereupon Shelley, without troubling to remove his clothes, obediently and optimistically jumped into the water and, floundering, had to be rescued. His inability to swim must have caused Shelley heartbreak: Trelawny wrote that the poet "never flourished far from water. When compelled to take up his quarters in a town, he every morning with the instinct that guides the water birds, fled to the nearest lake, river, or sea shore, and only returned to roost at night."

Perhaps it was his very love of water that got in the way of Shelley's surrendering to it, sinking into the object of one's desire being a fearful thing. The only time he was able to surrender without resisting was when he drowned.)

Suzanne taught me how to swim. Suzanne loves me and I love her. I never saw exasperation or impatience written on her face; she — who frolics with dolphins and dives without fear to the depths of the sea whose flowers are as familiar to her as dandelions — knew instinctively when to touch and support me, when to release me, when to encourage me to greater striving, when to accept that I could do no more. She never chided me or exercised the tyranny of practical good sense.

I lived in a water world with Suzanne in St. Croix. Her house was a glass box on stilts set in black rock. I opened my eyes in the morning every day to clean sea and untroubled sky, an immersion into purity.

The waves, whose sound I love, scared me: Suzanne taught me to swim in a pool over the sea, a pool the temperature of milky bedtime cocoa and the color of my mother's blue eyes.

I had taken swimming lessons before and on every occasion failed. In my imagination there was nothing so beautiful, so liberating, as swimming; in fact, I couldn't bear to put my face in the water (a form of suffocation) and I still can't: I need to see, I need to breathe.

One of the reasons that I married Mr. Harrison (I am assuming for the moment that it may be possible to extract reason from colossal muddle) was the ease and languor with which he floated. Like a rag doll. His apparent spinelessness, in the water, appealed to me; I interpreted it as a necessary passivity in the face of elemental force; it enabled me to see surrender as an active verb.

My high school had an Olympic-size pool; and to pass swimming lessons was a prerequisite for graduating. I don't know how I finessed my way out of this: the basement that housed the pool smelled and sounded like a vaulted claustrophobic anteroom to hell. Voices and echoes of voices bounced off tile walls — the antithesis of my dream of water: "stillness, and a gulf of air . . . / Wild air, world-mothering air / nestling me everywhere." And there was the horror of the bathing suit — regulation dark green woolen tank. I had firm, high, round breasts, but they were big (ripe, not overripe — had I only known that then!); they bounced. My body and mind protested — I would not have scratchy wet wool spread tight across the breasts I despised. Jiggling tits. So I lied (every week) and said (every week) that I had my period and couldn't swim. I sat in the stuffy smelly cavernous room wondering when my lies, my sins, would catch up with me and wondering if I could ever learn to behave like other people and wondering if I would ever swim.

(Graham Greene attempted suicide in an empty school pool — he swallowed twenty aspirins and recalled the suffocating effect: "I can still remember the curious sensation of swimming through cotton wool.")

I tried later in life to swim, lured by newspaper ads to a seedy hotel, the Kenmore, on East Twenty-third Street. An ex-con taught me to float on my back — which is the way I would have it (safely mothered on the surface of the water, water lapping at my eyes, but not threatening to suffocate me or to enter orifices I need in order to make my way coherently in the world). But when he left me to make my way on my own in the deep water, I panicked (he carried a long wooden pole with an iron hook at the end of it to fish me out — Moby Dick). And when he tried to get me to immerse my face in the water I panicked again and clutched at his thighs — which gesture he chose to misunderstand; I never went back. (The Kenmore continued its decline; its pool fell out of use and into disrepair; and the police closed the place — a haven for drug dealers — down.)

At Coney Island my guileless Grandma Concetta, her huge breasts floating merrily like mottled pink fish, sang "Ring Around the Rosie" and the Fascist youth anthem and jumped up and down with me (jiggle-jiggle), holding my hand as we ventured waist-high into the crowded sea (the brine not quite overwhelming the smell of baby oil and olive oil on greased bodies eager to be browned, the sticky-sweet insinuating smell of cotton candy, the exciting smell of cheap hot dogs and mustard); and I didn't learn how to swim.

I was fifty when Suzanne taught me how to swim (thirty-six when I learned to ride a bike). But good at jump rope and roller-skating, I find myself unable not to say. . . . My poor body, I defend its honor.

I cannot imagine the last decades of my life — I can't imagine how I would play them out — without this benediction, this sacred loveliness of water.

I discovered that I could float vertically — that I could hold my body upright in the deep water without moving, without thinking. In this

trancelike state I achieve a unique natal calm, a profoundly thrilling stillness. Nothing else exists. Consciousness is receptive but not
irritable.

(I still could not immerse my face in the water.)

I have fallen asleep floating in the water.

This loss of self-consciousness and of control is bliss.

It closely resembles death.

To the Chinese, water symbolizes the feminine unconscious. Immersion in water extinguishes fire and the masculine consciousness, which
is represented by fire.

One of the lies I tell is that I swam, in Libya, in and out of the Roman
underwater villas, skimming over gorgeous, ever-fresh mosaics. . . . I
didn't. I waded off the black shale rocks in little shallow pools — afraid.

Charlotte Brontë fainted when she first saw the sea. In Warren Miller's
book *The Cool World* a young black girl from Harlem sets off to California to gaze at the defining sea. She is amazed when she is told that
the Atlantic is at her own doorstep, she has never (this is the fifties)
heard of Coney Island. Sir Edward Mallory, climbing Everest, bathed
in Kashmiri rivers — because they were there; swimming was "an emotional and spiritual necessity" for him.

Well, of course it is; often in the water I say the Jesus Prayer: "Sweet
Lord Jesus, Son of God, have mercy upon us." Over and over I say it.
The water is a narcotic (a healing diffusion of warmth and sweetness);
and the prayer is a narcotic (stealthily, rhythmically warming, healing,
sweet). And swimming is an emotional necessity — which is why, sometimes, I avoid it, though I have an indoor swimming pool on the roof
of my building into which the sun falls at sunset, and from which the
New York skyline — north, east, south, and west — can be seen, and
over which planes fly and the moon shines and I race the planes,
backstroking faster than a 747 flies.

It is amazing to me how often we (I) avoid the occasion of happiness
and obdurately refuse to comply with our own necessities. Once I lived
across the street from the Brooklyn Botanic Gardens; and sometimes
— when I was deeply unhappy and knew that the cherry blossoms

would make me happy — I did not allow myself to cross the street into that world of color and filmy light.

I did not swim through Roman villas in Libya. Charles Sprawson (*Haunts of the Black Masseur: The Swimmer as Hero*) did. In Benghazi, he says, "when we dipped our masked faces into the water there emerged on the corrugated sand mysterious traces of the outline of ancient streets and colonnades, their sanctity disturbed by the regular intrusion of giant rays that flapped their wings somnolently among the broken columns as they drifted in from out of the shadowy gloom of deeper water."

I quite love this description (and envy him); but I hate the rays: they are underwater bats, they remind me of everything in the natural world I feared in Libya — and of everything the natural world was a metaphor for in my emotional life.

"I am still looking," the Australian swimmer Annette Kellerman said, "for my chest of gold in a cool dripping sea cave — or a mermaid combing her long green hair."

Imagine being in a hydrofoil sailing off the coast of Anzio to the island of Ponza just after a storm has abated: your whole world is a tunnel of green; the swelling green flecked with white is the skin of the hydrofoil — and there is nothing, absolutely nothing you can do but wait for a deliverance you are not sure you warrant or even want. Who would choose to leave a water world of liquid sunlight, pure, sensual, dangerous?

> *It seems to me that I discover and recognize myself when I return to this universal element. My body becomes the direct instrument of my mind, the author of its ideas. To plunge into water, to move one's whole body, from head to toe, in its wild and graceful beauty, to twist about in its pure depths, this is for me a delight only comparable to love.*
>
> — Paul Valéry

In Sicily, near Portopalo, is a nature and wildlife reserve — and a white-sand beach — to which one must proceed for a kilometer on foot (for Italians, who love their cars, this is a nuisance and an absurdity).

The heat makes me cranky. But I grow increasingly less petulant as I walk past the pale crystal magic of unworked salt flats; past a marsh, which adds a not unpleasant undertone of overripe decaying vegetable matter to the candid fragrance of ripe strawberries. White butterflies make small consternations among raspberry canes; papyrus whispers: a still delirium. No one is on the beach.

I walk a whole kilometer into the sea before my shoulders are immersed in water. The Ionian meets the Mediterranean here, it is like a friendly turquoise pond. The warm safe waters are so clear; I see my friendly feet.

In the Aeolian Islands, off the coast of Lipari, I see to the bottom of the sea from the oceangoing yacht in which for ten days I live a water life, a life of surrender to winds, current, cordial infinite air, and sun — a life of active trust; I see a red lobster pot on the floor of the ocean; I watch the pit of a greengage plum and its hairy flesh sink slowly to the bottom. I see my face reflected in the water.

Sun-dazed in a gentle place, the world all "brine and shine and whirling wind." Wild geraniums grow alongside the road above the sea. The soapy fragrance of lacy blue-green fennel mingles with the fresh green, pungent smell of wild mint.

At Campo Bianco there is a mountain of white pumice. (Abandoned loading jetties stretch into the sea.) Young men climb the white mountain like Sisyphus; they fall — leaping, sliding, slipping — like Icarus; they climb again and happily fall into the sea, a desired fate. White clouds of pumice blossom in the blue waters (we swim in milk).

Glass-blue days. At sunset we eat Sorrentine oranges, the delicious sticky liquid running down our chins and mingling with the salty sweat of our bodies. Then we swim again, over black rocks scoured by the sea in aqua waters: a rock garden.

Si lamentara: Stromboli rumbles, it laments. The light is honey sweet, lambent, pellucid, born of water and fire. Black night and a marvel of stars, "vaulty, voluminous, stupendous." Stromboli is showering arcs and arrows of pure red fire into the sky. The fire gushes up and then slides down its ordained path till, with the clink and splash of molten rock, it reaches the water: fire, rock, water, one chastening element.

The luminescent grotto waters of little Filicudi are warm and gentling like the waters of the womb, our first cave-home. I float: a fugue state; born again in water.

I am in turquoise water. I move toward sapphire waters, but they elude me, the closer I get the farther they recede, this is a trip into another country and I cannot find the border; where I am it is always turquoise no matter where I am.

Time is circular and continuous here.

"What would the world be, once bereft / of wet and of wilderness? Let that be left, O let them be left, wilderness and wet."

Rocks yearn.

Nothing is more democratic, less judgmental, than water. Water doesn't care whether flesh is withered or fresh; it caresses aged flesh and firm flesh with equal love.

In Budapest there is an outdoor thermal pool hotter than the body's temperature. Men and women walk to it like men and women in a parable: bare feet on icy snow, fur coats, and great billows of steam issuing from the waters. I somehow expect, when I am at this place — where men and women float cross-legged in sustaining water, and, on bobbing chessboards, play chess — to see or hear something supernatural, something naturally unnatural, a normal abnormality, counter to our understanding of what should be, but real: a boy soprano, countertenors, nightingales. A chorus of angels.

In Kerala every day I swim.

Men and women from the Emirates in dazzling white stroll across flowered hotel lawns, drinking in the last of the precious rains.

From heat and the yearning expectation of cooling rain arises an awareness of one's mind and body as instruments to be played by the centrifugal force of weather: "When the drum of the clouds thunders in heaven / and all the ways of the birds are thick with rain / the monk sits in the hills in ecstasy / and finds no joy greater than this."

The heat sears the back of my neck and the breezes fan it; I am in a sturdy little boat sailing through Kerala's linked backwaters (rivers, lakes, and estuaries), past duck pastures choked with purple hyacinth and skimmed by cormorants. In shallow water, women wiggle their toes in the sand for lazy fish, submerge, and pop the fish into their floating terra-cotta pots. Boys frolic in the water; the sun shines on wet varnished brown bodies.

A surreal composition on the island of Malipurum: salted silver fish and purple orchids; an impressionist composition: on dirt lanes the shifting black shadows thrown by ancient trees are fractured by piercing daggers of light against which men and women dressed in white shield themselves with black umbrellas. Cicadas saw. Scattered dwellings lie beyond scrims of plumbago and feathery calligraphic bamboo; white pumpkin flowers creep over raised wooden eaves, casting purple shadows.

Water is the gift of the gods. I float on the call of the muezzin, among red bamboo and orange butterflies. The water is as warm as fresh milk. The trees are black against the echo of the sun before I can bring myself to leave the pool . . . although I am afraid of the bats that fly in on the scented dusk.

The hotel pool in Fez is too cold, much too cold, to swim in at night. But my flesh feels stained by the stench of the tanneries (animal piss); and my body has been insulted by the imprecations of aggressive bazaar hawkers and a driver whose sycophancy cannot disguise his hatred of me, his loathing and contempt for all women. (He would marry, he says, but he "hates the mothers, all." He spits to underline his point.) I need an icy bath. P. L., the photographer with whom I am traveling, joins me; as we hold on to the side of the arctic pool, fat bubbles rise to the surface; we have both passed wind. "Ah," says P. L., "you get all the benefit of farts when the water is ice." He is right — we have for a moment warmed the water; and I warm toward him and know I will like this journey and find him to be a companionable mate.

In heavenly Lucignano, bathed in a delicious bath of medievalism and safe within its five concentric circles, there is a restaurant called Da Toto. We are served in the garden by the solemn children of the courtly proprietor, who ask, "Shall we make you the meal?" by which they mean, "Shall we choose what you are to eat?" to which the expected answer is yes. They relieve us of the burden of choice. In this garden grow basil and tomatoes and oregano next to gladioli, hot green peppers next to dahlias, a tangle like the tangle that is memory, as unchallengeable as memory, exactly right. Dandelions are as respected as mimosa. (This is the way the garden of memory grows, it is not hierarchical, everything that grows in it belongs in it.)

After the immense and impeccable meal, I float in the family's private pool. (Perhaps the proprietor has intuited the strength and seriousness of my longing; he turns other importuning diners away from his water preserve.) The courteous, smiling children, their work done, frolic at a comfortable distance. I float for hours. Around me are bell towers and roses. The children splash. I rest, absolutely still on the welcoming waters, afloat in children's laughter, the silken fragrance of roses, the chimes of church bells, the delectable and buoyant air. Larks sing.

Something terrible has happened.

It will pass.

It is difficult to describe prolonged, uncircumstantial biological panic: think of tumbling through eons of darkness, plummeting through an endless void; think of having only the moment, being immured in the moment, and the unendurable moment going on and on forever. The thrashing mind races nowhere; the catatonically still body understands its (endless and permanent) terror.

Now think of phobias as a kind of shadowy side effect of this terror, a lesser visitation of lesser demons:

I am in Tikal, the Mayan jungle ruins of Guatemala. One of the women who has flown in with me from Guatemala City (in a plane that also accommodated four standing farmers and burlap sacks with mysterious burdens and squawking chickens) announces that she is going to "schlep up" the pyramid. How I envy her normality. Or is it bravery? I don't know; I can't tell. To climb up the steps of this Mayan pyramid you have to hold on to a thick rope; I can't even permit my mind to imagine climbing *down* those steep and narrow steps, feet sideways, edging like a crab. I find myself alone on a little four-staired monument (a tomb, perhaps); and though the stairs are quite ordinary rough-hewn stone stairs, I can't walk down. I just sit. Awaiting deliverance the form of which I can't anticipate.

This is not a matter of will. It has happened to me before (and since), once when I left the office of a psychiatrist to whom my husband sent me; the elevator was broken, and I bumped down nine flights of steps on my ass. (Halfway down, it struck me as ridiculous that the man to whom I was going for help was the last man in the world I would ask to assist me down the stairs; I fired him.)

I dithered — anguished — a lot about getting a divorce but knew I would ask for one when Mr. Harrison (in a very bad mood indeed) grabbed my arm and forced me to go (blubbering) down the subway escalator at Fifty-third and Lex, the longest escalator in New York. "*Grow up,*" he said. The next day my arm was black-and-blue, but I was calm. I fired him.

In London, in Islington, I stood for three hours on a traffic island, waiting for a cab, knowing that to take the escalator down to the Angel tube station would be impossible. (My fear canceled my intelligence; it took me three hours before I knew enough to ask a shopkeeper to call a car for me.)

I could go on. And on. The week after my father died, I called my daughter to come and get me because I couldn't cross the avenue from which I called (I could see the white curtains billowing from our apartment as I made the call, it was just across the uncrossable street). . . . I once read a derisory story, meant to scathe, about Clare Boothe Luce's calling a cab to take her across a street — I liked her as a result; she did it in style. . . . When my mother died I forgot how to eat and spilled food all over myself and woke up in the morning crawling and making strangled noises deep in my throat; but that is another story.

I have gotten dizzy watching people on television walk unaided across wide stretches of empty space. (How do they stay rooted to the ground?) I once used up a ton of guts outside the Plaza Hotel standing, waiting for a cab in a snow flurry, quite sure that an errant thought would knock me off my feet, having no purchase whatsoever on the ground.

In water I am buoyant, weightless, unafraid.

I began to notice, after Jazzman entered my life, an unaccountable reversion to the panic-phobic state from which Prozac had redeemed me. For months and months after I moved to Manhattan — three years, perhaps — I walked and swam unafraid. I floated every day. I crossed Park Avenue at will. (I woke up every morning to the Chrysler Building and to East River light, amazing grace.)

Then Jazzman came back into my life, and I was happy; but the panic returned. "Mind over matter," he said — though I managed most of the time, owing in large part to his laziness, which kept him bed-, chair-, and taxi-bound, to hide my panic and my phobias from him; "mind over matter" (what a nit!).

It became true again, what my children had said of me: She can get to Afghanistan, but she can't cross the street to go to the post office.

(Nuns are always helpful when you ask for help to cross a street; they never ask questions. Nuns take your arm as if you are a blind person, which no doubt I am. . . . I have never asked a priest.)

There have been remissions. I went out to the West Coast to indulge a lifelong fantasy — I went to swim with Esther Williams. She had symbolized the perfection of natural action to me — elegant and intelligent and economical in all her tumbling, swanning, arching moves. I swam naked in her pool high above Los Angeles; I forgot that I was afraid.

I am afraid again.

I am practicing now to float on my back again — oh I want to sail through warm waters unselfconscious and once again unafraid. It's very odd. I don't know whether I have will in this matter or not. But I act as if I have (free) will, I have no choice. I don't know whether I can expect God's grace — how many times can He come to my rescue (why should He?) when I so often ignore Him? (Of course His *thereness* isn't altogether always a matter one takes for granted, like the air. And lately I have not been able even to take air for granted.)

When my son was little, he was away a lot in the summers, visiting his father, and Brooklyn stickball with the block's rough kids didn't come altogether easily to him. He struck out a lot. He came upstairs, locked himself in his room, cried; and then went back out again to hit the goddamn ball, snot and tears wiped from his face.

I model myself after him.

Every day now, and for the last several months — since I snatched my courage from my lethargy — I go to the pool, I try to float on my back and to navigate the pool. Oh but one shouldn't have to *try* to float, that's the whole point, it should be as natural as, well, breathing. I try to float. I am getting better. Some days I actually glide across the pool.

I tell myself it is never too late to learn how to live.

I act as if I have free will; I will myself to be receptive to God's grace.

I can still float vertically — I can suspend myself for hours on end without the invasion of a wayward thought or memory. I am *in* the water, free — and what do you think of that?

✿ L'ULTIMA

Edifice Wrecks
Climbing Jacob's Ladder

There are spigots in all the walls and on the ceiling — fire sprinklers — and they turn on as the black window frames turn blood red: Mommy! the girl cries. Mommy tries to stop it but she can't, the fire is enclosed in a milk-white globe, she gets a mild shock and walks away languorously, indifferently, in her nightgown. The gynecologist who is not a gynecologist but a butcher is snipping and cutting and pulling something out of the girl, a skinned pig, a bloody mass and other blobby bloody things. The house is shaking. The ceiling rots. The rot starts in the father's room. He is wearing a striped pajama top. The beams are rotten. Go away, he says. The rot spreads and great big holes appear in the walls, which are fancy, like Versailles (the stairs are mean, and the closets, too); the plaster falls. The ceilings part from the walls. The mother doesn't care. The girl cares about the closet, about the clothes, she is sorting out clothes and she yells out the window, Tell him I need five boxes and a moving trunk. The girl is on the telephone, she is having trouble breathing. Don't call the police, the mother says. The father appears dressed like a clown. He swoons, he jumps-falls-flies out the window. The girl closes her eyes and, a soft hand helping her, climbs down the narrow steps. Outside there are fire engines. The sidewalk is taped off. She walks away from the scene of the crime.

ACKNOWLEDGMENTS

I am deeply indebted to writers living and dead for nourishing my imagination and providing me with information, insight, titillation, amusement, and renewed connections to my past. I want especially to mention (in no particular order): Georges Duby; Paul Valéry; Dorothy L. Sayers; Milan Kundera; G. K. Chesterton, *Orthodoxy;* Henry James; Giuseppi di Lampedusa, *The Leopard;* Edith Wharton and Ogden Codman, Jr., *The Decoration of Houses;* Adele Davis, *Let's Cook It Right;* Carlton Fredericks and Herbert Bailey, *Food Facts and Fallacies,* and Carlton Fredericks, *The Carlton Fredericks Cookbook; The Poems of Gerard Manley Hopkins,* W. H. Gardner and N. H. MacKenzie, eds.; *Poesia Dialettale del Molise,* Luigi Bonaffini, Giambattista Faralli, Sebastiano Martelli, eds.; *The Poems of Emily Dickinson;* Reynolds Price, *Out on the Porch;* Martha Bensley Bruere and Robert W. Bruere, *Increasing Home Efficiency;* Catharine E. Beecher and Harriet Beecher Stowe, *The American Woman's Home;* Charles Sprawson, *Haunts of the Black Masseur: The Swimmer as Hero;* Kent C. Bloomer and Charles W. Moore, *Body, Memory and Architecture; What the Woman Lived: Selected Letters of Louise Bogan,* Ruth Limmer, ed.; Teilhard de Chardin, *The Divine Milieu;* Caroline Walker Bynum, *Feast and Fasting* and *Fragmentation and Redemption; The New Science of Giambattista Vico;* Douglas and Elizabeth Rigby, *Lock, Stock, and Barrel: The Story of Collecting;* Gavin Maxwell, *Lords of the Atlas;* Lady Lawrence, *Indian Embers;* Charles Allen, *Plain Tales from the Raj;* Steven Runciman, *The Sicilian Vespers;* H. V. Morton, *A Traveler in Southern Italy;* David Abulafia, *Frederick II;* David G.

Einstein, *Emperor Frederick II;* Kate Marsh, *Writers and Their Houses;* Alistair Moffat, *Remembering Charles Rennie Mackintosh;* Griffin and Meisel, *Clarice Cliff: The Bizarre Affair.*

The Metropolitan Museum of Art, the Victoria and Albert Museum, the Brooklyn Museum, the Hunterian Gallery, the Charles Rennie Mackintosh Society, and the Long Island Historical Society were congenial, invaluable, and in many cases thrilling resources.

I want especially to thank David Breul, editor and friend, for his kindness, trust, and support over the years.

John Herman has my love; and I am grateful for the energy of John Sterling and the enthusiasm and care of my good editor Dawn Seferian, and also of Larry Cooper.

I do not know how I could possibly repay my daughter, Anna Harrison, who led me sweetly and profitably to the words of the saints, whom she understands with her large heart and her discerning mind.

Often when I felt myself to be in trouble, I was rescued by the humor, the integrity, and the loving stillness of my son, Joshua. I thank him.